THE RAZ
BHAGWAN

Editing by Bodhisattvaa Ma Deva Barkha,
B.S., M.S., M.M. (RIMU), Acharya
Ma Shivam Suvarna, B.Sc., Ma Prem Gitika, M.A., B.Sc.
Typing by Ma Anand Shahida, Swami Prem Atirup
Design by Ma Dhyan Amiyo
Production by Swami Satyadharma, B.A.,
Swami Deva Anugito, Swami Prem Visarjan

Published by The Rebel Publishing House GmbH
Venloer Strasse 5–7, 5000 Cologne 1, West Germany

Copyright © Neo-Sannyas International

First Edition

Printing by Mohndruck, Guetersloh, West Germany

OR'S EDGE
SHREE RAJNEESH

All rights reserved

No part of this book may be reproduced or transmitted in any form or by any means electronic or mechanical including photocopying or recording or by any information storage and retrieval system without permission in writing from the publisher.

Distributed in the United States by
Chidvilas Foundation, Inc., Boulder, Colorado

Distributed in Europe by
Neo-Sannyas International, Zurich, Switzerland

ISBN 3-89338-015-9

Talks given
to the
Rajneesh International University
of Mysticism

Table of Contents

Session 1
Miracles
Are Bound To Happen   11

Session 2
The New Man:
A Citizen Of the World   23

Session 3
Just Like
The Open Sky   35

Session 4
First Be Selfish   47

Session 5
Existence Loves Imperfection   59

Session 6
Laughter
Is The Essential Religion   71

Session 7
When The Ocean
Has Called You   83

Session 8
Our Dance Is Forever   97

Session 9
Love Is Never Too Much   109

Session 10
With Trust
It Is Always Spring   119

Session 11
Bring The Dawn,
Dispel The Darkness   129

Session 12
God Is Also
Seeking You   143

Session 13
You Can't Hold On
And Clap Too   155

Session 14
Easy Is Right   167

Session 15
Once Coin, Two Sides   179

Session 16
Who Created God?   191

Session 17
Playing A Part
In The Movie   201

Session 18
The River
Needs No Guide   213

Session 19
Awareness
Will Not Go To War   221

Session 20
Each Human Being
Is A Longing Of Existence   233

Session 21
What Am I Doing Here?   245

Session 22
Don't Be Worried–
The Worst Will Also Happen   257

Session 23
It Is A Carbon Copy   267

Session 24
No Heaven,
No Hell,
No Doubt   277

Session 25
The Same Vicious Circle   285

Session 26
Live Fearlessly
Die Fearlessly   297

Session 27
This I Call
The "Razor's Edge"   307

Session 28
Truth:
The Greatest Surgery   317

Session 29
The Answer Is You   327

Session 30
A Little More Courage,
A Little More Love   341

Introduction

This series of discourses was spoken by Bhagwan Shree Rajneesh in the first months after His return to Poona, India. Nearly seven years before, Bhagwan had left the ashram in Poona–where in a few short years, His presence had drawn thousands of seekers from nearly every country in the world – and traveled to America. There, guided by Bhagwan's vision of a humanity living in harmony with nature, rich in both the material and the spiritual realms, His disciples created the commune-city of Rajneeshpuram, Oregon–history's most extraordinary experiment in human consciousness.

After five years of continuous harassment by the state and federal government, and a campaign of religious persecution orchestrated by fundamentalist Christian groups, Bhagwan was expelled from Amercia and the commune was dispersed. In the year that followed, Bhagwan was refused entry into virtually every European country, due to pressure from the American government and opposition from the leaders of traditional, orthodox religions. Finally, He returned to India – first to Bombay and then back to the Poona ashram.

For many longtime disciples the return to Poona was like returning to a childhood home – so familiar and yet somehow utterly different; different perhaps because we had grown, changed, matured. In the first Poona phase many of us had totally left our lives in the West and had come to Poona to be here "forever". Suddenly, overnight, our cozy home had dissolved and with it, many childhood dreams. Then in Rajneeshpuram, the new commune, we began again with a new strength and in five years set down roots which might have lasted a lifetime; but they did not. Within a tumultuous few months, five thousand disciples were thrust from their nest, young wings flapping madly–a quick lesson in life's insistence upon change.

Bhagwan has said that life is a *caravanserai* – just an overnight stay, and in the morning we move on. This understanding He has given us through first-hand experience. To live as a disciple with a Master such as Bhagwan Shree Rajneesh is to live on the razor's edge; one simply never knows where the path will lead. In these pages He says: "The world of love, the world of meditation is pure insecurity; it is moving into the unknown with no maps in your hand, with no guidebook to lead you – not knowing where you are going, not knowing where you are going to land finally…"

"To be in love with a living master is always risky, dangerous… The living master is a changing phenomenon; you never know what turn he is going to take tomorrow."

But wherever we land with Bhagwan, we are participating in a living process, a true mystery school. Many of the discourses in this book are a window to that mysterious process that happens between master and disciple. He says, "If you can experience me, my presence, if you can open your heart with a silent welcome, it is more than one can expect – because it is not a school where you are taught philosophy, religion, psychology; it is an alchemist's workshop where you are transformed into new beings." With such love, such ecouragement, Bhagwan urges us on into the unknown, towards that which cannot be known.

"And the time is ripe. For so many of my sannyasins, the first flowers of spring have started showing. More and more flowers will be blossoming… Words, I have given you many – that was a preparation. Seeds, I have sown many, and now that the spring is very close, you have to be courageous…" This book contains a true story, a story of the great love and immense trust between disciples and their Master as they move together along a path which is both hazardous and ecstatic – that path is the razor's edge.

With Love,
Ma Deva Aneesha
Poona, India
November, 1987

Session 1

Miracles Are Bound To Happen

*I am trying to get you to come back home.
You have gone faraway, wandering behind ephemeral things,
wandering behind dreams. And I want you to come back home
– because that which can give you contentment,
that which can give you fulfillment
is not out there, it is in here;
it is not in any other time, but now.*

February 25, 1987
Evening

Beloved Bhagwan,

All day, I have this melted sensation
like something inside me dissolving in the glow of Your love.
Discourse comes and it just expands to fill the silence,
leaving a breathing heart and a pair of ears hanging from nowhere.
It feels like being an orgasm.
Oh Bhagwan, are You even turning the dark night of the soul
into the light night of the soul?

Prem Amrito, it is exactly the definition of mysticism: the transformation of the dark night of the soul into a light night of the soul. It is my work and it is your work, too. All these people who have gathered here are in search of light, life, love, laughter; and all these divine qualities have been destroyed by centuries of exploitation – by all kinds of priests, bureaucrats, politicians, by all those who have been in some kind of power.

But they have not been successful in destroying you. They have been successful only in suppressing you; they have not killed you, they have only poisoned you. And your poison can be taken out, and you can become alive again – which is your birthright.

You are saying, "All day, I have this melted sensation." This is the beginning of disappearing- -disappearing into the whole. First, you will feel just as if you are melting, ice melting..."like something inside me dissolving in the glow of your love."

Something certainly is dissolving in everyone, more or less, except those few unfortunate ones who stand on the bank of a river and remain thirsty. But what is dissolving is not your reality; it is the unreal in which your reality has been repressed, covered. Once the unreal dissolves, the false disappears. Suddenly, you will have for the first time, an inner experience of sunrise – light all over the inner horizon of your sky.

"Discourse comes and it just expands." Spirituality is very contagious; if there are so many people around you in the same space, it helps tremendously. And if someone who has come back home is amongst you, his very presence starts giving you the direction, the dimension in which you have to expand, move, melt, merge.

"Discourse comes and it just expands to fill the silence." Perhaps this is the only place on the whole earth where so many people are sitting in immense silence – not only on the outside, but inside too. And silence gives space. Words, thoughts, are all disturbances.

Silence is an opening to the infinite.

You can expand to infinity – it all depends on your courage. And courage also comes as your experience grows, as you see that the more you expand, the more beautiful life becomes; the more you expand, the more love showers on you; the more you expand...everything takes on a new psychedelic dimension. It becomes more colorful, more alive, more dancing. The ordinary world suddenly starts changing into something extraordinary. The mundane becomes the sacred. And these are the most significant moments in life – when the mundane becomes sacred.

All the religions have been enemies of mankind for the simple reason that they have divided the mundane from the sacred. Rather than bridging them, they have been continuously conditioning the human mind that they are opposites, enemies, and you have to renounce one if you want to get the other.

If you want victory and success in the mundane world, you have to forget about the sacred completely. And to forget it, the best way is to deny it – it does not exist at all. Otherwise, how will you forget it? It will always remain somewhere in the corner, nagging you.

Just the other day, I was informed that in the Soviet Union – atheism is their religion – every child has to be conditioned from the very beginning in atheism. It is not different, it is the same: somewhere it is the Catholic religion, somewhere it is Protestant, somewhere it is Hindu, somewhere it is Buddhist. In the Soviet Union, it is atheist. Somewhere it is God, somewhere it is no God. But the society never leaves you anywhere to search for yourself. It gives you ready-made answers. And in life, ready-made answers are not only futile, not only poisonous, but almost murderous.

The information was about many countries within the Soviet Union which are Mohammedan – used to be Mohammedan. Now, officially they are all atheists. But they have not forgotten; something of the sacred still lingers – even against the whole propoganda machine of the Soviet Union, which is one of the most efficient, dictatorial, which allows no criticism, no freedom of thinking.

Those Mohammedans have to pretend that they are atheists. But in Mohammedanism, five prayers are prescribed every day – from morning till you to go bed. It is very difficult in the Soviet Union to do five prayers. They have changed the name of the five prayers; they don't call it prayer, they call it physical exercise. Five times every day...it is good for the body and for the mind. They cannot mention the soul.

Sixty or seventy years of continuous propoganda, conditioning – but the sacred is just standing by. And thousands of years of conditioning all over the world against the mundane, but the mundane has not disappeared. In India, they even reached to the extreme – they have been preaching for almost two thousand years that the mundane world does not exist; it is *maya*, it is illusion, it only appears.

I was staying with a shankaracharya, and he was discussing the illusoriness of the world. I told him, "There is no need to argue. You just pass through the wall. Don't go through the door. And it will be enough; I will be convinced and I will remain your devotee for my whole life."

He said, "Go through the wall? What kind of argument is this?"

I said, "It is not a question of argument. It will simply prove whether the wall is real or illusory."

You can condition the human mind, but the mundane is there. And even the person who preaches continually.... The first shankaracharya, Adishankaracharya, who created this theory of illusion and propounded it with great argumentation – he also needs food, he also needs water, he also needs clothes. And I am wondering why none of his followers ever objected, ever asked, "What is the need of these illusory things? And how can an illusory food become nourishment? And if it becomes nourishment, then to call it illusory is nonsense."

This was one side of the game: the people who wanted to emphasize spirituality had to deny the reality of the world which surrounds you everywhere. And there have been people who have been denying the spiritual, saying, "Man has no soul. He is just a robot created by nature, and when he dies, everything dies. So don't be bothered about the inner world; there is no inner. All that is real is outside, and all the talk about the inner is unreal, illusory."

On the surface, you may think these two parties are against each other. But my own understanding is different: they are using the same argument. They belong to the same category, to the same mind: choose one half – which half you choose is not the point, both are against the whole.

My effort is to make you aware that both are real, both are together in deep harmony. And the idea of their opposition destroys your life. Hence I say, the moments when you come to know that the sacred and the mundane are one – the sacred is the inside of the mundane, and the mundane is the outside of the sacred – then you have a total conception of reality.

"...leaving a breathing heart and a pair of ears hanging from nowhere." When you are absolutely silent and have become only a listening, naturally you will feel as if two ears are hanging from nowhere. This is the right way of listening, and "a breathing heart" deepens the silence; it does not disturb it.

Amrito, you are right when you say, "It feels like being an orgasm." It is. It is a love affair with the whole.

It is a meeting with eternity, and it is an orgasm that can remain with you twenty-four hours – day in, day out.

An enlightened man remains orgasmic in every moment of his life. Orgasm is no longer an incident that happens and disappears; it becomes his natural way of being. His blissfulness is so much, and he is so deeply in tune with existence that orgasm is no longer an incident, it is his very life.

"Oh Bhagwan, are you even turning the dark night of the soul into the light night of the soul?" That is the purpose for which we all have gathered here. This mystery school, or this university of alchemy, has only one purpose – to transform the baser metals into gold; to transform the dead into the living; to transform the dark into the light; to transform you from your mortality into the immortal.

Beloved Bhagwan,

When I was in Sweden, I felt my heart opening up for You,
filling me with a deep feeling of love and joy.
Now that I am in Poona, my heart seems to
be closed again, resisting Your love.
This fills me with sorrow. What should I do?

Carina Anderson, the time when you were in Sweden, I was just in your imagination. You were feeling your heart opening, but there was nobody to enter into your heart. You were feeling a deep fulfillment of love and joy, but that was all made of the same stuff dreams are made of.

Now that you are here, things are totally different. Keeping your heart open will make you afraid, because it is easy to let me in, but it is very difficult to throw me out.

I come into you like a guest, and soon you start feeling you are a guest and I am a host – hence, the fear. Here, you are resisting my love, and you are saying, "This fills me with sorrow." It is natural that it will fill you with sorrow – you must have dreamt so much, imagined so much, hoped so much and things have not turned out the way you wanted them to be.

You are asking, "What should I do?" Go back to Sweden. Poona, anyway, is not a good place to stay. And at least your heart was opening there. Although there was no guest knocking on your doors, at least you were imagining love, joy; and here you are closed, full of fear, and feeling sad and wondering what has happened.

So if you are a coward, then the easiest way is simply to go back to Sweden – as you enter the plane, your heart will start opening again and you will start feeling love for me. But don't return – enjoy your dreams. If you cannot enjoy the reality, why unnecessarily feel sad and sorrowful? But if you are courageous, then Poona cannot do anything to you. Then let your heart be open and don't be afraid of love.

In life, the only thing that one should not be afraid of is love.

But people are more afraid of love than anything else, because love is a kind of death. Your ego has to die. Only then will your heart be spacious enough for love to come in. But I warn you: beware! I come as a guest and soon I become the host. If you are ready to take the risk.... So many of the people here have taken the risk, and once they have taken the risk, they are grateful that this tremendous transformation became possible for them.

Whenever love comes in, it cannot be a guest, because it comes in and never goes. It becomes your very being, your very song, your very dance.

So either you can go right now back to Sweden and dream your dreams – but they are soap bubbles; you are simply wasting your time – or be here, take courage and accept the challenge: open your heart and let me in. Then I will be coming with you to Sweden – and on just one ticket, two persons! I have been traveling all over the world this way.

The governments and parliaments think that they are preventing me, but they don't know my ways – that wherever one of my sannyasins enters, I also enter with him. They can prevent me, but they cannot prevent my millions of sannyasins.

And I have distributed my love to everyone, deserving or undeserving, because that is my way of thinking. Everyone deserves love, just as everyone deserves breathing. Everybody is worthy of love, just as everybody is worthy of living.

Love is the nourishment of your soul.

You can choose...but don't be saddened, in sorrow. If you want to just imagine things, then you can imagine anything. It is easy for millions of people in the world to pray to God because it is all imagination. If by chance it happens that they meet God, then there will be difficulty. Then immediately they will want to escape, and they will start finding a thousand and one complaints. They will start laying many judgements upon God.

For example, if you meet God and he turns out to be Chinese, are you going to tolerate him – with five, six hairs in his beard, with long cheek bones? Or, who knows, maybe he is black. And maybe there is a possibility he is a woman...a black woman with a Chinese face! You will run back to Sweden so fast. It was good in Sweden, God was your imagination. Whatever you wanted....

In India, the god Krishna, in his temples...there are beautiful temples of Krishna all over India, and he is one of the most colorful men. He has to be given food two times a day, just as every Indian eats. Every afternoon he takes a nap. In the night, when he goes to sleep, the doors are closed.

It is your imagination; whatever you want to do.... If you don't give him food, he cannot lodge a complaint in the Bund Garden Police Station. The poor fellow is imprisoned already in a temple, and nobody knows...and nobody has ever thought about a cup of tea in the morning.

Times have changed. If Krishna were alive, he would have learnt to drink tea – it is not such a sin. But Hindus cannot offer tea to Krishna. They keep him in a swing, and the priest goes on pulling the rope of the swing so he is completely enjoying the swing. In rich temples, it is a golden swing, or a silver swing.

In one of the cities where I lived for a few months, there was a very famous temple of Krishna just in front of my house. So I used to go just to see what was happening there. I told the priest, "One thing you should remember: the whole day, keeping the poor fellow on the swing, and the rope is being pulled – the rope pullers go on changing but that poor fellow...the whole day – I think it will create nausea. You should be a little more compassionate."

He said, "But that's what the scriptures say."

I said, "You follow scriptures? Or do you have some intelligence, too? And if the scriptures say, 'Go on pulling the swing the whole day,' then at least take poor Krishna out for a morning walk outside in the garden – and go on pulling the swing as much as you want. Where are your scriptures? Is it written in them that Krishna has to be in the swing?"

He said, "That is not written."

I said, "Then it is your own idea – swing, do whatever you want. And this is idiotic: keeping the priests changing, now that electricity is available. Just plug the swing into the electricity and it will keep swinging – Krishna or no Krishna."

He said, "You should not say such things. It is irreligious."

I said, "I think that what you are doing is

irreligious."

In every country, in every religion, people worship dead saints, because dead saints are very easy. You tell them to lie down, they lie down. You tell them to sit up, they sit up. They are very obedient. But a living saint, a living sage, is not going to be obedient to you. You will have to be surrendered to him. But the imaginary god is surrendered to you – that's the joy.

So in Sweden, you must have been doing things to me of which I am not aware. Here you cannot do those things to me – I am not your imagination. But your imagination is not going to give you a new life. And your imagination is not going to open your eyes to the ultimate truth.

I can help you to be authentic, to be joyous, to be ecstatic, but you will have to pay the price. And the price is not much – I just want your dreams.

Give me your dreams, and I can give you reality.

Reality is already with you; your dreams are like clouds, hiding it. Just give me your dreams. I ask nothing from my disciples except their dreams, their lies, their falsities.

And once they are without any falseness, they don't need anything from anybody. They have everything within themselves. They have brought it with their birth.

So you can decide. Either you can go alone to Sweden, or if you want me also to be with you, then you will have to wait a little more, gather courage. If so many people with open hearts have not died, if so many people are ready and available for my love, for my blessings, for my being, for my presence.... And no harm has happened to them, except that they have become a little crazy. They sing more, they dance more, they laugh more, they love more. They *are* more. So you can choose.

Carina Anderson, be very careful in choosing, because you may not find a man like me again. Sweden will remain there. I am not going to be here always. And when you have come so far, just a little more, a little closer.... And you know perfectly well how to open the heart, because you were doing it in Sweden.

You know perfectly well how to be loving and joyful. Give it a try here too. Nobody is ever harmed by love, and nobody is ever harmed by opening the heart. Everybody has always become more enriched, more blessed.

But you can choose reality – or your dreams.

Beloved Bhagwan,

Once You said to me that I am energy and awareness.
I use this as a key.
The other day, while speaking about
the disciple touching the master's feet,
You said energy always moves downwards, like water.
I have felt energy showering down,
but I have also felt energy soaring upwards, like a flame.
Can you help me understand this?

Prem Shunyo, life has so many aspects, that it is almost impossible to contain all those aspects in one statement. When I said that energy always moves downwards, like water, it was in a particular context. The context was the disciple touching the feet of the master.

If he wants to get the master's energy he has to be humble, and available to the downgoing energy. Just as, in the East, for centuries the disciple has been touching the feet of the master, the master has been touching the head of the disciple with his hands. This way the disciple gets energy on his own accord, from the feet; and from the master's hands, compassion. And a circle starts happening. If the disciple is not holding himself back, then he will feel what Amrito was calling "orgasm," energy showering on the disciple from the master; but it is energy coming from above, downwards. This was the context, when I said all energy moves downwards.

But your experience is absolutely true. When the master's energy showers on the disciple, and if the disciple is totally ready, the energy is so much that the disciple becomes aflame; the energy becomes fire. And like flames, the energy starts moving upwards. You all have felt it without understanding it. Sometimes you feel your hands are moving upwards, in spite of yourself. You are not doing it. You are not the doer; your hands have become like a flame which wants to reach to the stars. This is the overflow of energy.

Ordinarily energy moves downwards; but if the disciple is able to attract the master's energy in such quantity that it starts flowing all around him, he cannot contain it – it is too much to contain. The very fact of abundance makes the energy move upwards.

And the feeling, Shunyo, is perfectly right. You say, "I have felt energy showering down, but I have also felt energy soaring upwards, like a flame." That is the second step. First, you have to be so humble – just like a valley – that from the mountains, rivers can descend into you. Once you have too much...you should remember that at a certain point, quantitative changes become qualitative changes.

For example, at one hundred degrees water suddenly starts evaporating, moving upwards. Ordinarily water flows downwards, but at a hundred degrees of heat a qualitative change happens. The whole direction changes; the water becomes a new phenomena: vapor. It is the same water – it starts moving upwards. Almost similar is the case if energy falling into you makes you so hot, so full...then you will feel a second step: the energy moving upwards like flames. So whatever you have experienced is not against reality.

What I was saying was only in a particular context. In Shunyo's context I can also be a witness. I have seen it, and many of you may have felt that whenever I come close to her, she starts moving her hands upwards – not only her hands upwards, but she starts saying things that...I don't think she understands what she is saying. The whole experience is just so much that it wants expression. Slowly, slowly, it is going to happen to everyone. But only when it happens is it meaningful to talk to you about it. I don't say many things to you. I will wait for the right moment, when you have some experience, so that my words don't just go above your heads but go directly like arrows into your hearts.

Beloved Bhagwan,

When You are dancing, sometimes You suddenly lift Your arms high
and stop in mid-air for a moment.
In that moment, for me, everything stops, disappears,
and then I feel myself lifted upwards, too.
It is an exquisite feeling. Bhagwan, what are You doing with us?
It seems that the formless is responding to the formless.

Prem Arup, you are right. It is the formless responding to the formless. Just like Shunyo, this is your experience and may be the experience of a few other people.

There are moments when suddenly I stop for a second, just to give you a taste – the taste when everything stops: time, space, mind, *everything* stops. But it is possible only if you are totally in tune with me and you are moving with me. If you are partially with me, then the experience will not happen. If you are totally with me and moving with me and then suddenly I stop, I give you a moment which is certainly exquisite, a moment of ecstasy.

You are asking, "What are you doing to us?" I am trying to get you to come back home. You have gone far away, wandering after ephemeral things, wandering after dreams. And I want you to come back home – because that which can give you contentment, that which can give you fulfillment is not out there, it is in here; it is not in any other time, but now. And the feeling of a stop – a total stop – is nothing but an experience of herenow.

I can give you only the taste, and once you have got the taste, then you will be in search of it. Then there is no way to prevent you. The most fundamental thing is a taste. You have heard words, beautiful words, but they have not driven you into a mad search. I want to give not only words to you, but some content. And that is possible only by giving you some taste.

And the time is ripe. For so many of my sannyasins, the first flowers of spring have started showing. More and more flowers will be blossoming. And you have to be very impatiently patient – with a deep longing, but without any demands. Because I cannot be here forever. And I have waited long enough; now it is time that I should start giving you the taste. Words I have given you many – that was a preparation. Seeds I have sown many, and now that the spring is very close, you have to be courageous, and total, and intensively with me – in my silence, in my joy.

It is time that the duality between you and me is dropped.

Those who are intelligent should drop it immediately. Those who are a little less intelligent will take a little time. I have a little time more to linger on your shore…but it cannot be very long.

Beloved Bhagwan,

Although You don't know me personally, everything is happening.
How is this possible?

Anand Prageet, I don't know anybody personally, but I know everybody essentially, I know everybody spiritually. Personality is a false thing. It is a mask: your name, your address, your profession, your photograph – passport size – your identity cards. What is your personality made of? – just these kind of things. Otherwise you come into the world without any name, without any address, without any religion, without any nation, without any race. You come as just a tabula rasa – so clean, so clear, crystal clear. That is your essentiality. But that is the essentiality of everyone, so it does not matter whether I know you personally or not. All personalities are false. And the essential being within you is the same.

The day I came to know myself, I came to know you too.

That's why everything is happening. I can understand your puzzlement, your problem: how is this possible? Because people think that unless you are known personally, how can I do anything for you? The reality is just the opposite: Unless I know you spiritually, I cannot do anything. And you don't know your own spirituality. You know your face, just the way the mirror shows it. Have you seen a house of mirrors, where there are different kinds of mirrors? In some mirrors you are so long, like a pillar; in some mirrors you are so small, like a pygmy; in some mirrors you even get afraid seeing your own face. But have you any guarantee that the mirror you have in your bathroom is the right mirror? And who decides what is the right mirror? But that is your only acquaintance with yourself.

There is a beautiful story about Mulla Nasruddin:

He had gone for a pilgrimage to Kaaba, the Mohammedan holy land. And there were millions of pilgrims – because it is expected by the Mohammedan scriptures that every Mohammedan, at least once in his life, must go to Kaaba; otherwise he is not considered to be a real Mohammedan.

So even the poorest Mohammedans sell their houses, sell their ornaments, their land, everything, because at least once in their life they have to go to Kaaba. So every year there is a great gathering. All caravanseries are full, all hotels are full.

Nowhere was there any vacancy, and Mulla was very tired. He clung to the feet of the manager of a hotel and he said, "Whatever you can do...but there must be some place in your big hotel, and I'm so tired – walking in the desert for miles. Just have mercy on me!"

The manager said, "I can understand your trouble, but all the rooms are full. Only one room can I manage to smuggle you into, because the man who is staying inside is snoring so loudly, he will not be able to know. You go silently and sleep. At least till morning that man is not going to wake up, and even if he wakes up, he will not find me. In the morning we will see – somehow we will persuade him."

Mulla went in; the room was a double bedroom. The man was snoring, so the manager left him there. And Mulla lay went on the bed with his shoes, with his cap, with his coat, everything – just as he was when he entered the hotel. Naturally it was very difficult to sleep with his shoes and his hat and his coat, and it was hot – Saudi Arabia is the hottest place – and on top of it all, the snoring man was by his side. He was snoring so loudly that even if you were at ease you could not sleep.

Mulla was tossing and turning – his tossing and turning woke up the man. And the man watched in the darkness of the room to see what was happening. Slowly, slowly he could see that Mulla had his shoes on, cap on, coat on...and it was so hot. He could not resist the temptation.

He said, "Listen, in the first place you have illegally entered my room. I have booked the whole room, for the simple reason that I snore so much that if somebody else is there he cannot sleep. And if he cannot sleep, then he creates trouble, and then I cannot sleep. But you kept silent for so long and suddenly you started tossing and turning. I opened my eyes; I said, 'My God, again another person!' But forget all about it – it is midnight, where will you go? But why do you have your shoes and cap on?"

Mulla Naruddin said, "There is a problem. The problem is that if I take off my shoes, and my cap, and my coat – and in fact I am accustomed to sleeping naked, and unless I am naked I cannot sleep – if I take off everything and go to sleep naked, you are also sleeping naked. That is the trouble."

"But what is the trouble? I am sleeping naked, you are sleeping naked."

Mulla said, "You don't understand. In the morning, how am I going to recognize who is who? Just to keep my identity, I was keeping my hat, my shoes, my coat. That way I will be certain that there is no problem: I am Mulla Nasruddin, this guy is somebody else. But both naked...."

The man said, "I will suggest one thing to you, because this way neither you can sleep nor I can sleep." And the man also thought that this was a strange type of man, who thinks that if he is naked he will lose his identity. He said, "Just before us, a family must have stayed in the room, and their child has left a doll. So what I will do is I will tie the doll to your feet, and then you can sleep perfectly well. In the morning you can see that the doll is on your feet, so you are Mulla Nasruddin."

Mulla said, "I'm so grateful to you." He dropped all his clothes, and the other man found that doll in a corner and tied it to the feet of Mulla. The man was laughing all the time inside, thinking "I have never come across such a man."

And then he had an idea in the middle...when Mulla was snoring, he changed the doll. He tied it to his own feet and went to sleep.

In the morning when Mulla looked at his feet, he jumped out of his bed, ran out of the room, naked, shouting, "One thing is certain: that man is Mulla Nasruddin. The problem is: who am I? Can anybody say? Can anybody recognize me? Where is the manager? He had seen me in the night, perhaps he can recognize me."

Your personalities are nothing but dolls tied to your feet. I don't have to know your personal life, your personality. I don't have to be acqainted with you personally; I know you essentially. By knowing myself, I have known you all. By dissolving my own problems I know your problems, and I know the key to how they can be dissolved.

The day I became aware of myself I came to know the sinner and the saint both. I have known those who are asleep, and those who have become awakened. So there is no problem in it. If you are here listening to me...and all that I am saying is: drop your personality, drop your ego.

Be humble, and be open. Be silent, be alert and conscious, and miracles are bound to happen to you.

And remember: I will not be responsible for those miracles. You yourself will be responsible for your miracles. You need not even feel thankful towards me. Your gratitude has to go towards the whole existence. I was just a stranger who met you on the way, and we talked a little, gossiped a little – I don't have gospels, but only gossips – and then we parted, you on your own way, I on my own way.

There is no need for me to know you personally, nor is there any need for you to know me personally. What is needed is an essential bridge between your being and my being. In silence that happens automatically.

Okay, Vimal?

Yes, Bhagwan.

Session 2

The New Man: A Citizen Of The World

*One thing is certain –
the old humanity is going to die.
If we can make the people of the world understand,
then a new kind of man can survive.
He will be a citizen of the world – no nations.
He will be religious – but no religion.
He will be scientific – but not destructive;
his whole science will be devoted to creation.*

February 26, 1987
Morning

Beloved Bhagwan,

One of the titles of the Master's Press is *A History of the Future.*
It is a book that puts together all the views
of the known prophecies about our future, and tries
to show what our world will be like in two hundred years.
Since Your views of the human race and this planet
are very specific, we would love to include Your views
of what man will go through and of how he will go through it.

Veet Niten, the first thing to be remembered about my attitude about the future is that all predictions are guesswork. The future remains always unknown and takes strange turns which no one would have ever conceived.

Moreover, my approach to life is to not be bothered with past and future. The past is no more, the future is not yet – all that we have got in our hands is this moment. The past is dead and the future is unborn.

Keeping this approach in mind, I would like to say a few words. First, there is every possibility that there will be no future as far as life is concerned. We are coming closer to a dead-end street. It is sad to recognize the fact, but it is good to recognize it, because then there is the possibility of taking a different turn. As things are moving today, the logical conclusion is a global suicide. There is only one hope: that life does not follow logic, that it is irrational. If it was rational, mathematical and logical, then you could not give more than twenty years to life on this earth.

The reasons are five:

First, the nuclear weapons are piling up every day. Right now, only five countries are nuclear powers. Within twenty years, twenty-five more countries will have joined the nuclear club. Thirty countries will have nuclear weapons. Already we have so much nuclear power that the whole earth can be destroyed seven times. And this will show you the insanity of man. Now what is the point of piling up more and more nuclear weapons?

Everybody is not a Jesus Christ, and everybody is not going to be resurrected again and again and again – seven times. The truth is, even Jesus himself was never resurrected, because in the first place he never died.

Just the other day the prime minister of the

Soviet Union, Gorbachev, said, "It is not possible to calculate how much destructive energy is already available." Just one submarine – and there are thousands of submarines moving underwater carrying nuclear weapons – just one submarine is equal to hundreds of second world wars. So the first problem is nuclear weapons.

The second problem is the immense rate of population growth. By the end of this century we will have seven billion people on the earth. And the earth is so heavily exploited that it cannot support that much population. Fifty percent of the population has to die simply of hunger. And just think, if fifty percent of the people die, what will be the situation of the living ones? There will be nobody even to carry their corpses to the graveyard; they will be rotting in your streets, in your neighborhood, even in your own house. The whole world will have become a vast graveyard, stinking of death.

No effort is being made by the politicians to prevent the population growth. On the contrary, a few rich countries of the West, for example Germany – where people are intelligent and can see that more population means more death, more population means more poverty, more population means more disease – have stopped producing children. And the politicians of those countries are giving incentives to produce more children because their population is decreasing.

They are not worried about the whole world. Their whole worry is…for example, Germany is losing three thousand people every day and thirty thousand immigrants are entering into Germany. The politician is not worried about the world, he is worried about his power, his country. If this goes on for twenty years – that their population goes on decreasing and immigrants go on coming more and more – the immigrants will be in the majority, they will be the rulers. So before it becomes a problem, the Germans have to start producing as many children as poor countries are doing. And the same is the situation of a few other Western countries.

The third problem is the disease AIDS, which is spreading like wildfire. And there seems to be no possibility, at least in the coming twenty years, of finding a cure for it. Scientists are more or less certain that there is no cure.

But no country is making celibacy a crime, and celibacy is the cause of the disease AIDS. It is the monks, the soldiers, the students, who are living separately from women, who become homosexuals – and homosexuality has created the disease. But homosexuality is only a symptom; the real problem is celibacy, *brahmacharya*.

Mahatma Ghandi has written a book, *Celibacy is Life*. Now somebody has to write a book, *Celibacy is Death*. And every country is trying to hide the facts: how many homosexuals they have, how many people are suffering from AIDS – because no one, no country, wants to be exposed to the world as homosexual. But you can see that every day people are dying from AIDS, all over the world. And AIDS takes time to ripen – it can take years – and then for death, at least two more years. If so many people are dying, millions around the world must be practicing homosexuality.

But it seems nobody has the guts to say that celibacy should be made a crime, and that those who are homosexuals should not be punished, but trained again to become heterosexuals. Every college, every school, every hospital, every institution that is concerned with human welfare should teach homosexuals, uncondition their mind from homosexuality and turn it to the natural way, the well-trodden way of heterosexuality.

All the religions are suffering from it, because they all teach celibacy. But no religion is ready to accept it, and whenever you don't accept an enemy you are giving more power to the enemy. Recognize it, so that you can find ways to fight with the enemy.

The fourth great problem that man is going to face in the coming twenty years is a collapse of the ecology. We are unaware of how we are destroying our own sources of life in different ways. Life needs an ecological balance, and that balance is being disturbed.

For example, around the earth is a layer of air. And just on the top of that layer is the ozone layer, which is a protective seal for the earth. But we have made holes in it by sending rockets to the moon and to Mars, which was absolutely unnecessary. You cannot manage the earth and you are starting to manage the whole universe.

The rockets, going out and coming in, have made holes and those holes are now turning out to be one of the most dangerous things – because the sun sends rays and all of the rays are not life-giving. That layer, the ozone layer, was returning those rays which would bring destruction and disease to the earth, and was allowing only life-giving rays. But we have made holes, not only with rockets, but by other means also, and now all those destructive rays are entering the atmosphere. Our atomic explosions have destroyed that layer; and there are many gases which scientists are producing – those gases have also created holes. Now the whole protective seal is no longer protective.

And it is not that the ecology is being disturbed from one direction alone. It is being destroyed by multi-dimensional methods. For example, because of the accumulation of carbon dioxide and man-made chemicals, the heat of the atmosphere has risen as it has never risen before.

For the first time there is a possibility that the ice on both the poles, north and south, has started melting. It has never melted before. If all the ice from the north and south poles melts, then all the oceans will rise by four feet. Cities which are ports, like Bombay, New York, or London, will be filled with water. But four feet...perhaps we can manage somehow.

The Himalayan ice has never melted, it has been eternally there. If the heat of the atmosphere rises a little more, then the Himalayan ice will start melting, and that is the greatest danger. And the heat is rising because nobody is listening, nobody is caring about anything. What happens to future humanity is nobody's concern – they are concerned with their power, their politics.

Atomic experiments continue, nuclear experiments continue. And it is a really horrible picture if the whole Himalaya melts; all the seas of the world will rise by forty feet. Perhaps four feet...somehow we can protect ourselves by creating walls or something, but forty feet higher.... The oceans will drown all your big cities, all your wealth, because they are all near the ocean.

A forty-foot rising of the oceans has immense implications. All the rivers will start moving backwards, because the oceans will not absorb them. The land will be flooded with water, and a flood will happen exactly like the one we read about in the *Old Testament*, which happened in Noah's time, when all life and everything got drowned. It has been, up to now, only a story; but the coming twenty years will see it happen as a fact. And there is nobody, and no way.... In that small story it was possible to create an ark, because sooner or later the floods would subside. But this is not a flood that is going to subside.

And the *most* dangerous thing is the fifth, which is man himself, with all his discriminations between black and white, between East and West, and a new discrimination has suddenly arisen between North and South. Humanity is divided by religions, by nations, by color, by race, and they are at each other's throats.

To avoid these five dangers, which man has never faced before, seems to be almost impossible – unless a miracle happens. But miracles happen only in stories, not in real life. And the most disturbing factor is that the intelligentsia of the world, the politicians of the world, the philosophers of the world are ignoring all these facts.

It happens in times of danger, that the only way to protect your peace of mind is to ignore the danger. This is called the "ostrich logic." The ostrich lives in the desert, a beautiful animal with a long neck, very colorful. Whenever the ostrich sees its enemies, other animals who can kill it, it has a strange logic – but very human. It simply digs a hole in the sand of the desert and puts its head inside the hole, because then it cannot see the enemy. And its logic is: if you cannot see the enemy, the enemy does not exist.

People are concerned about trivia, very stupid things, when great dangers are ahead. I hope that some sanity comes to humanity and life can be saved, but we will have to encounter all these five factors very carefully.

The world should have one government, there should not be any nations anymore. That way we can avoid any possibility of war.

The world should have only one kind of religiousness. Not one religion, just one kind of religiousness – a gratitude to existence, a loving heart, a meditative awareness. The most essential part of religion should be saved and Christianity and Hinduism and Buddhism and Jainism and Mohammedanism all should disappear from the earth. They are no longer needed; they have done enough harm. But now the harm is so much that they cannot be tolerated.

What is the need for nations? The whole earth is one.

Problems can be very easily solved if there is only one functional world government. Politicians will not like the idea because then they cannot go on bragging as presidents and prime ministers and cabinet ministers and parliamentarians do. If there is only one world government – and that too has to be functional, just like the post office or railway trains – somebody has to arrange things, so somebody should arrange things. And whoever is most capable technically, and scientifically to tackle the problem, should manage it – but not because of votes.

It is a strange situation that the most important things – your prime ministers, your presidents, your education ministers – are chosen by votes, votes of people who are absolutely ignorant of what they are doing. So there are education ministers who know nothing about education; there are prime ministers who have nothing to do with all these vast problems and don't even have the intelligence to tackle them.

You don't choose doctors, you don't choose surgeons: "It is a democracy, we will choose the surgeon; whoever gets the most votes will become the surgeon." Then instead of surgery there would be butchery and that is exactly what is happening.

Merit should be decisive, not the power of votes. And the meritorious should be *invited* because the meritorious are not the ones who are going to beg for votes. A man of merit has a certain dignity. Politicians don't have any dignity. They are beggars.

Although all the religions have been preaching celibacy, nobody raises the question:

Is celibacy natural? Is it humanly possible to be celibate? Can any scientist, or any medical expert, or any psychologist support the idea of celibacy? Nobody is going to say a single word against celibacy – that it is bringing all kinds of sexual perversions into humanity. Perhaps AIDS is only a beginning; even more dangerous diseases may be coming up.

And last I mention man. Man is not contemporary; he lives a thousand years back – and everything else has changed. His anger is the same, his fighting instinct is the same as when he used to have stone weapons. Now, the same man who used to have stone weapons has nuclear weapons. Man has not changed, and the technology has given him more and more destructive power.

If there is going to be a world war, it is going to be a push-button war. Nobody will be seen fighting in the field. Just from the White House, or from the Kremlin, the prime minister or the president simply pushes a button, and the whole world goes into the mouth of death. Nobody is going to win and nobody is going to defeat...it is such a stupid concept of war. Wars were fought for victory, but now the war is going to end all of them, friends and enemies, because both are capable of destroying each other.

It has been calculated that if the Soviet Union attacks America or America attacks the Soviet Union, which is more possible – in these last few months Ronald Reagan has shown his real face: he is absolutely stubborn, adamant, is not ready to stop creating more nuclear weapons – but whoever attacks first, the difference will be only of ten minutes; the other will be able to attack within ten minutes.

So the only thing is, who was ten minutes before and who was ten minutes after – no question of defeat, no question of victory, because there will be nobody left to write the history. It is a good idea, Veet Niten, to write the history now, because after twenty years perhaps there will be nobody to write history. You have a very beautiful idea, the history of the future. We have always been writing the history of the past; nobody has written the history of the future. But this is the right time to write it, because after twenty years there will be nobody to write it, and nobody to print it, and nobody to read it.

If you raise questions which are so dangerous, people will be annoyed with you. I have turned the whole world into my enemy for the simple reason that I go on pulling the necks of the ostriches out of the sand, and tell them that it does not matter whether you see the enemy or not. It is better to see, because by seeing you may have some way to escape, but putting your head into the sand you are absolutely defenseless. But the *shuturmurg,* this ostrich, feels very happy when his head is underneath the sand. If you pull his neck out he becomes angry, because again he has to see the enemy. Nobody wants to see the enemy. If we are fully aware of all the enemies....

Nuclear weapons have to be drowned in the Pacific Ocean, and the Pacific Ocean has to be banned for a few years to any kind of traffic. The Pacific Ocean is five miles deep; the name is also very significant, it means "peaceful". All the nuclear weapons, whoever possesses them, should go into the Pacific.

Celibacy should be a severe crime all over the world. All the monks and nuns should be allowed to marry each other, and it should not be thought that marriage or a love-relationship is against spirituality.

But people are so idiotic. Just the other day I came to know that the bishop of London, who ranks third in the hierarchy of the Church of England – the Archbishop of Canterbury is the first, he is the third, just one man is in between – has threatened the Church of England that if women are accepted as priests, then he will create a division in the Church of England. He will separate, with all those who are against women's initiation into becoming priests, bishops, cardinals.

People are concerned with such stupid problems. My feeling is that this is a way of avoiding the real problems. This is the ostrich's logic. For forty years continuously, there is a district in Maharashtra, Belgaum, where they have been fighting about whether Belgaum should be in Maharashtra, or it should be in Karnataka, another state on the border of Maharashtra. And they have been killing each other; riots have been happening, arson has been happening.

Strange people. What does it matter whether Belgaum is in Karnataka or in Maharashtra? And if you want to decide, let the Belgaum people decide it – they can vote on where they want to go. Under impartial observers this can be decided within two hours. For forty years they have been killing each other – and the problem remains where it was when the British left India. And I cannot conceive at all that, whether Belgaum is in Karnataka or in Maharashtra...what difference does it make? Maharashtra and Gujarat were fighting for Bombay. Gujaratis and Maharashtrians had been killing each other because...where should Bombay go, in Gujarat or in Maharashtra? Bombay will remain where it is.

I remember a beautiful story: When India was partitioned into India and Pakistan, on the border there was a madhouse. Obviously nobody was interested in that madhouse – thousands of mad people – but it had to be somewhere. The superintendent of the madhouse called a meeting of all the mad people and asked ,"You raise your hands whether you want to go to India or you want to go to Pakistan." They said, "We want to live here. We don't want to go anywhere."

The superintendent tried hard, "You will not be going anywhere, you will remain here." But the madmen could not understand. "If we will remain here then what's the problem? Then why are you asking, 'Who wants to go to India and who wants to go to Pakistan?' We are all friends and we want to remain here."

The superintendent could not explain to them the idea that their madhouse would belong to India, or it would belong to Pakistan. They said, "It does not matter. What is the problem? Why are you so worried?"

Finally it was decided that these people were not going to understand anything, so it was better to divide the madhouse into two parts. A wall was raised in the middle, and half the madhouse remained in India and half the madhouse became part of Pakistan.

I have heard that still the mad people climb on the wall from both sides and laugh at the whole matter, saying, "We are where we used to be. What happened to that 'going to India,' 'going to Pakistan'? Nobody has gone anywhere, and unnecessarily they have created this wall!" Small things go on keeping the human mind involved, so it cannot tackle the real problems.

I have told you there are five real problems which are going to destroy humanity. Solutions are very easy, but it is a big madhouse; nobody seems to understand.

All nuclear weapons into the Pacific.

The whole idea of celibacy has to be condemned as a crime, and the homosexuals have to be trained – they have become perverted – for heterosexuality.

But you will be surprised...the parliament of Holland prevented my entry into Holland, like many other countries. When the question was asked, the minister concerned answered, "Bhagwan has been prevented from coming into Holland: first, he is a dangerous man, he corrupts people's minds; second, in one of his statements he has appreciated Adolf Hitler." Out of context...I had made one statement, in which I had said that Adolf Hitler was a greater saint than Mahatma Gandhi. He never produced a single child, he was always going to bed early and getting up early in the morning, he was not using any kind of alcoholic beverage, and – you will be surprised – he was a vegetarian.

So I was simply joking, that if saintliness consists of these things then Adolf Hitler has defeated Mahatma Gandhi very easily. Mahatma Gandhi took the vow of celibacy after he had created four children. At that age one naturally wants to get rid of sex, because it is simply tiring. The American Medical Association has exposed that there are millions of people in America alone – to say nothing about the whole world – who have a migraine whenever they make love. They are doing great research into why they have a migraine after making love – after making love they should have a good sleep.

But to show you an example of conditioning: the scientists and the medical people who are doing the research into why the migraine happens are finding all kinds of causes, except the real cause. The real cause is Christianity, because sex has been condemned; so their minds are divided – half of their mind is against sex and half of their mind wants to go the natural way. This creates the tension.

I am not a medical man, I am not a scientist, but I can say with absolute authority that it is the condemnation of sex that is creating the migraine. Because the researchers are all Christians, they will find out many things, but they will not look at a simple psychological fact that no aboriginal ever has a migraine after making love. All these millions of people are Christian, and most of them are very pious and religious people. It is their religion that is creating the migraine because it is creating a split. And a migraine is nothing but a split in the head – one part wants to go, one part pulls back – naturally a migraine will be the result.

All condemnation of sex and all appreciation of celibacy should be absolutely stopped; otherwise we cannot get rid of AIDS. It is going to spread – it *is* spreading.

It is a simple fact that the earth is undivided. What is the need for so many nations, except that they fulfill so many people's ego trips? There is no other need. Why should Germany be afraid of immigrants, and give incentives to Germans to produce more children, when the earth is dying from overpopulation? If there was one world government we could shift population from one place to another place. Wherever the population starts decreasing, it should be replaced by the increasing population from other nations.

Once we accept that the world is one, then there is no need to destroy, every year, billions of dollars' worth of food in America, in Europe. They have to destroy it, and people in the East are dying. In Ethiopia one thousand people were dying every day, and at that very time in Europe they wasted two billion dollars in carrying their foodstuffs to be drowned in the ocean. If the world is one, and some countries are producing more and some countries have become barren, the food can be distributed very easily.

If religions disappear from the world, then many idiotic things will disappear with them. They are against birth control, although they know perfectly well that Jesus is the only begotten son of God – God created only one son in the whole of eternity. He must be practicing birth control; otherwise why only one son? – at least one daughter as well. But the religions are against birth control, they are against abortion, without any feeling for the danger of overpopulation – that the world will kill itself.

That death will be very cruel because it does not come immediately; when a person dies because of hunger, it takes months of torture and suffering. A healthy man can live without food for three months; then he will die, because the healthy man has a reservoir of energy in his body, which is for emergency purposes. But even the poorest man, the sickest man, will take a few days, a few weeks to die. Those few weeks of hunger are going to be absolute hell.

But religions are concerned with creating more children because more children means more power – power in two ways: more votes, and more fodder for your cannons in war.

For twenty to thirty years absolute birth control should be practiced. It is not a question of democracy, because it is a choice between life and death. If the whole world is going to die, what are you going to do with your democracy? Democracy will be the rule then – for the graves, of the graves, by the graves – because people will have disappeared.

Religions carry superstitions of all kinds which are hindering your intelligence, your vision, your possibility of creating a new man in the world.

One thing is certain – the old humanity is going to die. If we can make the people of the world understand, then a new kind of man can survive.

He will be a citizen of the world – no nations.
He will be religious – but no religion.
He will be scientific – but not destructive; his whole science will be devoted to creation.
He will be pious, compassionate, loving – but not celibate. That is a kind of lunacy. A celibate is a lunatic.

The new man will stop all kinds of experiments which are increasing the heat of the atmosphere around the earth, because the priority is *life,* not your experiments. The new man will not send rockets to create holes from which death-rays can enter into our atmosphere; there is no need at all. And if the need arises, then you should also be prepared to close those holes – the moment the rocket goes out, the hole is closed; the moment the rocket comes in, the hole is closed.

That is the only way to avoid the seas bringing the old story of the flood in which everything was destroyed...and now even Noah's Ark will not help, because the flood will never recede.

A new man without any burden of the past, more meditative, more silent, more loving...all the universities, rather than wasting their time on superficial subjects, should devote time to creating more consciousness in man. But football seems to be more important. It is one of the most idiotic games...and millions of people go mad when there is a football match.

I know one of my friends – he is a professor – he takes leave when there is a football match. If he cannot go to the match itself, then he sits in front of his television set. I was staying with him, he lives in Amritsar. Television came first to Pakistan, because Pakistan is an ally of America; it came to India almost twenty years afterwards. But Amritsar is only fifteen miles away from Pakistan, so they were enjoying Pakistani programs on television, even when in India there was no television.

I was staying with that friend, and I got fed up sitting in the room, because seeing a football match...it is so idiotic – millions of people are going mad, as if something very crucial is involved. And because the team that he was identified with was defeated, he threw his television set on the floor, he was so angry.

I said, "You must be an idiot! That I knew from the very beginning, but what is the crime of the poor television set?"

He said, "I became so enraged. It is absolutely unjust."

But I said, "It may be unjust or just, the television set is not concerned in it."

He said, "It is not a question of the television set. I was so angry, I wanted to destroy something."

In a Californian university, for one year they have been studying...that whenever there is a boxing match – which is the ugliest thing you can conceive of, people hitting on each other's noses.... Boxing proves Charles Darwin is right: man has come from animals and still has animal instincts in him. The report of the California university is very significant: whenever there is a boxing match, crime rates go fourteen percent higher immediately, and they remain at that level for at least one week – fourteen percent higher.

Just seeing people hitting each other, their own animal becomes alive – more murders, more rape, more suicides. It takes seven days for them to calm down, back to their normal criminality. Still, boxing is not banned. The same happens with football matches.

You will be surprised to know that American researchers have found that the crime rate is always on the increase. But a new phenomenon has started, and that is small children committing crimes, which has never happened before – thirteen-year-old boys, twelve-year-old boys trying to rape girls; ten-year-old boys, nine-year-old boys murdering, assassinating; seven-year-olds, eight-year-olds taking drugs – and in millions. Now drugs are not thought to be for adult people, but for primary school children.

But nobody seems to be concerned about why this is happening. It can be prevented. People use drugs because without drugs they are so much in anguish and anxiety drugs calm down their minds for a few hours. But again the problems are back. Unless meditation becomes an absolute in every educational institution, drugs cannot be prohibited. You can prohibit...they go underground. Man has to be taught some other ways of becoming calm and quiet and blissful, then there is no need for all these things.

A fourteen-year-old boy committing rape simply shows that you have to change your attitudes about sex. Boys and girls should be raised in hostels together; they should be allowed to make love with no inhibition. Up to a certain age there is no problem, because the girls are not going to get pregnant, so it is simply a game, a joyful game they can enjoy. But rape is a crime – and you are responsible for it.

By the time the girls are of the age that they can become pregnant, the pill should be available in every institution. And now there are pills available for men also; either the girl can take it or the boy can take it. In the past it used to happen sometimes that you had not taken the pill, and suddenly you met your lover – and man always thinks, "This is not going to happen to *me*...." But now they have found a new pill which can be taken after love-making. It is more secure.

Things should be thought about in a scientific way, not in a superstitious way; then there is a possibility of man's future. In many countries now they are declaring homosexuality a crime – that will make homosexuality go underground. This I call unintelligent. They should create special campuses for homosexuals, with absolute respect for their dignity. They can move to a special campus. Near every big city beautiful campuses should be available, where homosexuals can move, so that the disease does not spread among the general public. And among homosexuals there are many who are suffering from AIDS, so there should be a special section in the homosexual campus for the AIDS people.

No disrespect should be shown to them, but compassion. They are victims of religious ideologies. And there are doctors who are homosexuals, there are doctors who are suffering from AIDS. These doctors should be moved to those campuses. We can prevent the rest of humanity from being affected, and without destroying the dignity of the homosexuals or the people who are suffering from AIDS. It is so simple, and they will not be a burden on society. They can work, they can produce, they can do whatsoever they are skilled in; but they should remain in their own monastery. I call it a monastery, homosexual monasteries.

If we take a serious step against all these five dangers that are facing humanity, Veet Niten, there is a possibility of a new man, of a better man, of a natural man, of a healthier man, of a more religious man in the future...a world without wars, without nations, without religions...a world peaceful, loving...a world in search of truth, of bliss, of ecstasy.

But if these five problems are not solved immediately, there is no future possible.

You should start writing your book, *A History of the Future*, as quickly as possible, because most probably there is not going to be any future.

Beloved Bhagwan,

I really dig the idea of being a mirror,
but I am Italian.
Do You know the Italian mirror?
Once I was staying with two friends and a woman,
living in the same house.
One day the woman left.
She had written a message on her lover, Hugo's, mirror
with her lipstick: "Hugo ti amo" – "I love you, Hugo."
When the other guy went to the bathroom and saw the message,
he became envious.
So he put his finger in a pot of spaghetti
and wrote on the mirror with the tomato sauce:
"I love you, Sugo" – "sugo" means spaghetti sauce.
This is to give You an idea of an Italian mirror.
Now do You still want me to be mirror?

Sarjano, I still want you to be a mirror, but not an Italian mirror. There are more varieties of mirrors. Not only are Italian mirrors full of spaghetti sauce, even Italian heads are full of spaghetti. In this whole world I hate only one thing and that is spaghetti.

But you can be a German mirror, a Belgian mirror – the best of all mirrors is the Belgian mirror; and if you are going to be a mirror, why not be the best? But a mirror you have to be. And avoid spaghetti as far as possible, because that makes the Italians greasy. From every pore of their body you can see spaghetti coming out.

I love the Italians minus spaghetti.

Okay, Vimal?

Yes, Bhagwan.

Session 3

Just Like The Open Sky

*The moment the mind stops bothering you,
for the first time you are healthy, sane.
For the first time you are really born;
you are free from the imprisonment of thoughts and fears.
For the first time you have attained
to the most delicious phenomenon in existence –
freedom.*

February 26, 1987
Evening

Beloved Bhagwan,

A few months ago my friend and I were visiting his dying father.
Lots of people were around. His body was about finished.
To most people he was indifferent, but when everyone left
he suddenly opened his eyes and told us, "I feel like I have two bodies;
one body is sick and the other is completely healthy."
We told him, "That's right!
The healthy body is the real you, so stay with that one."
He said, "Okay," and closed his eyes.
As we sat with him, the sick energy around the hospital bed changed.
We couldn't believe this new energy;
it was as if we were in darshan with You...such beautiful silence.
I felt a bit strange saying these words
to someone who was really experiencing this.
Whatever I said wasn't really my experience,
just something I'd thought about.
After we left he improved for a while,
went home and died peacefully in his bed.
Beloved Bhagwan, even though I've been with You for ten years,
I felt so ignorant in front of this man who was ready
to let go of everything with such trust and clarity and peace.

Geeta, the experience that you went through always is possible when someone is dying. All that is required is a little alertness. The man who was dying was aware – not much awareness is needed for this experience.

At the moment of death your physical body and your spiritual body start separating. Ordinarily, they are so much involved with each other that you don't feel their separation. But at the moment of death, just before death happens, both the bodies start getting unidentified with each other. Now their ways are going to be different; the physical body is going to the physical elements, and the spiritual body is on its pilgrimage onwards, to a new birth, in a new form, in a new womb.

If the person is a little alert he can see it himself, and because you said to him that the healthier body is you, and the body that is sick and dying is not you.... In those moments, to trust is very easy because it is happening just before the eyes of the person himself; he cannot identify with the body that is falling apart, and he can immediately recognize the fact that he is the healthier one, the deeper one.

But you could have helped the man even a little more – this was good, but not good enough.

Even this experience of the man, of getting unidentified with the physical body, immediately changed the energy in the room; it became silent, peaceful.

But if you had learned the art of how to help a dying man, you would not have stopped where you stopped. A second thing was absolutely necessary to tell him because he was in a trusting state – everybody is, at the moment of death.

It is life which creates problems and doubts and postponements, but death has no time to postpone. The man cannot say, "I will try to see," or, "I will see tomorrow." He has to do it right now, this very moment, because even the next moment is not certain. Most probably he is not going to survive. And what is he going to lose by trusting? Death anyway, is going to take away everything. So the fear of trust is not there; time to think about it is not there. And a clarity is there that the physical body is getting farther and farther away.

It was a good step to tell him, "You are the healthier body." The second step would have been to tell him, "You are the witness of both the bodies; the body that is dying is physical, and the body that you are feeling is healthy is psychological. But who are *you*? You can see both the bodies...certainly you must be the third; you cannot be one of these two."

This is the whole process of the *Bardo*. Only in Tibet have they developed the art of dying. While the whole world has been trying to develop the art of living, Tibet is the only country in the world which has developed the whole science and art of dying. They call it the *Bardo*.

If you had told the person, "This is good that you have taken one step, you are out of the physical body; but now you have got identified with the psychological body. You are not even that; you are only awareness, a pure consciousness, a perceptivity...." If you could have helped the person to understand that he is neither this body nor that body, but something bodiless, formless, a pure consciousness, then his death would have been a totally different phenomenon.

You saw the change of energy; you would have seen another change of energy. You saw silence descending; you would have seen music also, a certain dancing energy also, a certain fragrance filling the whole space. And the man's face would have shown a new phenomenon – the aura of light.

If he had taken the second step also, then his death would have been the last death. In the *Bardo* they call it "the great death," because now he will not be born into another form, into another imprisonment; now he will remain in the eternal, in the oceanic consciousness that fills the whole universe.

So remember it – it may happen to many of you. You may be with a friend or with a relative, your mother, your father. While they are dying, help them to realize two things: first, they are not the physical body – which is very simple for a dying man to recognize. Second – which is a little difficult, but if the man is able to recognize the first, there is a possibility of the second recognition too – that you are not even the second body; you are beyond both the bodies. You are pure freedom and pure consciousness.

If he had taken the second step, then you would have seen a miracle happening around him – something, not just silence, but something more alive, something belonging to eternity, to immortality. And all of you who were present there would have been overwhelmed with gratitude that this death has not been a time of mourning, but it has become a moment of celebration.

If you can transform a death into a moment of celebration, you have helped your friend, your mother, your father, your brother, your wife, your husband. You have given them the greatest gift that is possible in existence. And close to death it is very easy. The child is not even worried about life or death; he has no concern. The young man is too much involved in biological games, in ambitions, in becoming richer, in becoming powerful, in having more prestige; he has no time to think of eternal questions.

But at the moment of death, just before death is going to happen, you don't have any ambition. And whether you are rich or poor makes no difference; whether you are a criminal or a saint makes no difference. Death takes you beyond all discriminations of life and beyond all stupid games of life.

But rather than helping people, people destroy that beautiful moment. It is the most precious in a man's whole life. Even if he has lived one hundred years, this is the most precious moment. But people start crying and weeping and showing their sympathy, saying, "This is very untimely, it should not happen." Or they start consoling the person, saying, "Don't be worried, the doctors are saying that you will be saved."

These are all foolishnesses. Even the doctors play a part in these stupid things. They don't tell you that your death has come. They avoid the subject; they go on giving you hope. They say, "Don't be worried, you will be saved," knowing perfectly well that the man is going to die. They are giving him a false consolation, not knowing that this is the moment when he should be made fully aware of death – so acutely and so impeccably aware that pure consciousness is experienced. That moment has become a moment of great victory. Now there is no death for him, but only eternal life.

Beloved Bhagwan,

When You said that now is the time
to drop the duality between me and You,
You gave me what I've yearned for from the moment I saw You.
I want to write this so that it is more real,
so that I can know more and more that this is my truth.
Beloved Bhagwan, I am not separate from You. There is no You – there is no me.
This feels so awesome to say – even more awesome to live.
Why? How to ever drop over my head?

Kaveesha, this is your truth. It will be better to say this is *the* truth, because the truth cannot be yours or mine. And I have known it from the very beginning, since you first saw me.

It is not a question of time – that one has to live with me for years and only then will he be able to feel that there is no I and there is no thou.

It is a question of sensitivity, not of time – of a clear perception, not of living many, many years with me.

There are people who have lived with me for years. In fact, the more they have lived with me, the more they have forgotten me completely; they have started taking me for granted. They will wake up only when I disappear from this physical body. Then they will feel a sudden shock – twenty years we have been together, what happened?

So it can happen in the first moment – it can happen any time. The only requirement is a clear perception. And Kaveesha, you have a very clear perception and a very loving heart. And from the very first moment you have not hesitated at all in opening all your doors, all your windows; you have been available to me.

I remember the first day I looked into your eyes, and I knew that somebody is there who is ready to disappear. If *you* disappear, you will suddenly realize that I disappeared long ago. So there is no I and there is no thou.

Kaveesha was born in a Jewish family, and she must be aware of one of the great Jewish thinkers of this century, Martin Buber. His most famous book, for which he received the Nobel Prize, is *I And Thou*. His whole philosophy is that people need a deep dialogue between I and thou.

He has written very logically and very rationally – he was one of the geniuses of this century – but his whole philosophy is wrong. He thinks the dialogue happens between I and thou. And I say unto you, the dialogue happens only when there is no I and no thou.

It is a very strange dialogue, of course, because we are accustomed only to a dialogue between two persons; and I am saying that when two persons disappear into one, only then there is dialogue, a heart-to-heart communion.

Martin Buber is dead; otherwise I would have traveled to Israel – he was very old – just to tell him, "There is still time for you; drop this idea of I and thou. Let there remain only the dialogue."

With Kaveesha there has been only a dialogue. And it is not that only now she has become aware of it; she has also been aware of it, but she wanted the seal of my authority on it – because one never knows whether one is dreaming or seeing the reality, whether one is imagining, or really the revolution has happened. Her question is just for her to become clear about it, so nothing remains clouded.

Yes, Kaveesha, this is the truth. Neither yours nor mine; just the truth.

You are saying, "Beloved Bhagwan, I am not separate from you. There is no you – there is no me. This feels so awesome to say – even more awesome to live."

It is such a great mystery to live that it is natural it will look very awesome – it is so overwhelming. But slowly, slowly, everything else becomes unreal and false before this simple reality – that there is no I and there is no thou.

It has happened between me and you, and soon you will see that it is happening between you and everyone else. This is only the beginning. It will be complete only when there is no I and no thou anywhere, when you are merged and melted into the ocean of the whole.

You have entered the door of the temple, and now there is no way of turning back. Just accept it as a gift of the divine in total humbleness and simplicity of the heart; otherwise it can become a heavy burden. The experience is too big, and we are so small.

It is almost as if the ocean has dropped into the dewdrop – just think of the poor dewdrop! When the dewdrop falls into the ocean, it is simpler; but once in a while the ocean also drops into the dewdrop – then it is tremendously awesome and overwhelming. But to whomsoever it happens, he is blessed, immensely blessed.

Just take it with deep relaxation, and with a humble heart, and soon it will become your natural way of life. Looking at the trees, or at the stars, you will find the same dialogue.

Beloved Bhagwan,

I feel as if I am almost letting go, but a part inside me,
small but very persistent, is holding on tight.
It creates a feeling of anxiety, a cloud of worry, a sense of incompletion.
Often, with You, the beauty of a single moment is so intense
that it turns into an ache and a longing.
Is it because my "yes" is not total yet?
And why does this create a sort of existential worry?
Nobody else seems worried.

Deva Surabhi, your question has its own answer in it – but this is how people are unconscious. You have not even thought a second time about what you are writing. You are writing, "I feel as if I am almost letting go." Do you see what it means? The moment let-go happens, it is not almost. Either it happens or it does not happen.

Let-go does not come in installments, and it is never "almost" – that too is "as if." Even the "almost" is not certain – uncertainty upon uncertainty upon uncertainty. "As if" is also not the beginning. "I feel" – it is not that I experience. Naturally, you will find yourself in tension and in anxiety.

And you ask me, "Is it because my 'yes' is not total yet?" What to say of your "yes" and its totality? You have not even dreamt about it; you have only heard about it, and you have seen people in a state of yes-ness.

You have also longed for it because you have seen the joy of those whose "yes" is total; you have seen their dance, you have seen their song. It is out of a competitive spirit – you don't want to be left behind. But you don't have any "yes" yet; otherwise, there would be no anxiety and no tension. "Yes" is a total let-go.

But my feeling about Surabhi is that she is a great thinker. I say great thinker because she is the only one who writes so many questions every day. I have to go on throwing away dozens of her questions, and then I start feeling that the poor girl is writing so many questions that I must choose at least one. So out of compassion I choose, Surabhi, your questions. Otherwise, they are not worth answering.

I would never have answered anybody else's question if he had written, "I feel as if I am almost letting go, but a part inside me, small but very persistent, is holding on tight." Even if a part of you is holding on tight, it is enough to destroy your whole idea of let-go. You cannot divide yourself into parts; even if one hand is holding tight, your whole body will have to remain there.

I have heard about a man who stole from the treasury of the king and was brought before the king. The man was certainly a very strange fellow because he did not deny it, although there was no eyewitness. He was not caught red-handed; he could have denied it – it was almost impossible for the king to prove that he had stolen from his treasury. But the man said, "Yes, I have stolen from the treasury, and whatever punishment you want to give, you can give. But remember one thing – only my hands have been involved in the stealing – I was just standing there and watching. I am the only eyewitness."

The king said, "You seem to be a very strange fellow. Your hands were stealing, and you were standing there, just looking."

The man said, "That's how I work. You can punish my hands, but you cannot punish me. That would be very unjust of you. And anyway, you don't have any other witness except me."

The king said, "You are not only a thief, but you seem to be very logical, too. Okay, I sentence both your hands to be kept for thirty years in jail."

The whole court laughed. The king said, "Now the poor fellow will be in difficulty because if his hands are in jail, how can he avoid not being in jail?" But the man laughed with the laughing court.

Seeing that he was laughing, the court stopped, because the man took off both of his hands – which were false – threw them before the king and said, "Goodbye. Thirty years, or three hundred years...as many years as you want to keep them, keep them."

But Surabhi, your parts are not false. If a false hand were holding tight, then things would be easy. You are an organic whole. An anxiety is being created because you are *trying* to let go. It is not a question of trying – because trying itself will be the hindrance to moving into the space of let-go.

Let-go cannot be tried. It is simply an outcome of understanding – you simply understand something.

For example, you see that your house is on fire. Then, you don't consult the *Encyclopedia Britannica* for how to get out of the house when the house is on fire; you don't give even a single moment for thinking. You just rush from wherever you can find a space to get out of the house – you may have to jump out of the window.

I have seen a man jumping out of his bathroom, naked, because the house was on fire. And nobody objected to it because you cannot follow etiquette and manners in a situation when the house is on fire. The poor fellow was in the bath under the shower. Do you think he should first put on his dress, make-up, and then go out of the front door? – just like a gentleman, jumping out of the window, in the house of another person, and that too, naked. But nobody took note of it. On the contrary, the neighbors brought a blanket and covered him.

Let-go is an instantaneous understanding: you see the futility of your effort. In that very seeing, let-go happens. It is not something, Surabhi, that you have to do – you are trying to do it. The same is true about love. These belong to the same category: let-go, love, meditation, God – they are not your doings. You are seeing people in a yes state, flowering, blossoming, in spring. You also want to be in that state, but you don't understand that "yes" is not a by-product of effort; "yes" is an outcome of deep understanding.

So while you are here, rather than fighting for "yes," try to understand what I am saying, what I am, what is happening here. Remain open and available, and one day – and one can never say when, it is unpredictable...one day – and there are not many days, there are only seven days, so there is no need to be worried.... Somebody may become enlightened on Monday, and somebody will become enlightened on Sunday – it doesn't matter. There is not much choice, only seven days....

So just relax, enjoy, forget all about achieving something: self-realization, enlightenment, God. Forget everything – we are not here to achieve anything, we are here just to enjoy these few moments that are available to us. It is another thing if while you are enjoying, suddenly you find God is dancing with you – that is another thing. You were not dancing for God, you were not waiting for Him; your dance was so beautiful, your dance was so total, your dance was so intense that the dancer disappeared.

In that moment you will find God dancing with you. And don't make much fuss about it – "God danced with me" – because if you make much fuss about it, you may not find the same dance again; you will be always, from the corner of your eyes, watching for when God comes. He never comes in this way.

There are millions of monks of all the religions in the world who are trying hard to get God to dance with them, but they never get even a glimpse of Him. And here you will find many people who have known what it means when God dances with you, what it means to say a total "yes" to existence.

It is not on your part an effort; you just drop the achieving mind which has been given to you by the society. It creates in the mind ambitions: ambition for money, ambition for power, ambition for prestige, ambition for God, ambition for heaven – but it is all ambition. In a mind which is ambitious for money and ambitious for prestige, ambition for God, ambition for enlightenment, ambition for nirvana are not different. They are all ambitions, all decorations for the ego. And God cannot be a decoration for your ego; neither can enlightenment be a decoration for your ego.

When you are not, then the whole existence starts showering thousands of flowers upon you from every dimension, from every direction.

Beloved Bhagwan,

The mind often tells me to beware of my greatest fear:
that any wrong move could result in a fall
and lead me away from Your love.
And yet, Bhagwan, I feel now as never before
that You are the breath flowing through me, the heart beating within,
that You are one with me when I rest behind my eyes,
that You are in the open sky between my breaths,
that You live within every fiber of my being –
absolutely inseparable and present.
O beloved One, I long to finally relax
and never worry about being separate from You.
Why do I still believe my mind and worry so much?
Or is it possible that what I am experiencing
is just an illusion? With tears of gratitude, so much more than I can contain,
I kiss this earth that gives You to us.

Maitri, mind is fear. Mind is a coward and is always concerned about security, safety, certainty. The world of love and the world of meditation is pure insecurity; it is moving into the unknown with no maps in your hand, with no guidebook to lead you, not knowing where you are going, not knowing where you are going to land finally.

Mind naturally always is worried, creating questions about where you are going, what you are seeking. Remain within the mundane world where things are objective and where superhighways exist which have milestones, which have maps, which have guidebooks, and you know exactly where you are going, and you know exactly where you will reach. But the world of love, the world of godliness, is just like the open sky. The birds fly, but they don't leave their footprints for other birds to follow. They don't make highways, superhighways, so that the coming generations don't go astray.

The human mind is always worried about going astray. So you have to learn one thing: that it is the nature of the mind to be worried. Just as you have five fingers...once you have accepted that you have five fingers, finished; you don't have to think every day, "...only five fingers?"

One of my teachers in the university had six fingers, and he was always hiding his sixth finger. It was very easy to expose him; I would just give a paper, a question, and he would have to take the question with the hand with the sixth finger, and the whole class would laugh. And on the note I had written, "This is just to expose your sixth finger."

When I did it the first time, he called me into

his room and asked me, "What kind of thing is this?"

I said, "What kind of thing were you doing? You started."

He said, "What do you mean, I started?"

I said, "You were hiding your sixth finger. And I simply wanted everybody to know that we have got a great teacher who has six fingers. Just *you* know that you have six fingers; let everybody know and be finished with it. Then there is no need every morning to worry about having six fingers. What is wrong in it? People are just missing one finger, that's all."

He said, "That's true. Why should I be afraid?"

I said, "But you go on always keeping your hands in your pockets." Even in public lectures he would keep his hands in his pockets – but I would approach with a paper. And he knew that there was nothing on the paper, but before the meeting he could not refuse it, he had to take it; he had to take his hands out. And both hands had six fingers. On the paper I used to write, "Just to expose your six fingers."

I said, "Once and for all, just show your six fingers to everybody, and ask everybody, 'Has anybody any objection?' And be finished with it. Why be worried?"

Maitri, mind will always create. I say *always;* in whatever state you are, it will always create – whether it is imagination or truth, whether it is a dream or reality, whether I am hallucinating or experiencing something existential.

Once and for all, tell the mind, "It is none of your business. If it is hallucination and I am enjoying it, nothing is wrong in it." The criterion should be the enjoyment, the ecstasy, the dance – if it is filling my heart with joy, then who cares whether it is true or untrue.

Otherwise, even if you become enlightened, your mind is going to ask, "First enquire whether your enlightenment is true, or just an exaggerated imagination." If it is imagination, then too it is a very good imagination; if it is a dream, it is a very sweet dream. It is better than having nightmares!

The mind has to be continuously put into its place – "You are not to be taken seriously at all. I am going to enjoy imagination, I am going to enjoy hallucination, I am going to enjoy illusion, I am going to enjoy dreaming – *I am going to enjoy.* You just keep silent, don't disturb."

The real thing is your being blissful, not the object, whether it is real or not. Your blissfulness is the criterion of its reality. But the mind is very clever and very cunning. Even if in this very moment it cannot distract you, it can start thinking and giving you ideas that you may go astray in the future; you may lose the path.

If you are here right now, then your next moment is going to be born out of this moment. It will be even more real. The future does not come from above, from nowhere; it grows within you. And if your present moment is full of love and full of juice and full of joy, out of this present moment will be growing your future; out of this life will be growing another life; out of this experience is going to grow your experience of the eternal.

But mind takes a little time, because you have listened to its fears and anxieties always. It goes on poking its nose into everything.

You have to be alert not to allow the mind to disturb your peace in the present, and the future will take care of itself. Because the future will always come as the present – and you know how to take care of the present – you know how to take care of all eternity because time cannot come to you in any other form than the present.

So let your blissfulness be the only criterion. If something is making you blissful, it is bound to be real – because from the unreal you cannot get blissfulness. And if your blissfulness goes on growing, then you are on the right path. Whenever you feel that your blissfulness is diminishing, then you are losing the right path. Then move back to the path where you were feeling more blissful – just a simple criterion, but it is enough for your whole journey, the whole pilgrimage.

Slowly, slowly, mind stops interfering, saying, "This Maitri has gone crazy; she does not listen to my sane advice." Nobody has attained to truth through the advice of the mind. Those who have attained to truth have attained by going against the mind, going beyond the mind, putting the mind aside.

One thing is certain, that mind is not going to deliver you anything that is of value. So just stop listening to it. It is a constant harassment. It does not allow you to sit silently even for a few moments. It will start asking you, "What are you doing? In this much time you could have earned so much money; you could have gone and seen your girlfriend or boyfriend – what are you doing here? At least you could have read the morning newspaper...wasting your beautiful morning."

Just go on pushing the mind aside – "You go on, meet the girlfriend, read the newspaper, but leave me alone." It is a parasite on you. But if you constantly go on throwing it away, slowly, slowly it will start not bothering you, saying, "This Maitri has gone beyond the boundary of sanity."

The moment the mind stops bothering you, for the first time you are healthy, sane. For the first time you are really born; you are free from the imprisonment of thoughts and fears. For the first time you have attained to the most delicious phenomenon in existence – freedom.

This place is not for the mind; this place is for those who can leave their mind outside the gate. Come inside, dancing and joyous. And when you go back, you can pick up your mind or anybody's mind – that will do, because they are all insane, and once in a while to change them is always good; you will have some new gossips to hear.

But here you have to be absolutely without mind. This is the only gift I can give to you: to help you to be without the mind. And then all the treasures of existence are yours.

Okay, Vimal?

Yes, Bhagwan.

Session 4

First Be Selfish

*Knowing thyself, you can be unselfish.
In fact you will be unselfish; it won't be an effort on your part.
Knowing thyself, you will know not only yourself,
but you will know the self of everyone.
It is the same; it is one consciousness, one continent.
People are not islands.*

February 27, 1987
Morning

Beloved Bhagwan,

This morning during discourse a great sadness overwhelmed me.
I feel so poor...there is nothing I can give You, not even my heart.
Slowly I surrender to my reality.
There is no need to pretend any longer.
A quiet peace and serenity descends,
and a warmth that is not mine follows in their wake,
leaving my sadness.
There is nothing I can give You, not even my heart.
Haven't You taken it long before?

Deva Gita, there is no question of anything to be given to me; on the contrary, you have to be receptive to what I am giving to you. It is true you are poor, but I am not poor. Let my riches be your riches, and let my mornings be your mornings, and let my nights, full of stars, be your nights too.

The very idea that you have to give something to me is absurd. All that you can do is to be receptive and available. When I knock on your doors, I should not find them closed – it is more than enough on your part. And when I take you into unknown territories you should come with me without any fear, without anything holding back.

You have all the money in the world but you are poor. I don't have any money in the world but I am rich – rich in my being. That's the only richness I recognize, because anything other than the inner richness is going to be taken away by death. It is not yours; it belongs to the world. The only thing that belongs to you is your own consciousness, and that consciousness is asleep. Just allow me to wake it up.

As far as your heart is concerned, you are right – I have taken it away long before. And when I take people's hearts, I don't take their permission. Hearts have also to be stolen. No permission is asked, because if you give your heart with permission, you can take it away any moment. The heart is always stolen. You become aware only later on when it is no longer there. And because you have not given it, you cannot take it back. You cannot even report to the Bund Garden Police Station that your heart has been stolen!

The moment you came to me, I took your heart – from the very beginning. Your mind I cannot take, because your mind is false; it is just like your shadow. I cannot take your shadow. I can take you, but not your shadow.

Your heart has been stolen long ago, but the mind never becomes aware whether the heart is inside or has gone out – because the mind has no connections with the heart. And the heart has to be taken away. That's what I call initiation. Now you have got only two things: a mind full of rubbish – even if you want to give it to me I will not take it – and a being which is asleep.

So two things have to be remembered, Gita. One, you drop your mind and allow me to wake your consciousness and you have not to give anything to me. I am so full, so abundantly full, that I can share my blessings with the whole universe, and still my fullness will remain the same. So instead of thinking of giving something to me, start thinking of receiving what I am giving to you – every moment, every day.

You are thirsty and I am full of cold water, fresh water, to quench your thirst. Take it. And this is a miracle: the more you take the water out of the well...fresh water is always coming into the well from hidden sources. A well from which water is not taken out is not granted fresh sources, and the old water becomes stale, and even poisonous.

Once you start feeling the fullness of your spiritual being, then go on giving to the deserving, to the undeserving – never discriminate! Whoever is ready to take, give it to him. And existence will always be giving you a thousandfold more to be shared.

Where disciples have to give to the master, there is no disciple and no master. Where the master has to give to the disciples, there exists a real mystery school. This is the gathering of those who are thirsty, who are searching and seeking. Giving something to me may fulfill your ego, but that is not the purpose here. Receiving something from me will make you humble, will make you more human.

So become a womb and receive your own awakening, your own new life, your own new birth, through my hand.

Socrates is reported to have said that the function of the master is that of a midwife.

He is absolutely right.

Beloved Bhagwan,

When You dance with us and we dance with You,
with a shake of Your head, the pillars of Chuang Tzu dissolve,
the roof falls away, and we take off!
Day after miraculous day I feel more empty and more melancholy,
as if, one by one, my very organs are disappearing.
Is this the surgery You speak of?

Deva Abhiyana, yes, this is the surgery I speak of. But it seems you are on the surgical table a little unwillingly; otherwise, why you should feel melancholy?

When you feel empty you should rejoice, because this emptiness is the only possibility of your spiritual growth. Only out of this spaciousness your potential can become actual.

This is the process of actualization.

You are saying, "When you dance with us and we dance with you, with a shake of your head, the pillars of Chuang Tzu dissolve, the roof falls away, and we take off! Day after miraculous day I feel more empty and more melancholy, as if, one by one, my very organs are disappearing."

You are just imagining that the pillars of Chuang Tzu disappear, that the roof falls off and you take off. If it was a reality, then when your organs start disappearing you should dance more madly; when you start disappearing you should be full of blissfulness. The pillars of Chuang Tzu and the roof can't help you even if they disappear.

Unless *you* disappear...but you are clinging to yourself, and you are afraid that your organs, one by one, are disappearing. Why be so calculative? This is not a place for calculation. Why be so retail?...organ by organ.

It happened in Ramakrishna's life: a very rich man from Calcutta came. He was a great devotee of Ramakrishna – at least he thought so. He had brought one thousand gold coins to present to him.

Ramakrishna said, "I will not reject you because I don't want to hurt your feelings, so I accept your one thousand gold coins. Now they are mine; will you do me a favor?"

The man said, "I am ready."

Ramakrishna said, "Take all these coins and throw them in the Ganges."

The Ganges was flowing just behind the temple where Ramakrishna used to live. The man was very much shocked. His gold coins...and he had collected them with so much effort. He hesitated.

Ramakrishna said, "Your hesitation says that you have not given them to me. These are my coins now; it is none of your business. You just throw them in the Ganges. You have given them to me, what does it matter? They don't belong to you whether I keep them or I give them to the Ganges."

The logic was clear. The man went very slowly, and it took hours. Ramakrishna waited and waited. And he asked one of his disciples, "Go and see what happened to that man. Has he committed suicide? Has he jumped with the coins into the Ganges? – because this is too much time. It should have taken not more than two minutes."

The man went there, and there was a great crowd. And that rich man was taking one coin after another. First he would throw it on the stone pavement to see whether it is absolutely twenty-four carat gold or not, and then he would throw it into the Ganges. Naturally it was taking a long time, and a great crowd had gathered – what is he doing? And he was enjoying.

The man reported to Ramakrishna, so he himself went and he told the man, "You seem to be very idiotic. When one collects money, naturally one has to collect it one coin by one coin. But when you are throwing them, why be retail? Why waste time? You could have thrown the whole bag, all one thousand coins, in one go. And why are you making this exhibition? What is the need of checking all the coins, whether they are pure gold or not? They are not yours! And when you are throwing them, whether they are pure gold or not does not matter. But I know what the reason is – parting with one thousand coins in one go is too much for you, so you are parting with one coin at a time – and that too, not without making an exhibition."

Abhiyana, you say, "My very organs are disappearing one by one." You must be reluctant. Somewhere deep down you must be clinging. The pillars of Chuang Tzu did not disappear one by one; the roof of the Chuang Tzu does not disappear part by part. It does not belong to you;

but your organs are disappearing only by...slowly, slowly. Are you ready for surgery? Or is there a deep hold-back? That hold-back is creating your melancholy.

When I read your question, I could not believe it. This is the moment to celebrate – feeling empty, feeling silent, all the junk has disappeared from you, feeling pure – you are ready for the guest to come. But because of your hold- back, although the temple is ready, you are not opening its doors; the guest is standing outside.

It is a contradiction to feel empty *and* melancholy, because emptiness is meditation; and the ultimate in emptiness is enlightenment. This is the most glorious and the most significant experience in man's life.

And what are you worried about – your organs? If they are melting and disappearing, let them melt and disappear. They are your prison; they are your cage. Once they have disappeared, your soul is free to fly like an eagle across the sun.

Drop this stupid idea of melancholy. Celebrate!

In all this dance and song and celebration, how can you manage to be melancholy? You are doing something impossible. Either your emptiness is false or your melancholy is just an old habit. And that's what my understanding is, sadness, misery, melancholy – these are your old habits. Although you are dancing, those old habits are also dancing within you. Throw them out!

They are pure poison. They have destroyed millions of people's lives and they have destroyed your life too. Get rid of them. They are polluting and poisoning your very being.

Just have an experience, a new experience, a new adventure of disappearing completely – wholesale. And you will be surprised – when you disappear completely the whole existence is yours. Right now only bones and blood and skin, these are yours. Not a great treasure.... If you meet your own skeleton, you will run away so fast – "My God, Deva Abhiyana is coming!"

In one of the medical colleges in Bhopal, one of my friends was a doctor, and I used to stay with him. He was very much afraid of ghosts.

I said, "Being a doctor, and that too in a medical college where there are so many dead bodies collected for dissecting, and you are afraid of ghosts!"

He said, "Well, what to do, I am afraid. From my very childhood, I have been afraid."

So I said, "One thing has to be done. Tonight you get the key of that great hall where you are keeping many dead bodies and we will go there and see – there must be ghosts. So many dead bodies, their ghosts must be around them."

He said, "I don't want to go there. I don't go there even in the day. In the night, never!"

I said, "But I am going; give me the key."

He said, "But why are you getting into unnecessary trouble?"

I said, "For your sake, because if I am going you will have to come with me; you are my host."

Very reluctantly, unwillingly, he went with me.

I had made an arrangement. I had told another doctor who was also friendly with me, "You lie down amongst the corpses and when I enter the door...you have not to do anything, you just sit up. Cover yourself with a white cloth so nobody will know – that will be enough."

I took my friend there, opened the door, and pulled him inside the room by the hand. I said, "Come in, there is nothing to be worried about, these are dead bodies, skeletons. You also have a skeleton within your skin. So there is no need to worry; you belong to the same category. Soon you will be dead and you will be in this hall. It is better to be acquainted with these people right now."

As we entered, the doctor not only got up, but he screamed. He screamed because he was not aware that I had put another man in there also. So while he was lying down there, the other man was getting up, going down, getting up, going down. The doctor was almost on the verge of death, because he was not aware that there was another man also; and the door was locked so he could not escape: it is better to remain silent – if this ghost becomes aware of him, he's going to torture him.

As we reached the hall he threw off his white cloth, jumped out and said, "My God! You have put me in such trouble. I was thinking it is a joke; it is not a joke! There is another ghost, a real ghost! And he's doing exercises. He gets up, lies down, gets up, lies down.... You don't know in what hell I've been for these few hours."

And my friend who had come with me, his face became completely white.

He said, "This is a doctor?"

I said, "Yes, he is your colleague."

He said, "What is he doing here?"

I said, "Well, I don't know, just ask him."

But he was not in a situation to say anything. He was stuttering because he was shooing the other ghost away.

I said, "Let us go to him." Nobody was ready to go to him. I went and pulled up his cloth.

They both looked at him and they said, "Another colleague? My God, should we look at the other corpses also? Do doctors come to sleep here in the night?"

I said, "It is better you become acquainted – once in a while come and sleep here, and see what the ghosts do in the night. Sometimes they dance, they sing, they play ping-pong. And one day you are going to be here, so it is better to be acquainted beforehand; otherwise you will be in much trouble."

All three left me there and escaped. I had not told the first doctor about the second, neither had I told the second about the first. When the first jumped up, the second was so shocked that he started trying to feel his heart, whether he is still alive or he is finished. And my host could not sleep the whole night, again and again he would come into my room.

I said, "What is the matter?"

He said, "I feel afraid."

I said, "There is no question of being afraid."

He said, "How did it happen, the two colleagues? Are they dead? Are they real? And what were they doing there?"

I said, "How am I to know? I am not part of your medical college. You should know better...."

But both those doctors stopped meeting me – even if I would pass them, they would close their doors. They all used to live in small cottages around the medical college, and I used to go for a walk in the morning. And I would knock on their doors, and they would look from the window and close the window, too.

Abhiyana, let your organs disappear. What are those organs – your head, your legs, your hands, your heart – let them all disappear; melt into the whole existence. Dance so totally that there is only the dance and no dancer. And you will not be a loser, because in those moments of disappearance of your personality, you will come to know your essential spirituality – your eternity. Then the whole universe is *you*.

That is the meaning of the Upanishadic seers who shouted from the housetops, *Aham brahmasmi* – I am the whole. This is the meaning of Al Hillaj Mansoor, who shouted in the marketplaces, *ana'l haq* – I am the truth.

But before you can know yourself as truth or

as the whole, you have to disappear. And in this beautiful melting pot where so many people are disappearing, you also should take a little courage.

Jump into the pot!
Forget yourself, just even for a few moments, and it will give you an insight into existence for which you have been searching for many lives.

Beloved Bhagwan,

I am haunted by a feeling of missing.
It's as if I am searching for somebody that I won't recognize –
and he's just nearby, leaping and waving and calling me,
but I'm just too dim and unaware to notice him.
However, having been back here with You for a few days,
I get the feeling that I might bump into him at any moment.
Could it be me?

Sharna, you have guessed well; it is you. So don't be afraid, bump into yourself. And you may think that you are just too dim and unaware to notice him – but you have noticed him; otherwise, from where does this question come?

You say, "I am haunted by a feeling of missing." It is a good beginning. Everybody is missing himself, but is not aware – not even dimly aware.

"It is as if I am searching for somebody that I won't recognize." That too is true. You don't know yourself, so how are you going to recognize yourself? Somebody has to introduce you to yourself. I'm here just to introduce you to yourself. You are working in England where people don't talk with each other without introduction.

I have heard...a man came out of the train very dizzy, feeling sick and nauseous. His wife had come to pick him up. She said, "What is the matter?"

He said, "The trouble is that I cannot sit in a train if my back is in the direction where the train is going. I become sick and dizzy because there is a contradiction – you are facing opposite to the direction of the train."

His wife said, "Then why did you not ask the other passenger who was sitting in front of you, and tell him your trouble? He would have readily exchanged seats."

He said, "I thought about it all the time, but the trouble is, nobody had introduced us. So how to start talking with the man?" The wife said, "That's certainly a difficulty. In England introduction is absolutely necessary."

After a few days, again he was feeling sick. When he came out of the train the wife said, "What happened?" He said, "The same thing; and this time it was even worse."

She said, "How can it be even worse than the last time?" He said, "This time, in front of my seat there was nobody. So whom to get introduced to and whom to ask to change the seat? It was empty."

It is immensely significant that you are missing something. Better would be to say, you are missing somebody; you are missing yourself. But this is a good beginning.

"It is as if I am searching for somebody that I won't recognize." It is true. You have never seen yourself, you have never met yourself. You don't know your original face; hence the function of the master – to convince you that this is you.

"But I'm just too dim and unaware to notice him." You are not, because you *are* noticing him.

"However, having been back here with you for a few days, I get the feeling that I might bump into him at any moment." At any moment you are going to bump into him. And he's your real self. You are phony, you are the shadow – he is the real.

"Could it be me?"

Yes, I repeat, it is you.

Everybody is living a phony life, and the real being is following you, waiting for the moment when you will understand that your whole life is false. But there must be something real; otherwise, there could not be anything reflected in the mirror. If there is reflection, reflection is not a reality, but there must be someone who is being reflected.

Get ready, and don't be afraid, because it is not your enemy, it is you; it is your very divine being. But there may be fear, because the moment you find your real being, your phony self will have to die, will have to disappear. And you have decorated it with so much care, educated it with so much trouble, have made it respectable, prestigious – all this will disappear, and the being which is just innocent like a child.... And you will have to start your life again from scratch; but it will be a real life.

Gurdjieff has written a book, *Meetings With Remarkable Men*. He explains what he means by a "remarkable man" as one who has found his real self, and is not living as a shadow but as a reality. But he has not found many – at the most two dozen people all over the world. He traveled all over the world in search of real men. Where there were billions of people, he could find only two dozen people whom he could say were authentic. What about the others? They were simply shadows, reflections in a mirror.

Gather courage, just a little courage. And it will be easier here than anywhere else, because many people here have bumped into themselves. And it has not been a disaster, it is not an accident; it has been a great opportunity, a great benediction.

Beloved Bhagwan,

The strongest thing in my Christian upbringing
was to be unselfish, not to think of myself.
Now, remembering myself and following the urge to turn inwards,
I seem to have to push through a layer of unease, guilt and confusion.
I know there is a big difference.
Would You speak to us about it?

Deva Vachana, all the religions have done immense harm to man's growth, but Christianity is at the top as far as harming humanity is concerned. They have used beautiful words to hide the ugly acts they are doing against you.

For example, unselfishness: a man who does not know himself, to tell him to be unselfish is so outrageously idiotic that one cannot believe that for two thousand years Christianity has been doing that.

Socrates says, "Know thyself; anything else is secondary." Knowing thyself, you can be unselfish. In fact you will be unselfish; it won't be an effort on your part. Knowing thyself, you will know not only yourself, but you will know the self of everyone. It is the same; it is one consciousness, one continent. People are not islands.

But without teaching people how to know their own being, Christianity has played a very dangerous game, and one which has appealed to people because they have used a beautiful word, *unselfishness*. It looks religious, it looks spiritual. When I say to you, "First be selfish," it does not look spiritual.

Selfish?

Your mind is conditioned that unselfishness is spiritual. I know it is, but unless you are selfish enough to know yourself, unselfishness is impossible. Unselfishness will come as a consequence of knowing yourself, of being yourself. Then unselfishness will not be an act of virtue, not done in order to gain rewards in heaven. Then unselfishness will simply be your nature, and each act of unselfishness will be a reward unto itself.

But Christianity has put the bullocks behind the cart – nothing is moving, everything has got stuck. The bullocks are stuck because the cart is in front of them, and the cart cannot move because no cart can move unless bullocks are ahead of it, moving it.

It happens to every Christian who comes here, that meditation gives a feeling of guilt – when the whole world is so troubled, when people are so poor, when people are dying of starvation, when people are suffering from AIDS, you are meditating. You must be utterly selfish. First help the poor, first help the people who are suffering from AIDS, first help everybody else.

But your life is very short. In seventy or eighty years, how many unselfish acts can you do? And when are you going to find time for meditation – because whenever you will ask for meditation, those poor are there, new diseases have sprung up, orphans are there, beggars are there.

One Christian mother was telling her small

boy, "To be unselfish is a fundamental of our religion. Never be selfish, help others."

The little boy – and little boys are more perceptive and clear than your so-called old boys—the little boy said, "This seems to be a very strange thing, that I should help others and they should help me. Why not make it simple? – I help myself, they help themselves." This fundamental of the religion seems to be very complicated – and unnecessarily complicated.

In fact, Christianity has condemned all the Eastern religions for the simple reason that to Christianity they look selfish.

Mahavira meditating for twelve years...he should be teaching in a school, or being a male nurse in a hospital. Although, naked, it will look a little bit strange. He should look after orphans, be a Mother Teresa and get a Nobel prize.

It is clear that no meditator has ever received a Nobel prize. For what? – because you have not done anything unselfish. You are the most selfish people in the world, just meditating and enjoying your silence and peace and blissfulness, finding the truth, finding God, becoming completely free from all prisons. But this is all selfishness. So the Christian mind finds it a little difficult to accept the idea of meditation. In Christianity there is no meditation, only prayer.

They cannot call Gautam Buddha a really religious man, because what has he done for the poor? What has he done for the sick? What has he done for the old? He became enlightened – that is the ultimate in selfishness.

But the East has a totally different outlook—and far more logical, reasonable, understandable. The East has always thought. "Unless you have a peace, a silence in your heart, a song in your being, a light radiating your enlightenment, you cannot do any service to anybody."

You yourself are sick; you yourself are an orphan because you have not found yet the ultimate security of existence, the eternal safety of life. You are so poor yourself that inside there is nothing but darkness. How can you help others? – you are drowning yourself. It will be dangerous to help others. Most probably, you will drown the other person also.

First you have to learn swimming yourself. Then only can you be of any help to someone who is drowning.

My approach is absolutely clear. First be selfish, and discover all that is contained in yourself – all the joys and all the blissfulness and all the ecstasies. And then unselfishness will come just like your shadow follows you – because to have a dancing heart, to have God in your being, you have to share it. You cannot go on keeping it, like a miser, because miserliness in your inner growth is a death.

The economics of inner growth is different from the outer economics.

A beggar was standing on the street and he stopped a car. He asked for something because he had not eaten for three days. The man in the car had just won a lottery. And looking at the beggar, he could not believe it – his clothes, although very old, dirty, showed that he came from a good family. His face, his language, all gave indications that he was educated.

He was so full of money at that moment that he took out a one hundred rupee note, and gave it to the beggar. The beggar looked at the note and started laughing.

The man in the car said, "Why are you laughing?"

He said, "I am laughing because soon you will be standing in my place. This is how I became a beggar. Once I used to have my own car; once I used to have thousands of rupees – but I went on distributing. It won't take a long time for you –

I will see you again."

The ordinary economics is that if you go on giving, you will have less and less and less. But the spiritual economics is that if you don't give, you will have less and less and less; if you give, you will have more and more and more.

The laws of the outside world and the inside world are diametrically opposite. First become rich inside, first become an emperor, and then you have so much to share. You will not call it even unselfishness. And you will not desire that any reward should be given to you – here or here-after. You will not even ask for gratitude from the man you have given something to; on the contrary, you will be grateful that he did not reject you, your love, your bliss, your ecstasy. He was receptive, he allowed you to pour your heart and your songs and your music into his being.

The Christian idea of unselfishness is sheer stupidity. The East has never thought in the same way. The whole East and its search for truth is very long. It has found one simple fact, that first you have to take care of yourself, and then only you can take care of others.

Vachana, you feel a certain guilt. You say, "I seem to have to push through a layer of unease, guilt and confusion. I know there is a big difference. Would you speak to us about it?"

It is a simple phenomenon. Christianity has deceived millions of people on a wrong path. In America, the fundamentalist Christians were the cause that destroyed our commune. Ronald Reagan is a fundamentalist Christian; and a fundamentalist Christian is the most fanatic, the most bigotted person you can find. We were not doing any harm to anybody. But the problem for them was that we were so happy, so blissful – they could not tolerate it.

Even here...the East has forgotten its own peaks of glory – the days of Gautam Buddha and Mahavira. Now it lives...even people who are not Christians are influenced by the Christian ideology. The Indian constitution says that charity consists of helping the poor, spreading education to the poor, making hospitals for the poor.

None of these three things will be found in the teachings of Gautam Buddha. Not that he is against helping the poor, but because he knows that if you are a meditator you will help, but you will not brag about it. It will be a simple, natural thing.

From this mystery school they have taken away the tax exempt status because they say it is not a charitable institution. To teach meditation is not charity. To open a hospital is charity. To open a school and teach geography and history is charity. And what are you going to teach in geography? – where is Timbuktu, where is Constantinople. Its Hindi name is *Kustutunia*. In history, what are you going to teach? – about Genghis Khan, Tamurlane, Nadirshah, Alexander the Great, Ivan the Terrible. This is charity.

But to teach people to be silent, peaceful, loving, joyous, contented, fulfilled is not charity. Even the people who are not Christians have become infected with the disease.

Mahatma Ghandi, at least three times in his life, was almost on the verge of becoming a Christian. And he was a Christian, ninety percent. Dr. Ambedkar, who wrote the Indian constitution, has been thinking for years that he and his followers – the untouchables – should become Christians. Finally he decided that they should become Buddhists.

But in the whole constitution you can see the impact of Christianity. In the whole Indian constitution there is not even the mention of the word *meditation* – which has been the only contribution of the East to the world, and the most precious contribution. The constitution reflects more what the Christian missionaries go on teaching. It does not reflect Gautam Buddha, it does not reflect Kabir, it does not reflect Nanak.

We have been fighting the case for years. But the problem is that the bureaucrats follow the words, not the spirit. They cannot accept it, that this is a charitable institution. And I cannot see that there can be any charity without meditation.

So your guilt is just a wrong conditioning. Drop it, without even giving it a second thought. I will make you unselfish by making you absolutely selfish. First I have to make you inwardly rich – so rich, so overflowingly rich, that you have to share, just as a raincloud has to share its rain with the thirsty earth. But first the cloud must be full of rain. Saying to the empty clouds, "You should be unselfish," is just irrational.

People even come here, well wishers, with good intentions. They say, "This is a strange ashram. You should open a hospital for the poor; you should collect the orphans; you should distribute clothes to the beggars; you should help those who need help."

My own approach is totally different. I can distribute birth control methods to the poor so that there are no orphans. I can distribute the pill to the poor so there is no explosion of population – because I don't see the point: first create the orphans and then create orphanages and then serve them and waste your life.

When I started speaking thirty-five years ago, India had only a population of four hundred million. And I have been saying since then that birth control is an absolute necessity. But all Christians are against birth control. And just within thirty-five years, India has more than doubled its population. From four hundred million it has gone to nine hundred million. Five hundred million people could have been prevented and there would have been no need of Mother Teresa, no need for the pope to come to India and teach unselfishness.

But people are strange – first let them become sick, then give medicine. And they have found beautiful ways. In every Lions Club and Rotary Club, they keep boxes for their members – if you purchase a bottle of some medicine and you are cured, and half the bottle is still there, you donate it to the Lions Club. This way they collect medicine, and then they are great, unselfish people; they are distributing the medicine. Service is their motto. But it is a very cunning service. Those medicines were going to be thrown away – if you are cured, what are you going to do with the remaining medicine?

It is a great idea to collect all those medicines and distribute them to the poor – and have a great feeling of being public servants.

In my vision, the thing that man needs first and foremost is a meditative consciousness. And after you have your meditative consciousness, whatever you do will be helpful to everybody; you cannot do any harm, you can do only compassionate and loving acts.

But even the Indian constitution does not accept a school of meditation as charitable. And this is the greatest charity possible.

I repeat again, Vachana, first be selfish. Know thyself, be thyself and then your very life will be nothing but a sharing, an unselfish sharing without asking for any reward in this world or in the other world.

Okay Vimal?

Yes, Bhagwan.

Session 5

Existence Loves Imperfection

*Perfection is the horizon of your consciousness;
it allures you, it challenges you, it calls you.
But remember, the distance will remain the same.
On the spiritual path there is no goal, only pilgrimage.
But the pilgrimage goes on becoming more and more juicy,
more and more beautiful, more and more ecstatic.*

February 27, 1987
Evening

Beloved Bhagwan,

You are a delicious bundle of mischief.
When You told us we would get a taste of eternity, a glimpse,
when we stop mid-flight, in mid-dance, at Your signal,
I thought a door would open,
and a beam of light would enter my darkness.
You ripped the whole door off!
I thought I was safe inside, and suddenly everything around me was gone – even me.
Since then there has been a giggling
fellow walking around in his old clothes,
looking for his house, using my name.
Shall I let him share our secret?

Devageet, it is time you realized that whenever I do something, I do it totally. I don't hold anything back. And that's my message to you too.

Do things with your whole heart, with as much intensity as you are capable of.

Anything done half-heartedly never brings joy to life. It only brings misery, anxiety, torture, and tension, because whenever you do anything half-heartedly you are dividing yourself into two parts, and that is one of the greatest calamities that has happened to human beings – they are all split.

The whole past has given you only one heritage, and that is schizophrenia. The misery in the world is not surprising; it is a natural outcome of our living always half-heartedly, doing everything only with one part of our being, while the other part is resisting, opposing, fighting.

And whatever you do with half of your being is going to bring you repentance, misery, and a feeling that perhaps the other part that was not participating was right – because following *this* part, you have attained nothing but a miserable state. But I say unto you: If you had followed the other part, the result would have been the same.

It is not a question of what you follow, which part; it is a question of whether you go totally into it or not. To be total in your action brings joy. Even an ordinary, trivial action done with total intensity brings a glow to your being, a fulfillment, a fullness, a deep contentment. And anything done half-heartedly, howsoever good the thing may be, is going to bring misery.

Misery does not come from your actions, neither does joy come from your actions. Joy comes when you are total. It does not matter what action you are involved in, misery is the outcome when you are partial. And living a life continuously half-heartedly is creating for yourself a hell every moment – and the hell goes on becoming bigger and bigger.

People ask, is there a hell somewhere, or is there a heaven somewhere? – because all the religions have been talking about hell and heaven as if they are part of the geography of your universe. They are not geographical phenomena, they are in your psychology.

When your mind, when your heart, when your being, is pulled in two directions simultaneously, you are creating hell. And when you are total, one, an organic unity…in that very organic unity, the flowers of heaven start blossoming in you.

People have remained concerned about their acts: Which act is right and which act is wrong? What is good and what is evil? My own understanding is that it is not a question of any particular act. The question is about your psychology.

When you are total, it is good; and when you are divided, it is evil. Divided you suffer; united, you dance, you sing, you celebrate.

Devageet, you are saying, "Since then there has been a giggling fellow walking around in his old clothes, looking for his house, using my name. Shall I let him share our secret?" Everything has to be shared. There should be no secret.

To have a secret is to have a wound.

One should live without any secrets. One should live without hiding anything. One should open one's heart to the wind, to the sun, to the rain. One should not ask whether the person deserves it or not. It is none of your business. If existence accepts that person, gives him life, what more can you give? If existence allows him, then who are you to prevent him from knowing something?

I am reminded of an ancient Tibetan parable: Deep in the Himalayas there used to live a very old sage. Only one thing was known about him: he never shared any secret, any experience with anybody. He never allowed anybody to become a disciple to him, for the simple reason that if you accept somebody as a disciple, then you have to tell him your inner secrets. He never allowed anybody to be close enough to know his hidden treasures.

People came from faraway places – because it is part of the strangeness of the human mind that the more a thing is unapproachable, the more people become obsessed with it. It was rumored all over the place that that old sage must have a great secret – that's why he does not even allow initiation to anybody as a disciple.

People asked him, touched his feet, cried before him, "Accept us as disciples and we are ready to do anything – whatever you say." But he always rejected. He seemed to be absolutely without any compassion.

There was just one young boy who used to cook food for him, bring things from the village nearby. When the day of his death came, he called the boy and said, "Go into the village and tell everybody that whoever wants to become my disciple should come immediately."

The boy said, "Whoever? But you always said, 'Unless somebody is worthy to receive, deserves to receive my secret, I am not going to give it to anybody.' What happened? You have changed your mind completely."

The old man said, "Don't waste time! Just rush to the village, and whoever is available, tell them 'The master is ready to accept you as disciples.'"

The boy could not believe it. Shaking his head because this seems to be so absurd…his whole life he denied, and now he is saying, "Any XYZ will do. You just bring them." He went, but he was thinking in his mind: Has he gone senile, has he gone mad? Something is certainly wrong, but if he says it, then there is no other way.

So he went into the village and he declared to the villagers in the marketplace, "Anybody who wants to be a disciple...the sage is ready. You come with me."

Nobody could believe it. But somebody was going to commit suicide...his wife was torturing him too much, and there is a limit to everything, and the limit had come. When he heard the boy, he said, "Okay, I am coming. What more can happen than suicide?"

Somebody was just having a holiday and thought, "There is no harm. We have heard so much about the great secret...." Just out of curiosity he also followed.

In all, eleven people came. And the old sage initiated all of them. The boy was standing there not believing his eyes. He said, "Master, what are you doing? You are not even asking what their qualifications are, what their qualities are."

The old man laughed and said, "To tell you the truth, up till now I had no secret. That's why I was avoiding people, that's why I was not initiating people – because once you initiate them.... I had nothing to give to them. Now I have it, and it does not matter whether the person deserves it or not. If existence accepts the person, who am I to be judgmental?

"Everybody is worthy. In this moment of joy, in this moment of ecstasy, when I have the secret, I want to share with anybody who is ready to receive it."

Always remember this parable. Whenever you have something, share it – and without thinking even for a single moment whether the person you are sharing it with deserves or not. Only think about one thing: whether you have *got* the secret or not.

If you have got it, share it. Spread the seeds to as many people as possible. Certainly a few seeds will fall on the rocks and will never grow. And some will fall on the footpaths where people walk continually: they will grow, but they will die. But some seeds will certainly find the right soil. And they will come to blossom, and they will bring thousands of seeds with them.

Don't waste your time, because nobody knows who is worthy and who is not worthy – murderers have become saints, criminals have become sages; sages have fallen and become criminals, saints have lost their way and become murderers.

Life is so mysterious that one cannot say what you are going to be the next moment. And you can decide the worth of anybody only by his past – but the seed is going to grow in the future. You are sharing your secret for the future, and the worthiness or unworthiness belongs to the past. And the future is always open. The saint can turn away, go astray; the murderer can become awake.

The future is so open and so flexible. The past does not decide it; hence, never bother about the past, always look to the open future. And everybody is worthy to receive the secret, because everybody is worthy to live, to breathe, to have a place in this beautiful existence.

Even the smallest blade of grass is as significant and important as the biggest star. The universe would miss it, even though it is a small blade of grass. Without it, the universe would have a little less beauty. Nobody else can replace it.

And as far as human beings are concerned, they are all unique, irreplaceable. Respect their uniqueness, and when you want to share your experience, open your whole heart.

Don't be a miser, because the more you give, the more existence will shower on you.

Beloved Bhagwan,

The other day when I was taking photos of You,
looking into the camera Your eyes slowly became bigger and bigger,
and You said, "Don't control, I am the captain of the ship."
Everything inside and outside of me started trembling and shaking,
including the camera. I felt that I really lost it.
All I could say was "Help! Where is the witness?"
I had to put the camera down, close my eyes and relax.
When I looked again, I suddenly recognized the witness
sitting in the chair, looking at me,
and zooming into the deepest core of my being.
Everything stopped, became sharp, clear and silent,
like a razor's edge.
Could You please comment,
my beloved and most beautiful Master?

Prem Turiya, you have taken training in photography, but perhaps the art of photography has never encountered crazy people like me. I know, I saw it. Sometimes my eyes start becoming bigger when I am looking into you – and perhaps you became afraid when the eyes started becoming bigger. Because you were taking *my* photograph, I was looking into you. I was also taking *your* photograph. Of course, my ways are different – without a camera.

And you heard it rightly – seeing you trembling and your camera also trembling, I said silently within myself, "Don't control." You were trying hard to control: "I am the captain of the ship, and however drunk I may be, my ship is always going towards the ocean." I have never felt for a single moment that there is a possibility of being lost.

The whole universe is ours.
Where can we get lost?

Wherever we reach will be our home. Once you have understood that the whole universe is our home, then the possibility of getting lost simply disappears. And if you try to control, there are problems with control....

In one of the universities where I used to teach, the vice-chancellor had a disease. He was ban old man, and his hands used to tremble, so he always kept them in his pockets.

Even while speaking before the students in the convocations, he would never bring his hands out of his pockets. But he was not aware that, because of his hands, his whole pants were shaking, which was even more ridiculous. Hands shaking...one can understand that you have a certain sickness. What can you do? But the pants shaking? Pants are never known to be sick.

So I told him one day, "Tomorrow is the convocation day and you will do the same again. Perhaps you are not aware that everybody is laughing; people are controlling their laughter because it doesn't look good. It is a serious affair, the convocation. But your pants shake so much that it is very difficult, particularly for the people who are sitting in the front, who can see your whole pants shaking."

He said, "My pants shaking? You never told me...."

I said, "I thought you must know. They are your pants, and you are putting shaking hands into the pockets. It is a natural, logical corollary that the pants will shake.

"So tomorrow, remember – because it makes the whole thing very ridiculous – you keep your hands out. And if you don't keep your hands out, I will come and take your hands out."

He said, "What?"

I said, "Tomorrow will be decisive...because people can feel compassion if your hands are shaking in old age; it is not something to be laughed at."

He said, "But I am very much afraid to keep them out."

I said, "Then I will have to come on the stage."

The convocation day came, and he was not courageous enough to keep his hands out. Now knowing perfectly well, he was trying to hold his pants from the inside, controlling, and this was making things even worse, because now everybody knew that he was holding the pants from inside, and the whole pants were shaking. They were shaking more than they used to shake. Before, it was only the hands and their vibration, but now he was holding the pants, so the pants were shaking really badly.

So I stood up. He said, "Sit! Sit down! You need not come." And he took his hands out. There was great laughter and there was great silence afterwards – what was the matter?

Just as I stood, he took his hands out and everybody saw that his hands were shaking. I said, "Now it is okay, you keep them out of the pants, and it is not a problem at all. Your hands are sick and you are old, but your pants are new and fresh and young. Because of your trying to control and hide, the young and fresh and new full pants are shaking like an old man."

He said, "I will keep them out, but you sit down. I had never thought that you would do that to me."

I said, "Just remember that I am here."

When Turiya was trying to control, I remembered my old vice-chancellor. The more she was trying to control, the more things were going out of control. It was good that she put the camera down and closed her eyes.

You need not be afraid if you see through your camera that my eyes are becoming bigger and bigger and bigger. I keep them almost half closed, just not to make people afraid. I open them fully only when I want to make Avirbhava afraid. And the moment I open them fully she shrieks, screams, tries to tell me, "Don't do this to me!" The moment I start moving towards her she starts controlling herself.

There is no need to control. If you had relaxed, there would have been no need to put the camera away. But you must have been trying to be physically perfect. Perfectionists are always afraid of committing mistakes, of doing something which is not technically right; and my understanding is that anybody who tries to be perfect in anything is bound to go insane. Perfection is not allowed by existence. Existence loves imperfection, because imperfection has the possibility of evolution.

Perfection means death. The moment you are perfect, there is no possibility of any evolution. This is something to be remembered: On the spiritual path, nobody ever becomes perfect. One is always coming closer to perfection, closer to perfection, closer to perfection, but never becoming perfect.

The distance between you and the perfection remains the same, just like the horizon. You can go towards the horizon, and you can feel, "Now I am coming closer, now I am coming closer," but the horizon goes on receding. The distance between you and the horizon remains always the same.

Perfection is the horizon of your consciousness; it allures you, it challenges you, it calls you. But remember, the distance will remain the same. On the spiritual path there is no goal, only pilgrimage. But the pilgrimage goes on becoming more and more juicy, more and more beautiful, more and more ecstatic.

Turiya is trying to make a book of my photographs. Forget the idea of being perfect. Just enjoy. Put your total energy into it, but don't expect that your photographs are going to be perfect. Imperfection has a beauty; imperfection is alive, and perfection is dead.

You are saying, "Everything stopped, became sharp, clear and silent, like a razor's edge." The path is just like the razor's edge, very sharp, and one has to be very relaxed to move on it. A little tension, a little anxiety, a little fear, and there is danger.

Have you ever observed one thing? In my childhood, I used to play a game. In my high school, there were two buildings, and between the two buildings there was at least a twenty foot distance. I had found a piece of wood, twenty feet long. First, I would put it on the ground and ask my friends, "Can you walk on it?" And everybody was able to walk on it without falling. And then I would put the same piece of wood on the two buildings, and except me, nobody was ready even to try.

I said, "This is strange, because you have walked on the same wood and you did not fall."

They said, "That was a different situation. Now it is so dangerous that if a little fear comes, if just one step goes wrong, you will fall nearabout thirty feet down."

I persuaded them by saying, "You can watch me; you should just not look this side or that side. You have walked on the wood...and this is my strategy: not to look here and there, just to keep totally concentrated on the wood, and go on. And I can go on for miles."

When one day I was persuading a few students, one new teacher, a chemistry teacher, who used to brag that he was a very brave man, just came by. I said, "You are a very brave man, perhaps you can try."

He said, "I can try." But then he looked down, there were thirty feet. He went two feet at the most, fell down, and had multiple fractures.

I went to see him in the hospital. He told me, "I have never seen such a dangerous fellow. What was the idea?"

I said, "You have been bragging so much.... Once you get well we will try a few more ideas."

He said, "What do you mean?"

I said, "You have just to say that you have been bragging because basically you are a man who is very much afraid. To cover it up, you are bragging, 'In the middle of the night, in the darkest forest, I can go alone. I am not afraid of any ghosts or any thieves, or any murderers.'

"It was you who provoked me to find something. And I had walked ahead of you, so it was not that I was not taking the risk. You thought that because I had walked, you would also be able to walk. That's where you were wrong.

"You started trembling from the first foot, but you could not go back. There was time, you could have jumped back, you had just taken two steps, but it was against your ego, so you went on and fell. It is not a multiple fracture to your body, it is a multiple fracture to your ego. Your body will be better within two or three weeks, but about your ego...never mention about your bravery again; otherwise...I have found a few other things."

He said, "I am going to resign from this school. This is enough. I don't want it!"

I said, "That is up to you. You can resign, but still we will try something."

And we managed to try. He resigned, and he took his luggage – he had no wife, no children, nothing. He had just come out of the university...a young man. I and few of my friends got hold of him. The station was two miles away from the city, so just in the middle, we got hold of him, and we made so much fuss, a great crowd gathered.

We said, "He's leaving his wife."

And he was trying to persuade the crowd, "I don't have any wife. These people are all lying, I am simply resigning and going."

I said to the crowd, "Just take him back to his home. He has a wife and three children."

The man said, "Leave me, because my train will be missed. I can't go back."

But then the crowd took over, and said, "You cannot go. First you come back home. Why should these children be telling lies?" And we were not just one, I had at least ten boys lined up who were saying, "Your wife is crying, your children are crying, and you are leaving them. This is not good."

The crowd caught hold of him – we all disappeared. He was shouting and screaming and saying, "I am not married, I don't have a child, I don't have any wife."

The crowd said, "First you come back home." He said, "But my train will be gone."

They said, "We are not concerned about the train. The train you can pick up tomorrow" – because there was only one train every day. "So it is only a question of twenty-four hours. First you come home."

And we had managed to find a very poor woman who had three children, and we had told her, "We are going to give you five rupees for just a little act."

She said, "But this is not a good act."

I said, "What is the harm? You just cover your face so nobody knows...." And in India, with the *ghunghat* you cover your head, and you cry. And I told the children, "You say, 'Papa, why are you leaving us?'"

He could not believe his eyes: there was a woman who was crying and holding his feet, saying, "Don't leave me, you have married me!" And the three children were crying, "Papa!" And the crowd said, "Now, what do you say?" He said, "Now, what can I say? I have never seen these children, I have never seen this woman, and they are sitting in my house."

We were all present there behind the crowd. Finally I told him, "The train is late, don't be worried." I took him aside and I told him, "This is just one of the devices. You will have to give five rupees to the woman, then you can go. Then I will take care."

He had to give five rupees to the woman. The crowd asked, "What is happening?"

I said, "They have compromised. He is going just for two days, and he has given money for two days expenses; then he will be coming back."

So they allowed him to go. And the woman told me later on, "If you have more of this kind of act...for just a five minute act, five rupees." And in those days five rupees was great money. One could live for one month on five rupees.

We went with the teacher, and he was so angry, he would not talk with us. And I said, "Don't be angry, because we can still try some other devices."

He said, "No more devices; I am fractured all over my body, my five rupees are gone, and I don't think that I am going to catch the train."

I said, "You don't be worried, the train has gone. You will have to wait in the waiting room, but we have made every arrangement...you will be comfortable there. In the night just be a little alert, be watchful.

I said, "We don't have much time, only one night. We tried many ghosts...only one ghost is ready."

He said, "My God!"

So in the night, in the waiting room...because in the night there is no train, and the station master goes away, and the waiting room is empty, and the whole platform is empty. He said, "Then I am not going to the station. I will lie down anywhere on the street, in the market, but I am not going to the station, to that empty place in the night."

I said, "You used to say that you don't believe in ghosts."

He said, "I used to say that, but seeing your devices...whether ghosts exist or not, some ghost will appear, and I don't want to get into any more trouble."

That man met me after twenty or twenty-five years. I asked him, "How are you?"

He said, "How am I? You made me so afraid that I decided never to get married, and never to have children, and never to be employed in any school; it is dangerous. My whole body has been destroyed, and that day you could have done even more harm, because the whole crowd was believing you."

I said, "That woman was ready to go with you, those children were ready to go with you. You yourself bribed them."

He said, "I bribed them? You suggested five rupees, and you managed to find those people. And I know that woman and those three children; they were just living in the neighborhood."

But I said, "Why were you trembling?"

He said, "Why was I trembling? I was trembling because that crowd might have forced that woman and those children on my head. My service was gone, and I would have had a family which was not concerned with me at all. That woman was so ugly, and you were so tricky that you told her to keep her face hidden behind the sari. But I have become so much afraid since then, I have not served in any school, and I have never said to anybody, 'I am a brave man.' I have accepted that I am a coward."

I said, "If you had accepted it before, this tragedy would have been avoided."

Everybody is afraid. It is not that you are afraid of *something*, you are simply afraid. Perhaps it is a deep-down fear of death in the very depths of your unconsciousness that surfaces as fear. And you try to control your life. In this controlling you go on repressing your fear deeper, but the fear is not going to be destroyed this way.

Relax and let your fear surface.

Turiya, what was making you afraid? Just something deep in you was touched. It has to be allowed to come to the conscious, because there is only one way to get rid of fear – to bring it to the surface, to the conscious, and to watch it.

You also became alert about it. You say, "I felt that really what was happening.... All I could say was, 'Help, where is the witness?' I had to put the camera down, close my eyes, and relax. When I looked again, I suddenly recognized the witness sitting in the chair, looking at me, zooming into the deepest core of my being."

That is not your witness. I was looking deep into you, but I am not your witness. Your witness is asleep inside you; you have to wake it up. So while you are dancing, singing, allow your own witness to watch your body clapping, moving, dancing, singing; allow your own witness to stand aside and see it all. Slowly, slowly, you will be able to witness all the contents of your unconsciousness, and this is the miracle of witnessing: If you witness, anything that has been repressed in the unconscious will disappear, will evaporate.

Once your unconscious is clean, unrepressed, you will have a dignity that you have never known, you will have a pride of being human, of being an individual, that you have never known.

You will have a joy, because now there is no fear, not even the fear of death; you are aware of something eternal running like an undercurrent in your consciousness.

That eternal, that immortal is your real self, is your reality. To know it, is to know all. Not to know it, you can be burdened with all the knowledge of the world, but still you are ignorant, because deep inside you, there is nothing but darkness – and in darkness, only death is hidden. Your witness will bring light, and when you have looked into every nook and corner of your being, you will be surprised: there is nothing to be afraid of – not even death, because death is a lie; it has never happened.

Life never dies, it only changes forms and goes on and on until it recognizes itself as totally awakened.

It goes on taking new forms; once it is fully awakened, enlightened, it merges with the universe, with the whole. That merger is the greatest ecstasy man has known. There is nothing higher than that, there is nothing deeper than that.

Beloved Bhagwan,

Whenever I watch Your gestures, Your hands,
something in me relaxes so deeply.
Whenever I look into Your eyes,
there is a shower of deep relaxation moving down my body.
It is like falling and dissolving into nothingness.
Sometimes, when I have these experiences,
there are thoughts following of what about love and ecstacy,
why don't I feel them as much?
Beloved Bhagwan, is my heart left behind somewhere?

Veet Kamal, I have been insistently emphasizing the fact that each individual is unique. It means each individual is going to experience his inner growth in his own way.

Never compare. To some it comes like love, to some it comes like music, to some it comes like dance, to some it comes like fragrance.

It is natural to compare when something is

happening to somebody else and it is not happening to you. Is there something wrong? No. Whatever is happening to you is so beautiful that you need not worry that love is not happening, ecstasy is not happening.

Always emphasize what is happening to you, so that it becomes more and more deep, more and more overwhelming. Perhaps its overwhelming depth will bring love too, will bring ecstasy too. If you focus on what is *not* happening, there is danger. The danger is that what is happening may be disturbed.

You say, "Whenever I watch your gestures, your hands, something in me relaxes so deeply." Enjoy this relaxation. There are millions of people who cannot relax. "Whenever I look into your eyes, there is a shower of deep relaxation moving down my body. It is like falling and dissolving into nothingness." That is something so valuable: Falling and dissolving into nothingness is what Buddha has called Nirvana.

Buddha has never talked about love, and has never talked about ecstasy, either. Perhaps they never came on his path. He has talked about nothingness as the ultimate: You become a nobody, just empty space. But the empty space is so full, it is not a negative phenomenon. It is tremendously positive. It is full of peace, of silence, of absolute relaxation.

You are moving absolutely rightly, but the human mind is always comparative. Somebody says he is so full of love, and you think, I am full only of nothingness, so perhaps my heart is left somewhere, or perhaps I don't have my heart. No, every flower has to have its own color, and every flower has to have its own fragrance, and neither roses should be compared with lotuses, nor lotuses should be compared with roses. They are all beautiful.

The variety itself makes this existence so rich. This is one of the fundamentals I would like never to be forgotten. All the religions, all the mystics of the world, have been quarreling because of their different experiences. But they have forgotten one thing, that every individual is so unique, the experiences cannot be the same.

Only one thing can be the same and that is a deep contentment. Whether it is love, or it is nothingness, or it is silence, or it is ecstasy, one thing is running through all of them like a hidden thread running through a garland of flowers – and that is a deep contentment.

If you are feeling a deep contentment, then everything is absolutely right. If love comes it is okay, if it does not come it is even better, because it may bring some trouble. If ecstasy comes, good; if it does not come, feel blessed, because the people who have been ecstatic have been almost mad. Ecstasy drives people mad.

I am neither for anything, nor against anything. My whole approach is that you should find a deep, relaxed contentment with yourself and existence. Then whatever else happens is just differences in your individualities.

Beloved Bhagwan,

Being with You now is overwhelming for me.
When You talk, I often cannot follow Your words,
but my whole being is just bathing in Your presence,
and everything in me wants to reach out,
to bow down to Your feet, in deep gratitude and love.

Sadhan, what is important is happening to you – that is, that being with me is an overwhelming experience for you. Words are not important. If you cannot follow my words, there is no need to worry about it. If you can experience me, my presence; if you can open your heart with a silent welcome, it is more than one can expect – because it is not a school where you are taught philosophy, religion, psychology; it is an alchemist's workshop where you are transformed into new beings.

So don't be worried about words, except when I tell jokes. If you miss the jokes, that is unforgivable. So listen well.

Father Mulligan was listening to confessions in his church one day, when he got very ill and needed to go to the doctor. He did not want to walk out on all the people waiting in line to confess their sins, so he asked a very old friend, a rabbi, to help.

He said, "Just sit in the booth and listen to their sins. It is very easy. They cannot see you, so they will not know it is not me." And he then told the rabbi the average usual sins and how many Hail Marys and Our Fathers to give as penance.

The priest left, and the old rabbi was doing great until a young man came in and confessed to having blow jobs. The old rabbi was puzzled as he did not know what penance to give, so he went quietly out the back door and saw a young altar boy lighting candles. He went up to him and asked, "What does Father Mulligan usually give for blow jobs?", to which the altar boy replied, "About five to ten dollars."

Okay, Vimal?

Yes, Bhagwan.

Session 6

Laughter
Is The Essential Religion

*Ego makes you sad, serious;
responsibility takes away your smiles, your laughter –
and to me laughter is the essential religion.
The capacity to dance and sing,
not separate from existence but as part of it,
is the very foundation of a real religious man.*

February 28, 1987
Morning

Oh Bhagwan,

Please cut my head off.

Mukta, do you think you still have your head? It has been cut long ago. Just the idea has remained. I will take the idea too. I had left it – otherwise people would feel a little disturbed to see you walking without a head. But if you want to enjoy that, it can be done.

This is my whole profession: cutting the head off but still leaving the idea that you have it, so you can move in the world and nobody freaks out.

Beloved Bhagwan,

Oh my beloved Beloved, each time You say we need not be grateful to You
there is an agony that rips through my heart
and it is almost unbearable.
The pain I only feel, but do not understand;
it feels like it is too much to ask my heart
not to be grateful to You, for it knows that without Your love
it would not have opened to life.
I understand a little, when You say to be grateful to existence,
and also realize I have forgotten existence many times.
You have always been like a window to existence,
and all is possible through You.
So please, Bhagwan, do not ask this impossible task
from my heart, for it suffers too much when You say
that we need not to be grateful to You.

Prem Patipada, I do understand your feeling. But I have been telling you this for two reasons: One, I should not be standing in any way between you and existence. Even as a window to existence I give existence a frame which it does not have; it is frameless and formless. If you are looking through the window, the frame of the window becomes the frame of the sky, of existence, which is frameless.

Secondly, it is man's strange mind – if you feel grateful towards me, somewhere, someday you may take revenge against me. It may not happen to *you* particularly; but it has happened to many who were as grateful as you are, and now they are as revengeful as they were grateful – in the same proportion.

The mind has a problem: if you are with me, enjoying my presence, enjoying my silence, it is very natural to feel grateful; but one never knows about tomorrow.

Our paths may separate, or you may be able to go only so far with me and then stop. Then you will have to find some rationalization for why you have stopped, or why you have separated from me and moved on another path. You are not in a state of consciousness which can simply say, "It was beautiful to be with him and I am grateful for that, but life takes strange routes; although I am now on a separate path, my gratefulness to him remains the same." That needs great consciousness.

What happens ordinarily is that the moment you are on a separate path, you start finding fault with me to justify why you are separate; and instead of being grateful you start being revengeful. You feel as if you have been cheated for so long, exploited, deceived. And then the wheel turns completely; where there was love, hate arises.

This is the ordinary human mind; either it can love or it can hate. When it loves it finds all the rationalizations to love, when it hates it finds all the rationalizations to hate. And when it hates it forgets completely those moments of love and gratitude.

To avoid your being sometime hateful towards me, I go on insisting: don't be grateful towards me. If you are not grateful towards me, even if you separate you will not be revengeful towards me – as if we were two strangers who walked on the way for a time and then our paths separated.

Right now it will be very hurtful even to think this. You are asking me not to say it again.... But you know those people also, who had also been in the same state of gratefulness as you are. But small things, very trivial, and your hate which has been waiting – while you were showing your love, your hate was hiding behind it, just waiting for the moment when your love disappears for any reason...then the hate comes with full vengeance. And just because you have to justify yourself, you even create lies – not knowingly, not consciously.

You have seen Shiva sitting here for almost seven years, and his gratitude was as deep as it can be. He would have died to save me. But you are not aware of the whole of your own mind. He came to the commune in America, but the whole setup had changed. He wanted, there too, to sit by my side, to have the same power. He used to think that he loved me – if he had loved me, then there would not have been any problem. He loved his own power. He was the chief guard in the ashram, but by the time he reached the commune, other guards, more efficient, had taken his place. He was not made the chief guard. Then all his love disappeared, all gratitude disappeared.

He has written a book against me now, full of lies, with no foundation in truth. But he has to justify why he has left. Still he is blind, still he cannot see that it was power that was keeping him here and it is power that is now taking revenge.

I have no complaint against anybody, but I understand your whole mind. You don't understand your whole mind. You only understand the part that is on the surface in this moment.

The whole commune was created by Sheela. And she did hard and great work – there is nothing except appreciation. But deep down she was very much worried, because she had taken the place of Laxmi – and the fear was natural that somebody else could take her place.

She never wanted me to see anybody else except her. When I was in silence for three and half years, only she was seeing me, reporting how things were going on. And everything was going perfectly well. She had a great managing capacity and absolute devotion.

When I used to go for "drive-by" she used to carry a gun by the side of my car; she learned to shoot, she got thirty people trained. And she was working from morning till late in the night. Nobody would have thought that she could say anything against me.

But as I started speaking, after three and a half years, people started sending questions relating to the work, relating to her dictatorial methods – that anybody who does not listen to her is immediately thrown out of the commune. And because only *she* was seeing me, I knew only as much as she related to me – and that was the part she chose.

So I said to her, "This is not right. I will have to see a few more people so that I can be aware of what exactly is going on in the commune. And if I find that you are doing something wrong, I can put you right." I started seeing two, three people once in a while – just to get an idea of whether Sheela is representing things to me exactly, and I found she was not being truthful. This was the point when she became afraid, afraid of those people who were seeing me. And the commune had become almost an empire in itself.

She would have died for me, but the day I declared that there will be no successor to me, that instead of a successor there will be a committee of enlightened people who will choose who is going to be in charge of the commune....deep down there must have been the hope that she was going to succeed me.

She started things which are inconceivable. She bugged *my* room, to be aware of what other people were telling me, what my answers to them were. And it was the *same* person who was moving with the gun to save my life. But the desire for power, which was unconscious up to now, and perhaps to her it remained unconscious.... But bugging your own master's room.... On the one hand trusting me totally – but bugging my room is not trust. She was afraid that I might be preparing somebody – in case someone could take better care of the commune.

She tried to poison Vivek, because she was the one who was taking care of my body...just to remove her, so that she could put in somebody who would only report what Sheela wanted – her own person. She poisoned Devaraj, my personal physician, to kill him, so that another doctor could be put in his place who would report to me only things which Sheela wanted.

Man's mind is such. And when she found that I had become aware that she had bugged at least two hundred houses in the commune, whomsoever she suspected may be capable of taking over her power.... She started tapping everebody's telephones, to find out if there was anybody who was against her.

When I became aware of all these things she simply escaped from the commune, leaving all the problems which she had created, and taking all those twenty people who were in charge of different departments. The day she left there was only food for one day in the commune, for five thousand people. Usually the routine was that food should be available for three months ahead.

She had created the commune; she could not

bear to see it in somebody else's hands. If she could not be in power...and it was all in her mind. There was nobody who was going to take her place.

I had no idea to replace her. I had certain ideas that things that she was doing should not be done. If you cannot trust your own people and you have to bug two hundred houses, then whom are you going to trust? If you have to tap everybody's phone, then it has become almost a fascist state.

I was going to tell her to remove all these bugs, all these tappings; I was not going to replace her. She was capable, and there was nobody else who was more capable than she was.

But in her own fear, because I had come to know all these things and now she had no answer – what answer could she give to me, why she had bugged my room? – she escaped with twenty people who were in charge of different departments, so that the commune would collapse: "If I cannot be in power, then nobody can be in power; the commune cannot exist." Man's mind is such.

Then she started writing and giving press releases, press interviews in Europe, saying things which were absolutely absurd. But she had to justify why she had left. And after she had been sentenced to four and a half years imprisonment, the first thing she said was, "In this jail I feel better than I did in the jail of Bhagwan's commune."

She was the whole, sole power. I simply used to come for one hour to talk to people. I had no idea how much money she had put into Swiss banks – she had never seen so much money: two hundred million dollars we had put into the commune. It was her secretary, who did not go with her, who said that she had been keeping at least thirty to forty million dollars in a secret account, in her own name, in Switzerland; and the money belongs to the commune.

Still I was not going to replace her. I was just going to change her ways, tell her, "This commune is a commune of love, of trust, of friendliness, and you are taking advantage, because I cannot look after small matters – money, and food, and land, and banks – you have to take care of."

Neither here do I know anything about how you have to manage. I know this much: that you love me and you will manage in a loving way.

But to justify herself – because people started asking, "Why have you left the commune?" – she had to find fault with me, to justify why she had left the commune.

So, Patipada, it is better to be fully conscious and let your gratitude be towards existence. Leave me aside – because I know any moment, any small thing may create a situation where you have to justify yourself. And to justify yourself you will have to invent lies against me.

Because you have been so grateful, the other side of your mind, which knows nothing of gratitude but only ungratefulness, will take over. You have loved me, now you will hate me with the same strength.

Knowing the games of the mind, I have always been saying that your gratitude should be towards existence. I am no more than a stranger you have met on the way. We talked a little while, just to pass the time. We can depart in a friendly way; there is no need to justify yourself.

When you are in love, it hurts to hear me saying to you that you need not be even grateful to me. But, Patipada, I am going to say it again and again so you don't forget it, because I don't want you to lie someday, to say things against me which you know perfectly well are wrong.

For example, Shiva was never my bodyguard; it simply happened as a coincidence. An Indian sannyasin attacked Laxmi and almost destroyed her nose. Laxmi is a small woman, so when I came to know about it I told Shiva, "You should be a bodyguard to Laxmi; wherever Laxmi goes you have to follow her." In evening initiation meetings Laxmi used to sit by my side to give me information about the person, and I had tõld Shiva, "Wherever Laxmi is, you have to be there," so he started sitting on the other side. He was not my bodyguard.

Now he is writing that he was my bodyguard and he knows every secret. He has never entered my room, not even once; there was no need. Someday he will repent what he has done, but then it will be too late; the people who are reading his book will be convinced of whatever he is saying. This can happen to anybody. And I don't want it to happen to *anybody*.

Teertha was hoping.... He was the first therapist to join the ashram; naturally, because he was the first, he became the chief therapist without any formalities. Nobody had told him that he was the chief therapist. It was just by coincidence, because he was here before anybody else – the other therapists came later on – that he managed to become the chief. And there was no harm in it; somebody had to take care of all the therapy groups.

When the commune dispersed he saw clearly that I cannot be in America – for fifteen years I cannot enter America. And in India the American government is pressurizing the Indian government that no foreign sannyasins should be allowed in.

Seeing the situation, he thought it was better to open an institute of his own in Italy. There was no harm in opening the institute in Italy. I had to tell my therapists that wherever they were they should continue to create institutes, communes, because all European countries have banned me.

I cannot enter into Europe, I cannot go to America, and foreign sannyasins cannot come into India.

Now there was no need to accept me as his master; there was a chance of becoming a master himself. So Teertha has become a mini-guru. He knows nothing about enlightenment. He has never meditated. Here he was involved with his groups, which have nothing to do with meditation. And I have told these therapists, "You should meditate," but it was against their egos, because they were therapists. Thirty or forty people were joining their groups, and they were the leaders. To meditate with the same people was against their egos; so they never meditated.

People must have been asking him, "Is your institute Bhagwan's institute?"

He said, "I have not been Bhagwan's disciple...."

Then what was he doing here? What was he doing in America? And the same has been done by Somendra, by Rajen, by a few other therapists – they are all therapists. Finding an opportunity that they can become mini-gurus.... But for that they have had to deny that they had anything to do with Bhagwan.

There were many reasons why I told you to drop the malas, to drop the orange clothes: First, so that you can enter this country; otherwise you cannot enter this country. Second, you will not be known to the world as my disciples, so there will not come any moment to deny it. I am simply trying to save you from telling lies, and making you absolutely independent even while you are here. You come here as friends – more than that seems to be risky. I will continue to do whatever I can do for you. I see not only your present – but possibilities in the future.

All these people are lying, and I don't feel it right to contradict their lies – they have been my disciples, I have loved them and I still love them. It is below me to contradict their lies. If their spiritual growth happens somehow, they may realize by themselves.

So, Patipada, there is no need to feel any pain. Whatever I say has a meaning in it, far-reaching, that you may not be able to understand right now. Gratitude is good – but to the trees, to the moon, to the sun, because you will never be in a position to be against the trees, against the moon, against the sun. But to be grateful to me is dangerous.

So I just want not to be in your way. I want to help you to move on the way – but I don't want to stand in your way.

My whole approach is to give you absolute freedom, so you never feel any revenge against me.

Beloved Bhagwan,

"What do I really want?" is a question to which I can't find an answer.
I feel I'm hiding behind phrases, such as "Get out of the way,"
"Go with the flow," and "The universe wants it that way."
Would You please help me
understand the difference between these phrases
and not taking responsibility for my own existence.

Atmo Sarvesh, do you know who you are? And if you do not know, how are you going to take responsibility for your own existence? When I say, "Let go," or "Go with the flow," or "The universe wants it that way," I am trying only one thing: to relax you, for you not to be tense. These are only devices to relax you, because only in deep relaxation will you come to know yourself. And once you know yourself, you will not be able to divide your responsibilities, your existence from other's existence – from the whole of existence.

The moment you know yourself, you become part of the whole existence – so organic a part that the question does not arise of taking responsibility. You will respond, but your response will not be a responsibility. Your response will be the response of existence itself, just through you – just as flowers belong to existence, but roses will come on a rose bush. They don't belong to the rose bush; ultimately they belong to existence. And only a stupid rose bush will think, "they are my flowers, my responsibility." But rose bushes are not stupid, they are utterly relaxed, they let existence take care. They are not separate from the earth, from the sun rays; they are joined in a thousand ways. The rose bush is only an expression of existence: So are you. But first know it! And only with a non-tense mind can one know oneself.

So relaxation or let-go are only devices. Once you are so relaxed, the way the trees are relaxed, you will find your roots in existence. All that you have is not yours – not even *you;* it is a flowering – existence has flowered in your individuality in a certain way. Existence loves variety, creates unique individuals, unique animals, unique trees.

Just for the last few days I have been seeing a bird. When I left for America it was not here, and I have never seen it anywhere else. It is so beautiful: pure white, with a black head and such a long tail – the bird is very small, the tail is almost six times bigger than the bird. Because the tail is so long, it cannot fly like other birds; it moves in air like a fish moves in water. I enquired...because it is a strange bird, I have never seen one so beautiful. It has made a point...every day when I am taking my food in the morning and in the evening it comes for certain. Shunyo told me that this bird is a rare bird; it is called the "bird of paradise."

I said, "It looks like a bird of paradise – it doesn't seem to belong to the earth. The beauty is so unique...with a small black head, and so snow-white, and the tail is so long that it cannot fly, it just hops from one tree to another tree. The way it moves is almost like a fish moving in water." I told Shunyo, "Watch, he cannot be alone, there must be a girlfriend or boyfriend – in this place he may be a bird of paradise, but he cannot be a saint!"

She says she has seen his girlfriend. She has a little small tail – that is the only difference. But I have not seen the girlfriend yet. It is my experience, if the girlfriend comes first to me the boyfriend is bound to come. But if the boyfriend comes first, then it is not necessarily so – the girlfriend even may become an enemy to me, jealous. The poor fellow comes alone. And every day I have been watching, looking; she must be sitting somewhere. But she is avoiding me.

This whole existence takes responsibility for the oceans, for the mountains, for the stars. Sarvesh, why should you be bothered about being responsible for your own self when you do not know who you are? It is just an egoistic desire.

Relax, know first who you are. In that very knowing you will know you are nothing but a part of this immense universe, and the universe takes care. Even if it takes care through you it is existence that takes care. You cannot take the credit for taking care of yourself. The ego desires that, the ego wants to be separate; it wants its territory to be demarcated. But you are so one with existence that ego is just an idea, a figment of your mind, it has no reality anywhere. And the moment you understand it, experience it – that there is no ego – you will be as happy as the birds singing, the trees taking a sunbath. All around you everything is immensely joyful.

Ego makes you sad, serious; responsibility takes away your smiles, your laughter – and to me laughter is the essential religion. The capacity to dance and sing, not separate from existence but as part of it, is the very foundation of a real religious man.

Beloved Bhagwan,

Please talk about the misuse of power.

Shantam Divyama, there is the famous statement of an English philosopher: "Power corrupts, absolute power corrupts absolutely."

I do not agree with him. My analysis is totally different. Everybody is full of violence, greed, anger, passion – but has no power; so he remains a saint. To be violent you need to be powerful. To fulfill your greed you need to be powerful. To satisfy your passions you need to be powerful.

So when power happens into your hands, all your sleeping dogs start barking. Power becomes a nourishment to you, an opportunity. It is not that power corrupts, you *are* corrupted. Power only brings your corruption into the open. You wanted to kill somebody, but you had not the power to kill; but if you have the power, you will kill.

It is not power that corrupts you, corruption you carry within yourself; power simply gives you the opportunity to do whatever you want to do.

Power in the hands of a man like Gautam Buddha will not corrupt; on the contrary, it will help humanity to raise its consciousness. Power in the hands of Genghis Khan destroys people, rapes women, burns people alive. Whole villages are burnt – people are not allowed to get out. It is not power...this man Genghis Khan must have been carrying all these desires in him.

It is almost like when rain comes, different plants start growing; but different plants have different flowers. Whatever is hidden in your seeds, whatever is your potentiality, power gives you a chance – because most human beings are living so unconsciously that when they come to power all their unconscious instincts have a chance to be fulfilled. Then they don't care whether it kills people, whether it poisons people....

You are asking me about the misuse of power. Power is misused because you have desires which are ugly, which are an inheritance from the animals.

In a better world the first things should be.... We waste almost one third of life in educating our children. In that one third of life, some time should be given to cleanse their unconscious; so by the time they graduate from their university, and they have some power somewhere – somebody will become a police commissioner, somebody will become a governor, somebody will become a prime minister – if they do not have anything in their unconscious that is poisonous, destructive, then power cannot be misused. Who is going to misuse it? Power is neutral.

My sannyasins in Italy have been trying for one year for a tourist visa for me, just for three weeks. And it has taken one year for the authorities, and they still have not been able to decide. Finally, a few days ago, a letter came: after one year the old application has become useless, a new application is needed.

They had filled in the application, I had signed the application, and just yesterday the Italian ambassador informed me that I have been given a ten day tourist visa – but there are conditions. I have never heard that tourist visas are given with conditions. The conditions are: "To report on what date, at what time, from which airport you will leave India and on what date, at what time, at what airport you will land in Italy; and the same for the return.

"In Italy, whichever city you are in, you should appear at the police station first, and inform them how long you are going to stay in the city. And before leaving the city you should go again to the police station, to inform them that you are leaving the city. Next city, again you have to go to the police station."

I have told Anando to write a letter to the prime minister of Italy: "Just a few months ago you were in India. How many conditions were put on you? And in how many police stations did you appear? And do you think I am a murderer, or a terrorist, or I am carrying bombs and dynamite?

"Let us know when you are coming back to India, so that we can give you a really good welcome. And I refuse to step in your land unless you apologize for making these conditions. It took you one year to figure out all these conditions; and then too you have not given the visa for three weeks, just for ten days. Ordinarily the visa is given for three months – and nobody has ever heard that such conditions have to be followed."

I have told Anando to write to him that, "It seems Benito Mussolini has not died yet. Your country is not a democratic country, it is still fascist. These conditions indicate, without any doubt, a fascist mind.

"So I will come to Italy if you apologize publicly; or I will come to Italy when you are no longer in power. And my people in Italy will try in every way to ensure that you are no longer in power. Just let the new election come, because I have thousands of sannyasins in Italy; and this is an insult to my thousands of sannyasins in Italy.

"The pope comes to India, and the president the prime minister go to receive him at the airport; he is not asked to appear at the police station in every city. And he himself has been here. But next time, if you come here as prime minister, then just inform us at what time and at what airport you are landing, so that we can reply to you about your conditions."

These people are not corrupted by power. These people are corrupted; power simply brings their corruption into action.

Power in itself is neutral. In a good man's hand it will be a blessing. In an unconscious man's hand it is going to be a curse. But for thousands of years we have condemned power, without thinking that power has not to be condemned; people have to be cleaned of all the ugly instincts that are hiding within them, because everybody is going to have some kind of power or other.

It does not have to be great power. You may be just sitting in a railway station selling tickets, but that too gives you power. You are standing at the window, and the man does not even look at you. He goes on turning his file – and you can see that he is not concerned with the file, he simply wants to show you your place. Even the peon sitting outside the collector's office behaves as if he is the president of the country – so it is not a question of where you are. Wherever you are, you will have some kind of power.

Aurangzeb, one of India's Mohammedan emperors, was so impatient that he could not wait for his father to die, or to become old, so that he could succeed him. He imprisoned his own father, and became the emperor of the country. His father had remained busy all his life. Now, sitting in the prison cell, he sent a message to his son: "At least arrange thirty boys, so that I can teach them the holy *Koran*."

And the comment that Aurangzeb made to his

courtiers is very significant. He said, "That old man does not want to lose power. Now he is no longer the emperor. But thirty students...teaching them the holy *Koran*, he will again have the power over those small children."

Psychologists say that people who are afraid of competing in life and becoming powerful, choose a simpler way: they become teachers in schools. Small children...and you can harass them, beat them, although it is illegal – but it happens all over the country.

Just the other day I was reading a report that there are cases found...but the government goes on hiding those facts. For the first time it has been accepted, because it has become too much, that teachers have hit the children so hard that they have become deaf for their whole lives.

One boy...his own father chained him; almost for ten years he remained chained, tied to a pillar in the house. He has almost become like an animal. He cannot stand up, he can only move on all fours; and because he was forced to live in darkness, he has lost his eyesight.

Even parents use power. Teachers use power, husbands use power, wives use power. It does not matter where you are.

If mankind comes to understand the deep psychological roots and changes man's unconscious so that there are no seeds, power can go on raining but there will be no flowers of corruption. Otherwise power is going to be misused always. And you cannot take power from people's hands; somebody must be a mother, somebody must be a father, somebody must be a teacher.

The only way is, to cleanse people's unconscious with meditation, fill their inner being with light. It is only meditation that gives you a clean heart, which cannot be corrupted. Then power can never be misused, then power can be a blessing – it is going to be creative. Then you are going to do something to make life more lovable, more livable; to make existence a little more beautiful. But that great day has not yet arrived, and to make an effort for that great day to arrive, all the power – addicted people are going to be against you.

It has been again and again asked of me, "Why is the whole world against you?"

They are all power-addicted people, and I am trying to make man a pool of serenity – peace and silence and love and ecstasy.

Okay, Vimal?

Yes, Bhagwan.

Session 7

When The Ocean Has Called You

*Joy is as infectious as any disease.
When you see a few people dancing,
suddenly you feel your feet are ready.
You may try to control them,
because control has been taught to you,
but your body wants to join the dance.*

February 28, 1987
Evening

Beloved Bhagwan,

What to do with the question
when there are no words for it?
And what to do with the secrets in our hearts
when there is no way to express them?

Krishna Priya, there is some misunderstanding. There is no question in the world which cannot be asked. Yes, there are answers which cannot be answered. A question always comes from the mind; hence the mind always finds appropriate words for it. But the answer comes from your very being, from your depths of silence where no words have ever entered. The territory of the words and language is the mind, and that is also the territory of the questions. Every question can be brought into words – only when you start feeling the answers, then the problem arises.

I have been watching you for almost ten years. You have gone through such a transformation that what you are thinking is a question, is not a question. You have come very close to the answer – that's why you cannot find words. But this is something that happens very rarely to very blessed souls. You should feel blissful, fortunate and grateful to existence.

The misunderstanding is also very natural, because the mind is well acquainted only with questions. When for the first time you are pregnant with an answer, it is a natural misunderstanding of the mind that there is some question because the answer, mind knows not, and the answer, mind cannot express.

You are saying, "What to do with the question when there are no words for it?" Then it is absolutely certain it is not a question. It is an answer, and you are not supposed to do anything at all.

A question has to be solved:
An answer has to be lived.

So what is arising in you – the peace, the silence, the joy that I can see in your eyes, on your face, the tremendous change...because you used to be very serious.... You have moved almost one-hundred-and-eighty degrees. You radiate joy.

Drop the misunderstanding that it is a question and rejoice that it is the answer. It will never find any words; it has never found any expression. Yes, your eyes may show it, your face may radiate it, your very gestures may have the grace of it, but words are too small and too trivial and too mundane – their approach is very limited.

The answer is beyond the mind. Those who go on seeking through the mind go on coming upon new questions. The very few people who have found the answer are those who have gone beyond mind, beyond words, beyond language.

You are saying, "And what to do with the secrets in our hearts when there is no way to express them?" Nothing has to be done; they will find their way of their own accord.

You have to understand one thing very clearly: there are things which you cannot do, but which happen. If somebody says to you, "love me"...now, love cannot be commanded, love cannot be ordered, and if – according to the order and according to the commandment – you make an effort to love, it is going to be phony; it cannot be an authentic reality.

What is arising in your being is thrilling your heart. It will find its own way to happen – in a dance, in a song, or in just deep silence which is not negative, but immensely full...in some creativity, or anything that you do – your being will find its way to do it in a new way that you have never done before, with great love.

You are not supposed to find expression for your experiences and the secrets that are arising in your being. They are far bigger than you; you cannot manage them. You are left far behind; those secrets, those answers happen only when you are not. Who is going to express them? Neither are there words to express, nor is there a person to express them. Now the experience itself will find its way, just as the rivers find their way to the ocean, just as roots find their way rising into trees and blossoming into flowers.

Looking at the roots and the flowers you may not see any connection at all – roots are ugly, and the flowers are so beautiful – but all the juice and all the color and all the beauty and all the fragrance that the flower has, have been given by the roots. The roots have been carrying those flowers for years in their womb. The seeds are never beautiful, but they can give birth to great beauty. You just wait....

I can understand your impatience, because you are too full and you want to shower just like a raincloud, but it is not within your capacity. Neither have you found it, nor is it in your hands to express it. On the contrary, it will be right to say *it* has found *you*. And now it will find its way in some creative act, in some loving act, in something that indicates that it is not coming from the mind. You have given it birth just as a woman gives birth to a child. She does not create it; it grows of its own accord, and a day comes when it comes out of the womb.

Every meditator has to remember it: One day you will be pregnant with God – whether you are man or woman does not matter – and the unknown will find its way. You are simply to relax and follow it.

You are not to become a guide, but you have to be guided by it. You have to become just a shadow. It becomes the reality and you become the shadow, and wherever the reality moves, the shadow moves. This is the experience everybody else is waiting here for. And the same question will be asked by many, sometime or other.

It is good, Krishna Priya, that you have asked it, because it is not only your question, it is going to be the question of many. Those who can be patient enough, those who can wait for the divine to take shape in their being, will have the same question, exactly in the same words.

But don't become tense because the experience is so new. And don't be afraid, because it may lead you in new ways which you are not acquainted with, untrodden by you ever before – not even dreamt, not even imagined.

This is the moment when trust is needed. Trust in existence, not in any belief system, not in any priest, not in any church, not in any holy book, but in existence. All around you the trees are so deeply trusting, the rivers are trusting, the mountains are trusting, the millions of stars are trusting. The whole existence is a tremendous experiment of trust.

And this is the right moment for you to become part of this immense experiment of trust. Let life lead your way. Give your hand to existence without any doubt and without any question. And never ask where it is leading you – it always leads to your destiny, and it never fails.

Those who cannot trust, they fail, because they think themselves wiser than the whole world, the whole existence. What is your wisdom? What is your intelligence? not even a dewdrop. And when the ocean has called you, trust it – take a jump and disappear into it.

Beloved Bhagwan,

You are the well.
All the time when I came there was fresh water
waiting for me, cleaning and purifying me,
taking me apart and putting me together
in a different, more beautiful way.
Now, for the first time,
I feel the courage to be so close
that I can see my face mirrored in Your water.
I'm afraid, Bhagwan, and also full of joy.

Chitbodhi, man is accustomed to misery; hence, he is never afraid of misery. However great, when misery happens, he knows it.

But man is absolutely unacquainted with joy. He has forgotten the very language of joy. His mind is full of tensions, anxieties, anguishes, anger, violence, jealousy. Nothing makes him afraid – they are all old companions, he knows them perfectly well. He has lived with them, although it has been a suffering, it has been a hell. But this is one of the significant factors to be understood about man: he can adapt himself to any conditions.

It happened in Egypt nearabout three thousand years ago: There was a monastery, and the monastery had an underground graveyard. Whenever any monk died, the great stone that was covering the way to the graveyard underneath was removed, and the monk's body was lowered down in deep darkness. The tunnel was miles long – a natural tunnel.

Thousands of monks have been lowered into that tunnel, and according to the Egyptian convention every monk was given some money, some clothes, and some food, because he was going for a pilgrimage. It was sixty feet deep and miles long.

It happened that a monk had not died, but was in a coma. Others thought that he had died, and they opened the graveyard, lowered the monk, closed the graveyard...and after a few hours the monk came to consciousness. He could not believe where he was – immense darkness, darkness so deep, as he had never seen, because not even a ray of light had ever entered into that tunnel. And such a stink, because so many dead bodies had become rotten – all around there were bodies and bodies, and they were all dead.

He shouted as much as he could, although he knew deep down that his voice would not reach to the monks in the monastery because it was sixty feet deep and then a huge rock always closed.... He had himself closed that rock many times. But as a last resort, he tried shouting with all his might, "I am alive!" But nobody heard it.

And you will be surprised to know the immense adaptability of man. You may think that he must have committed suicide – you are wrong. He lived in the hope that someday some monk will die, and the rock will be removed – then he can shout.

But meanwhile there was a little food that he has been sent with, and after that food, he started eating rotten food sent with other dead bodies which had become just skeletons.

It took ten years for another monk to die, although this monk was praying every day to God, "There are so many old monks...." But God has never heard anybody. Over the time of ten years he became a cannibal; he started eating the flesh of dead bodies. Not only that, he started collecting the money that had been given to each monk when he died, and the clothes – in the hope that when he would be rescued, he would take all these clothes and all this money.

And slowly, slowly he forgot that the graveyard was stinking; he forgot that he was living the ugliest life possible. For water, there was nothing else than the water that was coming from the rocks, and he knew that the water was from the gutters of the monastery. He started drinking that water; he could not have even touched it before, but there was no other way. The lust for life is so tremendous that man can manage.... That water which was coming was so dirty, but for him it was almost nectar; it was life-giving. And he was the only living man in that miles-long tunnel.

As he was moving around in the darkness, slowly, slowly his eyes became accustomed to seeing a little bit in the darkness. And dead people, just skeletons – nobody was there to prevent him, so he was searching everybody, finding money, clothes.

And when after ten years the rock was removed, he shouted back up. People had completely forgotten about him. They pulled him out, but he said, "First you pull up my clothes" – he had a big pile of clothes. People could not believe that.... Then he said, "Now pull up my money." So they pulled up his money – he had collected the money from thousands of people. After all his treasures were taken out, he came out.

It was difficult for him to open his eyes in the sunlight. He had grown such a long beard that it was touching the floor, and he was looking so healthy. People could not believe it and said, "How have you managed? You used to be very thin, and you have collected so much weight!" And when they heard his story they could not believe that a man can do this. When you think about it, putting yourself in his place.... First it is shocking, but soon you will understand that what he did, you would have done also.

He lived twenty years more. And again his eyes became accustomed to light. Now he himself could not believe that those ten years – it seemed almost like a nightmare that is ended.

Chitbodhi, you are afraid because you are feeling the first stirrings of joy. It is unknown territory. Your heart you are feeling for the first time. The heart is not just what the medical people say, or the physiologists say – a pumping station. The heart that the mystics and the poets talk about has nothing to do with the heart that medical science talks about.

Behind almost every physical organ there is a parallel to it – just behind it, a spiritual receptivity. Behind your eyes, there are eyes which see things, which these eyes cannot see. And behind your ears, there are ears which can hear music, that these ears cannot hear. And behind your physical heart, there is a spiritual heart which knows love – which this heart has no idea about – which knows joy.

The physical heart can be changed, and a plastic heart may be far better because a plastic heart cannot have a heart failure. There are, around the world, thousands of people moving about with an artificial heart. But that artificial heart cannot love. Just put two artificial hearts close to each other and see what kind of dialogue happens. Nothing will happen; there are just two dead things. They can do the function of purifying your blood, of taking in the oxygen, of throwing out the carbon dioxide; but love is neither oxygen nor carbon dioxide. Love is not a question of breathing – *everybody* is breathing.

So remember, whenever I talk about the heart, I am not talking about the heart medical science talks about – this is something behind it. Each of your senses has a parallel sense behind it.

If you hear me, you can hear in two ways. Either you can hear only with your outer ear, or you can hear with your inner ear too. When your outer and inner ear both hear, then it is listening; otherwise it is only hearing.

When your outer eyes and inner eyes both see, then the same existence becomes so psychedelic, so colorful.... The same tree is greener than it has ever been – and not only greener, each leaf has its own energy aura. The whole tree is surrounded by an energy aura, radiating rays.

In the Soviet Union one man has developed a new photography, Kirlian photography. He uses such sensitive plates that he can picture not only the trees in his plates, but trees with their energy aura surrounding them.

When your inner eyes are together with your outer eyes and there is a harmony, you will see this whole existence is a festival of lights, that everything is radiating light, is surrounded by beautiful light, soft...every man is surrounded.

And a man can be known by his aura. The ordinary man has only nearabout a one-inch aura all around his body, but as your meditation deepens your aura becomes bigger – two inches, three inches, four inches, five inches.

As your meditation deepens you are surrounded with more and more light coming from your inner being.

You have seen the pictures of Buddha or Jesus with a circle of light around their head, an aura, and people think that it is simply mythology. Now Kirlian photography proves it – it is not mythology. Kirlian photography says that that kind of round aura happens only when somebody has reached to his very innermost core, when somebody is awakened – a Gautam Buddha. Then his whole head radiates something of the eternal.

But when things start happening for the first time, one feels afraid. When a young boy, fourteen years old, becomes for the first time aware of his sexuality, he feels afraid, embarrassed, becomes very uptight, is worried: "What is happening? If somebody comes to know....And what am I supposed to do with it?" A new energy has become available of which he was not aware at all up to now. And when spiritual energy becomes available to you, it is a million-times-bigger phenomenon.... You feel joy, you feel blissfulness, and at the same time a trembling, a fear – but this fear will disappear.

It is a natural process. As you become more and more accustomed to the new state of joyfulness, fear will be reduced. Soon you will find there is no fear at all. And to be fearless is a tremendously great achievement, because fear is part of your death. If you become fearless, you have tasted something which is deathless.

In your joy you have come close to the deathless, in your joy you have come to your immortality.

You are saying, Chitbodhi, "You are the well. All the time when I came there was fresh water waiting for me – cleaning and purifying me, taking me apart and putting me together in a different more beautiful way. Now, for the first time, I feel the courage to be so close that I can see my face mirrored in your water. I'm afraid, Bhagwan, and also full of joy."

Give all your energy to joy, and fear will disappear. Ignore fear, don't pay any attention to fear, because the more attention you pay to it, the longer it will linger on. Pour yourself totally in the direction from where joy is arising, and fear will disappear just as darkness disappears when you bring light in.

Joy is light. And joy is the beginning of a great pilgrimage which ends in finding God. So go on – without any fear, because existence always protects those who trust it. Relax, give yourself to existence and allow the joy to overwhelm you. Let it become your wings, so that you can reach to the stars.

A joyful heart is very close to the stars.

It is only the sad and the sorrowful and the miserable who are going towards hell. They are creating their hell. The joyful and the singing and the dancing and the celebrating are creating their paradise by each of their songs, by each of their dances.

It is in your hands whether to create paradise or to fall into a darkness, into hellfire. These are not outside you; these both are within you. It all depends what you choose to be.

Choose to be divine, choose to be more and more a celebrant, choose to be festive, so more and more flowers can blossom in your being, and more and more fragrance can become available to you.

And this way will not only help you, Chitbodhi, it will help all those with whom you come in contact. Joy is as infectious as any disease. When you see a few people dancing, suddenly you feel your feet are ready. You may try to control them, because control has been taught to you, but your body wants to join the dance. Whenever you have an opportunity to laugh, join; whenever you have an opportunity to dance, join; whenever you have an opportunity to sing, sing – and one day you will find you have created your paradise.

It is not that one goes to paradise; paradise is

not somewhere in the sky – it is something that one creates around himself.

It is a good beginning.

With all my blessings, go deeper, in spite of any fear. Never listen to negative things, because if you listen to them they can poison you, they can destroy your joy – keep it pure, unpolluted. And here are people who will dance with you, who will celebrate, because you have taken the first step towards God.

And I want to remind you that the first step is almost half the journey.

Beloved Bhagwan,

This verse I send to You from "Gitanjali."
It is so beautiful, like You, Master.
"I know not how thou singest, my master,
I ever listen in silent amazement.
The light of thy music illumines the world,
The life breath of thy music runs from sky to sky,
The holy stream of thy music breaks through all
stony obstacles and rushes on.
My heart longs to join in thy song,
But vainly struggles for voice.
I would speak, but speech breaks not into song,
And I cry out baffled, ah, thou has made my heart captive
in the endless meshes of thy music, my master."

Chandra, Rabindranath Tagore, although he belongs to this century, echoes thousands-of-years-old longings and dreams of the East. He belongs to the seers of the *Upanishads*. He is the only man this century has produced whose words can be compared to the five-thousand-year-old *Upanishads*.

Those *Upanishads* were songs of the first seers of humanity, but it is a strange fact that truth remains the same. Everything changes, but the truth is eternal. Five thousand years of distance, but whatever Rabindranath sings, appears to be coming from the days of the *Upanishads,* of those days of humanity's childhood – so innocent and so pure.

Man was not yet corrupted by religions, organized faiths; man was not yet under the slavery of the priests; man was not yet divided into Hindus and Mohammedans and Christians and Jews. Humanity was still one.

The seers of the *Upanishads* were as innocent as every child is – it was easy for them to sing those beautiful songs of tremendous meaning. But for Rabindranath, being a twentieth-century man, it was certainly a miracle that he dropped five thousand years of knowledgeability and became a child again. Every mystic has to become a child again.

These few lines are from "Gitanjali," Rabindranath's book for which he was awarded the Nobel Prize. Gitanjali means "offering of songs."

Somebody asked Rabindranath, "Why have you chosen this title?" He said, "I don't have anything else to offer to God except my imperfect songs."

On his death bed, an old friend had come to console Rabindranath, and he told him, "You should be dying with absolute contentment, because you are perhaps the greatest poet in the whole world." In the West, Shelley has two thousand songs which can be put to music. Rabindranath has six thousand songs, and of far greater significance than any of the songs that Shelley has. That old friend was saying to Rabindranath, "You should die absolutely contented. You have achieved something – a peak no one has ever been able to achieve."

Rabindranath opened his eyes and said, "Keep quiet! – because I know I have not been able to sing the song I had come to sing. I am an utter failure. I am dying with tears in my eyes." And he did die with tears in his eyes.

He said to his friend, "I am praying to God! 'Give me a little time more, because in this whole life that you have given to me, I have been simply arranging my instruments. Now that the instruments are ready, you are taking me away – and the song that I have come to sing remains unsung.'"

The friend could not believe what Rabindranath was saying. He said, "Then what about your six thousand songs?"

Rabindranath said, "Those are all failures. Six thousand efforts to sing the song that I have come to sing, but each time I failed. I was trying hard to sing the song that was just on my tongue, but the moment I expressed it, it was something else. It was not the same quality, the same depth, the same beauty. When it was within me it was a living reality, and when it was spoken it was something dead. People have appreciated my songs, and I have been crying in my nights, 'Will I be able to sing it? Or I will always be a failure.'"

This is one of the fundamental qualities of greatness, because the longing and the dream are so high, and the human reach is so small. The longing is for the moon, and the human reach is so small that only small people can be contented about their creativity. The greater the man, the more he will feel he has failed.

Although Rabindranath has given such beautiful songs that there is no comparison, he had a comparison which nobody from the outside had any idea about. He had a song deep in his soul, very alive, ready to burst forth, and he always compared his songs with his inner feeling. He found that what he wanted to express had remained behind. Although he had been able to put together beautiful words, the life was no longer in them, the heart was no longer beating in them. They are faraway echoes of the song he wanted to sing.

I know not how thou singest, my master.
He is asking God Himself...
I know not how thou singest, my master.
I ever listen in silent amazement.
The light of thy music illumines the world,
The life breath of thy music runs from
sky to sky,
The holy stream of thy music breaks through
all stony obstacles and rushes on.
My heart longs to join in thy song,
But vainly struggles for voice.

I have got the song, but where is the voice?
Where are the words?

He is saying, "You have given me the song, but you have made me so poor that I don't have the voice to sing it" – and he was a beautiful singer, he was a great musician. He created a new kind of music altogether, which is called "Rabindra music."

India has a tremendously long history of great musicians; it has explored all the dimensions possible, and for hundreds of years nobody has been able to add anything new. Rabindranath has added a new dimension, but still his longing is so great that whatever he does falls short.

My heart longs to join in thy song,
But vainly struggles for voice.
I would speak, but speech breaks not into song,
And I cry out baffled...

When he was awarded the Nobel prize and he addressed the Nobel committee, he said, "You have awarded my tears. As far as the songs are concerned, I am still struggling to find voice for them."

Ah, thou has made my heart captive in the endless meshes of thy music, my master.

You have imprisoned me in endless meshes of music; I am unable to find the way out. I tried this way, I tried that way – my whole life I have been trying and trying and trying – but nothing seems to succeed.

This awareness makes him not only a poet, but a mystic too. In this whole century there have been many poets, but Rabindranath is a category by himself.

The poets, the painters, the musicians, the sculptors are very egoist people; they are continuously bragging about their painting, about their music, about their poetry. Rabindranath belongs to a totally different category – he is so humble. And I would like to say to you that the greater you are, the humbler you become. The higher the peak of your being, the deeper will be the valley by your side. The greater your being, the deeper will be your feeling that you could have done much more, but you have done so little.

The last words he said on his deathbed were, "I am worried. What will I say to God? – that you had sent me to sing just one song, and I could not even manage to do it."

This should also be the experience of all meditators, because the deeper your meditation goes, the more and more your ego disappears. Finally it leaves you just a nobody – anonymous, no name, no fame.

In that great nothingness, you become one with the whole universe.

Beloved Bhagwan,

It seems, that everywhere we are,
and now that we are in India,
the same stupid, silly, sky-rocketing charges are put on us.
These repressed beings –
poverty-stricken people, violent people, greedy people –
would threaten us with bulldozers
and forced entries into the ashram.
They also charge us with obscenity, drugs, etc.
Bhagwan, You have been too compassionate with all these idiots –
the blind, the deaf, and the dumb society.
Kindly put more light on this burning issue.

Gurudayal Singh, it is a right observation that the people are blind, that they are deaf, that they are insane, that they are utterly prejudiced, irrational in their beliefs. But because of all this, they need more compassion. You cannot say that because people are sick and ill the doctor should simply leave them. When people are sick and ill they need more compassion.

It is a great opportunity for you. In spite of their misbehavior, mistreatment, ugly lies, you can still remain silent, peaceful, loving and compassionate. And if you become enlightened in this society, the whole credit will go to the society. There is no need to be angry about them. What can they do? They have been handed down all this garbage for centuries. They are victims; they need all the compassion that is possible.

I would like you to remember Jesus. At the last moment on the cross he raised his eyes and hands towards the sky and said, "Father, forgive these people, because they know not what they are doing." In that moment Jesus reached his highest experience of life, his highest ecstasy. The love and the compassion that were in his eyes and heart for those who were crucifying him have made him go through a fire test, and he came out pure gold.

So I can understand...the world is going to be against me. It is not their fault, it is my fault. They are fast asleep, dreaming great dreams, and I am trying to wake them up. Naturally they are getting angry. They are living with their beliefs, consoled, and I am disturbing their beliefs. I am trying to say to them, "Your beliefs are only beliefs; you have to drop them and to search for truth on your own."

Because I am disturbing their consolation, the fault is mine. And of course they are in the majority. People ordinarily think that if so many people are thinking in the same way as they think, it must be true. But they don't know that truth is not to be decided by voting; truth is to be decided by experience.

The whole world may be against me, still it does not disturb me, for the simple reason that whatever I am saying is my own experience; I am saying it on my own authority. And those who are with me – and Gurudayal Singh has been with me for almost twenty-five years, a beautiful human being – naturally get worried and concerned, "What kind of humanity have we got? "

All the countries proclaim democracy, freedom of speech, freedom of movement, respect for the individual, and every country practices just the opposite. There is no respect for the individual; there is no respect for individual freedom of expression.

Just a few days ago, one of my friends was looking at the files of the CID department in New Delhi, because the chief of the CID department is his friend, and the chief was not aware that he is my friend also. He saw my name there...all kinds of charges, without any evidence.

The chief told him first, "He is a dangerous man." Now you should give some evidence. Have I killed somebody? Have I thrown any bomb or dynamite at somebody? Am I a terrorist, a murderer? But no, just this much is enough, "He is a dangerous man, and he has to be silenced."

My friend was very much shocked and he asked the chief, "What do you mean, 'he has to be silenced?' Do you mean he has to be assassinated, killed?"

He said, "No, that is not the meaning of it. 'Silenced' means we have to make every effort that no country allows him in, and we will not allow people coming from other countries to meet him. Naturally, he will not be able to corrupt people's minds."

My friend just jokingly said, "But have you any evidence that he has corrupted anybody's mind? And do you remember – the same was the charge against Socrates, that he corrupts people's minds?"

And just today I received from the police commissioner a new list in which he states that every talk that I deliver should be taped by the police. And before it is published they will scrutinize it; they will do the editing work. And he said, "I have come from Bombay – meeting my boss – receiving all these instructions."

One of my sannyasins has asked the parliament in Germany, "It is now over one year since you decided that Bhagwan cannot enter into Germany. In the first place, it was absolutely illegal to say that Bhagwan cannot enter into Germany. It was absolutely illegal – a man who has never been to your country, who has never broken any of your laws, who has done no harm to anybody in Germany.... Why should the parliament decide that this man cannot enter? Not only that, but his jet airplane cannot land on any airport in Germany, even for refueling. It is time that you withdraw it."

So it has been reconsidered, and today I received their reconsidered order. Again the same charges that, "He is a dangerous man, and his entry into Germany will disturb many people. He is on the list of the international police, Interpol, as a wanted man. So we cannot withdraw the order – the order is reinforced."

But I love the words, "He is a wanted man by the Interpol." At least some consolation – somebody, somewhere wants me.

Gurudayal, don't take these people seriously, because crucifixion is out of date. And they have committed that mistake once. By crucifying Jesus they created Christianity, and Jews are still repenting about it.

I am not saying this without any foundation. The attorney general of America, answering a press conference, said, "We did not put Bhagwan into jail because we don't want him to become a martyr. That will help his disciples to become more sympathetic, more loving towards him, more surrendered towards him. We cannot take that risk."

But the desire is clear – if the risk was not there, they would have liked to put me into jail for my whole life, or to kill me – but the fear that that may create a greater movement.... What I cannot do alive, their killing me may do.

In two thousand years people have learned something; otherwise there is no reason.... If they had poisoned Socrates, killed Mansoor, crucified Jesus, they could have killed me any day. The desire is there, but also a great fear: If they kill me, then my words and my people will become stronger, my death will bring them together. My people will become a force in changing the whole future of humanity.

So they are trying more sophisticated ways: silencing me.

They don't know that, according to me, they are only retarded people. If they can find a way of preventing my people, I can find a way of bringing my people there. For the whole year they have been trying to silence me, and I am still speaking. And all the governments of the world and all the religious heads of the world are together in the conspiracy against a single man – that shows how much intelligence they have.

I told my sannyasins, "Drop the orange clothes, drop the mala, so there is no identity left that you are sannyasins." Unless India wants to lose all its tourists, they cannot prevent my people from coming. Now my people are not sannyasins, but just tourists. And they cannot lose their tourists, because India earns nearabout fifteen million dollars per year from tourists. So all that I have to do is just tell my people, "Behave more stupidly, don't look intelligent."

Okay, Vimal?

Yes, Bhagwan.

Session 8

Our Dance Is Forever

*One has to remember that each beginning
has to be transformed not into a stopover forever,
but into a new beginning. And the journey is infinite,
so whenever you feel, "This is the place to stop,"
you will always be wrong,
because existence stops nowhere.
It simply goes on evolving.
It has no limits, no boundaries.*

March 1, 1987
Morning

Beloved Bhagwan,

It is so wonderful to be a river,
to sing and dance and celebrate with You,
but who wants to reach the ocean?
Sometimes much longing is there, but I really don't know for what.
I was so happy to hear You say
that You will recognize us in the universal consciousness.
But again, I have only a fantasy of what this means.
And who wants to be there
when this life is so incredibly wonderful.
Am I missing the point?
Is there something that needs to be understood? Please comment.

Anand Parigyan, I am sorry to say that you are missing the point. This life is beautiful, this existence is wonderful, this moment is ecstatic; but there is much more. This is only the beginning, and to stop at the beginning is very unfortunate. And deep down you are also feeling it; otherwise this question would not have arisen.

You are saying, "It is so wonderful to be a river, to sing and dance and celebrate with you, but who wants to reach the ocean?" But why has the question of the ocean arisen at all in you? Apparently it looks like you do not want to reach the ocean – the river is beautiful; its song is beautiful, its dance is beautiful. But melting into the ocean, it melts into a bigger song. Merging into the ocean, it merges into the universal music, into the eternal dance.

Rivers come and go; the ocean remains. And the whole dance of the river, its song, its beauty, is because of the ocean. It is dancing and is joyful because the ocean is coming closer every moment. If the same river is lost in a desert, all dance will disappear, all song will disappear. That will be a death.

The river is so tremendously blissful because it knows it is going to the ocean. At the ocean it appears on the one hand as if the river has disappeared, but in fact only the banks disappear – the river remains. And the banks are a bondage. The river was dancing, but its feet were chained. Those banks were its prison. The dance will remain, will become freer – so vast that perhaps you cannot see it, because the river is not going to disappear; it is going to become the ocean.

You have raised a significant question, because it happens to all those who follow the path. Even the beginning is so beautiful that many think they have arrived and there is no need to go any further.

One has to remember that each beginning has to be transformed not into a stopover forever, but into a new beginning. And the journey is infinite, so whenever you feel, "This is the place to stop," you will always be wrong, because existence stops nowhere. It simply goes on evolving. It has no limits, no boundaries.

Looked at from the point of view of the river – and you are not the river, you are just watching the river – it seems to be lost in the ocean. But you can say just the contrary – that the ocean is lost in the river.

Kabir, one of the great mystics of this country, when he was young and for the first time felt the melting and merging with the divine, he wrote a small poem – two lines of which are:

The dewdrop disappears
into the ocean.

Kabir is no more. Although Kabir had started to search, what he wanted to find has been found; but the searcher has disappeared.

Those lines are beautiful, but before dying, just on his deathbed, he called his son, Kamaal, and said, "You change those two lines. It is true that Kabir has disappeared. The seeker has disappeared; although what he had started out to find has been found. But the second line...I was too young, and the experience was too new.

"I am sorry that I wrote it, that the dewdrop has disappeared into the ocean. Now at my ripe old age, I can see that something just the contrary of what I had written had happened. So change it, write:

The ocean has disappeared
into the dewdrop."

Both are true, but the second has deeper implications. It is not only man who is in search of God. It is not only that man disappears in God; God is also in search of man.

And when the meeting happens, it is far more significant to say that the God disappears into the man. And you are aware of it; otherwise the question would not have come to your mind.

You are saying, "Who wants to reach the ocean?"

It is just like an old parable of Aesop. A fox was trying to reach to the fruits which were hanging, ripe, on a tall tree. But her jump always fell short. She tried hard, again and again, but she could not reach the fruits. A small rabbit was watching the whole thing. The fox was not aware that there was somebody watching. Tired, the fox moved away from the tree, and the rabbit asked, "Uncle, what happened?" And the fox said, "The fruits are not yet ripe. And who cares about fruits which are not ripe?"

There have been many sannyasins who used to live on the campus, in other houses, and sometimes they were moved to Lao Tzu. And they wrote a letter to me saying, "We owe an apology to You, because living in other houses, we were always thinking, 'Who cares to live in Lao Tzu.' But now that we have come to live in Lao Tzu, we know perfectly well that we were repressing our desire, our longing, to be in Lao Tzu, and just consoling ourselves, 'Who cares.'"

Parigyan, don't be like the fox in Aesop's parable. Don't say, "Who cares for the ocean." The whole dance of the river is for the ocean. It is moving from the mountain just like a newly married girl, running to meet her lover.

One of India's great emperors, Akbar, in his autobiography, *Akbar Namma,* has written many significant things. But one story is relevant to your question. It was an actual incident.

He had gone hunting in the forest, and then lost his way. The sun was setting – and that was the time for Mohammedans to do their prayer – so he sat under a tree to do Namaj, the

Mohammedan prayer.

While he was in the middle of his prayer a young girl ran by his side, almost hitting him as she went by. He could not speak; he was immediately very angry. In the first place nobody in his prayers should be disturbed. And he was not just anybody; he was the emperor of the country. And this girl had not even said, "I am sorry." She had not even looked back. She went rushing on to wherever she was going.

His prayer finished, Akbar waited for the girl, because she would have to come back to the village. Where she had gone, there was only deep forest for miles.

Finally she came back. Akbar was still angry, and he said, "You seem to be very rude, uncivilized – couldn't you see that I was praying? And I am not just anybody, I am the emperor of the country."

The girl said, "I am sorry, but as far as I am concerned, I never saw you. My body may have touched your body, but I don't even remember that your body touched mine, because I was going to meet my lover, who is coming after many years. I wanted to meet him just on the road that passes a few miles away. And I was so full of my lover and his sweet memories that I was almost not myself. So just forgive me. It was not deliberate on my part to disturb you; I was not even aware of it.

"But I want to ask you one question. I was going to meet just an ordinary lover. And you were praying to the greatest lover of the world, to God, and you were disturbed. You became angry, and you have been waiting here to punish me. It was not prayer. You were repeating those words just like a parrot; otherwise you would not have known who had gone by, who had touched you, you would have been so deeply involved with the ultimate beloved...."

Akbar was a very sensible man – perhaps the most sensible emperor India has known. He asked the girl to forgive him. And she had taught him a great lesson. He told her, "You are right. Your love was authentic. My prayer was false, just routine."

When the river is dancing and singing and rushing it is going to the ocean to its lover, to its ultimate beloved. There is nothing wrong in experiencing the beauty of this moment. But remember, this beauty has to grow more; each coming moment it has to bring more flowers, more songs, more dances.

And deep down you are longing for those; hence you say, "Who cares? Who wants to reach the ocean? Sometimes much longing is there." Longing for what? – because you have stopped your being from taking note that all your dance and joy is for the ocean. Now you cannot find the object of your longing.

"Sometimes much longing is there, but I really don't know for what." You yourself are preventing it; otherwise it is in your heart – the ocean.

"I was so happy to hear you say that you will recognize us in the universal consciousness." Again, the same thing. Mind goes on repeating the same mistakes. "But again I have only a fantasy of what this means. And who wants to be there when this life is so incredibly wonderful."

But do you think this is the limit? Do you think this is all? You know perfectly well. You may suppress it, but your being knows that this is not all. This is only the beginning – don't make it an end. In fact, there is no end. It is always beginning, reaching higher and higher, deeper and deeper, closer and closer.

But it is always beginning. And this is the grandeur of life – that you will never come to a full stop, because the full stop means death. It is good to have many commas and semicolons in your life, but don't have any full stops. Keep it open, and your dance will become richer, and your song will become celestial.

Sannyas is the pilgrimage – just the pilgrimage in search of something which you will many times think has been found, and again you will have to realize: this is a new beginning, not an end. From eternity to eternity, from one sky to another sky, we go on moving.

Our dance is forever.

You know you are missing the point; hence you ask, "Am I missing the point? Is there something that needs to be understood?" There is much that has to be understood.

And you are missing the point – it has to be consciously recognized. You become satisfied with so small, so little.

A spiritual seeker remains in a strange balance. He is contented with whatever he has got, but he never loses his discontent for more. It is a difficult point to understand, because it appears contradictory. It seems either you should be contented or discontented.

But the spiritual seeker is both: he is contented with whatever life has given, but he knows there is much more; hence, he is discontented too...contented with the past and discontented for the future.

Hence, he goes on discovering new treasures every moment.

Beloved Bhagwan,

The flowers that are blossoming around You
rejoice in the morning dewdrops, the sunshine,
in the silent, cool breeze.
A seed, like me, is in need of more tangible and basic stuff
like earth and water. These flowers got their soil and water
already in the past, but I missed.
But You are still my Master, so tell me,
is there no hope for me anymore?
Beloved Bhagwan, please help.

Deva Priya, it does not matter at what time you have arrived to me – in the morning, in the afternoon, in the evening, or even in the middle of the night – what matters is that you have arrived. You will have to be a little patient, because those who have come before are having flowers, fragrance, foliage.

But rather than becoming jealous of them, take courage from their experience, because the seed needs great courage. Unless the seed is ready to die in the earth there is no possibility of any sprout being born. The death of the seed is the birth of the plant. Seeing all those bushes and plants full of flowers will give you encouragement so that you need not be afraid. Your seed also contains many flowers, much future, much joy. And if I have been able to give other plants their basic needs like earth and water, I will become your earth, your water too.

But you are new and must be wondering whether this miracle that has happened to other trees is going to happen to you, or not. It all depends on you. If you are ready to die as a seed, as an ego, immediately you will start growing, blossoming. The spring always waits at the door – just you have to gather courage to disappear in the earth. And the master is nothing but an excuse for your ego to die.

You are afraid to lose your ego because you don't know, if you lose your ego, what will remain. But look around – and you are aware that people are blossoming. They were also in the same state in which you are, but they arrived in the morning and you have come in the evening.

In India we have a proverb: If a man is lost in the morning and comes back home in the evening, he should not be called "the lost". He has arrived, what does it matter whether it was morning or evening? All that is significant is arriving home.

I am going to be your earth and I am going to be your water – just as I have been the earth and water to others. Allow your seed to disappear. The moment the disciple disappears in the master, spring has come. Then thousands of flowers will be yours. Right now, also they are with you, but only as a potential. They need actualization; and for actualization the seed has to die.

It is one of the mysteries of life, that the seed protects your potential until it finds the right soil. But the seed is blind. It is a protective layer, but the protective layer can become an imprisonment if you start clinging with it. Say goodbye to it. Be grateful to it that it protected you till you reached the place where you could discard it. And you can come out of it with all your glory, with all your beauty.

Every man is born with the potential of the divine in him; no man is there without the potential.

There is a beautiful story about Gautam Buddha's past life, when he was not yet awakened, when he was himself a seed. But another man, his name was Deepankar, had become a buddha. His name is beautiful – *Deepankar* means full of light. And thousands of people were coming to Deepankar to listen to his words, to sit at his feet, to have his blessings, to find a discipline from him and an encouragement.

The man who was going to become Gautam Buddha in the next life also went to see him. He was so beautiful, so silent, so serene, so blissful, that the man who was going to become Gautam Buddha in the next life, although he had come with all kinds of skepticism and doubts, forgot all his skepticism, forgot all his doubts, and fell to the feet of Deepankar Buddha. His very presence was enough to dispel the darkness of his skepticism. But he was very much puzzled – as he stood up, Deepankar Buddha bowed down and touched the feet of this unknown man.

He was puzzled, and he said, "My touching your feet is perfectly right. I am wandering in darkness; you have arrived and you are full of light. I had come with many doubts, but just seeing you, looking into your eyes, they all have disappeared. I have never felt such silence, such serenity. It is perfectly right for me to touch your feet in gratitude. But what have you done? Why have you touched *my* feet? – an ignorant man, unconscious of his own self?"

Deepankar laughed and he said, "Don't be

worried. It is only a question of morning and evening."

The man said, "What do you mean by morning and evening?"

Deepankar said, "I arrived a little earlier, but I can see you...you may not be aware, but I can see that by the evening you will also have arrived. In the next life you will become awakened, enlightened. It does not matter – the seed has become actual in me, in you it is a potential, but the value is the same. And more emphatically I have touched your feet, so that you can remember when you become a Gautam Buddha, that anybody who comes to you is also a Gautam Buddha of some future life.

"I have touched your feet so that you never forget the reverence for every human being, however lost. He may be a murderer, he may be a criminal – it does not matter. It is only a question of time. But everybody's spring is going to come. One day all beings have to become awakened. They can delay it, they can postpone it, but they cannot cancel it."

Buddha used to tell that story again and again to newcomers: "Don't be worried. I myself was worried, and when Deepankar said this to me it gave me such an upsurge of energy, such a confidence, that if Deepankar says that next life I am going to become a buddha, I have already become a buddha. It is only a question of time – and time does not matter; the whole eternity is available."

Beloved Bhagwan,

My life seems to hang from a single thread,
and that thread is You. Day by day the feeling grows,
and now I find myself caring about only one thing:
being as close to You as possible for as long a time as possible.
While the totality of the feeling frightens me a little,
overwhelms me, I would not wish it any other way.
Although I feel like I am dying, I am so glad.
Beloved Bhagwan, am I imagining things again?

Deva Surabhi, it is not your imagination, for the simple fact that you are saying, "Although I feel like I am dying, I am so glad." It is a basic truth of spiritual life that before you really know what life is you have to die to the old, which you had been taught is your life. It was phony, false. It was more or less acting in a drama, and sometimes the drama can become too much.

It happened that after the murder of Abraham Lincoln...one hundred years had passed, and the whole year was celebrated in his sacred memory. A drama was prepared, which moved all over America all through the year, playing the same drama based on the life of Abraham Lincoln. And it was a rare coincidence that they could find a man who looked like Abraham – he was lean and thin and tall and ugly. Abraham Lincoln was not a very beautiful person, as far as his face is concerned. As far as his being is concerned, he was one of the most beautiful persons.

When he was fighting in the election for the presidentship, a little girl suggested to him, "If you grew a small beard, that would make your face look more beautiful," because he had marks on his face from small pox. First he laughed, but he thanked the girl and he thought it over. And he grew the beard, and with the beard his face took a totally new shape.

This man had the beard, had the same kind of eyes, the same nose, the same height; so he was given the part of Abraham Lincoln. Abraham Lincoln used to stutter a little once in a while, so he was taught to stutter. He was also a little lame – one leg was a little longer than the other – so they tried to make one of this man's legs a little longer by traction, pulling it – just a little longer so he started walking like a lame man.

They trained him to speak the way Abraham Lincoln used to speak – one hundred year-old language, words which were in fashion in those days. And he proved to be a perfect actor. Anybody could have misunderstood, seeing him, that he was Abraham Lincoln.

And for one year he was moving around the whole continent playing the same drama, three times a day – in the morning, in the evening, in the night. The poor man got so much obsessed with it that when he came home he still walked the way Abraham Lincoln used to walk; he still talked in one hundred year- old language, and he still stuttered.

His wife, his children, his father and mother all laughed. They said, "You have done enough – one year – now, drop it. And let your other leg also be lengthened so that you stop this business of walking like a lame man. And there is no need to stutter."

But he said, "I am Abraham Lincoln."

First they thought he was joking, but soon they realized it was not a joke. He had started believing that he was Abraham Lincoln. They tried in every possible way...but once he had seen the glory of being the President of America and one of the greatest men of history, he was not ready to descend down back to being an ordinary human being.

He was brought to the psychoanalyst, but to no effect; he would behave just like Abraham Lincoln. And he would ask the psychoanalyst, "What is missing in me that you are so worried? What is the problem? Why am I not accepted as Abraham Lincoln? You show me any fault...." And it was true, there was no fault.

Finally the psychoanalyst said , "This is beyond...this is not a case of mental derangement. He has become obsessed, and he will understand only when he has been assassinated. But then there will be no point. And if you assassinate him, perhaps he may think that he was right – even dying, he will die exactly like Abraham Lincoln. He has died many times on the stage, although the assassination was false. But he knew how to fall, what to say, what Abraham Lincoln's last words were. Even if he is assassinated, he will do his act to the very last."

You will think that this is a rare story, but the fact is, you are all living a personality which has been imposed on you.

My father used to introduce me to guests: "He is very obedient," and I would immediately tell the guest, "He is saying something absolutely wrong. I am not obedient."

And he would tell me, "That at least in front of the guests, you could have remained silent."

I said, "I cannot, because this is the way people are falsified. If I go on accepting that 'I am obedient, I am obedient, I am obedient…' I may start being obedient, which is not true. You should introduce me saying 'This boy is very disobedient.' Then I will remain silent, because you are saying something true."

He said, "But it looks very awkward to introduce your own son to somebody saying, 'He is very disobedient,' as if disobedience is a quality."

I said, "It *is* a quality. Obedience is just a kind of death. The person has no individuality of his own; he has become only an actor. And I don't want to become an actor."

There was a fair just a few miles away from my village. I went to the fair. My father was worried, and he came in search of me. He knew that I must have gone to the fair. He was worried because in that fair there were prostitutes, magicians, gamblers and all kinds of things used to happen. And the fair continued for one month.

So he got hold of me on the third day, and he asked me, "Why did not you tell me that you want to go to the fair?"

I said, "Because I wanted to go."

For a moment, he was silent, and he said, "If you wanted to go…that's what I am saying, that you should have told me."

I said, "I could not afford to tell you, because then going to the fair would have been impossible. I really wanted to go. So you make it a note in your mind that when I don't ask for something, that means I *really* want to do it. And when I ask about something, I do not care whether you say no or yes – it does not matter.

"So any nonessential thing I will ask, but any essential thing I am not going to ask – because, why commit a double crime? First, I am going whether you say yes or no, and then there is a second crime, that I am disobeying you. At least I came to the fair without disobeying anybody, just obeying myself."

Without your being aware, your parents, your teachers, your neighbors, your friends…all are putting things around you, creating an image of you. And because the image brings respect, honor, you start holding it. But you don't know it is the death of your real being. You become an actor; life becomes a drama where you smile when your heart is not with your lips, where you cry, but those tears are crocodile tears.

I used to live with one of my father's sisters. Her husband's sister died – she had come for treatment, and she had also been living in the same house. She had been old, crippled, and it was a burden on the family, so nobody was really sad about her death – in fact everybody said privately, "It is good. For the family it is good, and for her also because she was suffering too much." But you cannot say these things publicly.

I used to sit outside on the lawn, and my father's sister told me, "Whenever somebody comes – neighbors come, relatives come…." For at least a few days this whole drama continued. So she had told me, "Whenever you see that some relative is coming…" just to give consolation about her…. And nobody needed the consolation; in fact, the death of the woman had consoled everybody.

But my father's sister had to cry and weep, so I had to push the button: "Get ready." Because it is not easy when you don't want to cry, but in India it is easy. She used to pull her ghunghat down so you could not see her face, and she used to keep water…. The moment I would push the button, she would immediately put a few drops of water on her face, pull down her ghunghat – cover her face in the sari – and would start talking about how untimely it was that the old woman had died.

I was amazed at the whole thing.

One day a very close relative came and I did not give the signal. I told the man, "You go in." And she was not prepared. She was very angry at me saying, "I could not manage...I could just pull my ghunghat down, but I could not show the tears. What will the man think?"

I said, "What happened...I think something must have gone wrong with the electricity. It is not my fault, I had pushed the button."

She said, "Then you should take care that nothing goes wrong, because I was in such an awkward position. I was sitting with a friend, laughing and enjoying, when the man entered. Suddenly I had to change from laughing to crying, and I could not manage the tears. Then to put the water on in front of him would have been too much."

You are living acts, but you are not allowing your reality to function.

Surabhi, your personality has to die, has to be discarded, so that your individuality, in its authenticity, starts functioning. To be an individual is a beautiful experience, and to be just carrying a bogus personality around yourself is nothing but misery.

Because of the personality, your individuality cannot grow. Slowly, slowly, you become so identified with the personality that you forget the individuality – you become Abraham Lincoln. But however accurately you become Abraham Lincoln, it is not going to give you joy, contentment, blissfulness, because you are false, and these things don't happen to anybody who is false. Be sincere and be truthful, and your joy will know no bounds.

You are saying, "Although I feel like I am dying, I am so glad." This statement is possible only if you are really going through the process; otherwise you would not have been able to put this contradiction together.

It is not your imagination. Allow that which is dying; help it to die – the sooner it dies the better. Then whatever remains will be your innocence – the individuality that you had brought into the world, but which the world corrupted. It corrupts, and it succeeds in corrupting everyone because small children cannot do anything.

Listening to the birds, I remember.... Just outside my classroom in the high school there were beautiful mango trees. And mango trees are where cuckoos make their nests. This is the cuckoo that is calling, and there is nothing sweeter than the sound of a cuckoo.

So I used to sit by the window, looking out at the birds, at the trees, and my teachers were very much annoyed. They said, "You have to look at the blackboard."

I said, "It is my life, and I have every right to choose where to look. Outside is so beautiful – the birds singing, and the flowers, and the trees, and the sun coming through the trees – that I don't think your blackboard can be a competitor."

He was so angry that he told me, "Then you can go out and stand there outside the window unless you are ready to look at the blackboard – because I am teaching you mathematics, and you are looking at the trees and the birds."

I said, "This is a great reward you are giving me, not a punishment." And I said goodbye to him.

He said, "What do you mean?"

I said, "I will never come in, I will be standing every day outside the window."

He said, "You must be crazy. I will report to your father, to your family: 'You are wasting money on him, and he's standing outside.'"

I said, "You can do anything you want to do. I know how to manage things with my father. And he knows perfectly well that if I have decided then I will remain outside the window – nothing can change it."

The principal used to see me standing outside the window every day when he came for a round. He was puzzled at what I was doing there every day. On the third or fourth day he came to me, and he said, "What are you doing? Why do you go on standing here?"

I said, "I have been rewarded."

He said, "Rewarded? For what?"

I said, "You just stand by my side and listen to the songs of the birds. And the beauty of the trees.... Do you think looking at the blackboard and that stupid teacher...because only stupid people become teachers; they cannot find any other employment. Mostly they are third class graduates. So neither do I want to look at that teacher, nor do I want to look at the blackboard. As far as mathematics is concerned, you need not be worried – I will manage it. But I cannot miss this beauty."

He stood by my side, and he said, "Certainly it is beautiful. I have been a principal for twenty years in this school, and I never came here. And I agree with you that this is a reward. As far as mathematics is concerned, I am an M.Sc. in mathematics. You can come to my house anytime, and I will teach you mathematics – but you continue to stand outside."

So I got a better teacher, the principal of the school, who was a better mathematician. And my mathematics teacher was very much puzzled. He thought that I would get tired after a few days, but the whole month passed. Then he came out, and he said, "I am sorry, because it hurts me continuously the whole time I am in the class that I have forced you to stand out here. And you have not done any harm. You can sit inside and look wherever you want."

I said, "Now it is too late."

He said, "What do you mean?"

I said, "I mean that now I enjoy being outside. Sitting behind the window only a very small portion of the trees and the birds is available; here all the thousands of mango trees are available. And as far as mathematics is concerned, the principal is teaching me himself; every evening I go to him."

He said, "What?"

I said, "Yes, because he agreed with me that this is a reward."

He went directly to the principal and said, "This is not good. I had punished him and you are encouraging him." The principal said, "Forget punishment and encouragement – you should also stand outside sometime. Now I cannot wait; otherwise I used to go for the round as a routine, but now I cannot wait. The first thing I have to do is to go for the round and stay with that boy and look at the trees.

"For the first time, I have learned that there are better things than mathematics – the sounds of the birds, the flowers, the green trees, the sun rays coming through the trees, the wind blowing, singing its song through the trees. Once in a while you should also go and accompany him."

He came back very sorry and said, "The principal told me what has happened, so what should I do?" He asked me, "Should I take the whole class out?"

I said, "That would be great. We can sit under these trees, and you can teach your mathematics. But I am not going to come in the class, even if you make me fail – which you cannot do, because I now know more mathematics than any student in the class. And I have a better teacher. You are a third class B.Sc., and he is a first class gold medalist M.Sc."

For a few days he thought about it, and one morning when I went there I saw that the whole class was sitting under the trees. I said, "Your heart is still alive; mathematics has not killed it."

But every child has to follow so many things, so many people, that by the time he has grown up, become adult, it is too late – the personality has taken over, and the individuality is forgotten.

Surabhi, let the individuality die. It is not individuality that you have been thinking of, up to now, as your individuality – let it die. It is simply personality; and when it has died, without leaving any trace behind, you will find yourself. For the first time you will meet yourself, and that meeting becomes the beginning of spiritual growth.

It is not your imagination. The personality may be telling you, "It is all imagination." I don't believe in imagination. I destroy all kinds of imaginations so that you can know your consciousness without any dreams, without any projections, without any imaginations – just pure awareness. And that pure awareness is the door to the divine.

Okay, Vimal?

Yes, Bhagwan.

Session 9

Love Is Never Too Much

*My vision of a real humanity is of pure individuals:
relating to each other but not tied in any relationship;
loving to each other but not being possessive of each other;
sharing with each other all their joys and all their blessings,
but never even in their dreams thinking of dominating,
thinking of enslaving the other person.*

March 1, 1987
Evening

Beloved Bhagwan,

How is it possible that You love us so much?
Is it possible that You mean me, too?
When I allow myself to feel Your love, to let myself be loved by You,
there is so much pain and so much gratitude that I cannot say it.
Thank You, Bhagwan.
Suddenly I see that there has been this fear my whole life
not to be part of it, not to belong, not to be in Your family.
Is it possible that I am already in it?

Sambodhi Amrita, I do not love you, I am simply love. One loves when one is not love himself. Then love is only a passing moment; it comes and goes.

The day you realize yourself, your very being becomes love. It is no longer a relationship, it is no longer addressed to anyone in particular; it is simply overflowing in all directions and all dimensions. And it is not something on my part, that I am *doing* it. Love cannot be done. And the love that is done is false; it is only pretension.

You are asking me, "How is it possible that You love us so much?" I am simply helpless, I cannot do otherwise. It is just my heartbeat. My love is my life; nobody is excluded from it. It is so comprehensive that it can contain the whole universe...you too.

You are saying, "When I allow myself to feel your love, to let myself be loved by you, there is so much pain and so much gratitude that I cannot say it."

Perhaps you are not aware of many aspects of love. One is that when too much love descends upon you, its very intensity appears like pain. You must have heard, once in a while it happens that just out of sheer joy somebody dies of heart failure. The joy was too much and his heart was too small.

I will tell you a story: A very poor man had made it a habit to purchase, every month, one ticket for the lottery. He had been doing that for almost twenty years.

In the beginning the family, the friends, used to ask him, "Why are you wasting your money? You earned just one rupee with so much hard labor, changing your blood into perspiration. You go on wasting every month one rupee, and you have not won any lottery." But slowly, slowly they dropped advising him; it had become almost a routine habit. In the beginning he used to think that some day the lottery would come up in his name, but by and by he even forgot that too. Just like a robot, the first day of the month would come and he would purchase a ticket.

And one day it happened, the lottery came up in his name for twenty-five lakh rupees. He was not at home. The wife became very much afraid when she received the message that the lottery had come up in her husband's name. She was a Christian – she ran to the church. She was afraid: "This is too much. He has not seen even twenty-five rupees together...twenty-five lakhs! He is sure to die just out of too much happiness. So I should pray to God, and also I should ask the priest some way to save his life. Poverty has not been able to kill him, but this richness will kill him immediately."

The priest said, "Don't be worried. I am coming with you and I will tell your husband when he comes home, very slowly, slowly, 'You have won one lakh rupees.' When I see that he has absorbed that, I will tell him, 'In fact, you have won two lakh rupees.' And when I see he has absorbed that and is still alive, then I will say, 'You have really won three lakh rupees.' Slowly, slowly I will reveal the whole truth about the twenty-five lakh rupees."

The wife said, "If you can save his life, I will give one lakh rupees to the church." And the priest said, "One lakh rupees?" And he dropped flat on the earth, dead! He had never hoped that anybody was going to give him one lakh rupees.

Anything for which you are not prepared – it may be bliss, it may be joy – will be so intense in the beginning that it is bound to appear just like pain. You are well-acquainted with pain, you know it; that is the closest experience.

When love comes to you without asking, and when love comes from a source which you have never expected, never thought of, never hoped for, you never had the idea that you deserve it or you are worthy of it.... When it is a relationship, it is a very superficial phenomenon. But when you come across somebody who *is* love, the whole ocean has poured into your heart. It feels as if you are bursting, dying. It is immensely painful. But at the same time you can feel the distinction. It is very close to pain, but it is not pain.

Your being understands things which your mind does not understand. Experiences come that your mind will say are painful, but your being will not accept this, because it is not pain, it is too much blissfulness. The problem is that you are not accustomed to so much love, so much joy; hence on the one hand you feel pain, that is the interpretation of your mind, and on the other hand you feel gratitude – that is the interpretation of your being.

Whenever there is any conflict between your mind and your being, trust the being, because the being is vast and can understand experiences which the mind is incapable of. The mind is a small entity; your being is as vast as the whole universe. If you go on listening to your being and not paying attention to the mind, slowly, slowly you will see, pain has disappeared. The pain is the intensity of joy; it is too much joy, and you have to make space for it.

Hence my insistence that if you continue to meditate – and meditation and love happen together to you – there will be no pain at all. Meditation makes your consciousness wider, expands it, makes it as big as the sky. It can contain infinite love, infinite joy.

Your meditation is not, Amrita, yet so vast. But I am helpless. I cannot give you love in installments according to your capacity; I can give you only my undivided wholeness. You have to be prepared. Your pain shows your unpreparedness, but your gratitude shows that you are capable of being prepared. Just a little meditation, just a little more silence, just a little more serenity and you will be able to dance with joy. The more intense the joy is, the greater will be the dance.

You have also raised a very significant question: "Suddenly I see that there has been this fear my whole life not to be part of it, not to belong, not to be in your family. Is it possible that I am already in it?"

The first thing is, I don't have a family. I have people whom I love, who love me, but there is no binding of any family ties. Nobody belongs to me, neither do I belong to anybody. Everybody here has his own individuality, totally pure, without any kind of imprisonment in the name of love, in the name of religion, in the name of nation, in the name of race – beautiful names but only hiding ugly prisons.

It is good that you have been afraid all your life, "not to be part of it, not to belong, not to be in your family." I don't have any family. And you should remember not to belong to any family at all.

My vision of a real humanity is of pure individuals: relating to each other but not tied in any relationship; loving to each other but not being possessive of each other; sharing with each other all their joys and all their blessings, but never even in their dreams thinking of dominating, thinking of enslaving the other person…a world consisting not of families, not of nations, not of races, but only of individuals.

Only a world where families have disappeared and nations have died and races are no longer existent can have beauty, and can have immense possibilities for human growth. Otherwise all your relationships are destructive, because they are all possessive – your love is followed by your jealousy, your love is full of suspicion, mistrust. Everybody is trying to keep the other remaining within his control. It is a very strange situation where everybody is a prisoner and everybody is a jailer too. You are the jailer, you are the jail, you are the jailed, and you are trying to manage all three functions simultaneously. Certainly your life has become a mess!

Amrita, at least here you need not be afraid. It is not Italy, and it is not a Mafia. Mafia simply means "the family." Here, everybody is an individual – loved, respected, accepted as he is. Nobody is expecting him to be somebody else; no ideals are provided for you to imitate, no discipline is given to you so that you become a robot, a mechanical personality, repeating actions, words and never meaning really….

You say to people, "I love you," but you have never thought exactly…do you really mean it? Your words have become so phony, your actions have become so false, your faces have become masks. You have completely lost your originality.

My effort here is to help you to discover your original face. And that is the greatest thing that can happen to any human being, to know his original face, because that is the face of God.

Beloved Bhagwan,

There is a word that has often touched me deeply.
By just remembering it from time to time
it feels as if it can heal wounds,
and it brings stillness and contentment.
This word is suchness.
Would You like to talk about suchness?

Sadhan, it is certainly one of the most significant words in the whole language. It started with Gautam Buddha. The language that Gautam Buddha used was Pali. It has died; now it is no longer a living language. But a few words were so important that they have remained alive in other languages.

The Pali word for *suchness*...because *suchness* is only a translation of that word; in English there has been nobody who has used that word or experienced the taste of that word. The Pali word is *tathata*. And because of the word *tathata*, one of the names of Gautam Buddha is *tathagata*. He was the first to use that word and give it so much meaning and depth.

The English word *suchness* perfectly translates the Pali word *tathata*. If you understand its meaning, just the very understanding of the word is certainly going to bring great healing to you, great silence, great peace. But try to understand from Gautam Buddha, because he is the original source of that certain meaning.

If somebody came to Gautam Buddha and said, "I am blind".... if the same man had gone to Jesus Christ, perhaps he would have done a miracle and given the blind man his eyes. But I say unto you that Gautam Buddha did greater miracles. They are so great that most often you have completely missed their meaning. If somebody came and told him, "I am blind, in both my eyes"...Buddha would say, "I am not blind, but I have seen the whole world, and the real joy and the peace that I have found has been found with my eyes closed. Accept your blindness as a blessing.

"I have to close my eyes, your eyes are already closed. And even if people who have eyes close their eyes, images which they have seen with open eyes go on disturbing them. You are fortunate, your blindness is a blessing in disguise. Accept it as a gift of existence. This is the way existence wants you to be. This is the meaning of tathata – that it is perfectly alright that you are blind; nothing is missing, just you have to learn how to use your blindness for your spiritual growth.

"People who have eyes have to learn how to use their eyes; you have to learn how to use your blindness. And I say to you that you are in a better position. Relax, and feel grateful to existence that it has not given you all the distractions which are possible when you have eyes. You are already without any distractions, without any images. Your insight is already calm and quiet."

Because this was Buddha's attitude about everything, tathata became his very foundation of religion. When Buddha's teachings were translated into English, they were not able to find right words for many things. But it is a great coincidence that suchness has the same flavor as tathata.

You are blind – such is the case. Accept it in its total suchness. Don't try to be miserable about it, because millions of people have eyes, but what have they done with their eyes?

I would like to tell you one story about Jesus which was not compiled by the Christians, because it is a very strange story. When they were compiling the New Testament, three hundred years after Jesus' crucifixion, they left out many things for the simple reason that it was so difficult first to explain them, and second to avoid contradictions. This is one of the stories that has been left out, but it has been preserved by the Sufis.

The story is…Jesus enters into a town and he sees a young man going after a prostitute. His eyes are full of lust, his whole presence stinks of passion. Jesus prevents the young man and says, "Are you aware of what you are doing?"

The young man suddenly becomes angry and he says, "I was blind. It was you who cured my eyes; otherwise I was not aware that there are prostitutes. You are responsible for it. By giving me eyes you have given me so many troubles. When I was blind, everybody was sympathetic to me. When I was blind I had no responsibilities. People were very loving and very kind – they were providing food, clothes, shelter. By giving me eyes you have taken away all their kindness, all their sympathy, all their love. Now I have to work the whole day to earn my food. And what do you suppose, when I see a beautiful woman and my passion arises? – what should I do?"

Jesus had never thought about it, that a blind man would be so angry because his eyes are cured. Jesus was very sad. Leaving the young man because he had no answer for him, he entered the town and he saw another man who was completely drunk and had fallen in the gutter. Jesus shook the man and asked him, "Is life given to you to waste in such ugly ways?"

The man opened his eyes and he said, "Right – you are the man who made me alive; I had died. And now there are so many problems and so many anxieties that without drinking I cannot even sleep. Why did you make me alive again? I had died! And who gave you the authority? I had not asked you."

Jesus was really shocked. He was thinking he was doing a service to people, and things have turned out to be just the opposite. He did not go into the town; he felt so miserable. He went out of the town to meditate and to pray to God, "Give me clarity – what should I do?" As he was going out of the town he saw one man was trying to commit suicide by hanging himself from a tree. Somehow he prevented him.

The man said, "You have come again. Why are you continually after me? Once before I committed suicide – you are a strange fellow. I am tired of life, I don't want to live, but you saved me. It would be better if you save others. I don't want any savior, just let me die. And remember that I don't want to be revived back to life. You did it once, but now I am preventing you myself."

The whole story has been dropped out of the New Testament because the whole story would have been a great trouble to Christian theologians. Their whole religion depends on the miracles of Jesus; they go on praising the miracles of Jesus, and this story seems to be just contradicting all the miracles.

Gautam Buddha's approach was whatever happens, allow it to happen, and accept it with your total heart. This is how existence wants it to be. Remain in this attitude of suchness…such is the desire of the whole, and I am part of the whole; I cannot go against the desire of the whole.

Certainly if you understand it, it will give you tremendous insight and be a great help in your meditations. It will help you not to resist existence, not to fight against the current, but just to go with the current. Allow the river to take you to the ocean.

Sadhan, you are right when you say, "There is a word that has often touched me deeply. By just remembering it from time to time it feels as if it can heal wounds, and it brings stillness and contentment. This word is *suchness.*" Just try it in moments of turmoil, in moments of pain, in moments of misery. In the darkest nights of your life, just try, "Such is the will of existence, and I am part of it. I will relax with it. If this is the will of the whole, so it will be."

Sufis have preserved the story because Sufis have a similar attitude to Gautam Buddha. If you listen to a Sufi mystic you will be surprised about one thing. In each sentence he uses certain words, and they are, "God willing." If you ask him, "Can I come to see you tomorrow?" – just a simple thing – he will say, "You can come, God willing. It is not in my hands. What is going to happen tomorrow I cannot predict. As far as I am concerned, I am ready, you can come. But remember, neither I can decide for tomorrow, nor you can decide for tomorrow. We can only hope."

They use the words *God willing* so much that when I used to see Sufi mystics I told them, "This is too much. Each sentence either begins with 'God willing' or ends with 'God willing' or in the middle of it, 'God willing.' Don't you get tired of it?"

The man said, "God willing, sometimes I get tired, sometimes I don't get tired, but it all depends on God. Nothing is in my hands."

Gautam Buddha has no God; his approach is more sophisticated. If somebody insults him and his disciples become angry, he says to them, "You don't understand, such is the case. That man could not do anything else. If you had been brought up in the same conditions, in the same situations, you would have insulted me also. And I can see so clearly that he does not have any bad intentions. All that he could do, he has done. And all that I can do, I am doing. He can insult me; this is his suchness. I can still feel love and compassion for him; this is my suchness."

The suggestion of Sadhan is so great, it can be helpful to you all.

Just remember – not as a word but as a feeling – suchness. Then there is no grudge, no complaint, no desire that things should be different than they are. A tremendous acceptance arises. This acceptance is real and authentic religiousness.

Beloved Bhagwan,

Cleaning the house, preparing the tea, being in joyful anticipation –
then You are right in front of me, showering Your love on us,
and from time to time I see myself closing the doors and the windows
as fast as possible and escaping from the back door.
Beloved Bhagwan, this old fear of receiving love and staying open,
this old voice saying, "this is too much for me"
seems so ridiculous and out-of-date. How to drop them?

Veet Kamaal, the first thing to be remembered is that the fear of love is not, and can never be, out-of-date. It is as new as love. You don't say love is out-of-date, although millions of people have loved. Still, when love happens to your heart it is fresh, absolutely new, as if you were the first lover in the world. The fear that follows love is love's shadow.

You want love, but you don't accept the shadow of it. If your insight grows deeper, you will accept the shadow too; it is part of love. The fear is as natural as love. The fear is, who knows? – love is so beautiful in this moment, so nourishing, so fragrant, what about the next moment? The next moment is just coming in, and one cannot be in control of experiences like love. It is a breeze that comes, and you can enjoy it and you can dance with it, but you cannot hold it in your fist.

Hence, the fear that as soon as it has come it may go. But if you meditate on the whole problem...if it has come – the breeze, the love, the joy – existence is not exhausted; it will be coming again and again. And the more mature you become, the more is the possibility of love coming to you. And your maturity will soon be that you don't close the windows and doors to keep love imprisoned – that is childish.

If you close all the doors and all the windows, even the freshest breeze will die, even the strongest and youngest bird will start hitting its head against the walls, running here and thither, trying to find a way out, because nobody in existence wants to be imprisoned. Even if you make a prison of gold, then too, nobody wants to be imprisoned. And the fear is that the love will come and will go – you cannot control it.

There are only two ways. One is that of the immature person, who will close his windows before love enters in so that he is safe from the misery, from the pain, from the fear that love may leave him. He has closed the doors and windows; he is safe, but this safety is very costly. And because he wants to be safe and he is afraid, love may be strong enough...it may be a storm and may open the windows and doors. Not to take the risk, you say you close the doors and windows and you escape from the back door. This is the way of the immature person.

The mature person will make as many doors and as many windows in the house as possible, or perhaps he will live in the open where breezes are continuously coming and flowing. And each time the breeze goes, he knows deep in his heart that this is only a moment of rest; a fresher breeze with more fragrance will be coming. And as it goes on happening again and again, one becomes more and more mature, and the fear fades away. It becomes just what it is – a negative shadow; it has no existence.

You are asking, "Cleaning the house, preparing the tea, being in joyful anticipation – then you are right in front of me, showering your love on us, and from time to time I see myself closing the doors and the windows as fast as possible and escaping from the back door. Beloved Bhagwan, this old fear of receiving love and staying open, this old voice saying, 'This is too much for me,' seems so ridiculous and out-of-date. How to drop them?"

There is no need to drop them, they will disappear on their own accord. You have just to grow more in maturity and understanding – your conceptions are not right. No love is too much for anyone. And if it feels too much, that means you are not trying to expand your consciousness. And what is meditation for? Love is a test – if it feels too much, that means your consciousness is too small.

Rather than being worried about love, you should be more concerned about expanding your consciousness...a few more acres are needed. And whenever you feel it is too much, always remember, you need more space. Love is never too much, it is always that the space is too small. Your insistence should be on the space, because that is in your hands, to make it bigger or not.

Love is not in your hands.

Love is something that comes from beyond.

But you can make a bigger space to allow that love. Drop this idea, "This is too much." Love is never too much.

Secondly, you are thinking about love intellectually. That's why you say it seems so ridiculous and out-of-date. If you look through intellect the fear appears to be ridiculous, because love is not going to harm you, why are you afraid? But love is going to destroy something in you which you have been strengthening your whole life – your ego. That is the fear. It is not ridiculous, it is significant. Create more space, and say goodbye to your ego. And then there will not be this idea that this fear is ridiculous, that it is out-of-date.

These are intellectual condemnations, but they don't help; they simply make you feel that you are very intelligent. Love does not need your intelligence, love needs your heartfulness.

And these conceptions of ridiculousness, being out-of-date, these are not of the heart. Heart knows nothing about ridiculousness, about being out-of-date; these are your mind games. And love is a phenomenon which has nothing to do with the mind.

And, Kamaal, as far as I am concerned, your strategies won't work, because I may start entering from the back door. You may be caught red-handed escaping from the back door. So keep all your doors and windows open, otherwise I will have to tell Neelam. Then what? "Whenever Kamaal tries to close the doors and windows, you start opening them."

Women listen to me very obediently. And I can trust Neelam; moreover, she is my secretary. If I say, "Open all the doors and windows!" she is not going to listen to you, Kamaal.

Beloved Bhagwan,

I went inside to wait for the guest, and the host was there.
In a wild panic I closed the door and ran away.
When I realized what had happened, I crept back:
Host was gone, guest was gone, only a beautiful fragrance remained.
But why such a panic?

Krishna Priya, it is a beautiful question and very relevant to almost everybody. She is saying, "I went inside to wait for the guest, and the host was there. In a wild panic, I closed the door and ran away." You think, you have been told to think, that God will come as a guest. It is a poetic metaphor. But in fact, God is already sitting in you as a host – who do you think you are?

So the question is beautiful; she says, "I went inside to wait for the guest to come" – because God has always been conceived as someone outside, who is going to come. The fact is, he is already inside you, he is *you*, he is the host.

"In a wild panic I closed the door and ran away." Naturally, if you are thinking that the guest will come, you are thinking yourself to be the host. And if you go inside your house and you find the host is sitting there, naturally, there will be panic. Then who are you? The host is sitting there, the guest is going to come, and who are you?

Out of panic, out of fear, she says she escaped. "When I realized what happened, I crept back: Host was gone, guest was gone too. Only a beautiful fragrance remained."

In language, in words, we have to speak in dualities – the guest, the host, the soul, the God, the individual, the universal – but in reality, there is no duality, there is only oneness. Neither the host is there, nor the guest is there. And when both disappear, what remains is just a fragrance, just an eternal fragrance, a silence full of fragrance. This is what the seers of all the ages have called *samadhi*. All duality is gone. Because of the duality you were not able to see the beauty of oneness, of an organic unity; you were not able to see the light, the clarity, the immortal life force.

Priya is asking, "But why such a panic?" The panic is of the mind, the panic is of the ego because now the ego cannot remain. The ego follows the politician's rule – divide and rule. If you remain in a split, the ego goes on becoming more and more powerful. The more you are fragmented, cut into pieces, the more the ego is happy, and the more your mind is powerful – because it has become the master and it has reduced the master into a slave. But when the guest and the host disappear, all dualities fall down; there is no function left for the ego, and no function left for the mind.

The panic is of the mind. Just wait a little. As the mind will be gone, the panic will also be gone. The panic of the dying ego...just let the ego die, and the panic will disapppear. And where you were full of panic you will be full of blissfulness, full of benediction.

Okay, Vimal?

Yes, Bhagwan.

Session 10

With Trust, It Is Always Spring

*You cannot do anything about it,
you simply go on remembering and watching.
Trust is enough.
If love also joins it, it will become more juicy,
have more flowers, more perfume;
otherwise trust, in itself, is enough.*

March 2, 1987
Morning

Beloved Bhagwan,

Was Rabindrinath's longing, his creative angst, the very thing
that in the end became an obstacle to his enlightenment?
Am I also destined to die with tears in my eyes,
and a pocket full of songs?

Milarepa, a poet is not in search of truth. His search is for beauty, and through the search for beauty nobody has ever become enlightened. One can become a great poet, a great painter, a great singer, a great dancer; but on the path of beauty, enlightenment is not possible.

The seeker of truth, and only the seeker of truth, attains to enlightenment. And this is the miracle of enlightenment, that once you have discovered truth, then beauty, the good, and all that is valuable simply become available to you.

Beauty cannot lead to enlightenment, but enlightenment opens your eyes to all dimensions and all directions.

Rabindranath was very close to enlightenment, but his search was not for enlightenment – he was searching for the beautiful. And the search for the beautiful, deep down, is the search for expressing beauty – in words, in music, in dance, in any kind of creativity.

The seeker of beauty is really seeking a vision which he can reproduce in his poetry, in his song, in his painting. Always the search is inner, but the goal is somewhere outside. And that's the problem for all great creative people: they come to know, but then expression becomes difficult; they come to experience beauty, but how to share it? You may see a roseflower and be suddenly overwhelmed by its beauty, but how to share it? How to express it?

The concern of the artist is expression; the concern of the seeker is experience. Neither of them is able to express, but because the seeker of truth is totally concerned with experiencing, he comes to enlightenment, and he can die with a smile on his face, with fulfillment, whether he has been able to say something about it or not – that is not his concern, that is not his angst, his anxiety.

The artist also comes to know what he is seeking, but his problem is that basically, his interest in seeking beauty is for expression – and expression is almost impossible. At the most you can stutter a little bit – all your songs are stutterings of great poets. They look beautiful to you, immensely meaningful and significant, but to the poet...he knows he has failed.

All artists, either in the East or in the West, have felt an immense failure. They have tried their best, and they have produced great pieces of art – for us they are great pieces of art, but for them they are faraway echos of their experience. Hence, they die either mad....

Almost seventy percent of painters, dancers, poets have gone mad. They have made too much effort. They have put too much tension into their being, so that it brought a breakdown, a nervous breakdown. And many of the artists have even committed suicide. The wound of failure became unbearable: to live any longer and to carry the same wound, and feeling again and again...became too difficult, and it was better to destroy oneself. And those who have not gone mad or committed suicide, they have also not died in a blissful way.

In the East, we have defined the ultimate values as three: *satyam, shivam, sundaram*. *Satyam* means truth – that is the highest. The seeker, the mystic follows that path. Then comes *shivam*: goodness, virtue. The moralist, the saint, the sage – they follow that path. And *sundaram* means beauty. The poets, the singers, the musicians – they follow that path.

Those who attain to truth automatically come to know what is good and what is beauty. Those who follow good, neither come to know what is true, nor do they come to know what is beauty. The followers of good – the moralists, the puritans – also never achieve enlightenment. All that they achieve is a repressed personality – very beautiful on the surface, but deep inside very ugly. They have great reputation, honor, respect, but inside they are hollow.

The people who follow *sundaram*, beauty, are inside fulfilled, utterly fulfilled, but their misery is that that is not their aim: just to be fulfilled. They want all that they have experienced to be brought into language, into paintings, into sculpture, into architecture. Hence, even though they have experienced beautiful spaces they remain anxiety-ridden.

The people who follow beauty are most often not very respectable – not in the same sense as the saints are. They are very natural people, very loving and very lovable, but they don't have any ego, any idea of holier-than-thou; they remain just simple and ordinary.

These three values have been for centuries followed separately. So the people who have become enlightened have never painted, have never made beautiful statues, have never composed music; they have never danced. They have never followed the dictates of the society, they have never followed the conventions of the society; hence most of them have been crucified, poisoned, killed – because people want you to be a puritan, a moralist. In people's eyes morality is a social value, truth is not. Beauty is for entertainment; they don't take it seriously.

I have been trying in many ways to open new doors – this is one of the most important doors. I want you to be a seeker of truth, but when you have attained to truth you should not be without songs and without dances. Beauty is a little lower value than truth, but the man of truth can express beauty more clearly than the poet, than the painter. For the higher, the lower is always understandable – not vice versa.

The man who has attained truth should also

take care that his life radiates godliness, goodness. It may not be in tune with the morality of the society – it cannot be, because that morality is created by blind, unconscious people, just as a convention. For the man of truth it is not convention, it is simply his life. In utter nudity, he should make his life available to existence, to people, so that the ordinary morality of convention slowly, slowly changes into a real and authentic morality of a man who knows the truth.

The man of truth should not look at poetry and music and dance as just entertainment for ordinary people. He should make it a point, because he has risen to a height from where he can see beauty in its absolute glory. He can contribute many riches to existence: each of his words can be a poem in itself, each of his silences can become celestial music, each of his gestures can indicate towards the most beautiful phenomenon, grace.

But this has not been so up to now – they have all followed their paths separately. I want *my* people to seek the truth, because by seeking it the other two will become available on their own accord.

But remember, when you have experienced truth don't forget that it is part of your compassion to give humanity new dreams of goodness, new visions of morality, ethics, which are not of the marketplace, which are not only conventions. And he should not forget that his truth is so deep inside him that the unconscious people will not be able to have a taste of it – he should create beauty in all possible dimensions.

Once in a while it has been done. For example, when the Taj Mahal was created...it was not the work of great architects, but it is the most beautiful architecture in existence. Shahjehan, the emperor who was creating it as a memorial grave for his beautiful wife, Mumtaz Mahal – hence the name Taj Mahal – searched for years for Sufi mystics, who have no concern for beauty. He asked the Sufi mystics, "Although it is something lower, and you are not interested in it – and why should one be? – just for my sake, you design the Taj Mahal. The architects will make it, but the design should come from those who have known beauty in its fullness, from a height."

George Gurdjieff used to say that there are two kinds of art. One is subjective art – ninety-nine percent of art in the world is subjective: you are simply pouring your feelings, your desires, your longings, your dreams, into whatever you are making.

But once in a while there is objective art – only one percent. What he calls objective art is art created by those who were not artists, who were realized people. They created music to help meditation – it was not for entertainment. They created poetry to convey that which cannot be conveyed by prose. They sang, they danced, to give you just a glimpse of their ecstasy, of their inner dance, of their joy, their blissfulness.

In India, there are many places which have objective art. Even Gurdjieff had to mention them, although he was in the West; he was born in the Caucasus, but when he was talking about objective art, he had to fall upon India.

Indian classical music is not just for entertainment. Listening to it, you start going deep into yourself. It is not for all, it is only for those who are ready for an inner pilgrimage.

He mentioned the Taj Mahal, too. On the full moon night, when the moon comes just in the middle of the sky, the Taj Mahal becomes the greatest object of meditation that man has created. You just sit silently and look at it, and just looking at it your thoughts will subside. The beauty of it is so enormous that your mind simply feels at a loss. It cannot grasp it, so it becomes silent.

The caves of Ajanta and Ellora, the temples of Khajuraho, Puri, and Konarak…all these he mentions as objective art – objective because they are not an effort to express feelings or ideas, they are devices, so that for centuries to come people will be able to have the same taste, the same feeling, the same joy.

The pyramids in Egypt are part of objective art. Just in the beginning of this century, when excavations were begun in the pyramids, a cat was found dead inside. The pyramid was three thousand years old – perhaps when they were closing the pyramid, the cat had remained inside and died. For three thousand years the cat had been there, dead, but its body had not deteriorated. That was a miracle: three thousand years, and the body of the cat was as if she had just died.

The scientists were puzzled. Finally it was discovered that the shape of the pyramid is the cause. That particular shape of the pyramid is tremendously capable of preserving things as they are. Even if you put a dead body inside, it will be preserved. Nothing else is needed, because the shape of the pyramid changes the direction of the rays of the sun, and in that change of direction the miracle happens.

Now there are small plastic pyramids, glass pyramids available in the market. And people who are very much health-oriented, they just sit inside that pyramid. A small pyramid, portable – you can fold it, keep it in your suitcase – and wherever you want you can fix the pyramid up like a tent, and just sit inside it for one hour. And you will feel as immense a well-being as you have ever felt.

The possibility is that if these pyramids are used widely, man's life can be prolonged. If it becomes a routine exercise for every child, in every home, in every school, in every college, life can be stretched up to three hundred years. Just one hour every day inside the pyramid, and you are not to do anything, just sit there. It is helpful in both ways: It will preserve your life, and that one hour of well-being will give you a deep feeling of meditation. The people who created the pyramids must have been mystics who had come to such a clarity, to see things which are not available to us.

I want *my* people to be seekers of truth. But never forget that you have to bring a revelation into the moral codes of humanity, too. You should not feel satisfied that you have found the truth, and you have found what is good. You should make your good as much manifest and available to humanity as possible.

The same is applicable to beauty. One feels a great loss…if Buddha had painted, or composed music, or sang songs, or once in a while danced with his disciples, the world would have been immensely enriched.

I say to you, remember in those moments when you realize the truth that a great responsibility has fallen on your shoulders: you have to change the ordinary morality into a spiritual code, and you have to change subjective art into objective art. This will be the new expression of the contemporary mystic, and it will make a new breakthrough for the future.

Milarepa, you are asking, "Am I also destined to die with tears in my eyes, and a pocket full of songs?" If you remain interested only in songs and music, you will die with tears in your eyes, and those tears will not be of joy.

Let your search be for the truth, and only on the margin go on practicing your music, composing your songs; so when you reach to your enlightenment you are articulate enough to bring beauty to expression. Then you can go laughing, fulfilled, without any tears.

Beloved Bhagwan,

Can one meditate too much?

Shanti Animisha, there are things which you can never do too much. For example, you cannot love too much; more is always possible, and there is no limitation anywhere.

I am taking the example of love because that will be easily understood. The same is true about meditation: you cannot meditate too much, because silence knows no bounds – it is an abysmal depth. You can go on and on, and you will find there is always much more to be explored.

There comes no point in meditation when you can say, "Now it is the full stop." There is no such thing as a full stop, because you are carrying the whole sky within your heart, a whole universe in your being.

Meditation is trying to find the ultimate limit. You always feel that you are coming closer to it; you are always coming closer, and closer, and closer. It is always coming closer, but you never reach it, because the limit that you seek is just like the horizon – you can go towards the horizon, thinking that it looks only a few miles away at the most, where the earth and the sky are meeting, but they do not meet anywhere. So as you go on, your horizon also goes on receding; you will never reach to the horizon. What is true about the inner consciousness is also true about the outer space.

Albert Einstein used to think, when he was young, that there must be a limit somewhere – because mind cannot see the unlimitable. It may be very far away, millions and millions of light-years away, but it must be there. But as he continuously worked on the stars and space, slowly, slowly he became aware that there is no limit at all.

And there cannot be, because a limit needs something else to make a limit out of it. For example, your house has a fence because there are other houses in the neighborhood. Your fence cannot exist if there is nothing beyond it.

Space is a nothingness in which stars are moving, millions of stars – three million stars have been counted up to now. You may or may not be aware that in the night when the sky is absolutely clear of clouds and you see the stars, you don't see more than three hundred – but even three hundred seems to be so many. And if you don't believe me, try to count. It is a very difficult task – from where to begin? And again and again you will be coming to a point: have I counted this star or not?

Scientists have figured out that with the eyes only three hundred stars at the most can be seen. And there are three million stars. That is not the limit of the stars, that is the limitation of our scientific instruments – because three years ago there were only one million. Then we improved our instruments, and there were two million, and then we improved our instruments, and there were three million.

Einstein said, "It all depends how refined the instruments we have are. Go on refining your instruments, and the stars will go on becoming more and more available to you."

And these stars are in a very strange situation, which was not known before Albert Einstein. He has given us so many new insights: that all these stars are running away...as if you are running away from your home, farther and farther. Scientists have not been able to find the center of the universe, but there must be some center, it seems, from which the stars are running away, farther and farther, with tremendous speed – at the same speed as the speed of light: one hundred eighty-six thousand miles per second.

Hence, the new idea has come of an expanding universe. It is no longer a fixed thing, it is continuously expanding – and expanding into what? An immense nothingness, pure space; and that space has no limit. And we don't know whether we will be able to know about all the stars, because it will all depend on our instruments. Every day, many stars are being found.

This expanding universe can give you a parallel: inside there is an expanding consciousness.

In meditation you start feeling the expanding consciousness – there is no limit to it.

You cannot do too much. Whatever you are doing is always too little. And it will always remain too little. These are the mysteries of existence.

The scientist becomes aware of the outer world, the mystic becomes aware of the inner world. And the inner world is far richer.

Beloved Bhagwan,

I loved the story about the sun and darkness.
As far as my watching is concerned, instead of being a sun, I feel more like I am carrying an old Indian flashlight, having to make an effort to push the button.
I hear You talking about not making an effort, not trying, but letting it happen.
The problem is, when I don't push this button there is no light,
and what is happening on its own is darkness.
Beloved Bhagwan, could You put some light on this effortless effort,
as far as watching and awareness are concerned?

Veet Kamaal, first, a few corrections to your question. You are saying, "I am carrying an old Indian flashlight with me." It is not old, even the latest Indian flashlights will do the same. You have to learn how to behave with any product that is being made in India!

You say that you have to make a great effort to push the button. You need to keep with you a steel rod, so each time you want the flashlight on, *hit* the button. It is no ordinary flashlight made in Germany, it is made in India. Pushing it will be a tremendous wastage of energy.

I have heard a story.... In an Indian factory, one day the machines suddenly stopped. The mechanics tried everything, but nothing was helpful. A man was just standing outside, watching all this. He came in and he said, "If I can start this machine, are you ready to pay my price for it?"

The owner was losing so much money, because it had been almost three days that the factory was closed. He said, "What is your fee?" The man said, "Not much, just ten thousand rupees."

The owner said, "You are asking too much." The man said, "It is up to you to choose; you will be losing thousands of rupees every hour. Then I can go."

The owner said, "No, I will give you ten thousand." The man said, " In advance."

The owner said, "You are a strange fellow. Can't you believe me?" The man said, "In India, the old proverb of the Sufis is applicable: Trust in God, but first tie your camel. Just don't let the camel move in the desert because you trust God. Trusting is very good, but tie down the camel also. I believe and I trust you, but still in advance is better."

The poor owner had to give ten thousand rupees. The man brought a big rod, went around the factory, and at a certain point he hit the machinery so hard that the owner jumped. He said, "What are you doing? Are you a mechanic? I have never seen such kind of...." But the machines started working.

The owner said, "Just for hitting, ten thousand is too much." The man said, "It is not a question of just hitting. It is a question of where to hit. That needs wisdom."

So Kamaal, first drop the idea you have, that it is an old Indian flashlight. Even the latest will behave just like the old. India follows the ancient way.

You are worried, because you say, "I hear you talking about not making an effort, not trying, but letting it happen. The problem is, when I don't push this button there is no light, and what is happening on its own is darkness. Beloved Bhagwan, could you please put some light on this effortless effort, as far as watching and awareness are concerned?"

First, you have to understand that darkness has its own beauty, its own depth, its own silence, its own song. And if, without doing anything, only darkness is happening, then remember what Sadhan had asked yesterday – that such is the case. Remember the word *suchness,* and relax.

Perhaps the darkness may become even deeper and darker – and don't rely on any flashlight. Depend on patience, and watch the darkness. It is far more cooling to the eyes, resting to the heart, relaxing to the being. And as the darkness becomes deeper, remember: before the dawn it becomes the darkest.

So, when the darkness is becoming deeper, rejoice; it means the dawn is very close by. You simply go on watching. It will become the darkest, and then slowly, slowly, the sun will start rising from the East, with psychedelic colors all over the horizon. The birds will start singing, the trees will start swaying in the wind – life has come again back to the earth. Sleep is gone, you are awake.

Just as darkness has to be watched, so watch the morning, watch the light, watch the beautiful colors. The question is not what you are watching, the question is that you are watching. Your inner growth is not concerned in watching something special; you can watch anything. You can watch just darkness, nothingness, but the watcher should remain there; it should not fall asleep.

And the dawn is sure to come – then too you have to watch. Night or day, suffering or blissfulness, life or death, you remain just the watcher.

It needs no effort; it is simply remaining alert.

And I think that, in darkness, you will be more alert than in light. You can try it: go into the forest in the middle of the night, and then try to sleep. You will not sleep. You would rather sit watching – a slight movement around somewhere in the darkness, a leaf falling from the trees, or a bird suddenly flying in the darkness, and you will jump up with all your awareness.

Darkness is a perfectly good space to be aware.... You need not carry that flashlight made in India, and make a great effort to push the button; sometimes, even with the button pushed, there will be no light, because the batteries are also made in India. India makes really mysterious things. You can enjoy them, but you cannot rely on them. There is no need at all.

The watcher has to be a pure watcher. For example, right now, what effort is needed to be silent, to be watching, to be listening to the birds. There is no effort in it, you are just relaxed. And remember, relaxation is not an effort.

In America, there is one great best-seller book, entitled, *You Must Relax!* When I read the title, I said, "My God, You *must*...then relaxation also becomes an exercise." Then you force yourself into relaxing. And what kind of relaxation will come out of it? Either you relax, or you don't relax, but there is no question of any *must*. "Must" implies effort, doing, forcing – but for the American mind, perhaps there is no contradiction in the title.

Here you have just to relax – no must, no should, no great effort on your part. Relaxation is a natural phenomenon. The trees are relaxed, the birds are relaxed; even though they go on singing their song, it is coming out of their utter relaxation. And you are relaxed, and you are not making any effort for it.

Beloved Bhagwan,

During the eight years I have been Your disciple, my trust in You
and existence has become stronger and stronger.
My love for You is very changeable –
sometimes being with You, my eyes are full of tears;
sometimes there is a deep silence, like waves drowning me;
and sometimes it looks like nothing is happening.
Is trust coming from my being, and love from my heart?
Can You please shine Your light on what is happening?

Devadip, your question has its answer in itself. You have clearly distinguished between the heart and being. Trust belongs to being. Being is always the same; it is part of eternity. And because trust belongs to being, it does not change the way love changes.

Love belongs to the heart, and heart is very moody. Sometimes you are full of love, and sometimes utterly empty, sometimes dancing, and sometimes with tears of joy; and sometimes nothing happens. The heart is very seasonal – one season comes and it is raining; another season comes and it is summer; another season comes and it is winter. And seasons go on changing, so love goes on changing.

Unless a great revolution happens in your being, that your love also dives deep and becomes one with trust...then there are not two things, trust and love, but only trust-love. Then there will always be the same peaceful joy, the same silent love energy; but love has to be joined with trust.

You cannot do anything about it, you simply go on remembering and watching. Trust is enough. If love also joins it, it will become more juicy, have more flowers, more perfume; otherwise trust, in itself, is enough.

You should not pay too much attention to the changes of love. Accept them; it is the nature of love. And with acceptance, slowly, slowly the love will go deeper and will join hands with trust. And once love and trust are together, trust is so powerful that it transforms the very nature of love itself. But love has a dance in it, a beauty in it, a nourishment in it, of its own. Trust will become more beautiful, more nourished, more juicy, more blissful. So the joining will be a great radical change in you.

But you should not try to do it; you cannot do anything. All that is possible for you is to go on becoming more and more strong in your trust, and accept all the seasons of love with the same attitude – whether it is smiling, whether it is giving tears to your eyes, whether it is an empty desert, or whether it is a garden full of flowers. Whether it has a song to sing, or is just silent, accept all its seasons.

Love is a changing energy, and nothing is wrong in it. With your acceptance, one day there will be a quantum leap in your being, and love will join with your trust.

Meanwhile, make your trust more and more strong. Then trust will transform the changeability of love; all seasons will disappear, it will be always spring.

With trust, it is always spring.

Okay, Vimal?

Yes, Bhagwan.

Session 11

Bring The Dawn, Dispel The Darkness

*With our deep meditation and gratitude for existence,
it is possible that this earth can remain
growing with more consciousness, with more flowers;
it can become a lotus paradise.
But a tremendous struggle
for a great revolution in human consciousness is needed,
and everybody is called for that revolution.
Contribute all that you can.*

March 2, 1987
Evening

Beloved Bhagwan,

Why have human beings gone through this struggle
since the very beginning? Were there not already
highly developed civilizations living on this earth?
And yet their consciousness got lost
and man had to start all over again.
Right now it seems to be a particularly dark period.
Is there such a cosmic law that says,
"Only out of the mud the lotus can grow"?
And will this earth ever become a garden of flowers?
In deep gratitude and love.

Prem Jaldhara, the question that you have asked has tremendous implications in it.

First, there have been many civilizations before our civilization which have reached to even higher peaks, but they all destroyed themselves because all those civilizations, including ours, have been growing in a deep imbalance. They developed great technologies, but they forgot that even the greatest technological progress is not going to make man more blissful, more peaceful, more loving, more compassionate.

Man's consciousness has not grown with the same pace as his scientific progress, and that has been the cause of all the old civilizations destroying themselves. There was no outer cause, no outer enemy – the enemy was within man. He created monsters as far as machines are concerned, but he himself remained very retarded, unconscious, almost asleep. And it is very dangerous to give so much power to unconscious people.

The same is happening today. Politicians are the lowest kind as far as consciousness is concerned. They are clever, they are cunning, they are mean, too; they make every effort for a single goal – how to be more powerful. Their only desire is for more power – not for more peace, not for more being, not for more truth, not for more love.

And what do you need more power for? – to dominate others, to destroy others. All the power accumulates in the hands of unconscious people. So on the one hand, politicians in all the civilizations that have developed and died – it would be better to say have committed suicide – had all the power in their hands. And on the other hand the genius of human intelligence was searching for more and more technological, scientific ways, and all that they discovered finally had to go into the hands of the politicians.

It was Albert Einstein who wrote a letter to President Roosevelt. He had escaped from Germany. In Germany he was researching atomic theory for Adolf Hitler, but reluctantly, because he was a Jew, and Adolf Hitler was killing Jews in such vast numbers that it seemed unbelievable. A single man killed six million Jews inside Germany. During the second world war Adolf Hitler was responsible for killing maybe fifty million people.

Seeing the situation – of course Albert Einstein was not going to be killed, he was too valuable – he escaped from Germany. He did not want to make the atom bomb for Adolf Hitler. It was a simple human reaction – so many of his people, his friends, had been killed. He wrote a letter to President Roosevelt of America: "I can come to America and I can create the atom bomb. I have the whole secret with me. And whosoever has the atom bomb is going to be the victor in the second world war." Immediately Roosevelt invited him and created all the facilities to make the atom bomb.

By the time the atom bomb was ready, Roosevelt was no longer president; Truman had come in his place. Germany was defeated, and it was only a question of seven days at the most – that's what all military experts of the world agree – before Japan was going to surrender. There was no way…because all the power had been coming from Germany. Japan was only an associate. And even American generals advised Truman, "Now there is no need to use atom bombs. With ordinary bombs, within seven days, Japan will have to surrender." But Truman would not listen.

Again Albert Einstein wrote a letter, saying that now there was no need. But now who cares about Albert Einstein? The bombs are in the hands of the president. And Truman, for no reason at all, bombed two cities of Japan, Hiroshima and Nagasaki. Big cities…each city had more than one hundred thousand people, and within five minutes all those people had evaporated. Such destruction had never been heard of. And it was a destruction which was not needed.

Truman was in a hurry. He was afraid that if Japan surrendered, then there would be no opportunity to use atomic bombs, which had been created with so much money. And he would not be able to show the whole world that America was the greatest power, that he was the man who holds the key to the greatest power. Those bombs on Hiroshima and Nagasaki were not meant just to defeat Japan. Their basic purpose was totally different – an ego fulfillment for President Truman: "I am the greatest, the most powerful man in the whole world, and my nation has come to the top." This has been happening again and again.

Before the second world war, nobody was ready to believe that such destructive weapons had ever existed. In the old scriptures of India, the story of the Mahabharata, the great Indian war of five thousand years ago, is just mythological. It was inconceivable that such powerful weapons were available five thousand years ago. But since the second world war it is now absolutely clear from the description in the Mahabharata, that they had discovered something close to atomic energy. They destroyed a great civilization, but the destruction came from within their own civilization.

Again we are moving towards the same situation. The destruction is not coming from some other planet, we are preparing our own graves. We may be aware, we may not be aware – we are all grave diggers, and we are all digging our own graves. Right now there are only five nations who are in possession of nuclear weapons. And nuclear weapons are millions of times more powerful than the second world war atom bombs. Now scientists say that compared to modern nuclear weapons, the second world war atom bombs seem to be like fire-crackers.

By the year 2010, twenty-five other nations will also be nuclear powers. It is going to be beyond control – thirty nations having so much destructiveness that a single nation could destroy the whole earth. A single crazy man, a single politician, to show his power, can destroy the whole of civilization; and you have to begin from ABC. And the destruction is not only of humanity. With humanity die all the companions of humanity – the animals, the trees, the birds, the flowers – everything disappears, everything that is alive.

The reason is an imbalance in our evolution. We go on developing scientific technology without bothering at all that our consciousness should also evolve in the same proportion. In fact, our consciousness should be a little ahead of our technological progress.

If our consciousness were in the state of enlightenment.... In the hands of a Gautam Buddha, nuclear weapons are no longer dangerous. In the hands of a Gautam Buddha, nuclear weapons will be turned into some creative force – because force is always neutral; either you can destroy with it or you can find ways to create something. But right now our powers are great, and our humanity is very small. It is as if we have given bombs into the hands of children, to play with.

You are asking, "Why have human beings gone through this struggle since the very beginning?" It is the imbalance between the inner and the outer. The outer is easier; and the outer is objective. For example, one man, Thomas Alva Edison, creates electricity, and the whole of humanity uses it; there is no need for everyone to discover it again and again.

Inner growth is a totally different phenomenon. A Gautam Buddha may become enlightened, but that does not mean that everybody else becomes enlightened. Each individual has to find the truth by himself. So whatsoever happens on the outside goes on accumulating, piling up; all scientific progress goes on piling up. Each scientist is standing on the shoulders of other scientists. But the evolution of consciousness does not follow the same law. Each individual has to discover it by himself; he cannot stand upon the shoulders of somebody else.

Anything objective can be shared, can be taught in the schools, in the colleges, in the universities. But the same is not true about subjectivity. I may know everything about the inner world, still I cannot hand that over to you. It is one of the fundamental laws of existence that the inner truth has to be discovered by each individual by his own efforts. It cannot be purchased in the marketplace, nor can it be stolen. Nobody can give it to you as a gift. It is not a commodity, it is not material; it is an immaterial experience.

One can give evidence by his individuality, by his presence, by his compassion, by his love, by his silence. But these are only evidences that something has happened inside him. He can encourage you. He can tell you that you are not going inside in vain – you will find treasures as I have found. Each master is nothing but an argument, an evidence, an eyewitness. But the experience remains individual. Science becomes social, technology becomes social; meditation remains individual. That is the basic problem:

how to create balance.

All the civilizations in the past.... A civilization existed on Atlantis, a vast continent that was drowned in the Atlantic Ocean. It was thought that that too is mythology, but recent researchers have proved that still there are remnants five miles deep under the water, of great cities. And the same happened with another continent, smaller than Atlantis – Lemuria. That too was drowned in the ocean.

It seems to the superficial observer that it must have been a natural calamity – perhaps a great earthquake, a movement of the earth, an entering of the ocean into those great cities, volcanoes – but something natural must have happened as a calamity. But as far as I can see, those natural calamities are also caused by us.

Just the other day I received news about one of the most beautiful forests in Germany, the famous Black Forest. Rumors have been coming for years that a part of it is dying; trees are simply dying for no visible reason. And the government of Germany has been hiding the facts. But just now the thing has become too big; you cannot cover it up. Fifty per cent of the forest has died. And the reason is not natural. The reason is the use of certain gases in the factories. Those gases are mixing with vapors, and when it rains the water becomes acidic. So if it falls on a tree, that tree dies immediately – it is poisoned. Maybe half the Black Forest is completely dead. The remaining half cannot survive either, because those gases are still being used.

The scientists have calculated that around the earth there is a two hundred mile thick layer of air surrounding the globe. And in the air is a layer of ozone, which is very protective; it protects life on the earth. *All* of the sunrays are not good for life. The ozone layer returns a few rays – those are death rays; if they enter the atmosphere they will destroy life. And only those rays are allowed through by the ozone which are not against life, but life enhancing.

But stupidly, we have made holes in this layer by sending rockets to the moon – which is a simple exercise in stupidity. When the rockets went, they made great holes in the ozone layer, and when they came back they again made holes. Russia and America both have been competing in creating those holes, and only just now they have become aware that those holes have taken away some of the protective layer. Now death rays are entering into the atmosphere.

When this civilization is destroyed, people may think it was a natural calamity. It is not. We have created it.

Because of the accumulation of carbon dioxide and other gases, the temperature of the earth's atmosphere has begun to rise, and that is creating a new problem. The ice at both the poles, south and north, is melting for the first time because the temperature has never been so high. Before, the ice remained eternally settled.

Scientists calculate that by the end of this century, all the oceans of the world will have risen by four and a half feet. There have never been any floods of the oceans – and this will be a permanent rise. Cities like Bombay and New York, which are on the seashore, will be filled with four and half feet of water.

This is only one calculation of one group of researchers who are working at the north pole and south pole. A third group is working on the Himalayan ice, which has been eternally there. If the temperature rises just one degree more, then the ice from the Himalayas and the Alps will start melting. And that will be a real calamity, because it will raise every ocean by forty feet. It will drown almost everything that we know as civilization; all our great ports, great cities, all will be under water. Anybody researching later on would find it to be a natural calamity – it is not. It is our own stupidity.

We can learn much, seeing what is happening, and then we can think introspectively about other civilizations which have disappeared, either through war or through calamities which apparently look natural. But I don't feel that they were natural. Those civilizations must have done something stupid that caused the calamities.

"Were there not already highly developed civilizations living on this earth?" There were, but they all got into the same mess in which we are entering; they all got into the same darkness in which we are entering. "And yet their consciousness got lost and man had to start all over again." Their consciousness was not lost – they had no consciousness. They had just the same superficial consciousness as we have.

What are you doing to prevent the calamity that is coming closer every day? The death of this earth is not far away – at the most, twenty years, twenty-five years. And that is a very optimistic attitude; for the pessimist it can happen even tomorrow. But even if we give twenty-five years to you, what are you going to do to help human consciousness rise in such a way that we can prevent the global suicide that is going to happen?

It is coming from many directions. Nuclear weapons are one direction which is almost completely ready. Any moment...and it is going to be a push-button war. It is not a problem of sending armies and airplanes.

Just the other day the prime minister of the Soviet Union declared that there are thousands of submarines underneath the ocean, moving around the world. Each submarine is carrying so much nuclear power that it is equal to one thousand second world wars. One submarine...and there are thousands of submarines, Russian and American, underneath the water. The explosion can happen just by accident. There is no need for any war, just by accident....

That is only one direction from which we are about to destroy ourselves. The second is creating the holes – because those experiments continue. Now the moon is not the target, now has Mars become the target. And there is nobody to protest against all these experiments – because they are not going to help human happiness or human life in any way. Why waste energy? And why create unnecessarily destructive situations? All those gases that are rising in the air and creating acid rain....

From another dimension, the disease AIDS is spreading so fast that there is every possibility it will destroy almost two-thirds of humanity without any war. And if the oceans are filled with all the ice that the Himalayas hold, and that of the south and north poles and the Alps and other mountains, we will be drowned, just as Atlantis was drowned and Lemuria was drowned.

The only possible way to avoid it is to create more meditativeness in the world. But it is such an insane world that sometimes it seems almost unbelievable.

The police commissioner of Poona has asked that police officers should be allowed to tape every one of my discourses; they will scrutinize and edit them, and they will tell us what parts should be kept in and what parts should be left out. One has never heard that police officers can even understand what meditation is.

The commissioner has been saying that respected citizens of Poona should make a committee, and they should come as a commission and go through all our meditations, our therapy groups, our discourses, and they should produce a report on whether what is happening is right or not. Who are the respected citizens of Poona, and how much do they know about meditation? How much do they know about psychotherapies? How much do they know about themselves?

But this is the world we are in. Seeing such absurd expectations, one loses all hope for the future. Rather, tell the people of Poona to come and meditate here, send the police officers to participate in therapy groups, to participate in meditations – because there is no other way.

If somebody is doing Vipassana, what can you observe? Whatever is happening, is happening so deep inside the person...with closed eyes he is sitting silently. These people can only report to the newspapers that I am teaching people to be lazy, sitting and doing nothing. Naturally they cannot see what is happening inside. They do not know anything of what has happened in one hundred years in the world of psychology, and they do not know anything of what has happened in ten thousand years in the world of meditation – how many methods have been created, how deep man has reached.

Who are these respected people? Their respectability may be because somebody has made a hospital, or somebody has opened a college, or somebody has donated to the orphans, to the poor. All these things are perfectly good – we have no objection. But because of these things they don't become experts in meditation, and they don't become experts in therapy.

They cannot even repeat twelve names of the enlightened people of the world, and they want to edit what I am saying. What will be their criterion? They know nothing of the interior world. They know nothing about the highest peaks of consciousness. They may have never heard the names like *tathata, anatta*. But such is the insanity of man that he even wants to judge Gautam Buddha and Mahavira and Basho and Sarmad, not knowing even the ABC's of them.

This is the only effort that we are trying to make: to raise the consciousness of a few individuals, and send them to faraway corners of the world to help, wherever they are, in raising the consciousness of humanity.

If, in the coming twenty years, man goes through a revolution, attains a new consciousness, perhaps, what has been happening up to now can be avoided for this civilization. We should make every effort to avoid it.

Lastly, Jaldhara, you are asking, "Right now it seems to be a particularly dark period." It is, and it will become darker and darker unless everybody becomes a light unto himself and radiates light around himself; unless everyone starts sharing his light and his fire with those who are thirsty and hungry for it. The dawn is not going to come automatically. You have to be fully alert to make every possible effort in helping consciousness.

Before the oceans rise forty feet, at least we have to make consciousness rise forty feet. The world needs at least two hundred enlightened people. Those will be the two hundred lighthouses where millions can be satisfied in their thirst for truth. It is a great struggle against darkness, but also a great opportunity and a challenge and an excitement. You have not to become serious about it. You have to do it lovingly, dancingly, with all your songs and with all your joy, because that way only, it is possible to bring the dawn and dispel the darkness.

Yes, Jaldhara, this is true. There is a cosmic law that says "Only out of the mud the lotus can grow." The politicians, and the priests of all the religions, the governments and the bureaucracies, all are creating enough mud. Now we have to grow lotuses. You have not to be drowned in their mud; you have to sow seeds for lotuses. The lotus seed is a miracle, it transforms the mud into the most beautiful flower.

In the East the lotus has been almost worshiped for two reasons. One, that it arises out of the mud – every man is just mud. The English word *human* simply means mud. The Arabic word *admi* simply means mud because God made human beings out of mud. But there is a possibility of growing a lotus flower. It is the biggest flower. It opens its petals only when the sun rises and the birds start singing and the whole sky becomes colorful. And as the darkness comes and the sun sets, it again closes its petals. It is a lover of light.

Secondly, it has a very beautiful quality – its petals, even its leaves, are so velvety that in the night dewdrops gather on the petals, on the leaves. In the early morning sun, those dewdrops shine almost like pearls – far more beautiful, creating rainbows around themselves. But the most beautiful thing is that although they are resting on the petals and on the leaves, they don't touch the leaf. Just a small breeze comes and they slip back into the ocean, leaving no trace, no wetness on the leaves or on the lotus petals.

The lotus flower has been very symbolic to the East, because the East says you should live in the world but remain untouched by it. You should remain in the world, but the world should not remain in you. You should pass through the world without carrying any impression, any impact, any scratch. If by the time of death you can say that your consciousness is as pure, as innocent, as you have brought it with you at birth, you have lived a religious life, a spiritual life.

Hence, the lotus flower has become a symbol of a spiritual style of living. Untouched by the water...it grows from the mud in the water, and yet remains untouched. And it is a symbol of transformation. Mud is transformed into the most beautiful and the most fragrant flower this planet knows about. Gautam Buddha was so much in love with the lotus that he called his paradise "the lotus paradise."

Jaldhara, with our deep meditation and gratitude for existence, it is possible that this earth can remain growing with more consciousness, with more flowers; it can become a lotus paradise.

But a tremendous struggle for a great revolution in human consciousness is needed, and everybody is called for that revolution. Contribute all that you can. Your whole life has to be given to the revolution. You will not have another chance, another challenge – for your own growth, and for the growth of this whole beautiful planet.

This is the only planet in the whole of existence which is alive; its death would be a great tragedy. But it can be avoided. You have to become the soldiers for this revolution to avoid the criminal forces, the evil forces, which are getting ready to destroy us.

I would like to end my answer with a beautiful reference. The people in America destroyed our beautiful commune, which was an oasis in the desert, which we had created with immense effort – five thousand people continuously working for five years. But America could not tolerate such happy, joyous, dancing people – so serene, so calm, so peaceful. They did everything illegal and everything criminal, but they had the power, and they destroyed the commune.

Now they have made a memorial, a marble memorial as a symbol of their victory. But unconsciously they have written a sentence on the memorial which I loved, which I would have suggested to them to write. The sentence is, "Evil forces win only when good people remain silent." That sentence is in our favor. That memorial they have made really says something about what happened: evil forces have won because the good people remained silent.

America is full of good people. If they had raised their voices, the commune could have been saved. But it is the weakness of good people everywhere; in private they will say, "It is perfectly good," but in public they will join the crowd.

Good people don't have guts. Bad people have guts. This is the trouble.

So just a few bad people have been ruling the whole of humanity, and millions of good people, seeing destructiveness, seeing violence, seeing criminality, just remain silent. They don't want to get involved in any trouble. The bad people are in search of trouble; the good people avoid trouble.

We have to learn one thing, and that is, to fight for the truth, fighting for that which is beautiful, fighting for that which is good, fighting for God. I want my sannyasins to be soldiers of God; otherwise there is no hope for humanity.

Beloved Bhagwan,

When I was a student at a Japanese Buddhist university
I heard the word *consciousness*.
Beloved Bhagwan, what does it mean?

Kranti Satbodha, consciousness you already have, but only in a very small proportion. It is just like an iceberg – one tenth is above water and the rest is under water. Just a little bit is conscious in you.

I am saying something and you are listening to it; without consciousness it is not possible. These pillars of Chuang Tzu Auditorium are not listening – they don't have consciousness. But we are aware only of a very small piece of consciousness.

Meditation is the whole science of bringing more and more consciousness out of darkness. The only way is to be as conscious as possible twenty-four hours a day. Sitting, sit consciously, not like a mechanical robot; walking, walk consciously, alert to each movement; listening, listen more and more consciously, so that each word comes to you in its crystal clear purity, its definitiveness. While listening, be silent, so that your consciousness is not covered by thoughts.

Just this moment, if you are silent and conscious you can hear small insects singing their song in the trees. The darkness is not empty, the night has its own song; but if you are full of thoughts then you cannot listen to the insects. This is just an example.

If you become more and more silent, you may start listening to your own heartbeat, you may start listening to the flow of your own blood, because blood is continuously flowing all through your body. If you are conscious and silent, more and more clarity, creativity, intelligence, will be discovered. There are millions of geniuses who die without knowing that they were a genius. There are millions of people who don't know why they have come, why they lived and why they are going.

It happened...George Bernard Shaw was traveling from London to some other place in England. The ticket checker came and Bernard Shaw looked in all his pockets, opened his suitcase – he was perspiring – the ticket was missing.

The ticket checker said, "I know you, everybody knows you, there is no need to be worried. You must have put it somewhere, don't be so tense". Bernard Shaw said, "Who is being tense about the ticket?" The ticket checker said, "Then why are you perspiring and looking so nervous?"

He said, "The problem is that now the question arises of where I am going. It was written on the ticket. Now, are you going to tell me where I am going? Who is going to tell me?"

The ticket checker said, "How can I tell you where you are going?"

So Bernard Shaw said, "Then you should go and leave me alone. I have to find the ticket. It is a question of life and death. Where am I going? I must be going somewhere, because I have come to the station, purchased the ticket, entered the compartment. So one thing is certain, I must be going somewhere."

This is the situation, most people never come to know – their consciousness is a hidden treasure. One does not know what it contains unless you awaken it, unless you bring it into light, unless you open all the doors and enter into your own being and find every nook and corner. Consciousness in its fullness will give you the idea of who you are, and will also give you the idea of what your destiny is, of where you are supposed to go, of what your capacities are. Are you hiding a poet in your heart, or a singer, or a dancer, or a mystic?

Consciousness is something like light. Right now you are in deep darkness inside. When you close your eyes there is darkness and nothing else.

One of the great philosophers of the West, C.E.M. Joad, was dying, and a friend, who was a disciple of George Gurdjieff, had come to see him. Joad asked the friend, "What do you go on doing with this strange fellow, George Gurdjieff? Why are you wasting your time? And not only you...I have heard that many people are wasting their time."

The friend laughed. He said, "It is strange that those few people who are with Gurdjieff think that the whole world is wasting its time, and you are thinking that we are wasting our time."

Joad said, "I don't have much longer to live; otherwise I would have come and compared."

The friend said, "Even if you have only a few seconds more to live, it can be done here, now." Joad agreed. The man said, "You close your eyes and just look inside, and then open your eyes and tell me what you find."

Joad closed his eyes, opened his eyes and said, "There is darkness and nothing else." The friend laughed and he said, "It is not a time to laugh, because you are almost dying, but I have come at the right time. You said that you saw only darkness inside?"

Joad said, "Of course."

And the man said, "You are such a great philosopher; you have written such beautiful books. Can't you see the point, that there are two things – you and the darkness? Otherwise, who saw the darkness? Darkness cannot see itself – that much is certain – and darkness cannot report that there is only darkness."

Joad gave it consideration and he said, "My

God, perhaps the people who are with Gurdjieff are not wasting their time. This is true, *I* have seen the darkness."

The friend said, "Our whole effort is to make this "I," the witness, stronger and more crystallized, and to change the darkness into light. And both things happen simultaneously. As the witness becomes more and more centered, the darkness becomes less and less. When the witness comes to its full flowering, that is the lotus of consciousness – all darkness disappears."

Satbodha, we are here in a mystery school, doing nothing else than bringing more and more crystallization to your witness, to your consciousness; so that your inner being, your interiority, becomes a light, so full and overflowing that you can share it with others.

To be in darkness is to be living at the minimum. And to be full of life is to live at the maximum.

Beloved Bhagwan,

Sometimes while reading a poem by Kabir
there is an experience of "aha,"
even though the mind doesn't always comprehend it.
Sitting with You in darshan I was reminded of this poem:
Ignorance shuts the iron gates
But love opens them.
The sound of the gates opening
Wakes the beautiful woman asleep.
Kabir says, "Don't let a chance like this go by."

Prem Prasado, Kabir is one of the most rare human beings who has ever been on this earth. He belongs to the highest category of mystics. And strangely enough he was absolutely uneducated, uncultured, an orphan. But although living the poor life of a weaver, he has also woven some golden poems of tremendous beauty. His words are raw but very pregnant.

Ignorance shuts the iron gates.

This word *ignorance* has a beauty. Ordinarily you may not have thought about it in this way. You have always thought about ignorance as absence of knowledge; but its true meaning is, ignoring yourself, ignoring that which can become your knowing, which can become your wisdom. And the whole day, the whole life, you are continuously ignoring yourself.

You are taking care of everything, every trivia, but never taking any note of the most precious thing that you have – yourself. And Kabir is using the word in the same sense. Ignoring yourself is the only ignorance. It shuts the iron gates.

But love opens them

These are the words of a man who knows. If

139

he was only a learned man he would have said that knowledge opens the doors. But instead of knowledge, only a man who knows can say, *but love opens them.*

The mind is going to remain in ignorance; it cannot get out of it. The iron gates are closed. The mind can become knowledgeable, but it cannot become wise. It is only the heart which opens the gates. It is only love that makes you wise.

The sound of the gates opening
Wakes the beautiful woman asleep.

Now these are symbolic words. According to Kabir, your soul is the sleeping woman. He is using the word *woman* for your soul, your consciousness, because only the feminine qualities are authentically spiritual qualities. Beauty is feminine, honesty is feminine, sincerity is feminine; all that is great within your consciousness is feminine. Even the word *consciousness* is feminine.

In English it is difficult, because in English you don't make a difference in words, you don't make a difference between male and female in each word. But in any language that is born in the East, each word has the distinction: *consciousness, awareness, samadhi, sambodhi,* all are feminine. And the man of love and compassion starts having a feminine beauty and a feminine grace. The male is a little barbarous. His qualities are that of a warrior, fighter, egoist, chauvinist, fanatic, fascist. The male qualities are qualities of a Nazi.

It is not strange that Germany is the only country which calls its own land the fatherland. The whole world calls their countries the motherland – Germany is a special case. It is time they should change it; they should stop calling it the fatherland because that gives male qualities the priority.

Friedrich Nietzsche was thought of by Adolf Hitler as his master, although Adolf Hitler had not the intelligence to understand Friedrich Nietzsche – whatever he understood was simply misunderstanding. But there were a few points for which Friedrich Nietzsche was also responsible.

He said in a letter that the most beautiful experience of his life was when he saw, one day in the early morning when the sun had risen, a batallion of soldiers with their shining guns, and heard the harmonious sound of their steps: "I have never seen such a beautiful scene, nor have I heard such beautiful music as the music of the soldiers and their boots going in harmonious parade." Nietzsche also is responsible; these types of pieces Adolf Hitler collected from Nietzsche. The soldier became the real human being, and all the qualities of a warrior became the qualities of a superman.

But the East has always been aware that man and his qualities may be utilitarian, useful, but they don't have the sensitivity, the softness, the lovingness, the compassion of the woman. That is why Kabir says,

The sound of the gates opening
Wakes the beautiful woman asleep.
Kabir says,
"Don't let a chance like this go by."

I also say to you, Prem Prasado, Don't let a chance like this go by. We are making every effort here to wake up your woman, to wake up your consciousness, to wake up your grace, to wake up your beauty. Don't let a chance like this go by.

Beloved Bhagwan,

I am afraid to ask You this question
for I feel Your answer could really destroy me.
Your sword is so sharp these days
that even the sound of the "whoosh" can make me tremble,
but I must ask no matter what.
Why don't You answer my questions?

Prem Patipada, I am not answering your questions deliberately. First, you have been part of the gang which destroyed the commune. You were aware of many things; you never came to me to tell about them. You were aware even that my personal physician was being poisoned, that efforts were being made to kill Vivek, my caretaker.

You remained part of the gang, a small group which wanted to have absolute power in the commune. And anybody who was not with them, their argument was, was against them. You knew everything, still you never came to tell me. Even when I started speaking, you could have written questions informing me about all these things. You never did that.

On the contrary, when Sheela left with her small criminal group you also left the commune, writing to me in a letter, "Bhagwan our paths are parting and perhaps I will never be able to see you again." You may have forgotten your letter; I don't forget so easily. I can forgive – I have forgiven you – but I cannot forget. And you have been here since that letter, twice; you came to Bombay, you have come here.

And you are afraid, not because I am going to destroy you – you are afraid because I am going to expose you.

That's why I have not been answering your questions, because you have not even offered an apology to me. And you owe an apology not only to me, but to the whole commune.

Beloved Bhagwan,

I have been with You for the last six months and now
the moment has come that I am forced to leave.
To be honest, this is the only way that I would leave.
My whole being is shaking.
My heart is broken and my eyes are full of tears,
but nothing can take away what I feel in Your presence.
I am not good at expressing what I feel;
it is just a feeling of thankfulness.
Thanks, Bhagwan, for everything.
Thank You for allowing me to stay in Your house,
thank You for Your beautiful gift,
and especially thank You for being so compassionate with me.

Dhyan Aum, there is no need to be full of tears because you have to go. Always remember that every going is a beginning of coming back; otherwise how will you come? So rather than emphasizing going, always emphasize coming. Go laughing, and if you love tears then the tears have to be of joy. Just for your laughter I will tell a joke.

A young lady finds herself to be pregnant. Luckily she has a friend who is a surgeon in a hospital. "Don't you worry," says the friend, "I will help you."

So she goes to the hospital to give birth to her baby. A Catholic priest who went to the hospital to have a gall bladder operation is very astonished to wake up from the operation with a newborn baby beside him. With some reluctance he finally accepts the surgeon's explanation that it is his baby.

In the end he takes the child home and raises it as his child. When he comes to die he calls the now grown-up child to his deathbed and says, "My child, before I die I must tell you the truth. You have always believed that I am your father; I am not. In fact I am your mother. Your father is the bishop."

Okay, Vimal?

Yes, Bhagwan.

Session 12

God Is Also Seeking You

*Search has to be from both sides;
otherwise both sides will be waiting.
Existence has a balance about everything.
Your waiting is not enough;
your longing, your search is categorically needed.*

March 3, 1987
Morning

Beloved Bhagwan,

Is it really true that God is also searching for me?
Can I wait for him to find me?

Sat Vijaya, it is absolutely true that just as you are seeking God or truth or the beloved, he is also seeking you. The search is never one-sided. And any search that is one-sided is never going to be fulfilled. But your question is, "Can I wait for him to find me?" – then he will also wait to search for you.

Search has to be from both sides; otherwise both sides will be waiting. Existence has a balance about everything. Your waiting is not enough; your longing, your search is categorically needed.

One of the Sufis' sayings is: if you take one step towards God, he takes one thousand steps towards you. But at least one step on your side is absolutely necessary.

And your one step is far more important than the one thousand steps of God, because by "God" is not meant any person; by God is meant the intelligence of this whole universe, the consciousness of the whole universe.

You have a very small proportion of consciousness. Your one step is far bigger than the one thousand steps of God, because existence has infinite intelligence. So waiting alone won't do. Just waiting is a state which is not alive; there has to be tremendous longing, a thirst from every pore of your being. Unless God becomes a question of your life and death, the meeting is not possible.

Almost everybody will be prepared to wait – that means on your laundry list God is the last item, when you have done everything of the world. And that is not possible, even in eternity; something or other will be left undone. God has to be your first priority. It has to become a kind of haunting in your heart. Breathing in, breathing out, there has to be a remembrance: whatever you are doing is nonessential, and the essential part is to go deep down in meditation.

Never think of God as someone outside you. That is a wrong beginning – because where will you search for him? The outside is so vast; you don't have the address or the phone number. In the infinity of existence, in which direction will you search for him? How will you find that you are on the right path? Millions of paths...how are you going to choose? What will be the criterion?

Because of this misconception that God is outside, religions became organized around priesthood, around a holy book, around certain dogmas – because that at least gives you some feel for where you have to search: you have to go to the church, you have to do a certain prayer, you have to go to the synagogue, you have to find your path in the holy scriptures. The idea of God outside has led the whole of humanity into tremendous confusion.

He is within you. Better will be if I say: He is your within, your very interiority, your very center of being. You are on the periphery of your individuality. Move inwards.

First you will meet the thoughts. Don't get involved in them, just ignore.... Buddha has used the word *upeksha*, ignoring, as a certain guaranteed method; otherwise you are going to get caught in the net of thoughts. Don't fight, just go on your way as if mind is empty. And if you can ignore the mind it becomes empty.

The more attention you pay to the mind, the more nourishment you give to the thoughts. If you can pass the boundary of the mind without disturbing – and it is not an arduous thing, just a little knack of ignoring – then you will come into the world of feelings, emotions, moods, which are more subtle than the thoughts. You have entered from the mind and its territory into a deeper area of your being, the heart.

Continue the same method, ignore your sentiments, emotions, moods, as if they don't belong to you. As you pass the boundary of the heart you enter the boundary of your own being. That is the temple of God. And the moment you enter the temple, certainly he takes those one thousand steps towards you.

Those one thousand steps are symbolic. He comes towards you as light, as the very essence of beauty, as blissfulness, as silence, as peace. And he comes with so much force, almost like a flood, that you are drowned in it.

You will find God, but you will have to lose yourself; that is the price. It is not much. How much do you think your cost-price is? In fact, any animal in the world is more costly than man. When man dies, nobody is ready to purchase him. When an elephant dies, then thousands of rupees.... When any animal dies, even the dead animal has some utility. It is only man who dies, and all that you can do is either burn him or bury him – just to get rid of him. Rather than bringing some money to you after death he withdraws some money from your pocket.

So there is no need to be afraid if you are lost, drowned, because in the temple of God only one can exist – either you or he. Duality is not possible there, because duality is conflict. And the experience of God is that of immense harmony. That harmony can be achieved only if you allow yourself to be drowned in the flood that comes from all sides – of joy, of bliss, of ecstasy.

The feel of dying in the flood of God is the most exquisite and the most sweet experience – the last, the highest, the greatest; there is nothing beyond it.

But it is not going to happen by just waiting. You will have to go inside your own being. He is present there always; he is your life, he is your all. You are just a small ray of light from that immense source. So when you get drowned in him, it is just that the ray has returned back to the sun. One has come home.

If God is understood the way I am telling you.... And I am not a thinker; it is not my hypothesis, it is my experience. I have passed through that death and I have found that it appears to be death from one side, but from the other side it is resurrection. You disappear as a small creature and become a vast creativity. You don't lose anything and you gain everything.

But the organized religions don't want you to be aware of this fact, because their whole business depends on an outside God. Then the priest is needed, the temple is needed, the mosque is needed, the church is needed; then the *Holy Bible* is needed, then some interpreters are needed, and then all the millions of priests around the world become your mediators with a fictitious God somewhere in the sky.

The Vatican pope has declared it a sin to confess directly to God; you have to confess to the priest. And of course it has to be a catholic priest – only he is authorized to have a direct communication with God. You cannot pray directly, you cannot ask forgiveness directly.

Do you see the cunningness, the meanness, the whole strategy of exploitation? The priest becomes more important than God himself. On the one hand these people go on calling you children of God, and on the other, children cannot directly communicate with their father; a priest is needed as a mediator. The reality is, there is no God outside; it is the invention of the priest. And he has invented a great business. For centuries he has been exploiting men, whether they are Hindus or Mohammedans or Christians or Jews – it does not matter.

There is only one thing every religion insists: that a direct relationship with God is not possible. They don't give any reasons why. I have seen trees praying directly to God; the rivers and the mountains and the stars don't have any priests, the flowers and the birds don't have any priests. Do you think this whole existence except man is not related to God? It is more related to God than man. It is only man who has gone astray.

Have you ever heard in any religion, in any country, a story that God expelled a few trees out of the garden of Eden? Or a few animals, or a few birds? It is only man who is expelled.

The story is significant. It simply means that the whole of existence is rooted in God. Only because man has a thinking mind, he has wandered far away. Mind is capable of wandering anywhere – you can be sitting here and your mind may be wandering somewhere in America or somewhere in Germany, or somewhere in Japan, or maybe on the moon.... There are all kinds of lunatics.

It is very rarely that you are here, very rare to be in the place where you are. Your mind is always wandering somewhere else. It is never here, it is never now. This wandering mind has taken you away from your own inner being. And this has become a great opportunity for exploitation. All over the world, like mushrooms, priests and religions and holy books have appeared.

There are three hundred religions in the world. They differ on every point except one point, and that is, the priest is an absolute necessity. Any intelligent person can see that these religions are not for you, these religions are for the priesthood. They are parasites – catholic parasites, protestant parasites, Hindu parasites, they come in all sizes and all shapes!

My effort here is to make you free from the chains of the priesthood. The moment you are free from the chains of the priesthood, you are no longer Christian, no longer Hindu, no longer Jew.

You are simply and purely human beings. You have already come very close to your home; the priest was distracting you.

An ancient story says that the old devil is sitting under a tree, having his morning tea, and a young disciple comes running, very much disturbed. He says, "What are you doing? You are sitting here, drinking tea, and our whole business is in difficulty. One man on the earth has found the truth!"

The old guy laughed. He said, "You are too young, you don't know all the secrets. Don't be worried, my people have reached there." The young disciple could not believe his eyes, could not believe his ears. He said, "I am coming from there, I have not seen anyone of our people."

The old devil said, "There is no need to send our people. I have created the priests. And they are surrounding the man. Now they have become a wall between the man and the people. Whatever the man says, the priest will interpret it and distort it.

"Truth has been found many times," said the old devil, "but while priests exist, truth will be found and lost again, because the priests immediately start interpreting, making organized religions around the truth – churches, temples, mosques – and the truth is lost in their interpretations, in their commentaries.

"What commentaries can they make? They don't know the truth. Truth needs no commentary, it is pure experience. Either you know it or you don't know it; there is no third position. That's why I'm so much at ease. Just sit down and have a cup of tea."

The story is significant. Beware of the priests, beware of organized religions, beware of others telling you what is truth. Nobody can tell it to you. You will have to find it yourself.

And it is so close to you that you have not to go on a faraway journey. You have to go in silence, in profound peace, beyond words and beyond feelings, and suddenly you find the temple of consciousness. And as you enter into it you disappear.

Only God is.

That is your authentic reality.

God is your very soul.

Beloved Bhagwan,

I love this little Zen story,
as it also has the flavor of Your childhood stories.
Ikkyu, the Zen master, was very clever even as a boy.
His teacher had a precious teacup, a rare antique.
Ikkyu happened to break this cup and was greatly perplexed.
Hearing the footsteps of his teacher,
he held the pieces of the cup behind him.
When the master appeared, Ikkyu asked,
"Why do people have to die?"
"This is natural," explained the older man,
"Everything has to die, and has just so long to live."
Ikkyu, producing the shattered cup, added,
"It was time for your cup to die."

Gayan, Ikkyu is one of the most important Zen masters of Japan. There are many stories about him which can open new doors for you to contemplate and meditate. This is the first story about his childhood, when he was not a master yet but used to serve another master.

He was doing small little things for him. But a man who is going to become enlightened has from the very beginning a clarity, a sharpness and an intelligence that people with great effort cannot even attain in their old age.

This story is beautiful. Ikkyu was very clever as a boy. The man who is going to become enlightened is bringing with him from his past life almost ninety-nine percent of his enlightenment. Just a small part was left and death came over him. Such people die consciously. And because they die consciously they know that death is a reality only from the outside; as far as the inner experience is concerned, it is just a changing of the house. Life continues.

Even in the mother's womb the man who is going to become enlightened shows indications of intelligence. This seems unbelievable, but the Buddhists, the Jainas – two great authentic paths which have produced more enlightened people in the world than any other religion – both have this idea that when a child is in the mother's womb he gives indications that he is not an ordinary unconscious child.

Scriptures describe exactly how he gives indications: He gives certain dreams to the mother. He is one with the mother's body; he can project certain dreams.

And for thousands of years the East has been looking into the phenomenon of enlightenment. For example, the white elephant is a very rare quality. Perhaps not one of you has seen a white elephant – except in language. When you want to condemn something you say, "It is a white elephant, I don't want it. It is unnecessarily expensive." The child in the mother's womb, who is going to become enlightened in this life, gives her again and again the dream of a white elephant.

Upon that, the Buddhists agree, the Jainas agree – because they both have worked hard to find what kind of indications the conscious death of a person will bring to the mother into whose womb he has entered.

There are many other dreams upon which they have agreed – because they have been repeated so many times, and it has been only when the person was going to become enlightened. So it is not only cleverness, it is consciousness. I will not say it is just cleverness. Cleverness is ordinary; it is available to anybody. There are thousands of boys and girls who are clever.

Whoever has written the story, Gayan, has no idea of enlightenment; otherwise this word would not have been used. It shows consciousness, it shows awareness.

"His teacher had a precious teacup." Remember again, it is not said in the story that his *master* had a precious teacup – because the esoteric traditions of all mystery schools make a distinction between the teacher and the master. The teacher simply teaches you philosophies, theologies – he transfers to you the knowledge that is contained in the scriptures – but he himself is not enlightened. He is a knowledgeable person, a learned person. But it is not his own experience.

"His teacher had a precious teacup." In China, in Japan they have made it a great art. Just yesterday one of my sannyasins from Spain brought me a very precious Chinese teacup. It is antique; it was produced in the thirteenth century – very fragile, but very beautiful. To have lived so long with such fragileness – it is very thin.... And because the tea ceremony has become a religious phenomenon in China and Japan, all monasteries have beautiful tea ceremony temples – in the garden, surrounded by ponds, beautiful trees, birds, swans, peacocks.

And the tea ceremony is a religious phenomenon; it is not something mundane. The way you drink tea is a mundane thing. The way tea is served in a Zen monastery is sacred. And to transform the mundane into the sacred is a great art.

You have to leave your shoes outside. You sit inside in a circle, listening to the samovar making its sound, the boiling water, the birds singing outside, the breeze bringing fragrances of flowers. Nothing is spoken; it is a meditation.

And the hostess will bring rare antique cups which may have existed for hundreds of years. They have survived so long because they are being taken with such respect and reverence in the hands. And the tea is poured.... Then people don't just start drinking the tea. First they will smell the aroma, and then slowly, slowly, as if they are doing a prayer they will sip the tea. And because the cups and everything are sacred, they can survive for hundreds of years.

Our cups are far stronger, thicker, but are broken so soon. You cannot find in any other country cups a thousand years old, still in use and young and fresh. In silence the tea is sipped. And they all bow down – the hostess bows down to the guest. With care, with love they put their cups back. And slowly, slowly the guests depart. Not a single word is uttered, only gestures.

This is symbolic of a certain deep insight that if you want, your whole life can become a sacred phenomenon. If tea drinking can become sacred, then why should anything else remain mundane? In the world, people who don't understand Zen...even making love is not sacred; it is something ugly, full of guilt, condemnation.

People are loving each other because of a biological urge, not as a spiritual act of meeting with your beloved.

I have always thought, whenever I have come across any reference about the tea ceremony, that my people should create a love ceremony. It should not be a hit and run affair. You should have a temple, a love temple in your house, where nothing else is done. You go there only to play music, to dance, to sing, to burn incense. And love has not to be made deliberately. You are just listening to music and dancing and singing, and the whole room is full of fragrance, the incense. And if love happens spontaneously, not a cerebral thing that you have been thinking about...it is thinking that makes it ugly. If it is pure spontaneity it becomes the greatest prayer you can find in human life – the most precious meditation.

I call it a love ceremony.

Ikkyu happened to break this cup and was greatly perplexed. He was a small child, and those cups are very fragile. Hearing the footsteps of the teacher he held the pieces of the cup behind him. When the master appeared, Ikkyu asked, "Why do people have to die?" This is not cleverness, this is great intelligence. Why do people have to die?

"This is natural," explained the older man. "Everything has to die and has just so long to live." Ikkyu, producing the shattered cup added, "It was time for your cup to die." He has made an accident into a profound experience. By bringing death into it, first he has stopped the mouth of the teacher – now he cannot say anything. If everything has its time and then it has to die, he has to accept that the precious cup has died.

But it is not just a story. Ikkyu, when he himself became a master, used to tell about this incident many times – that death is a natural phenomenon, that one should not be worried about it, and one should not be sad about it. The only thing that one can be sad about is a life unlived.

You go on dragging yourself without living – that is unfortunate. You are vegetating; you are not singing the songs that you have come to sing, you are not dancing the dance that is lying in your potential, fast asleep; you are not bringing your intelligence to its highest peak.

You will be surprised that even our so-called great geniuses only use fifteen percent of their intelligence. Eighty-five percent of their intelligence remains unused. And this is about our great geniuses – talented people use nearabout ten percent, and the common masses use not more than seven percent. One wonders, if people were using their intelligence to its full, the world would be a totally different place – far more alive, far more rich, far more beautiful.

The only thing that one should be sad about is that you are not living, but just passing time. Death is not something to be sad about – if it comes to a fulfilled life, if it comes to a life as a crescendo, its climax, it has a beauty of its own.

I want my people to live totally, and to live intensely, to burn their life's torch from both ends together. If they can manage to live a total and intense life in each of their acts, their death will be something of a greater beauty than their life has ever been – because death is the highest peak, the last touches of the painter on the painting. That's why I have been saying that death should be celebrated just as life should be celebrated. Both are natural, both are gifts.

Life is tiring; a time comes when you are spent. Death comes as a great help. It is nothing but relaxation, a deep relaxation. And it is not the end, it is only the beginning of a new life. If you think of it as an end, you will feel miserable – think of it as a beginning of a new life. Just a little difference of emphasis, and your whole experience changes its color, its beauty. Where there was sadness there will be joy, and where there were tears of misery, pain, anguish, there will be tears of fulfillment, contentment, blissfulness. The same tears with a new meaning, the same tears with a new music; the same death, but with a totally different taste.

When Ikkyu died himself, he collected all his disciples and asked them, "Just tell me some new way of dying, because I am not interested in imitation. People die on their beds; I don't want to die on the bed." The bed is the most dangerous thing – 99.9 percent of people die there, beware! So whenever you go to bed, remember: This place is very close to the graveyard. His disciples knew that he was a crazy man – now, whoever has ever bothered about how one dies? People simply die....

Ikkyu asked, "Has somebody a suggestion?"

One man said, "You can die sitting in the lotus posture." Ikkyu said, "That is not new. Many other masters have died in that posture. Suggest something new, novel!"

One man said, "You can die standing." Ikkyu said, "That looks a little better." But a disciple objected; he said, "Although it is not well known, I know one Zen master who has died standing. So you will be number two." Ikkyu said, "Then reject it. Suggest something new. I want to be first!"

One of his disciples suggested, "Then there is only one way. You die standing on your head, in a head stand, *shirshasam*. Nobody has ever tried it." Ikkyu said, "That is right. That suits me! I am so grateful to you." He stood on his head and died.

Now the disciples were in trouble. They knew what to do when somebody dies on a bed – that his clothes have to be changed, that he has to be given a bath, new clothes have to be put on him, and then he is taken to the funeral – but what to do with this man who is standing on his head? He has not even fallen, and he is dead!

They tried in every possible way to find out whether he was dead or alive. He was dead, but there was no precedent, so they didn't know what procedure should be followed.

Somebody said, "I know his elder sister, who is also a Zen mystic. She lives in a nearby monastery. And he was always respectful to her. I will call her, perhaps she can say something. It is better to enquire before we do anything wrong."

The sister came, and she was very angry. She came and she said, "Ikkyu, you have been your whole life mischievous; at least in death, behave! Just lie down on the bed!" And Ikkyu jumped up and lay down on the bed and died. And the sister simply went out. She did not bother that he had died.

In the East it is not thought good to not follow the order of your elders, and particularly at such a moment. The disciples were amazed, because they had tried everything – the heart was not beating, the pulse was not there, they had moved a mirror in front of his nose, and there was no shadow of vapor. What had happened?

As the sister shouted at him, he immediately jumped, and just like an obedient child lay down on the bed and died! Even death is a game. And the sister did not even wait for the funeral.

To those who know that life is eternal, death means nothing. It is the death only of your physical body, not of your consciousness. And particularly a man like Ikkyu is not going to be reborn; he will not be again encaged in another body. He will be moving into the eternity, into the ocean of the consciousness of the whole existence.

It is a moment of celebration.

Beloved Bhagwan,

I came here confused, not knowing who I am.
For many days sitting near You
I have heard my heart asking and Your voice answering.
Every day You have heard my words and my questions.
Now I sit in Your presence, my heart is quieter.
Sometimes just a jump of joy, a desire to dance
or to give You a hug, nothing else...no questions, no answers, no problems.
Bhagwan, am I sleeping again?

Anand Shobha, you are saying, "I came here confused, not knowing who I am. For many days, sitting near you I have heard my heart asking and your voice answering. Every day you have heard my words and my questions. Now I sit in your presence, my heart is quieter, sometimes just a jump of joy, a desire to dance or to give you a hug, nothing else...no questions, no answers, no problems. Am I sleeping again?"

No, Anand Shobha. You were sleeping before, when you were full of confusion, when you had no idea of who you are, when there were so many questions to be asked, so many answers to be received – that was the time of your sleep. As your heart became quieter, your awakening came closer.

Now you say, "Sometimes just a jump of joy, a desire to dance or to give you a hug, nothing else...no questions, no answers, no problems."

You are blessed, because the confusion has gone, the clouds have disappeared and the sun is shining bright. When there are no questions and no problems you cannot be asleep; it happens only when you are alert and awake. So it is not that you are falling asleep. You were asleep, and you have come out of it.

Now rejoice, dance, sing as a gratitude to existence. What else can we do to show our gratitude? Words are useless, because existence does not understand any language. It understands only your joy, your blissfulness, your ecstasy...not in words, but in your experiencing them.

So don't hold back. This is the only way and the only possibility, to dance so madly that the dancer disappears and only the dance remains. And existence will understand it. Sing so totally that the singer is not left behind, but is completely drowned in the song, becomes the song itself. And existence will understand it. Existence has its own existential language – this is the existential language.

I have heard about two generals, after the second world war, sitting in a restaurant in London. One was a German and the other was an Englishman. The German general was saying to the English general, "I cannot figure it out, why we got defeated in the second world war. We were more powerful, and we had been winning for five years continually. What went wrong?"

The English general laughed. He said, "Nothing went wrong, just one small thing you forgot. And that is, our British armies were always going to the field, to the front, after praying to God, 'Lord, give us victory.' The Lord was with us. Our prayers proved more powerful than all your power."

It was time for the German general to laugh. He said, "You must be stupid. Do you think we were not praying? We were also praying, and the Lord was with us continually for five years."

The English general said, "In what language were you praying?" The German said, "Of course in the German language."

The British general said, "That is the problem. God does not understand German! Except English, he does not understand any other language."

But this is the attitude of all the races, of all the countries of the world. Jews think God knows only Hebrew, Hindus think God knows only Sanskrit, and Mohammedans *know* that God knows only Arabic.

But I would like to tell you that God does not know any of these languages. These are all manufactured by man. God understands only that which he has made. He understands these birds and they are not speaking English, nor German. God understands even the silence of the trees, the fragrance of the flowers, the song of a river descending from the mountains, the eternal peace that reigns in the Himalayas. These are the languages that God understands.

You be silent, you be joyful, you sing a song, you become a dance. I am not saying dance, I am saying *become* a dance, and your prayer has reached to the farthest source of existence.

There was one Sufi mystic, Jabbar. The English word *gibberish* comes from Jabbar, because he used absolutely absurd language. It was not a language at all. He went on inventing any sound, any word, anything. Nobody could understand what he was saying. It was just like small children playing, when they start learning to speak – making any sounds – even the sound makes them happy. And many times his disciples said, "Why do you bother? You go on inventing sounds, words that do not exist in any language, in any dictionary...."

But mystics are mystics. He never changed his idea. People used to think that soon nobody would come to listen to him. But they were amazed, he had more disciples than any other contemporary mystic. And people were puzzled: what is happening?

What was happening was something really great. Listening to Jabbar, your mind had nothing to do. You could not interpret, you could not say, "It is right, it is wrong." You didn't know what it was. Naturally, listening to him your mind stopped – that this man is mad and you cannot figure it out, what it is. No comma, no semicolon, no full stop; he simply went on and on. He must have been very inventive.

And he enjoyed it very much. He would laugh as if he had been telling a joke, and again he would start. The gathering of his disciples increased, because just sitting near him, listening to his gibberish, their minds became silent. And that was the purpose, that was his device. And when their minds became silent, they were in meditation.

The moment the mind becomes silent, your whole consciousness is clean, pure. And that cleanliness, that pureness is your godliness. Many more people have understood God through Jabbar's gibberish than through great learned scholars. I have never heard that anybody has experienced God by great learning.

But Jabbar must have been a very unique man. It is very unfortunate that there was no way of recording in those days; otherwise whatever he was saying could have become one of the holiest scriptures. Nobody would have been able to understand it – but you don't have to understand anything, you have just to be silent, you have just to be absent.

So any way, either singing or dancing, whatever makes you absent, immediately you will be filled with God's presence. Suddenly you will become aware of your own inner light.

The last words of Gautam Buddha were, *appo deepo bhavo:* Be a light unto yourself. And those words were said to his chief disciple, Ananda, who had been with him for forty-two years, just like a shadow, non-stop, day out, day in. But he had not become enlightened. And many others who had come afterwards had become enlightened.

So he was crying, sitting by the side of Buddha, saying, "You are leaving us." Buddha declared, "I am going to die today. As the sun sets, I will withdraw my consciousness from my body and dissolve into the universal."

Ananda burst into tears. He said, "What will happen to me? I have been with you for forty-two years and I am yet unenlightened; and now you are going. And you are going forever, you are not going to return in any other body, so there is no question of meeting you again."

Buddha said, "That is the barrier. You think *I* can make you enlightened – that's why these forty-two years have gone by and you have not attained. Perhaps after my death, within twenty-four hours you may become enlightened. For these forty-two years there was a hope that *I* would do something. Nobody can do anything. Be a light unto yourself."

Those were his last words. As he died, Ananda did not move from the place, and within exactly twenty-four hours he became enlightened. He could have become enlightened any day. Those forty-two years he was hoping that as he was the chief disciple of Gautam Buddha, he need not do anything.

But the death of Buddha came as such a shock that his whole mind stopped. The other disciples were worried that he may go mad. He had loved Gautam Buddha so much, and he was an elder cousin-brother to Gautam Buddha. And he had followed him, serving him...he may go mad. And the way he was sitting – almost frozen, like a statue. They thought that it was intolerable for him to see Gautam Buddha dead.

But what had actually happened was, Ananda had not gone mad, Ananda had also died with Gautam Buddha. His mind stopped the moment Buddha stopped breathing.

In this nothingness, in this silence, he became aware of what Buddha had said as his last message. He saw his own inner flame, his own inner light. And after twenty-four hours, the first thing he did was, he laughed.

Somebody asked, "Why are you laughing?" He said, "I am laughing because I was waiting for Gautam Buddha to do something, and the thing I was waiting for had been always inside me. I could have turned inwards any moment and it was mine."

Anand Shoba, this is a blissful moment for you. Don't hold back. Be total in your dance, be total in your joy, be total in your blissfulness. It is the moment of awakening. It is your dawn.

Okay, Vimal?

Yes, Bhagwan.

Session 13

You Can't Hold On And Clap Too

*It is an existential reality
that if you drop all clinging,
your whole life will disappear
and you will find yourself a totally new life –
with new visions, new longings, new desires,
new light, new challenges, new stars calling you for the pilgrimage.*

March 3, 1987
Evening

Beloved Bhagwan,

These last days, I have come from discourse
shaking and quivering from inside out.
It comes after You have left.
Although my body trembles, it doesn't feel like fear...
or not any fear that I have known before.
The image that comes is of me hanging by my fingertips
to a window frame high in the sky, with nothing beneath it.
There is no house, just a window frame
and You are leaning out and dancing and singing madly.
It is so inviting, that I forget myself
and start clapping and singing, too.
After You have gone, my survival mechanism
comes running and trembling, trying to take over again.
Is this what is happening, beloved Bhagwan?

Devageet, a very ancient Sufi story.... A man has lost his way in the dark night, in a thick forest. He cannot see any sign anywhere that he is close to some village, some town; but he cannot stay either. It is so dark, and the fear of wild animals....

Trembling, he gropes his way along and falls into a ditch. Afraid, because in the darkness he cannot see how deep the ditch is, he clings to the roots of a tree.

The night becomes colder and colder, and he is shivering and trembling. His hands are becoming almost frozen with cold. And now the ultimate fear grips him, that there are not many more moments to his life. His hands are slipping from the root, he cannot keep them tight, he is almost paralyzed...and finally, it happens.

The root is lost, and the man falls. But the whole valley is filled with his laughter, because there was no ditch – just six inches below there was plain ground. And half of the night he unnecessarily struggled and tortured himself. He has not only found the plain ground – that was the road.

Devageet, you are in the same situation. You say, "It does not look like fear." It is not fear; it is death itself.

The image that comes is of you hanging by your fingertips to a window frame high in the sky, with nothing beneath it. There you are not right. In the darkness you cannot see that just beneath it is the way – only six inches you have to fall.

Only for six inches, you have to accept death.

But the image is correct...there is no house, just a window frame. That is absolutely true about me. I am just a window frame, and those who trust me are going to be in the same situation in which Devageet is.

I try my best to invite you to dance, and if you are mad enough you are going to start clapping, at least. And that is the moment when you forget that you cannot hold on to the window frame and clap too. The moment you start clapping, the window frame is lost; your hands have slipped from the root.

Those six inches seem to be a long journey, because it is sure death. You are falling, in your mind, into an abysmal depth. It is another matter that nobody dies. Just for six inches...how much time does it take? Perhaps a few seconds, or not even a few seconds, and the whole valley will be filled with laughter – *your* laughter.

You have found the way, just by *not* clinging to anything, even to a window frame which is hanging in the empty sky. Every temptation is there to hang onto it. Against that temptation I have to persuade you at least to clap. And soon you will know that you have passed through a death and reached to a new life, a new path. It is a resurrection.

The Christians have committed a great mistake by making the resurrection of Jesus a historical fact. It is not a historical fact. It is an existential reality that if you drop all clinging, your whole life will disappear and you will find yourself a totally new life – with new visions, new longings, new desires, new light, new challenges, new stars calling you for the pilgrimage.

That Sufi story was not written by a story writer. It is the experience of all those who have lived with a master, who have dropped everything and are just clinging to the master – his love, his trust. And now the whole art of the master is, somehow, to make you clap. Once you have lost the window you have found the door to the divine.

Gautam Buddha used to say, "When you burn a candle, first the flame burns the wax of the candle, but there comes a moment when all the wax has disappeared...the candle also disappears."

The master first helps you to be unattached to everything, and brings your total energy in a deep trust...very single-pointed, holding the hand of the master. Now that is your only protection, and for this protection you have dropped all other protections.

But you don't know that the master is going to drop you one day into an abysmal depth – which only appears abysmal. It is only six inches from the mind to your heart; that is the distance.

And once you have reached to your heart, you have found the way to your being.

Now, your ultimate realization is not far away.

Devageet, whatever is happening to you is beautiful. Allow it to happen, and help others also. Finally the clinging with the master has also to be dropped.

Gautam Buddha has said, "If I meet you on the way, cut off my head immediately." It is one of the most strange statements made by any master ever. What does he mean? He means that as you go deeper in your meditation, the whole world will be left behind, but the love that has become stronger and stronger every moment with the master will be the last barrier.

Between you and existence, the last barrier is going to be the master. And Buddha is absolutely right, "Don't think even for a single moment. If you meet me on the way, immediately cut off my head. Once I am removed from your way, you have found your home."

The master is a device himself. First to help you un-cling to other things – money, power, prestige; and then finally to help you with the final un-clinging, to the master himself. And you will be immensely grateful that the master did not block the way.

This is the only criterion whether the master is real, authentic – or phony. The phony master will try to make you go on clinging to him. Your clinging to the master gives him his ego nourishment.

Only the authentic master can help you be free of him.

To make you free from the world is very easy, but to make you free from the master himself.... And he has to do it himself; he has to manage in some way that you start clapping and fall from the window frame. The fear will last for only a few seconds, and suddenly you are on a new ground, in a fresh consciousness, in a more profound understanding, in a blissful realization of your eternity. All fear disappears because all death disappears.

Fear is the shadow of death, and unless you know that you are deathless you cannot be free of fear. And unless you are free from fear you will not know what freedom is. All these things are interconnected.

Devageet, whatever is happening is exactly what should happen.

Beloved Bhagwan,

Most of the time I live on the surface,
my ego is dominant and I think the whole time.
Then once in a while, when I see You in the morning discourse,
or when I feel close to You, I feel great love
and my heart opens, and I get a taste of what is possible.
Beloved Master, please help me to change myself.

Anurag Sudeha, you are saying, "Most of the time I live on the surface." That is the reality of the whole of humanity, so you should not feel sad about it. It is where humanity is stuck – on the surface.

There are depths beyond depths, but the fear of the unknown, the fear of losing the known and entering into unknown dark waters prevents people. They start making their whole life superficial. They love superficially, they live superficially.

There are at least six thousand holes in your lungs, but you breathe by only two thousand holes. Four thousand holes, which are deeper, never come into contact with fresh air, with oxygen, with life. They remain filled with stale carbon dioxide. Not only metaphorically, but physiologically too, you breathe very superficially. Perhaps there, too, is some deep-rooted fear.

Only in Japan have they worked to find out, for centuries...and that is their speciality, their uniqueness, their contribution to the world. Just as India has been trying to find out the center of your life, Japan has been trying to find out the center of your death.

Both have discovered that just below the navel, two inches below the navel...the Japanese call the center of death *hara*. That is why in Japanese suicide is called *hara-kiri*. Hara-kiri is the least painful way of committing suicide, because you are directly forcing the dagger into the very center of death. It takes only a split second. Everything else is far away from the death center.

Perhaps man is afraid of taking deep breaths because if you take deep breaths you will not be breathing in the chest; on the contrary, your belly will start rising up and down where the death center is.

If you have observed Indian statues of Gautam Buddha you will see a very athletic body. The belly is almost missing, the chest is big – just like a lion whose belly is small and chest is big. That was the conception of the athletic body. But if you see the Japanese statues of Buddha, you will be suprised that he has such a big belly. What happened? Why did Japan create...Gautam Buddha was not a Japanese, why did they create the statues with big bellies? – because Japan has an understanding which India has never bothered to discover: one has to breathe from the belly.

In all other kinds of gymnastics developed all over the world, you are taught that you should pull the belly in and force your chest forwards; fill your chest with as much air as you can, but pull your belly in. Aesthetically it looks beautiful. The big belly does not look very beautiful.

But the question before the Japanese was totally different. It is not a question of beauty; the question is that if you breathe deeply, so deeply that the belly comes up and down, your chest will relax. Your belly is bound to become bigger, but a strange phenomenon happens as you start breathing from the belly – you feel tremendous relaxation. It is a kind of meditation. You are so close to death, and just as a dead body relaxes, you start relaxing. And the closer you are to death, the farther away you are from the mind. Mind stops thinking.

So in Japan the first exercise for meditators is breathing from the belly, which goes against all gymnastic rules, but it has a tremendous spiritual value. Your mind relaxes, your body relaxes, and oxygen reaches to all the holes of your lungs, forcing out dead carbon dioxide. It brings a tremendous release of liveliness, playfulness, laughter. Whenever you laugh deeply it is called "belly laughter."

Unless your belly also laughs with you, your laughter is superficial. It is a Jimmy Carter smile – just an exercise of the lips. It is possible without any difficulty. You can stretch your lips ear to ear. That's what poor Jimmy Carter was doing, and the whole day. I have heard that his wife used to close his mouth at night, because the whole day remaining in the same pose is bound to create a static situation, and the lips of Jimmy Carter must have lost elasticity.

I have heard the story – I don't know whether it is true or not, because I don't have any evidence for it, but it is beautiful – that one day his wife forgot to close his mouth and he went on smiling, and a mouse jumped into his mouth. The wife just saw the tail of the mouse going in; the whole mouse had already gone in. She phoned the doctor, not knowing what to do. And he was still smiling!

The doctor had never come across such a case. He said, "There is no precedent, and I have never come across, in any medical book, any such case. But just try one thing while I am reaching there – because it is snowing and it will take almost half an hour to reach to your house – you just hang above his mouth a piece of cheese. Perhaps the mouse may come back, smelling the cheese."

So she ran into her kitchen and brought a piece of cheese from the fridge. But by the time she came back, what she saw almost gave her a nervous breakdown. She saw a cat going inside, because the cat was in search of the mouse! She phoned the doctor again: "The situation has changed."

But the wife of the doctor said, "The doctor has left, he must be on his way. And this case is even more unprecedented. I don't know anything; I cannot even suggest anything. This is just my opinion, because I am not a doctor, but try to find a mouse. Instead of cheese, now a mouse is needed. Hang it over his face; perhaps the cat may come out."

By the time the doctor reached there, Jimmy Carter's wife was hanging a mouse over his face. The doctor said, "I had told you to hang a piece of *cheese.* Are you mad or something?"

She said, "But the whole situation has changed. By the time I had brought the cheese, I saw a cat was going in, and this was your wife's suggestion."

He said, "My God, a cat is also in? Then you are doing right!"

People are smiling without any meaning in it; it is superficial. People are saying things to others which they don't mean, and they have never thought...that's why they are saying these things.

One of my professors was so talkative that he even used to talk in his sleep. His wife complained to me, "He loves you so much, perhaps you can tell him that, at least in the night, stop lecturing the class. But he goes on talking, and does not allow anybody in the house to sleep silently."

And he had a very loud voice – he was known as "the loudspeaker." He never used one. Even in addressing five thousand people, there was no need for any loudspeaker.

The wife said, "Not only we cannot sleep, even the neighbors...."

And the whole day...in the class he was talking, in the common room he was talking, in the cafeteria he was talking. I told him, "Have you ever thought about how much energy, how much fuel you are burning in talking so much? And nobody wants to listen to it. In fact they feel tortured--people want to escape from you. I have seen people turning into other roads, seeing that you are approaching. Nobody comes to see you in your house; and if you go to somebody else's house, the wife says that her husband is out – and he is in. Everybody is avoiding you, and you are not gaining anything out of it."

He thought for a moment, and he said, "You are right. Once in a while I also wonder why I go on talking."

I said, "You try this just for one day, and you will find so much joy – talk telegraphically. Only use the absolutely necessary words, just like when you give a telegram. Then you don't go on writing like a letter; you use the absolutely essential words – ten words at the most. And your telegram is more effective than your long letters, because in those ten words you have condensed your whole message. The impact is going to be deeper. "So," I said, "you try it."

"But," he said, "How to stop...I go on forgetting. The moment I see somebody, I forget."

So I gave him a round marble stone, a small ball, and told him, "Keep it in your mouth, so you cannot speak."

He said, "You seem to be very dangerous. Even at times when it is necessary to speak, first I will have to take out this ball. Anybody will laugh – 'Why were you keeping this ball in your mouth?'"

I said, "There is no hurry, your house is not

going to be on fire. It is not that you will have to face an emergency. You try it."

I persuaded him – he tried it just for one hour. The whole university was amazed – what has happened? People were saying, "Good morning," and he was simply waving his hand. He could not say even, "Good morning." And everybody was worried about this man – silent for one hour completely, sitting in his chair. But he enjoyed it so much that when I asked for my ball back he said, "I cannot give it."

I said, "What are you going to do with it?"

He said, "I am going to keep it in my mouth even in the night, to give a surprise to my neighbors, to my family, to my children, to everybody – because they will all be waiting for my speech in the night, and I will be sound asleep."

And he said to me, "This is strange. Because I am not speaking, fewer thoughts are coming to my mind; I'm feeling so calm and quiet. You have invented a great thing, this marble ball." He told me, "You should market it. If everybody carries it, there will be so much silence in the world."

I said, "You carry it for a few days, and then try without it, because this should not become an addiction."

After ten days he tried, and was successful. He came to me in the middle of the night to tell me, "The whole day today I have not used your ball. And I have come to give it back to you with great thankfulness, because these ten days I have known for the first time so many things – the silence of the night, the songs of the birds, and an inner tranquility. And I wonder how this can happen only by this marble stone. It has done magic."

I said, "It is not magic or anything. You had become accustomed to talking. Without talking you felt as if you were missing something."

People, when they are nervous, immediately start searching in their pocket for the cigarettes. It is not different from my marble ball. The marble ball is cheaper, more aesthetic, less harmful. But smoking cigarettes is just a way to continue using your mouth, your lips. There are people who have discovered chewing gum – such a nonsense activity. But these are substitutes for talking.

To avoid talking, it is better to chew gum, because at least you are not interfering with somebody else's life – it is your teeth, you can chew as much gum as you want. But just a little understanding, and neither the cigarettes nor the chewing gum are needed.

A little taste of silence, and you will enjoy all those moments when you are not needed to talk, when you can sit silently. And remember one fundamental law of existence, that if you can deepen your experience in any one dimension, you become capable of deepening your experience in other dimensions to the same extent.

For example, if you can deepen your silence, you can deepen your love without any difficulty, because it is the same process. You can deepen your laughter, you can deepen your vitality. Your life can become not just a superficial, formal thing, but something that contains depths beyond depths. Just to sit by the side of a man who has looked deeply, you will find yourself moving into deeper waters.

Your observation, Sudeha, is right, that most of the time you live on the surface. Most of the people do the same. You say, "My ego is dominant and I think the whole time." Thoughts are basic constituents of the ego. The more thoughts you have, the stronger is your ego. That's why when a meditator comes to a point where mind stops completely, his ego also disappears.

Ego is nothing but the collective name of your thoughts. It is not a separate entity, it is just the collective name. All your thoughts are just the bricks...out of those bricks, the house of the ego is made.

As you stop your thoughts and start moving into a space of no-mind, of non-thinking, you will not find the ego there. You will be there, but there will not be any sense of "I-ness," only a pure "is-ness." And it is a great achievement.

It is a tremendously valuable achievement to lose your I, and just to feel a simple existence, a pure "is-ness." It is the beginning of experiencing God. As your "is-ness" becomes more and more crystallized, you become aware that you are not and God is; you are not, and the universal consciousness is.

And because you are not, there is no question of your death – you have never been, in the first place, so how can you die? And this "is-ness" that you are feeling now, in the silence of no-thought, has always been here. You have been part of it from eternity, and you will remain part of it until eternity. This is the experience of the immortal soul.

The seers of the *Upanishad* have the best expression for it. They call man, *amritasya putrah:* sons and daughters of immortality. You are not born out of a mother's womb; you are not born out of a father, a mother; they have been just a passage for the immortality to take shape. They have given you your blood, your bones, but they have not given you your life. Your life has always been here.

Sudeha, while your ego remains dominant you will remain on the surface. If you want to know the deeper realities and mysteries, then you have to watch your thoughts. Just by watching, they start coming less and less to you. And a day comes when you find you are there without any thoughts. That is the greatest day of your life. To be more accurate, that is the birthday of your being. From that day, you start living on deeper levels, where life has its roots.

And it is possible, because you feel it when you come close to me. You say, "I feel great love and my heart opens, and I get a taste of what is possible." It is my invitation to you. If you can feel the opening of the heart, then you are not a difficult problem. If you can feel love, and even the awareness that this is the taste of what is possible, then you have almost reached to the door of the temple.

Nobody is preventing you; and the doors are always open. Don't ask me, "Beloved Master, please help me to change myself." There is no need to ask me. You are moving in the right direction, just a little more courage....

Chidananda has sent me a small joke.

How many psychoanalysts does it take to change a light bulb? Only one, but it all depends on how much the light bulb wants to change. In fact, no psychoanalyst is needed to change a light bulb. Anybody can change it, just the light bulb has to be ready. If the light bulb resists change then it is very difficult; if it runs around and jumps and escapes....

You are asking me to change you, and what do you think I am doing? Do you think that first I take your permission? In fact, before you asked me to change you, I had already finished my work. That's why you are having the taste, that's why you are feeling the opening of your heart.

This is invisible surgery, so you don't see it clearly. It is not something objective, it is something subjective that I am doing every day, twenty-four hours. And it is not work as far as I am concerned; I have just to continue radiating my love towards you, wherever you are, and the revolution in your being is going to happen. It has already happened, just it will take a little time for you to recognize it. But the first recognition has come to you.

Just go on feeling more and more close to me. And when your heart opens, don't hold back; let it open totally. And when you feel the taste, don't be afraid, because that taste is going to transform you totally. It is going to bring a new man in your place.

Be ready. Things have started moving inside you – you don't have a stone heart. And I am absolutely certain that it won't take a long, long time for you to recognize that your ego has evaporated, and your thoughts have fallen like dry leaves.

Just this evening, I saw that dry leaves are falling from the trees like rain. In the same way, thoughts fall. You cannot see them, but I can see them. When you are clapping and dancing and swaying, I can see that thoughts are falling all around you.

There are a few idiots sometimes who come here. They are observers, and I know that they are idiots because when your rotten thoughts are falling they are collecting them. When you will be going light with wings, light, ready to fly, they will be loaded with all your rubbish and crap to their houses, feeling themselves very learned.

Avoid...whenever somebody is going really mad in clapping, keep alert that he does not drop his thoughts on you!

I heard about one psychoanalyst.... A man was brought to him. The man had got an insane idea that very slimy creatures, small creatures, were crawling all over his body; and he was throwing them away all the time, the whole day.

His family became worried. His business was going bankrupt because people thought, "This man is absolutely mad and unbelieveable. You cannot trust him." And he was not interested in anything. Customers were standing there, and he was throwing his...with such disgust on his face.

The psychoanalyst said, "Don't be worried," to the man's family. He said, "You go, leave him with me. He will need a few sessions." The psychoanalyst tried to explain to him that the creatures were just imagination, hallucination, but he was not listening; he was throwing them off all the time, because they were crawling all over his body. This was not a time to understand psychology and things like that, and he was coming every day. The seventh day, he said, "Because I am so much involved with these slimy creatures, I cannot even hear you, exactly what you are saying, so can I pull my chair close to you?"

The psychoanalyst stood up, and he said, "Wait! Don't put those slimy creatures on me, because for two nights I have not slept – the whole night they are crawling on me. And I pray to you that you find some other psychoanalyst, I am finished. You finish somebody else! And such dirty, slimy creatures...from where did you get them? Being seven days with you has been enough. Now I have to first get rid of my own creatures, then I will see you. Don't come here again!"

I can see when, for example, Devageet is throwing off his slimy creatures, one should be alert – you can get them. He is becoming a man from a gorilla; you may become a gorilla from a man! It is only a question of thoughts – just the idea has to get in you, that you are a gorilla. So beware of Devageet. He has finished, he has come out of his gorillahood, but that gorillahood is here. Somebody may get into it.

There are all kinds of idiots – just out of curiosity to see what is in it.... Going in is easy, getting out is very difficult.

Beloved Bhagwan,

When You were talking about suchness the other day,
it felt so good. It felt like nourishing me from the inside,
and making me face the reality of having to leave
this incredible oasis for a little while.
But then, being happy to have my mind under control,
my body freaked out totally, and now I feel like
a stupid little girl again, lying in bed with a big cold,
unable to dance with You in discourse, just before leaving.
Suchness was the key to calm down my mind.
Do You have another key for me to calm down my body, too?
Why does my body freak out so easily whenever things
get a little much? How can I break this old pattern?

Nandan, the golden key of suchness is no ordinary key; it is a master key. It can work for the mind, it can work for the heart, it can work for the body. Just the body will take a little longer.

When you heard me talking about suchness, first your heart calmed down, felt the cool breeze of suchness, a deep acceptance of existence. But as the heart calms down, it starts changing your mind. The mind is going to be number two. It will take a little longer time than the heart.

But the same key will work, and your mind will also cool down. The body will be the third, because this is the position: your being is your center, and closest to your being is the heart; then is the circle of the mind, and then is the outer circle of the body. The body is the farthest from your being, so things reach there a little late.

So lying down in your bed, allow the body also to feel suchness, that if it is suffering from a cold it is okay. A cold is not a disease but a cleansing.

The inner mechanism of your body has a layer of mucus. It is a kind of lubricant to make your body function more easily, more smoothly. And just as in any mechanism you need a change of the lubricant once in a while – at least once a year, or twice a year. The mucus which has become old and is not as efficient as it used to be has to be thrown out, and the body grows new mucus.

A cold is not a disease, that's why there is no medicine for colds. If it was a disease, a medicine would be possible – hence, the saying, "If you don't take the medicine your cold will last for seven days, and if you take the medicine then your cold will last for one week."

Medicine or no medicine, it is not a disease, it is a cleansing. So accept it, and even when there is a certain sickness in the body, don't resist it. Use medicine, but the whole attitude, the whole psychology will be different.

Medicine can be used with two different, almost diametrically opposite viewpoints. One is to destroy the disease; that is a negative attitude.

That is the attitude almost everybody lives with.

One who understands suchness will not take that attitude. His attitude will be that perhaps this illness is needed at this time. You don't reject it. You are taking medicine only to help your body to accept the disease, to give your body enough strength so that you can live with the disease in suchness. You are not taking medicine against the disease; you are taking medicine to help your vitality, your health, to be strong enough so that you can accept this disease as a friend, and not create any antagonism.

And you will be surprised that this idea of suchness helps you in the turmoils of your heart, emotions, feelings, in the confusions of your mind, and in the sicknesses of your body.

You are worried because you have to leave. But I have told you: always look through the eyes of suchness, that you are leaving to come back. And distance always creates greater longing, more love. So when you come next time, you will be coming dancing, more joyfully.

Chidananda has sent another joke:

Do you know which are the three categories of infertile people? The first are the surgeons, because they only work in their rubber gloves. The second are the lawyers, because they only work with their tongues, and the third are the Italian communists, who are coming and coming, but they never come.

But, Nandan, you are neither Italian nor communist – you are going to come! So just go; go in order to come back as soon as possible. Go dancingly! We should make everything a celebration. Going also should be a celebration, because it will give you a chance to come back with more joy, with more bliss, with more longing of the heart.

Distance never destroys love, it always enriches it.

Okay, Vimal?

Yes, Bhagwan.

Session 14

Easy Is Right

*Going against the stream is difficult,
but going with the stream is not difficult.
So either choose the easiest things in life, the most natural things in life,
and you will be right;
or if you want to begin the other way,
remember the criterion that the right has to
produce easiness in you, relaxedness in you.*

March 4, 1987
Morning

Beloved Bhagwan,

I love this poem by Chuang Tzu:
"Easy is right. Begin right and you are easy.
Continue easy, and you are right.
The right way to go easy is to forget the right way
and forget that the going is easy." Would You like to comment on it?

Anand Shanti, Chuang Tzu is very rare – in a way the most unique mystic in the whole history of man. His uniqueness is that he talks in absurdities. All his poems and stories are just absurd. And his reason to choose absurdity as his expression is very significant: the mind has to be silenced. With anything rational, it cannot stop; it goes on and on. Anything logical and the mind finds nourishment through it. It is only the absurd that suddenly shocks the mind – it is beyond mind's grasp.

His stories, his poems and his other statements are so absurd that either people simply left him, thinking that he is mad.... Those who were courageous enough to remain with him found that no other meditation is needed. Just listening to his absurd statements, the mind stops functioning. And that is the meaning of meditation.

Meditation is not of the mind.

Most of the Western translations of treatises from the East on meditation have fallen in the same track. They have used the word meditation as if it is concentration. And in fact the English word *meditation* seems to be synonymous with concentration.

English has three words – concentration, contemplation, meditation. None of them comes even close to the Eastern word *dhyana*, that became in China *ch'an* and in Japan *zen*. The root is the Sanskrit word *dhyana*, and it will be very good for you to understand the distinction. In concentration your mind is focused, narrowed only on one object.

A famous story about one of the great master archers.... Arjuna says that his teacher, Dronacharya, was giving the final examination of his disciples. He had put a dead bird far away on a tree as a target.

He asked one of his disciples, Duryodhana, "What are you seeing?" Duryodhana said, "Everything! The trees, the sun rising behind them, the bird that you have put as a target. I am seeing everything."

Dronacharya asked another disciple; he said, "I see only the bird." He is more concentrated. Duryodhana has his mind spread all over the place. The second disciple says he is seeing only the bird. But the master is not satisfied.

He asks Arjuna, "What are you seeing?" Arjuna says, "Only the eye of the bird that you have told us is going to be the target. I don't see anything else." His concentration has come even more narrow. And for an archer, this kind of concentration is needed. But meditation is not archery.

Contemplation is not being concentrated on a single object, but thinking about the same object from every possible aspect. For example, somebody is contemplating about love – what does it mean? He remains confined to a certain line of thinking, not to a certain object, but to a certain subject.

And "meditation", in all the languages of the world except the Indian, Chinese and Japanese, also gives the feeling.... The archer is concentrated, but he is not concerned with the eye, the bull's-eye. His concern is how to shoot the arrow so that it reaches the eye; his concern is not to miss the target.

Meditation, as far as Western languages are concerned, is going deeply into one object – thinking, in its deeper implications. Contemplation was linear; you were thinking about a subject from all possible aspects, but the mind was moving. In meditation the mind is not moving. It is similar to concentration without any arrows. Your thoughts are the arrows, but they are hitting the same subject deeper and deeper and deeper – not in a line, not horizontal but vertical.

There is no word in Western languages which can translate the word *dhyana* absolutely and adequately. "Meditation" has been chosen because there is no other word, but it is a wrong choice. Out of the three words, it is the best, but *dhyana*, *ch'an* or *zen* have a totally different meaning: mind has stopped.

In concentration mind has narrowed, in contemplation it is flowing in a line on a particular subject, in meditation it is concentrated, and instead of arrows it is throwing thoughts deeper and deeper into the same object. But all three processes belong to the mind.

Dhyana means the mind has been put aside. There is no concentration, there is no contemplation, there is no meditation. It is a state of no-mind; it is absolute silence, not even a small stirring of any thought.

In the East, so many devices have been tried...how to stop the mind chattering continuously, how to bypass it, how to stop it, how to go beyond it. Chuang Tzu has his own, unique contribution. He talks to his disciples in absurdities, and the mind cannot tackle them. The mind needs something reasonable, rational, logical; that is its territory. The absurd is beyond it.

I have told you the famous story about Chuang Tzu: One morning he woke up with tears in his eyes, so sad and so depressed. His disciples had never seen him sad or depressed or with tears; he is an enlightened master...what has happened? They all rushed and enquired, "Can we be of some help?" Chuang Tzu said, "I don't think so." They said, "Still, we want to know what is the problem that is torturing you so much. You are beyond problems!"

Chuang Tzu said, "I used to be, but last night I saw a dream and it has disturbed my whole attainment, achievement, self-realization, enlightenment – everything has gone down the drain."

They said, "Just a dream?" He said, "It was not just a dream, it has shattered me into pieces." They said, "Still, please tell us the dream!"

The dream was that Chuang Tzu saw that he had become a butterfly. All the disciples laughed. They said, "Unnecessarily being depressed and crying and tears and thinking that your enlightenment and self-realization have all gone down the drain.... It is an ordinary dream, nothing to be worried about it. In dreams people see themselves becoming many things, but a dream is a dream."

Chuang Tzu said, "I understand that a dream *is* a dream. The problem is that I am worried, who am I? If Chuang Tzu in his sleep can dream that he has become a butterfly, a butterfly in her dream can see she has become Chuang Tzu. And now I am puzzled. Who am I? – a Chuang Tzu or a butterfly?

"If Chuang Tzu is capable of dreaming himself to be a butterfly, you cannot cancel the possibility of a butterfly taking a nap on the rose bushes and dreaming that she has become Chuang Tzu. Who can prevent her? And the question is, have I awakened, or is the butterfly dreaming that she is Chuang Tzu? You tell me who I am! – the butterfly or Chuang Tzu."

They were all at a loss...what to say? This man goes on finding such absurd things. Millions of people for millions of years have been dreaming, but nobody has raised this question. You have been dreaming, but have you ever raised this question? – that when you wake up perhaps it is the beginning of a new dream.

What makes you so certain that you are not dreaming? – in the dream you were so certain that you are a butterfly, and now you are so certain that you are Chuang Tzu. There is no difference in certainty. In fact when you are awake the possibility of suspicion is there, you can doubt; but when you are dreaming, there is even no doubt at all, no suspicion, no question mark – you are simply a butterfly.

He said, "Sit down and meditate and find out the answer – who am I?" They looked at each other – how to meditate upon it, how to think about it? It is unthinkable, it is beyond the mind. His closest disciple, Lieh Tzu, had gone out to the nearest village. He returned he saw the whole scene: Chuang Tzu in tears sitting on his bed, all the disciples with closed eyes, their minds completely stuck.

What can the mind say about it? The question is absurd. He asked one of the disciples who was near the door, "What is the matter? It seems to be really serious! I have never seen such seriousness here. And why is our master crying? Has somebody died or something?"

The disciple said, "He has created a new absurdity. Nobody has died and nothing has happened; he is torturing us and nothing else! Now we have to meditate upon it." And he told him the problem. Lieh Tzu said, "Don't be worried. You meditate; I am coming."

He went out, brought a bucket full of ice-cold water and poured it on Chuang Tzu. And Chuang Tzu said laughingly, "If you had been here before you would have saved all these idiots! They are looking so serious, as if they are really thinking. And you would have saved my tears and my misery. Just wait; don't pour the water, it is too cold."

Lieh Tzu said, "Has your problem been solved or not?" Chuang Tzu said, "It is solved – you are my successor!"

It is not a question to be solved by the mind. The mind is absolutely impotent.

Chuang Tzu has hundreds of stories and he must have had a very strange kind of genius – even to invent those stories is not easy – but his teaching was very simple. And those who remained with him, all became enlightened. That is a rare phenomenon. He defeated even his own master Lao Tzu – a few people became enlightened, but most of Lao Tzu's disciples remained in their old ignorance. He defeated Gautam Buddha – a few of his disciples became enlightened, but that was a very small proportion, because he had thousands of disciples and not more than a dozen became enlightened.

Chuang Tzu has a rare position in the history of mystics. All his disciples became enlightened. He would not leave you unless you had become enlightened. He was so much after you that finally people decided that it was better to become enlightened. Every day new torture...the only way to save yourself is to become enlightened. But his method was very simple, and this poem, Anand Shanti, tells in a very aphoristic way his whole approach.

Easy is right. Nobody has dared to say it ever. On the contrary, people make the right as difficult as possible. To you, who have all been conditioned by different traditions, the wrong is easy, and the right is arduous. It needs training, it needs discipline, it needs repression, it needs renouncing the world, it needs renouncing the pleasures....

Lies are easy, truth is difficult – that is the common conditioning of humanity. But Chuang Tzu is certainly a man of tremendous insight. He says, *Easy is right.* Then why have people been making right difficult? All your saints have been making right very difficult. There is a psychology behind it: only the difficult is attractive to your ego. The more difficult is the task, the more the ego feels challenged.

Climbing Everest was difficult; hundreds of people had died before Edmund Hillary reached the top alive. For the whole century groups upon groups of mountaineers had been coming, and when Edmund Hillary reached, there was nothing to be found! Just at the very peak there is not even space enough...only one person can stand there, on the highest point. He was asked, "What prompted you? Knowing perfectly well that hundreds of mountaineers have lost their life during one hundred years, and not even their bodies have been found...why did you try this dangerous project?"

He said, "I *had* to try. It was hurting my ego. I am a mountaineer, I love climbing mountains, and it was humiliating that there is Everest and nobody has been able to reach there. It is not a question of finding anything, but I feel so immensely happy."

What is this happiness? You have not found anything! The happiness is that your ego has become more crystallized. You are the first man in the whole history who has reached Everest; now nobody can take your place. Anybody who will reach there will be second, third...but you have made a mark on the history; you are the first. You have not found anything, but you have found a deep nourishment for your ego. Perhaps Edmund Hillary himself is not aware of it.

All the religions are making the right difficult, because the difficult is attractive – attractive to the ego. But the ego is not the truth; The ego is not right. Do you see the dilemma? The ego is attracted only towards the difficult. If you want people to become saints you have to make your right, your truth, your discipline very difficult. The more difficult it is, the more egoists will be attracted, almost magnetically pulled.

But the ego is not right. It is the worst thing that can happen to a man. And it cannot deliver to you the right, the truth; it can only make your ego stronger. Chuang Tzu is saying in a simple statement the most pregnant statement: *Easy is right*. Because for the easy, ego has no attraction.

If you are going towards the easy, the ego starts dying. And when there is no ego left, you have arrived to your reality – the right, the truth. And truth and right have to be natural. Easy means natural; you can find them without any effort. Easy is right means natural is right, effortlessness is right, egolessness is right.

Begin right and you are easy, contiue easy and you are right. They are just two sides of the same coin. If, beginning to live a right life, you find it difficult, then remember, it is not right. If, living the right, your life becomes more and more easy, more and more a let-go, flowing with the stream....

Going against the stream is difficult, but going with the stream is not difficult. So either choose the easiest things in life, the most natural things in life, and you will be right; or if you want to begin the other way, remember the criterion that the right has to produce easiness in you, relaxedness in you.

Continue easy and you are right. Never forget for a moment that the difficult is the food for the ego, and the ego is the barrier that makes you blind to see, makes you deaf to hear, makes your heart hard to open, makes it impossible for you to love, to dance, to sing.

Continue easy. Your whole life should be an easy phenomenon. Then you will not be creating the ego. You will be a natural being, just ordinary. And to Chuang Tzu, and to me also, the ordinary is the most extraordinary. The people who are trying to be extraordinary have missed the goal. Just be ordinary, just be nobody.

But all your conditionings are so corrupting; they corrupt you. They say; to be easy is to be lazy, to be ordinary is humiliating. If you don't try for power, for prestige, for respectability, then your life is meaningless – that has been forced into your mind.

Chuang Tzu in these simple statements is taking away all your conditionings.

Continue easy and you are right. Never for a moment get attracted towards the difficult. It will make you somebody – a prime minister, a president – but it will not make you divine. Easy is divine.

I have heard about an American super-rich man. He had all the things the world can offer and he had been striving all his life to be on the top; now he had reached and was feeling stupid inside because there was nothing on the top. If Edmund Hillary was intelligent enough, he must have felt stupid standing on Everest...for what have you been trying? The man who walked on the moon must have looked very embarrassed, although there was nobody to see him.

This man had come to the top as far as money is concerned, and as far as money can purchase, he had purchased everything. And now he was looking stupid. What is the point of it all? Inside he is hollow. He has no time to give to his inner growth, no time even to be acquainted with himself.

He dropped all his riches and rushed towards the East to find the truth, because three-fourths of his life was almost gone – just the tail has remained, the elephant has passed. But if something could be possible there were a few days left. He rushed fast. He went from one master to another master, but nobody could satisfy him, because whatever they were saying was again another trip of the ego. And he was well acquainted with that trip.

It does not matter whether you are accumulating money or whether you are accumulating virtue, whether you are becoming respectable here or you are becoming respectable hereafter – it does not matter, it is the same game. Whether you are becoming a world-famous celebrity or a world-worshiped saint, there is no difference; both are ego numbers.

And they were all telling him difficult disciplines and difficult, arduous ways of finding the truth; they were all saying, "It may not be possible in this life, but start anyhow. In the next life maybe…. The journey is long, the goal is a faraway star."

But now nobody could deceive him. He had found that just becoming somebody special is an exercise in stupidity. Finally he heard about a saint who lived in the Himalayas. And people said, "If you are not satisfied with him, you will never be satisfied with anybody. Then forget the whole thing."

So tired and tattered, walking for miles, finally he found the old man. He was very happy seeing the old man, but was shocked. Before he could say anything, the old man said, "Are you an American?"

He said, "Yes, I am."

The old man said, "Very good. Have you got any American cigarettes with you?"

He said, "My God, where have I come! I have come to seek truth, to find the right…." He pulled out cigarettes and the old man started smoking.

The American said, "You have not even asked me for what I have come here, tired, hungry…."

He said, "That does not matter."

The American said, "I have come to find the truth!"

The old man said, "Truth? You do one thing, you go back. And next time when you come, bring a lot of American cigarettes, because here in this place it is very difficult to find cigarettes. And I am an easy-going man, I don't make any effort; people come on their own. But I like the best cigarettes. Here Indians come with beedies…."

"But," the man asked, "what about my search?"

The old man said, "Your search? This is the discipline for you: go back, get as many cigarettes as you can get and come back and remain here with me."

He asked, "Any discipline?"

The old man said, "I am an ordinary old man – no discipline, no religion, no philosophy – I only like to smoke cigarettes. You come here, and slowly, slowly you will also become just as ordinary as I am. And I tell you, to be ordinary, with no pretensions, is the right."

And as the man was going back, puzzled, the old man said, "Listen, at least leave your wristwatch here, because I don't have any wristwatch so I don't know the time, what time…. And anyway you are coming back, so you can bring another wristwatch." Chuang Tzu would have liked this old man.

Easy is right. Begin right and you are easy. That has to be the criterion. If you feel uneasiness, tension, then what you have started cannot be right.

Continue easy and you are right.

And the last part is something never to be forgotten. *The right way to go easy is to forget the right way* – because even to remember it is an uneasiness. *The right way to go easy is to forget the right way and forget that the going is easy.* What is the need of remembering these things?

Relax to such a point…be as natural as the trees and the birds. You will not find in the birds that somebody is a saint and somebody is a sinner; you will not find in the trees that somebody is virtuous and somebody is full of vices. Everything is easy – so easy that you need not remember it.

I agree with Chuang Tzu with absolute,

unconditional, categorical attunement. I would have loved to meet Chuang Tzu. If I were given the opportunity to meet one of the mystics of the whole human history, Chuang Tzu would be my choice. I have named this place Chuang Tzu Auditorium.

He was very much misunderstood. It is obvious...because he was destroying all the priests, all the popes, all the *imams,* all the *shankaracharyas*; he was destroying the so-called great commandments for being right, and destroying them so easily. He was one of the most natural men the world has seen. He has not given any discipline, he has not given any doctrine, he has not given any catechism. He has simply explained one thing: that if you can be natural and ordinary, just like the birds and the trees, you will blossom, you will have your wings open in the vast sky.

You don't have to be saints. Saints are very tense – more tense than sinners. I have known both. and if there is a choice I will choose the sinners as a company rather than the saints. Saints are the worst company, because their eyes are full of judgment about everything: You should do this and you should not do that. And they start dominating you, condemning you, humiliating you, insulting you, because what they are doing is right and what you are doing is not the right thing. They have poisoned your nature so badly that if real criminals have to be found they will be found in your saints, not in your sinners. Your sinners have not done much harm to anybody.

I have been visiting jails, meeting the criminals, and I was surprised that they are the most innocent people. And perhaps because they are the most innocent they have been caught. The cunning ones are doing far greater crimes, but they are not caught. Every law has loopholes. The cunning ones find the loopholes first; the innocent ones get caught, because they don't have that cunningness.

It is really strange that when America forced me into jail without any cause.... And since they had no cause, and no reason to keep me in jail, they tried, as long as they could manage, to keep me in jail before the trial began, because once the trial began they didn't have any evidence for anything.

But pre-trial they kept me for twelve days. It was a good experience to know...I had known criminals, prisoners, but only as a visitor – and this was a totally different experience, to be one amongst them. And it is surprising that I was taken to five jails just to harass me – for twelve days they went on changing jails – but to me it was a good experience.

All the inmates of the jails received me, welcomed me. Behind their bars they were waving their hands and shouting, "Bhagwan, don't be worried, truth is always victorious." And they were showing me the sign of victory from every cell, whenever I would enter a jail or I would get out of a jail.

They would send me small notes: "We love you. We don't know you, but we have seen you on the television. We have heard you and we know you are innocent." Looking into their eyes and looking into the eyes of the law enforcement authorities, one could see the difference...who are the real criminals? The jailers, the marshals, the judges, they were the real criminals. You could see it in their eyes, in their faces.

To torture me they refused to supply vegetarian food because no vegetarian has ever been in their jails – "So we don't have any arrangement." And when the inmates heard it, they started bringing fruits, nuts, milk, which was given to them, and they would say, "Bhagwan, you take it. We can eat non-vegetarian food and it hurts us that you are hungry, that you are starving and we cannot do anything." My cell was full of fruits. And I used to tell them, "I cannot eat so many fruits, I cannot drink so much milk."

But they would say, "Don't take this opportunity from us. You are not going to be here for long. Tomorrow they will move you again."

And they would bring cuttings of my photographs from newspapers to be signed in their name, because this will be their memory – "We have lived with you, even if it was only for one day or two days."

It is a very strange world in which we are living. Here criminals are rulers, here criminals are politicians, here criminals become presidents, vice presidents, prime ministers, because except the criminal, who wants power? An authentic human being wants peace, wants love, wants to be left alone, wants freedom to be himself. The very idea of dominating others is criminal.

Chuang Tzu is right that if you feel any tension, then remember, whatever you are doing is not right. And he is the only man who has given such a beautiful criterion, *Easy is right. Begin right and you are easy. Continue easy and you are right. The right way to go easy is to forget the right way and forget that the going is easy.*

Relax into nobodiness.

And this is also my message to my sannyasins: be natural. You don't have to be Christians, you don't have to be Hindus, you don't have to be Mohammedans – these are all ways of creating difficulties – you have to be just natural like trees and birds and animals.

Become part of this relaxed universe – so relaxed that you forget all about easiness and you forget all about rightness. To me, this is enlightenment.

Beloved Bhagwan,

What is culture? Is it an inner phenomenon?
Is it something like an Indian culture and a Western culture?
Could You please comment?

Narendra, culture to me is the grace that comes to anybody who is being natural. Culture is neither Indian nor Eastern nor Western. The things that are called Eastern culture, Western culture, Indian culture are all phony; they are a kind of deception. How can culture be Indian or American or Russian? Culture is the radiance of a natural man, his graceful behavior, his effortless naturalness.

But these cultures that are being talked about are trainings – trainings to make you fit into a certain society, at the cost of making you unnatural, uneasy, tense, anxiety-ridden.

I will give you a few examples. In China, for centuries, the women from their very childhood...when the woman was just a baby, they used to put iron shoes on the feet of the baby to keep her feet small. If the woman belonged to the highest and the richest society, to royal families, then they were almost incapable of walking, because their feet remained small and their bodies were allowed to grow. Those small feet were not capable of carrying the body of the woman. But it was culture. People appreciated the smallest feet as the most beautiful.

Just by seeing the feet you could decide to what kind of society she belongs: the poor, then she has big feet; the middle class, then smaller; and the highest class, very small. Royal family women were absolutely unable to walk; they were crippled in the name of culture. But nobody for centuries ever thought that the feet had to grow in proportion with the body; otherwise walking would become difficult. It was absolutely unnatural; it was painful.

Every society has imposed ideas on people, strange ideas. But once your mind is contaminated, you never think that it is absolutely nonsensical. In India, on Hindu holidays, or special occasions, they make a special drink – never drink it! Even if they offer it to you, simply refuse. They have given it a beautiful name, *panchamrit* – five nectars. And what are those five nectars? – cow dung, the urine of the cow, the milk of the cow, the curd from the cow and the purified butter called ghee. All five things from the cow...and people drink it with great joy. It is Hindu culture; the cow is the mother.

In Mahatma Gandhi's ashram there was a man, a well-educated man, professor Bhansali. He became almost a great saint, for the simple reason...for eating cow dung for six months and not eating anything else. Eating cow dung, drinking cow urine, that was his only quality. But even Mahatma Gandhi praised him, saying that he is a great saint. And when I saw him I told him, "You are an idiot!" But I said, "Don't be worried, in my vocabulary saints and idiots are synonymous."

If you look around the world, everywhere you will find such stupid things, but they are part of the culture. In Calcutta, in the temple of the mother goddess Kali, every day animals are butchered, sacrificed. And then their blood and meat is distributed as a gift from God to the devotees who gather there.

It goes on happening even today. And people drink that blood and that meat, feeling very grateful to God. I was there and I asked the head priest of the temple, "What happens to the animals you sacrifice?" He said, "They are fortunate, because an animal sacrificed at the feet of the mother goddess Kali goes directly to paradise."

I said, "Then why don't you sacrifice your father? Why take any risk? Sacrifice your children, sacrifice your wife, sacrifice yourself and go directly to heaven, because if you die a natural death there is no certainty. You may go to hell! Be compassionate to your old father."

He said, "What kind of man are you?"

I said, "I am simply giving you advice. If you are certain that animals sacrificed go to paradise, then you will not be shocked by sacrificing your father. This is such a short-cut."

But people go on deceiving others and getting deceived themselves. There have been Christian monks – and they still exist – who used to have shoes made in a special way. Inside the shoes there were nails, so that when they put on those shoes the nails would go in to their feet and create dozens of wounds in their feet. And with the wounds from the nails they would go on walking. And they were thought to be great saints because they were not attached to the body.

In Soviet Russia before the revolution, there was a Christian sect which went to the logical end of celibacy. Celibacy is a crime, because celibacy is unnatural. It has produced all kinds of perversions, homosexuality...and it has finally produced AIDS, which is another name of a slow death for which there is no cure.

That certain sect in Russia was the most respected sect of the Christians. Every year at Christmas time they would gather in their churches and they would cut off their genital organs. Men could cut off their genital organs; women could not remain behind, so they started cutting off their breasts.

And inside the church there would be a pile of genitals and breasts and people were covered with blood – and there are people who are touching their feet and worshiping them because they are great celibates. This is the logical conclusion, because now, even if they want, they cannot deceive people. And it was thought to be one of the most spiritual disciplines.

These are not cultures; these are all superstitions.

I know only one thing which can be called culture, and that is when your mind is absolutely silent and your being starts radiating joy – joy in ordinary things, joy in being nobody.

Let us repeat Chuang Tzu: Easy is culture. And anything that makes you uneasy is stupid.

Jews and Mohammedans have circumcision. They cut the foreskin of the genitals of small children. It is their culture.

I have heard about a bishop who lived opposite a rabbi, and they were continuously in competition. All religions are in competition with each other, and they are all teaching that you should not be competitive. And we are so blind that we cannot see that they teach, "You should not be competitive," and they are all competitive.

They say, "God is love," and they are all creating crusades, religious wars. Religions have killed more people than anybody else – in the name of God, in the name of love. And our blindness must be great that we cannot see that in the name of God and in the name of love crusades cannot be arranged. People have been burnt alive.

So both the bishop and the rabbi were in great competition. And one day in the morning the rabbi saw that the bishop has brought a new car, a new Chevrolet. He was jealous and hurt; it was very insulting. And then he saw the bishop coming out of the house with a bucket full of water, and he poured the water on the car. The rabbi could not contain his curiosity. He asked, "What are you doing?" The bishop said, "I am baptizing it. Now this car is Christian."

You cannot compete with Jews. The second day the rabbi brought a Cadillac. The bishop looked at the Cadillac, felt very much hurt – "What to do with this rabbi? He is always ahead!" And then he saw the rabbi coming with the garden scissors!

The bishop could not contain *his* curiosity. He came close and he said, "What are you doing?" The rabbi was cutting the exhaust pipe! He said "I am doing circumcision. Now this car is a Jew."

A simple man, contented with his ordinariness, joyful just as he is, accepting himself and all that he has without any judgment – with a deep feeling of suchness that this is how existence wants me to be – is the only cultured man, because he will have a grace and a beauty which these people who are trying to become somebody cannot have.

You can have grace only if you relax in whatever you are. The roses have culture, because they are not competing with the lotuses. Even the smallest blade of grass has a grace and beauty, because there is no competition. It is not worried about why it has not been made a rose bush. It is utterly satisfied with being itself.

This satisfaction creates an aura of grace. And this grace is neither Indian nor German nor Chinese; this grace is neither capitalist nor communist nor fascist. This grace belongs to the natural human being who has dropped all kinds of conditionings – Christian, Hindu, Mohammedan, Jewish – and who lives not bothering to be in tune with the society, but in tune with existence. Then the music of existence flows through him, then the fragrance of existence surrounds him. It is not something to be cultivated, it is something you are born with; just give it an opportunity to grow.

Don't hinder its progress. Have you ever seen any deer which is not graceful? Have you seen any eagle which is not graceful? It is only man who has to cultivate it.

It is strange, because man is the highest part of existence which has evolved consciousness. Grace will come just like a shadow; you don't have to cultivate it. Anything cultivated is going to be phony. Only something natural that arises from your very being is going to be authentic, sincere, honest.

Okay, Vimal?

Yes, Bhagwan.

Session 15

One Coin, Two Sides

*Love needs immense consciousness.
Love is a meeting of two souls,
and lust is the meeting of two bodies.
Lust is animal; love is divine.
But unless you know that you are a soul,
you cannot understand what love is.*

March 4, 1987
Evening

Beloved Bhagwan,

When I first came to You and looked into Your eyes, I saw myself.
After some years, looking into Your eyes
I felt myself inside my body, each cell of my body
and that 'something else' inside dancing with aliveness.
Last night I looked in Your eyes and I saw.
There was no one there. What a relief.
Oh Bhagwan, I am so glad You are not there.
Can You say something about this,
and this mysterious relief that there is no "thou" in my Master?

Maitri, the eyes are the doors of human consciousness. They are the most unphysical part of the physical body. That's why a blind man gets more sympathy and compassion than somebody who has no legs, somebody who is dumb or deaf. They are also missing a certain sensitivity, but they don't get the same sympathy as a blind man. And the reason is that eyes are the very windows of your soul.

People don't look into each other's eyes. The average time psychologists have decided that is allowed, is three seconds. To look more than that is thought to be offensive. It has to be understood why looking more than that is offensive: Because you are trespassing the individual's privacy, his very consciousness.

Only lovers can look into each other's eyes without offending each other. But lovers' eyes don't have much depth, because their love is nothing but lust; it is a biological urge, very superficial. It does not need your consciousness. In fact, the more unconscious you are, the more you are in the grip of biology.

But to look in the eyes of the master is a totally different phenomenon. There is no question of any biology, any physiology, because the very existence of the relationship between the master and the disciple is not part of biological programming. It is the only relationship that is not of this world. Naturally, the eyes of the master will give you many, many experiences at different stages of your growth.

You are saying, Maitri, "When I first came to You and looked into Your eyes, I saw myself." You were so full of ego. My eyes became just mirrors; you could only see the reflection of your own ego. You were too much concerned about yourself, about your own growth, about your own spirituality, about your own enlightenment. You had come to me, not for me, but for yourself. Naturally, my eyes reflected the state and the space you were in.

"After some years, looking into Your eyes I felt myself inside my body, each cell of my body and that 'something else' inside dancing with aliveness." You had moved a little closer to me. Your ego was not so prominent. On the contrary…something else, something unknown, dancing with aliveness was felt.

Your meditation has deepened, and this something else is your consciousness, for which there is no name. The aliveness and the dance and the joy indicate that now your mind is no longer reflected, but your no-mind. Your ego is no longer reflected, but your egolessness. But still you are reflected. So you have come closer to me, but not very close.

You are just in the middle between me and you. You have left your ego behind, but you have not arrived into my being. You are on the way. The first flowers of the spring have started blossoming – the aliveness, the dance, and the feeling of something else that is inside the body, the very life, the very consciousness, your very being – but still you are concerned with yourself.

"Last night, I looked in your eyes and I saw. There was no one there." You came really close. There has been no one for many years – just a pure nothingness, just an immense space; nobody is occupying it. For the first time you moved from yourself to me. For the first time you were not seeing something reflected of you; for the first time you were seeing something that is within me; for the first time you had really seen.

"What a relief. Oh Bhagwan, I am so glad you are not there. Can you say something about this, and this mysterious relief that there is no 'thou' in my master?" Experiencing the empty mirror within me, reflecting nothing, nobody present there, no "thou"…you must have been puzzled – why are you feeling such a relief? The relief is felt because the moment you cannot see "thou" in me, your "I" has also disappeared. That is one coin, two sides: What is "I" in you creates "thou" in me.

The moment you saw that there is no thou, you felt a relief without understanding clearly why this relief was there. This relief appeared to be mysterious, but it is very simple, there is no mystery in it. Seeing no thou in me, for the first time, without being aware, you lost your ego; they both disappear together.

It is certainly a joy to find a master in whom there is no person, but only a presence, because the person is mortal, and the presence is divine and immortal. That which appeared to you as absence, nothingness, emptiness, soon will be realized as the presence of the divine. The moment the ego dies, God is born.

So Maitri, one step more and your journey is complete. Some day you will see, looking into my eyes, the feeling, the taste of godliness. Then you have arrived home, then the disciple has gone through a transformation – he has become a devotee. And that is the highest stage on the path of spiritual growth.

The master does not exist; the disciple exists, and slowly, slowly the master has to persuade the disciple to disappear.

The whole function of the master is to make you also empty, absent of yourself, so that God can be present in you. And eyes are certainly the only doors, the only windows from where you can reach to the ultimate depths of consciousness.

Just one step more…you have been going perfectly right, but don't stop here. The emptiness has to become fullness, the absence has to become presence. In that moment the master is not there, the disciple is not there – just a merging of two flames into one flame.

This is true communion, the true meeting. This is the communion for which everybody is longing, unknowingly. And this is the communion which is causing continuous strife between lovers. It cannot happen between lovers, but the deep-down desire is for this moment, this peak of becoming one.

Because lovers expect to become one and cannot become one, it creates tension and fight. And each one of them feels that the other is betraying, the other is keeping a distance, the other is not allowing the merger. The same is the attitude of the other, but it is natural. If you are intelligent, you will not fight. You are trying to fulfill a longing which lovers cannot manage to fulfill. It is possible only when your love is no longer biological.

Between the master and the disciple there is love, but it is no longer biological; it is spiritual. It has nothing to do with your chemistry, with your hormones, with your physiology. Its concern is with your consciousness. When two consciousnesses meet the joy is infinite, and the joy is forever – there is no separation. Once two consciousnesses meet, they meet for eternity.

This seed, this longing, everybody is carrying within himself. And those few people who happen to meet a living master are really blessed. Millions of people in the world go on worshiping the dead saints. This kind of meeting is impossible with a dead saint, because looking into the marble statue's eyes, you will not see anything.

Yes, once, when the master was alive, it was a totally different matter. Before Gautam Buddha died, he said to his disciples, "Do not make a statue of me because once I am gone, I am gone. The statue can go on deceiving you for centuries."

For five hundred years no statue was made. Instead of a statue in the temples, there was only, carved in marble, the bodhi tree under which Gautam Buddha became enlightened – just a symbol. But as time passed statues started appearing. Now there are more statues of Gautam Buddha than anybody else. And the poor fellow had said in his dying statement, his last wish, "My statues should not be made at all."

Rarely have there been people with such clarity like Gautam Buddha, knowing that it is better that people search for a living master rather than worship a dead statue. But people find it easier to worship a dead statue than to be in love with a living master, because to be in love with a living master is always risky, dangerous. You cannot rely.... The living master is a changing phenomenon; you never know what turn he is going to take tomorrow, and you cannot dominate him.

People try...hundreds of people have tried even with me, with all good intentions – what I should say, what I should not say. Their ignorance is such that they don't understand that if they are wiser than me, then why are they following me? They are my followers, advising me – what I should say and what I should not say, what I should do and what I should not do. They have come to me to be transformed and they are trying in every way to transform me!

Naturally, by and by, these people disappear, but with a dead master they are perfectly at ease. When they say to the dead master, "Lie down," the dead master lies down, "Sit up," the dead master sits up, "Now it is time to take your food, now it is time for worship...." The dead master is just a toy in their hands. Whatever you want to do with Gautam Buddha as a statue, you can do.

You will be suprised to know that even the statue of Gautam Buddha is not his own – the face has been taken from Alexander the Great. But

Buddha cannot prevent it. It was five hundred years after Gautam Buddha had died that Alexander came to India. He was a beautiful man – almost like a statue – and he impressed the Indian sculptors. There was no photograph of Buddha available, no painting, so there was no difficulty – the statue that you see of Gautam Buddha made in India is the statue of Alexander the Great; it is his face, it is his nose.

Gautam Buddha must have looked far different, because he was born just on the boundary between India and Nepal. He may have looked more like a Nepalese than like an Indian. And you can see it: the Japanese statue of Buddha is different, the Chinese statue of Buddha is different.

Now it is in your hands; Buddha cannot do anything. Whatever you want – a long nose, closed eyes or open eyes – it is up to you. The poor guy cannot prevent you. This is the time for him to sleep, but you have fixed him into a lotus posture. The whole night he is sitting in a lotus posture, and do you think that Gautam Buddha used to sit in a lotus posture the whole night? – twenty-four hours in a lotus posture?

And now you can do anything you like...once a master dies people start editing his words according to their own idea of what he should have said. The day Buddha died, just the next day, there were thirty-two schools immediately, thirty-two sects differing about what Buddha had said. Now the Sinonese Buddhist does not agree with the Tibetan Buddhist, neither does the Tibetan Buddhist agree with the Japanese Buddhist, nor does the Japanese Buddhist agree with the Indian idea of Buddhism.

Now it is in your hands. And Buddha was absolutely right: "Don't make a statue of me, and be a light unto yourself. Search and seek, and if you can find a living master, then don't let me hinder you, because all living masters are exactly the same. Their faces may be different, their languages may be different, but their grace, their awareness, their truth is exactly the same."

It would have been a great blessing to humanity if every great master had told his disciples, "When I am gone, search for another living master." And he should have made the criterion that the living master is one who does not listen to you, and who does not fulfill your expectations.

But your so-called saints are all fulfilling your expectations. It is a very strange game – they are worshiped, but the reason for their worship is that they fulfill your expectations. By fulfilling your expectations they have shown clearly that they don't have their own individuality, they don't have their own consciousness, they don't have their own style of life. Just for the sake of respectability they are ready to follow those who are their followers, and this game is being continued all over the world.

Maitri, you have been observing your experiences very accurately – just one step more and there will be nothing to be said, just pure silence.

Beloved Bhagwan,

To me, You are like the purposeless glad ocean
that twice a day comes and goes,
showering us with Your energy like the waves of the sea.
I could wish for nothing more than this joy
of knowing that each day You will be with us again in the evening,
and when night comes I go to my bed feeling filled,
contained, and so much loved.
In my sixty-seven years I have wandered so far away from myself.
Could this miracle that is happening
within and without be that at last I am on my way home?

Deva Vachana, yes, it is true, at last you are back home. Your understanding about me is absolutely correct: I am just as purposeless as the waves of the ocean, or the flowers in the garden, or the stars in the night.

Purpose is a very mundane thing – machines have purposes, the electricity has purpose, and the effort of the society is always to reduce human beings also to a purpose. From my very childhood I have been criticized by my elders, my teachers, my professors for a simple reason – they used to ask me, "What are you going to become?"

But I said, "Why should I become, I am already whatever I am; becoming means going away from being. The people who *become* lose their being, lose their home. I am perfectly at home."

My elders used to say, "You are good for nothing."

I said, "That is perfectly right, everybody should be good for nothing – then life will be just a blissful dance. You never ask the roseflower, 'What is your purpose? Why are you dancing in the wind? Why are you so beautiful? Why are you spreading your fragrance? What is the purpose? What are you going to gain? How much is it going to help your bank account?'"

My professors were continuously worried because I was never reading the textbooks. I was reading a lot, all kinds of strange things, and I was also dragging my professors into discussions which, according to them, were purposeless. Again and again they would say, "Look, you are taking the whole class away in a purposeless direction; you are not going to be examined for it and you are not going to get your degrees for it."

But I said, "Who cares for degrees? We are here to become more alert, more silent, more joyful; we have come here to discover ourselves – who cares for degrees? You have got so many degrees, but you don't know anything about yourself and you are trying to teach us to be purposeful."

The whole society is geared for purpose: "You should be productive, you should be of some help." Just being yourself, a beautiful dance of your being, is not acceptable by society. You have to be a prime minister, you have to be a president, you have to be successfully rich; then the society appreciates you. And the reality is that all these successful people are nothing but beggars. Inside their being there is nothing but darkness, not even a small flame of light – their whole life is without love. At the most they pretend to be loving, but their activities in life destroy their lovingness.

A man who is greedy for money cannot be loving, because the greed for love is possible only if you drop the very idea of compassion. The more money *you* have...somebody, somewhere must be becoming poorer. You have to keep yourself completely closed about the poverty that you are creating by accumulating money. How can you love your own children? How can you love your own wife? You love only money. A man of greed is bound to become loveless; he loses all juice, he becomes dry.

Man is not a machine. And I am not saying that you should not be creative; I am saying you should be creative, but not productive. And those two are totally different things. All creation is purposeless, and all production is for some purpose. If your creativity, as a by-product, serves some purpose, that's another matter. It will serve something, but your basic longing should not be for production; it should be for creativity, and the joy of creativity.

For example, you can be creative in architecture. You can make a beautiful house, not just for the purpose of living in it, not just a shelter from the rain, and from the summer heat, and the cold, but as a creative piece of art. It may serve some purpose, but that is secondary. The priority should be that you are creating a beautiful piece of art – not just a house, but a temple...a temple where beauty dwells, a temple where meditation becomes so easy and so natural, a temple where love grows. Its purposes are secondary. But in the society, the whole educational system reduces every human being into a machine – produce more!

Your observation is right, Vachana, I am purposeless. And my whole philosophy of life is to enjoy purposelessness – beauty for beauty's sake, truth for truth's sake, love for love's sake. The man who is always thinking of purposes, even if he loves, it has some purpose behind it.

I have heard about a man who was in a great inner conflict. Two women were in deep love with him, and both were trying to get him to marry them. One was very beautiful, but absolutely poor; the other was immensely rich, but also immensely ugly. And there was great conflict in the mind of the man – what to do? If he thinks about purpose, then the ugly woman should be the choice. If he thinks about love, beauty, then the poor woman should be his choice.

Everybody who was friendly to the man was suggesting to him, "Beauty is just for a few days...once you become accustomed, you become immune to it. And who knows? Tommorow your beautiful wife may suffer from smallpox, may have breast cancer – anything can happen. Beauty is very fragile, and anyway one day she will become old and beauty will become only a long-away forgotten dream.

Be practical and be pragmatic, marry the ugly woman. She has money, and money can do anything in the world. Money is the greatest miracle invented by man. As far as her ugliness is concerned, for that much money it can be tolerated. And anyway, always come home late – when it is dark, whether the woman is beautiful or ugly makes no difference. And always remember that you can take her to a plastic surgeon, but don't forget money."

The people who are continuously concerned about being practical, pragmatic, are the lowest kind of human beings. The highest kind of human beings are very impractical, unpragmatic. And the mystics, the poets, the philosophers, the people who have raised human consciousness to the level at which we are now, who have made us different from animals, they are all purposeless.

Vachana, in your sixty-seventh year you are still young, fresh, because you can see the point so clearly that I am, "As purposeless as the glad ocean that twice a day comes and goes, showering us with energy like the waves of the sea." It is absolutely without any purpose, I simply enjoy being with you, I enjoy sharing my heart with you. There is nothing to be achieved through it, just the sharing in itself is my reward.

And you say, "I could wish for nothing more than this joy of knowing that each day that you will be with us again in the evening. And when night comes, I go to my bed feeling filled, contained and so much loved. In my sixty-seven years I have wandered so far away from myself, could this miracle that is happening within and without me be that at last I am on my way home?"

Not just on the way, you are already in the home. And you had never left the home – that is the point which is the most significant to be understood. You say that in sixty-seven years you have wandered far away from yourself. That wandering is only dreaming; you never go away from the home, nobody can go away.

It is just in sleep that you can wander, go to the moon, but when you wake up you will find you are still in your bed in your own room. What happened to the moon? And in the dream you may have worried much: "I have reached the moon. My God, now how am I going to get back?" There seems to be nobody to even enquire to about when the next train leaves, and whether there is any train, any station – nobody is there.

You may have been having a nightmare. How will I reach my home? And the nightmare can be so impressive that people wake up perspiring, trembling, their heart pounding. Although they are awake, and they know they are in their room in their bed...they have not gone anywhere, but it takes a little time for them to settle and forget the nightmare, and to have a little laugh – how stupid I am that I took that dream so seriously.

All your wandering, Vachana, has been only a dream of wandering – everybody's wandering is just in their dreams. The moment you wake up, and you are waking up, you will find you have never left the room, even for a single moment – because your being is your home, how can you leave it? You are it.

But it is good, although it is very late, sixty-seven years. But however late it may be, even before dying, if just for a second one becomes awake, he is equal to Gautam Buddha. Gautam Buddha may have been awake for forty-two years, and you may have been awake only forty-two seconds – that does not matter. What matters is that you are not dying in sleep. And whenever you wake up, it is morning. Just a single moment of total wakefulness is the most precious experience possible to the human mind.

This wakefulness is also purposeless. It has to be deeply understood that in life anything that is significant – love, beauty, virtue, silence, wakefulness, enlightenment...all are useless things. They are intrinsically valuable, but they don't have any price tag on them. You cannot sell them; you cannot make money out of them. They themselves intrinsically are so blissful that only a very few people have moved in the direction of these purposeless values. But these are the only real people; they are the very salt of the earth. The others are only wanderers in dreams. Their money, their respectability, their power, their position...all will be taken away before death.

But your love, your silence, your consciousness, your awakening, no death can even make a dent in those values. They cannot be taken away. This should be the criterion: that which cannot be taken away by death is the real treasure; that which can be taken away by death is just an illusion. It may last for years, but it is an illusion.

Death is the criterion, the fire test. Anything that passes through death without being destroyed is the real value. And the man who has values like this is the richest man, although he may be a beggar on the street.

I am reminded of a story: A king used to go every night into the city for a round to see how things are going – of course, in disguise. He was very much puzzled about one man, a young, very beautiful man, who was always standing under a tree by the side of the street, the same tree every night. Finally, the curiosity took over, and the king stopped his horse and asked the man, "Why don't you go to sleep?" And the man said, "People go to sleep because they have nothing to guard, and I have such treasures that I cannot go to sleep, I have to guard them."

The king said, "Strange, I don't see any treasures here." The man said, "Those treasures are inside me, you cannot see them."

It became a routine thing for the king to stop every day, because the man was beautiful, and whatever he said made the king think over it for hours. The king became so much attached and interested in the man that he started feeling that he was really a saint, because awareness and love and peace and silence and meditation and enlightenment, these are his treasures which he is guarding; he cannot sleep, he cannot afford sleep. Only beggars can afford....

The story had started just by curiosity, but slowly, slowly the king started respecting and honoring the man, almost as a spiritual guide. One day he said to him, "I know you will not come with me to the palace, but I think of you, day in, day out. You come to my mind so many times, I would love it if you can become a guest in my palace."

The king was thinking that he will not agree – he had the old idea that saints renounce the world – but the young man said, "If you are missing me so much, why you did not say it before? So bring another horse, and I am coming with you."

The king became suspicious, "What kind of saint is he? – so easily ready. But now it was too late, he had invited him. He gave him his best room in the palace which was preserved only for rare guests, other emperors. And he was thinking the man would refuse, that he would say, "I am a saint, I cannot live in this luxury." But he did not say anything like this. He said, "Very good."

The king could not sleep the whole night, and he thought, "It seems this fellow has deceived me; he is not a saint or anything." Two, three times he went to look from the window – the saint was asleep. And he had never been asleep, he was always standing under the tree. Now he was not guarding. The king thought, "I have been conned. This is a real con man."

The second day he ate with the king – all delicious foods, no austerity – and he enjoyed the food. The king offered him new clothes, worthy of an emperor, and he loved those clothes. And the king thought, "Now, how to get rid of this fellow?" Just in seven days he was tired, thinking, "This is a complete charlatan, he has cheated me."

On the seventh day he said to this strange fellow, "I want to ask a question." And the stranger said, "I know your question. You wanted to ask it seven days before, but just out of courtesy, manners, you kept it repressed – I was watching. But I will not answer you here. You can ask the question, and then we will go for a long morning ride on the horses, and I will choose the right place to answer it."

The king said, "Okay. My question is, now what is the difference between me and you? You are living like an emperor, but you used to be a saint. Now you are no longer a saint."

The man said, "Get the horses ready!" They went out, and the king many times reminded him, "How far are we going? You can answer."

Finally they reached to the river which was the boundary line of his empire. The king said, "Now we have come to my boundary. The other side is somebody else's kingdom. This is a good place to answer." He said, "Yes, I am going. You can take both the horses, or if you like, you can come with me."

The king said, "Where are you going?" He said, "My treasure is with me. Wherever I go, my treasure will be with me. Are you coming with me or not?"

The king said, "How can I come with you? My kingdom, my palace, my whole life's work is behind me."

The stranger laughed and he said, "Now, do you see the difference? I can stand naked under a tree, or I can live in a palace like an emperor because my treasure is within me. Whether the tree is there or the palace is there makes no difference. So you can go back; I am going into the other kingdom. Now your kingdom is not worth remaining in."

The king felt repentance. He touched the feet of the stranger and said, "Forgive me. I was thinking wrong thoughts about you. You are really a great saint. Just don't go, and leave me like this; otherwise this wound will hurt me my whole life."

The stranger said, "There is no difficulty for me; I can come back with you. But I want you to be alert. The moment we reach the palace, the question will again arise in your mind. So it is better – let me go. I can give you some time to think. I can come back.

"To me it makes no difference. But to you it is better that I should leave the kingdom; it is better. In this way at least you will think of me as a saint. Back in the palace you will again start doubting, 'This is a con man.' But if you insist, I am ready. I can leave again after seven days when the question becomes too heavy on you."

There are values which are intrinsic; they are part of your being – to discover them is the real discovery. And there are things outside you – to waste your life in collecting them is the most idiotic act one can do. But that kind of act is respected, because the society lives on the outside.

Your individual is within you, and your individual is capable of becoming a source of eternal ecstasy. It is purposeless.

To understand the purposelessness of great values, and to live them, is the way of the sannyasin.

You are not just on the way back home; you have never been out of the home. You have just fallen asleep and dreamt about wanderings – sixty- seven years you have been dreaming. It is your wakefulness that is making you feel so filled, so contained, and so much loved.

Beloved Bhagwan,

I feel we all use the word *love* like another four-letter word –
not really knowing at all what this state is.
Can You please talk about what love really is?

Kendra, you are right. The way people use the word *love* is exactly like a four-letter word, obscene – because to call it lust would be offensive.

If you say to someone, "I lust for you," you can't expect that that woman is going to have any respect for you. She will say, "Lust? Then get lost!" But if you say, "I love you," then everything is good.

And deep in your mind you are simply lusting. It is a biological desire to use the woman but a beautiful word hides the ugly reality. The problem is that people are not aware of what love is, so they are not only deceiving others, they are themselves deceived. They *also* think it is love.

Love needs immense consciousness. Love is a meeting of two souls, and lust is the meeting of two bodies. Lust is animal; love is divine. But unless you know that you are a soul, you cannot understand what love is.

I cannot tell you what love is, but I can tell you how to find your soul. That's my whole work: to help you meditate, to help you become more aware, alert, so that slowly, slowly you start seeing that you are not just the body, that you are not just even the mind, that there is something else hidden behind it all, which is your real life. And once you become aware of your real life, your being, you will know that the joy of being is so overflowing that one wants to share it with someone who is receptive, someone who is available, with someone who is ready to open his heart.

The meeting of two consciousnesses is love.

Discover your consciousness and you will find what love is. It is an experience, and there is no way to say anything about it, more than that which I have said. The meeting of two consciousnesses merging into each other brings the greatest orgasm the universe allows.

But before that, you have to move away from the body and the mind and the heart, and reach to the very center of your being.

Once you have reached to the center of your being, you will find love radiating from you. It is not something to be done by you. It will be just as if the sun has risen and the flowers have opened, and the air has become filled with their fragrance.

Love is a by-product of meditation.
Only meditators know what love is.

Okay, Vimal?

Yes, Bhagwan.

Session 16

Who Created God?

"Who created the world?"
And Yagnavalkya laughed,
thinking that this woman was asking a childish question.
But he was wrong.
He said, "God created it –
because everything that exists
has to be created by someone."

March 5, 1987
Morning

Beloved Bhagwan,

A few nights ago in darshan, sitting very close to You,
I was suddenly flooded with the words "Bhagwan, I'm sorry,
I'm sorry," over and over again until I was so filled
with pain and regret I could hardly sit in front of You.
Now, after Patipada's question, the feeling has returned
and I feel sick with a remorse which I don't understand.
I feel as if I have failed You or hurt You
in some unforgiveable way, and knowing that You
will never forget my stupidities weighs heavy on my heart.
Beloved Bhagwan, I'm sorry,
and I don't even really know what for.

Deva Aneesha, there is nothing for you to be sorry for. It is just your love, and your sensitivity that is making you feel remorse and sorrow.

I had answered Patipada, and certainly I am wounded and hurt; but not by you. You simply felt my being wounded and hurt, and that's why you are puzzled, why you are feeling sorry and sad. But Patipada is not feeling sorry or sad – just thick-skinned.

She has also written a letter to me, saying, "I looked deep into myself, and I don't feel that I have to be sorry for anything, that I have to apologize to the commune or to you."

And she was one of the members of the criminal gang that was the root cause that American politicians used to destroy the commune. She was aware that even my room was bugged by Sheela, and I had asked Sheela, "Is my room bugged?"

She flatly denied it, but I could see from her face – she became pale, and she said, "Tomorrow I can bring the electricians to check it, but it is not bugged." And Patipada knew all these things.

I have loved you so much, I have trusted you so much, and this is the reward you give me – you bug my own room. And she does not feel that she owes an apology. I have not been saying that she has done these things, but the group that was doing them...she was part of it. At least she could have informed me, she could have enquired whether I have ordered Sheela to bug my room. But still she is not repentant about it.

You are very sensitive. Your love is great, your trust is immense. You have not done anything, neither were you aware of anything that was being done; but you have felt my wound, and that feeling is disturbing you.

My wound is: I am the first person in history who has given women not only equality in my communes, but even superiority. *You* have not failed me, but my opinion of women has certainly gone down.

I was trying to compensate, because man has tortured woman for centuries – made her feel inferior in every way. My effort was to bring woman to her natural status; but a group of twenty women proved far uglier than twenty men would have proved. They have not only destroyed the commune, they have destroyed their only friend in the whole world, who has given them superior status and a more spiritual consciousness.

Perhaps, Aneesha, you are feeling bad because you are also a woman, and the wound was created by women. It is simply a reflection, because of your sensitivity. Otherwise – you are completely innocent; you don't need to be sorry at all. You have not failed me, you have not hurt me – there is no question of forgiving you. You have proved what I have been trying to prove – that woman can rise higher than man. She has far finer qualities.

But I can understand those twenty women also – Patipada included – because for centuries women have not been in power, and I put only women in power. Centuries of repression...and they forgot completely the man who had put them in power – that they were betraying him. But it is just unconsciousness.

In Patipada's letter she writes, "I don't feel that I owe any apology to you, or to the commune." And still she ends the letter with, "I put my head at your feet." For what? If she cannot even say "I am sorry," then putting her head at my feet is just words without meaning.

But all this happened unconsciously, so I am not angry, just wounded. I don't want you to feel repentant; I just want you to be more conscious. That's why I asked her for an apology: that would have made her more conscious.

When you are repressed for centuries and suddenly you get power, there is every possibility of misuse. And that's what happened. But I am still of the opinion that the woman carries in her heart more sensitivity, more love, more compassion. Given the chance, these old, repressed things will disappear. Therefore I am still giving that chance.

And, Aneesha, you proved my trust was right. You are not even aware what you are feeling sorry for; you have not done anything wrong. It is just a reflection, because a group of women did immense wrong, not only to the commune, but to the coming humanity. By their apology nothing will change; what they have destroyed in their unconsciousness is destroyed. But by their apology some understanding may come to them. And I want women not to be repressed in the future; they should be treated on equal terms. I was even making them superior, just to compensate for those thousands of years – but they behaved so unconsciously and so stupidly. But I was aware of the possibility....

I was reading a joke. It will be good for you, Aneesha. Two Irishmen, Paddy and Sean, were flying to Poona. The plane took off, and they were just settling down with their first drink when the captain's voice came over the intercom, "Engine number one has failed, but there is nothing to worry about. We can run fine on three engines, but we will be arriving in Poona one hour late."

Paddy looked at Sean, and they had another drink. Ten minutes later the captain's voice came again saying, "Engine number two has failed, but we can run fine on two engines. We will arrive in Poona two hours late." Sean looked at Paddy, and they had another drink.

Ten minutes later the captain's voice came on again, "Engine number three has failed, but there is nothing to worry about. We can run fine on one engine, but we will be arriving in Poona four hours late."

Paddy looked at Sean and said, "I hope that the last engine does not fail, or we will be up here all night."

What they did was very Irish, unconscious.

Your question is beautiful, and shows the beauty of your heart. It does not matter that a few women betrayed the trust and the love that I have showered on them. They cannot be taken as the criterion for all the women of the world.

I am a stubborn fellow. I will continue, in spite of the wound, to give woman every possible opportunity which she has been denied in the past. And there will be more women like you, Aneesha, who will come to the surface. And they will prove my point that you are absolutely equal to men, there is no question of inferiority. Perhaps something may be superior in you, because you are the mother of man. The man has your blood, your bones, your marrow; all that the man has is a contribution from the woman. It was out of fear that woman might prove superior that man started putting her down.

It is now up to you not to be bothered about the past – that which is gone is gone – but to be ready for the future, and prove to man and to the whole of humanity that man need not be afraid of you; he can trust you. And you can be of immense help in the evolution of man.

Beloved Bhagwan,

Whenever I hear or read about Meera, the enlightened princess,
who gave up her palace to devote her life to the beloved,
dancing wildly in the streets, my heart is full of joy.
Also, I notice that only very few
enlightened women are known to us.
Beloved Master, would You like to talk about women's enlightenment?

Sadhan, more women could have been enlightened than men, but man has not allowed them to reach to those heights. He has kept them, enslaved them as second-class citizens. He has not allowed them education; he has not allowed them freedom of movement in society; he has not allowed them even to listen to the religious scriptures. He has tied them to the home, which has become almost a prison while he is free.

And for centuries he has used the woman just as a reproductive mechanism, just to produce children. You may not be aware that in the past the woman was constantly pregnant – because out of ten children only one survived; nine died. Just to have two children twenty children had to be produced – and that is not a part-time job. The woman's life has been almost a constant torture, because every pregnancy is a torture. Nine months she suffers, and then she has to bring up the child – that is tedious. And before the child is even a few months old she becomes pregnant again. And man has never thought what he is doing to her – treating her like cattle.

Around the world, all the cultures have misbehaved with women. Even a great culture like China has not accepted the idea that the woman has a soul. She is only a reproductive machine. In China, for centuries, if the husband killed his wife it was not considered to be a crime – even murder was not a crime because the woman had no soul. It is almost like destroying your table, or your chair, or your washing machine. You cannot be dragged to the court as a murderer because you have destroyed your chair. It was your chair, and you have every right to keep it or to destroy it.

The woman has been possessed almost like a commodity. The Indian scriptures say that while the woman is a child, the parents should be in possession of her; when she is young the husband should be in possession of her; when she is old her own sons should be in possession of her.

In such ugly situations it was almost impossible for women to become enlightened. They were not even living, they were being used. And the most insulting thing in the world is to be used.

No religion has shown any respect to women. I sometimes wonder what kind of religions we have produced. Even the finest people, like Gautam Buddha, were not ready to initiate women into sannyas. Buddha was more afraid about his male sannyasins... that if women become sannyasins the celibacy of his male sannyasins will be in danger. What kind of celibacy is it? – so fragile, not confident of itself. And it is not surprising that these monks created homosexuality in the world. You can avoid the woman, but by avoiding the woman you cannot destroy the sexuality of man.

Mahavira, a man of tremendous compassion, who brought the concept of non-violence to the world, is very violent about women. He says that a woman cannot become enlightened as a woman. First she has to earn enough virtue to be born as a man, and then there is a possibility of her being enlightened. But as a woman he absolutely denied the possibility.

Jesus talks of love so much, but when he chose his twelve apostles he did not include a single woman – although there were three women who were very close to him...far more understanding than those apostles. And it is a historical fact to be remembered that when he was crucified, all his twelve apostles disappeared, afraid that if they were caught, perhaps the same treatment would be given to them too.

But those three women: Mary Magdalene, and she was a prostitute, but listening to Jesus she went through a transformation; she dropped her profession, and she was one of the most beautiful women in Judea – Jesus' mother, Mary, and another woman follower, Martha: they remained near the cross. They showed more courage. And those three women were the ones who brought the body down from the cross – all those twelve apostles were hiding, they were not coming out.

But still Christianity has not given any recognition, any respect, even to Jesus' mother. But Christianity is not at fault – even Jesus himself was not respectful. One day he was speaking in a marketplace, a small crowd surrounding him, and his mother, who had not seen him for years, came to see him. And somebody shouted to Jesus, "Your mother is standing outside the crowd. She wants to see you."

And Jesus misbehaved. He said, "Tell that woman...." Now, it is ugly. He could not even call her "mother." "Tell that woman that I don't have any mother, I don't have any father here on the earth. My father is in heaven."

The same is true about other religions. Man has been preventing women from any spiritual growth.

It is a miracle that even in spite of all this suppression and slavery a few women became enlightened. They are proof that Mahavira is wrong, that Buddha is wrong, that Jesus is wrong. For you, Sadhan, I have been looking for the names of all the enlightened women. There are not many, only five in the whole history of man.

One is Gargi. Five thousand years ago, when the *Upanishads* were being written, it was the childhood of mankind, and man had not yet become so brutal against women. The emperor of the nation used to call, every year, all the wise people for a contest. He was himself very philosophically-minded. In fact, no enlightened person would have gone to those contests; they were childish, although there was great reward. And it happened one year that the emperor declared that he would give one thousand cows, with their horns covered with pure gold and studded with diamonds to the person who won the contest.

Yagnavalkya was one of the most famous and learned men of those days. And he was so confident of his victory that when he came to the campus where the debate was being arranged, he looked at the cows. Those one thousand cows with gold-covered horns, studded with diamonds, were looking really beautiful in the sunlight. He told his disciples, "You take these cows to our place. It is unnecessary for the poor cows to stand in the hot sun."

The disciples said, "But first you have to win." He said, "That I will take care of."

Even the emperor could not prevent him. And all those thousands of wise men who had gathered – they could not prevent him. They all knew that it was impossible to beat him in argument. His disciples took away the cows.

And it was almost the moment when he was going to be declared the winner, when a woman named Gargi...she was waiting for her husband who had also gone into the debate, and it was getting late; so she went herself to call him. She entered the campus and she saw the whole scene – that the cows had been taken away even before victory.

And she said to the emperor, "Don't declare his victory. Just by chance I have come here, to look for my husband. But this man needs somebody who really knows, and I am ready to have a discussion with him. He is only a learned man, but learning has never known truth."

Those were more beautiful days, when even a woman could challenge the most learned man. And the emperor said, "Then I will have to wait. You can discuss."

She asked only simple questions. She asked, "Who created the world?" And Yagnavalkya laughed, thinking that this woman was asking a childish question. But he was wrong.

He said, "God created it – because everything that exists has to be created by someone."

This was the time for Gargi to laugh. She said, "You are caught; now you are in trouble. Who created God? – because he also exists, and everything that exists needs a creator."

Yagnavalkya saw that he had got into difficulty. Because if he said another God created him, the question will remain the same: Who created that other God? You can go on answering for a thousand times, but the question will remain the same: Who created the first God? And if there was somebody to create him, he cannot be called the first.

Yagnavalkya got so angry that he pulled out his sword and said, "Woman, if you don't stop, your head will fall on the ground!"

But Gargi said, "Put your sword back into the sheath. Swords cannot be arguments." And she told the emperor, "Tell this fellow that those one thousand cows should be returned."

It was so insulting to Yagnavalkya that he never again participated in any discussion. And Gargi took those one thousand cows back from Yagnavalkya.

She was the first known enlightened woman.

The second woman went through a very difficult phase. Her name was Mallibai and she belonged to the Jaina tradition. Mahavira and all the twenty-three great masters of Jainism had declared that a woman cannot become enlightened. But Mallibai, who was a Jaina, became enlightened, and gave the evidence and the proof that their argument was simply male-chauvinism. They had to accept her as the twenty-fourth great master. But they played a trick: when she died they changed her name.

So even Jainas don't know that of the twenty-four statues in their temples, one statue is of a woman. They changed her name from Mallibai to Mallinath; it becomes male. And they changed even the statue; the statue is not of a woman, the statue is of a man.

When I came to know about it, I was very angry with the Jaina monks. Whoever visited my place, I used to ask, "Which one of these twenty-four statues is Mallibai? – because they are all men's statues. You are deceiving the whole world. You have even changed the name of the woman just to keep your ideology intact."

But Mallibai must have been a great woman. It is not easy to follow the Jaina path. It is hard, very harsh. To become a *tirthankara*, a great master, one has to even drop one's clothes – no possessions, not even clothes. Mallibai must have been a very courageous woman. She lived naked, and proved that their whole theory was wrong. But after her death they managed – and these are religious people, cunning and deceptive.

The third is a Mohammedan woman mystic, Rabiya al-Adabiya. She seems to be the most significant Mohammedan mystic. Mohammedans don't allow women in their mosques; they have to pray outside the mosque. Women are treated exactly like cattle. Mohammed himself married nine women, and allowed every Mohammedan to marry at least four women – just to produce more children, so that Mohammedanism would spread. But he never thought about a simple problem, that if you marry nine women – nature produces men and women in equal numbers, it has a subtle balance – what about those eight men who will not get a wife?

So in Mohammedan countries homosexuality is tremendously prevalent, although the punishment for homosexuality is death. Knowing that the punishment is death, still homosexuality is much more prevalent in Mohammedan countries than anywhere else.

You have heard that in Africa homosexuality and the disease AIDS is spreading like wildfire. The parts where AIDS is spreading like wildfire are Mohammedan. It has nothing to do with Africa, it has something to do with the Mohammedan idea that one man can marry four women. So people who can afford...and four is not the maximum limit, it is the minimum limit.

The Nizam of Hyderabad in India, just before the Britishers left, had five hundred women. This kind of stupid behavior...and it becomes even more stupid because the Nizam had a big state,

Hyderabad; he was a king, and the tradition was that his son would be the successor. When the father dies, he will inherit as his wives, all the wives of his father, except his own mother. That is his inheritance. The woman is something like a thing, money, land – but not a human being.

Rabia al Adabiya is the only Mohammedan woman. who reached to the point of enlightenment. And she was really a courageous woman. It needs courage. The stories of her courage are many.

Once a great mystic, Junnaid – who was afterwards the master of Al Hillaj Mansoor, the famous mystic who was killed by Mohammedans...Junnaid used to sit in front of the mosque, tears rolling down his cheeks.... Five times a day a Mohammedan has to pray, and five times Junnaid was found sitting in front of the gate of the mosque, raising his hands to God above, and asking him, "How long is it going to take? When are you going to open the doors? I have been waiting and praying for years."

One day Rabiya was passing, and Junnaid was praying with the same words: "Open the door, I have waited enough, I am a frail human being, my patience is not infinite!"

From the back Rabiya hit Junnaid on his head and said, "You idiot!" – and Junnaid was known as a great learned scholar – "The doors of God are always open. Why are you unnecessarily wasting your time? Get in! The doors of God are never closed. And I say it on my own authority, because I have been in and out so many times." She must have been a very courageous woman.

Another mystic, Hassan, was staying with her. And in the morning he wanted her holy *Koran*, because he had not brought his own copy – knowing that there must be one with Rabiya al-Adabiya. Rabiya al-Adabiya gave him her copy. He was shocked, because in many places she had corrected the holy *Koran*. It is a great sin – the holy *Koran* cannot be corrected, it is written by God.

Hassan called her back: "Rabiya, somebody has destroyed your holy *Koran*. Corrections in the holy *Koran*...? It has never been heard of, never been thought about."

She said, "Nobody has distorted it. Those corrections have been made by me, and I had to make them." And she looked at the correction which Hassan was reading. The statement in the *Koran* is that you should hate the devil. She had crossed it out.

He said, "I don't understand."

She said, "It is very simple. I am now so full of love that it does not matter whether God comes before me, or the devil – they will both receive love, because I don't have anything else to give. Hate I don't have to give. And this is my copy of the *Koran*. From where can I get hate? Hate has disappeared; my whole energy of hate has become love. Now it does not matter – God will receive the same love as the devil: I am helpless: I had to cross out this line, because it is no longer relevant to me."

This woman Rabiya was seen once running in the marketplace with a burning torch in her hand, and in another hand a bucket full of water. People gathered and asked, "What are you going to do?"

She said, "I am going to do the thing that should have been done before. I am going to burn this idea of heaven above in the sky, and I am going to drown this idea of hell beneath the earth. Both are bogus; they are not part of geography, they are inside you.

"And it all depends on you, whether you live in hell or you live in heaven. Living in hate, in anger, in jealousy, in depression, you are living in hell.

"And living in love, in compassion, in truth, in

sincerity, you are living in heaven."

The fourth is another Mohammedan woman from Kashmir. Her name is Lalla. She was one of the most beautiful women…Kashmir has the most beautiful women in the whole of India. Not only is the land beautiful, but the people are also very beautiful.

Lalla remained naked, disowned everything, renounced everything – still, no police commissioner came to her to say that this was obscene. On the contrary, in Kashmir they have a proverb: "We know only two words which are meaningful; one is Allah, and another is Lalla." They have raised Lalla equal to God, Allah.

When I was in Kashmir visiting many times, I heard from many Mohammedans: We don't know anything comparable to these two words: Allah and Lalla. She was respected so immensely – her songs are so beautiful. I have asked one of my friends in Kashmir to translate them, because they are in Kashmiri. But even hearing them…they have such music. I don't understand Kashmiri, but whenever I have gone to Kashmir I have found somebody who can sing Lalla's songs. They have such depth that although I don't understand the language, I understand the feeling, the vibe. And Lalla must have impressed the whole of Kashmir as nobody has ever impressed Kashmir.

And the fifth, Sadhan – you have mentioned her – is Meera. Perhaps she is the most significant of all the women who have become enlightened. Her songs…each word is pure gold. It is coming from the very source of enlightenment.

She was a queen, but she could not remain imprisoned in the palace; neither could her husband or her family tolerate her in the palace, because even to her husband she had said, "You forget all about being my husband. I have been in love with God from my very childhood. If anybody can claim to be my husband, it is God. But he cannot claim, because with him I am one."

Naturally, the family also wanted to get rid of her…and she also wanted to move in the streets, to sing her songs, to dance her dances, to spread her blissfulness as far and as wide as possible.

Two stories I would like to tell you about her. In Vrindavan, there is the greatest temple of Krishna. The priest of the temple was a celibate; and as all celibates are sick, psychologically sick, he was also a sick person – sick in the sense that he would not allow any woman inside the temple. Only men could come inside the temple – women had to worship from the outside.

He had not seen a woman for twenty years. This kind of celibacy is nothing but tremendous repression, so much fear of women, that even seeing a woman you are afraid you may lose your whole life's effort.

When he heard that Meera was coming to dance in the temple before Krishna – and she was one of the most beautiful women you can conceive of – he put two guards with naked swords at the gate, saying, "Don't allow her in. Even if she has to be murdered, don't be worried."

Meera came dancing and singing, and the guards became so overwhelmed by her love, by her joy, by her ecstasy, that they forgot their business – why they were standing there. And she danced, and entered into the temple.

The priest was worshiping Krishna. On a plate he had candles, and he was worshiping with those candles. As he saw Meera, the plate fell – and he could not believe…what had happened to the guards?

She was drunk with the divine, and she danced before Krishna. The priest stopped her and asked her, "How dare you? You know that no woman is allowed here. And the guards are at the gate, they should have prevented you."

Meera laughed, and she said a very significant

thing. She said, "I used to think that only God is a man and everybody else is a woman. Today I have found there are two men – you and God.

"What kind of love you do you have? If you cannot become simply the loving heart of a woman, all your worshiping is just hocus-pocus. Whom are you trying to deceive? I don't see that there is anybody who is a man. Only God is a man, and we are all his beloveds. You are also a woman. Join me in the dance!"

Only these five names.... It is a crime on the part of man that he has prevented women from becoming enlightened. He has not given them a chance, otherwise my feeling is that there would have been more enlightened women than men, because for man there is a difficulty – his head.

The woman has a direct contact from the heart. Man's journey is a little long – first he has to struggle with the head...that can take years. And unless he comes to the heart, he cannot move towards the being.

The woman is already at the point of the heart. In that way she has a superiority; and more women would have become enlightened.... But the crime is on man's head – and it continues.

Just a few days ago, I heard that in England there is going to be a great conflict. The Church of England is on the verge of splitting in two, because the orthodox bishops and cardinals are against initiating any woman as a priest. A few intelligent people think that this is ugly. Why cannot a woman be a priest? The bishop of London has threatened that if women priests are initiated he is going to take the major part of the Church of England with him, because he is absolutely against women being priests.

What to say about enlightenment? Women cannot even be priests! And it is not only in England. You will not find women priests anywhere in the world. Man has created every barrier. It is not only against women, it is against the whole humanity; because women constitute half of the earth. Half of humanity is being prevented from being religious.

Among many of my efforts, this is one of the major projects – that as far as religiousness is concerned there should be no discrimination between men and women.

And perhaps this is the only place where there is no discrimination. But because of these things, the whole world is against me. But I am ready – let the whole world be against me. Sooner or later they will understand that I was fighting for them, and they were against me; I was trying to improve the whole consciousness of humanity, and they condemned me.

But perhaps that is the destiny of every rebel.

And I am not a one-dimensional rebel – I am a multi-dimensional rebel. About *everything* I am rebellious.

Okay, Vimal?

Yes, Bhagwan.

Session 17

Playing A Part In The Movie

*No rationalization can be absolutely consoling.
There is bound to remain the doubt,
"perhaps I am befooling myself."
And that's what you are doing.
You have never been out of the movie.
Even when you became a watcher....*

March 5, 1987
Evening

Beloved Bhagwan,

I sometimes fail to watch my mind with detachment.
Indeed, I sometimes revel in adding juicy tidbits
to my otherwise unguided fantasies just for the fun of it.
This does help me to shed more light on my desires,
but I sometimes wonder if I didn't get lost in the movie
somewhere along the line, and still haven't found my way back out.
That is, if I was ever outside in the first place.
Beloved Bhagwan, could You please speak on the foibles
of finding the workings of one's own mind
a form of entertainment?

Anand Ashubodha, you are saying, "I sometimes fail to watch my mind with detachment." It means more often you do not fail; but the truth is, if you succeed even one time to watch the mind, then you cannot fail. So it is a misunderstanding on your part that you fail sometimes; you fail all times. Sometimes, when you think you have succeeded in watching, that too is only a thought, not a witness.

I can remind you – many times, in sleep you can dream you are awake. There is no problem in it, only in the morning when you will *really* be awake, then you will see the difference – that the dream *can* manage to give you the feeling that you are awake. It is only a dream awakening, not a true authentic awareness.

I can say it with absolute authority, because once you know the witness, there is no way to lose it, even if you want. Once you have become a watcher of your mind, then all these rationalizations that you are giving in your question will not be needed. As the watcher becomes more and more crystalized, dreams disappear.

But you are saying, "Indeed, I sometimes revel in adding juicy tidbits to my otherwise unguided fantasies just for the fun of it." These are rationalizations. When you are dreaming you cannot add anything to your dream, you cannot add juicy tidbits. You are fast asleep. Your fantasies are going to remain unguided, because the guide is no longer there, not yet at least.

But this is the cunningness of the mind, that it may even console you that you are fully aware – not only aware, but you are guiding your fantasies just for the fun of it. And it becomes clear in your question: "This does help me to shed more light on my desires, but I sometimes

202

wonder if I didn't get lost in the movie somewhere along the line, and still haven't found my way back out. That is, if I was ever outside in the first place."

You also have suspicions about your rationalization. No rationalization can be absolutely consoling. There is bound to remain the doubt, "perhaps I am befooling myself." And that's what you are doing. You have never been out of the movie. Even when you became a watcher, you were just playing a part in the movie.

Because you are so interested in being a watcher, your mind can give you even that. It is a safety device of the mind, to allow you to feel that you are the watcher: don't be worried, you are outside the dream; you can even guide it a little bit, you can make it more funny, more juicy.

And you are asking me, "Could you please speak on the foibles of finding the workings of one's own mind a form of entertainment?" The problem is that if you are a watcher there is no mind, and if there is a mind you are not a watcher, and for the entertainment both are needed to be together – and this is existentially impossible.

Either you can be part of the drama that the mind is playing – but at the same time you cannot sit in the hall and see the drama – or you can sit in the hall. But your mind is incapable of facing your awareness. It simply disappears – it is very shy. Leaving you alone, the screen of the mind becomes empty. So there is no possibility of entertainment.

I have heard that at one railway station, on the platform, a few people were waiting for the train. The train was late, it was the middle of the night, and they were all puzzled about one person who was sitting in his chair and really rejoicing about something. Everybody was watching him: What is going on? because sometimes he will throw something with his hand, sometimes he will smile, sometimes he will almost start giggling.

Finally they all said, "We have to ask him. The train is late, and this man is driving us crazy with what he is doing." So they went to the man and they said, "It is not right on our part to interfere, but now we cannot resist anymore. What exactly are you doing? Sometimes it seems you are throwing something away, sometimes you seem to be smiling and enjoying, sometimes you giggle, sometimes you put your hand on your mouth, as if you are worried that others may hear the laughter – and we don't see anything on this ugly station platform."

The man said, "Your question puts me in a very embarrassing situation, but I will have to answer it because you all seem so interested. It was not much, I was just telling jokes to myself. Finding nothing else to do – the train goes on being late – I started telling jokes to myself."

They said, "If you were telling jokes, then what were you throwing away?"

He said, "Sometimes old jokes which I have heard before – I was throwing them and saying, 'Get lost! don't bother me.'"

They could not understand whether that man was sane or insane, because any joke that he would be telling to himself must be old – at least for him. And he said, "Sometimes it is so juicy that I smile, and sometimes I am afraid that you may become aware of what is happening inside me, so I put my hand over my mouth."

They said, "All your actions have been maddening the whole crowd. We were disscussing only one thing, what is happening to this man? And you are enjoying so much relaxing in the chair...."

Entertainment you can have – but then you cannot be the watcher. And if you want to be the watcher, you cannot have the entertainment. In fact, who needs entertainment? – only a miserable person. Who are the people who are lining up in front of movie houses? – all kinds of miserable, tense, worried, tired people, crushed by life – wanting for at least three hours to forget all the problems and all the worries and all the anxieties and get lost in the movie.

Entertainment is for the miserable – not for the blissful, not for the meditator, not for one who is aware. He is having so much joy within himself that no entertainment can enhance it; on the contrary, the entertainment may become a disturbance. If you are peaceful, silent, then any kind of entertainment is just a disturbance. But if you are too full of thoughts, and noisy, the entertainment gives a relief for two, three hours; you forget yourself.

It is good that in movie houses when the film starts, it is dark. In that darkness people cry, people weep, people laugh; they are not worried, because nobody is seeing them. But why are they crying? – because on the screen there is nothing, except a play of light and darkness. But some tragic scene, and tears come to their eyes. They have become absolutely identified, part of the story.

Their life is so negatively empty that they would like to fill it with something. It may be a movie, a circus, it may be alcohol or some other drug – for the simple reason that they can forget this world and all its problems. But by forgetting them they are not solving them; after three hours the problems will be back with vengeance. After the whole night remaining drunk, in the morning they will have all the problems *and* above all, the hangover, a migraine – that is an additional gain. All the problems are there, all the worries are there...perhaps they have grown in the night.

I have told you many times that Jews have suffered the most in the whole history of man, and because of this suffering they are the people who have the best jokes in the world. Just something to laugh at; otherwise their life is just tears. To avoid the tears, something is needed that can make you laugh.

I have worked hard to find one, but in India we don't have a single original joke. Ten thousand years, and we don't have a single joke which we can say is our own. All jokes are imported, and most of them are from the Jewish tradition.

Jews have beautiful jokes. And the reason is not that they are very happy – just the opposite. The reason is that they have lived in such tragic times. Since the times of Moses – almost four thousand years – they have suffered and suffered. And there seems to be no end to their suffering – they are still suffering in Israel.

But you will be surprised: in this whole long history of suffering, they have somehow managed themselves, they have not gone mad. Their jokes have saved them; but their jokes have not solved their problems.

I will tell you two Jewish jokes. A rabbi finds himself sharing a railway compartment with a Roman Catholic priest. After some time, the priest leans forward: "Excuse me, rabbi, but is it true that men of your faith may not eat pork?"

"Yes, Father, you are right," replies the rabbi.

"And tell me, between priests, confidentially, have you ever tasted it?"

"Well, as a matter of fact, a long time ago, I *did* taste some bacon."

"And did you like it?" asked the priest.

"Yes, I must admit, I did."

A little while later, the rabbi leans forward, "Excuse me, Father, but is it true that priests are not allowed to have any sexual relationship with a woman?"

"Yes, rabbi," the priest replied, "you are quite right. It is forbidden to us."

"And tell me, between priests, have you ever

indulged?" asked the rabbi.

"Well, as it happens, no, I have not."

"Hmm, pity," says the rabbi, "it is better than pork."

The second joke: Moses arrives at the Red Sea with the Israelites. The pharaoh and his army are in hot pursuit. He calls his public relations office, "Abe, where are the boats? You schmuck! Where are the boats?" Moses screams.

Abe says, "Boats? Who said anything about boats?"

"I need boats to cross the water, you idiot! What do you expect me to do – part the water and walk through it?"

"Hey, Moses baby, now you are talking! If you do that, I will get you two whole pages in *The Holy Bible.*"

A long, long history of troubles, tragedies, torture that seems to be unending, has created a tremendous amount of jokes, but those jokes are just to hide the tears.

Friedrich Nietzsche is right when he says, "Whenever I laugh, you can be certain that I am hiding my tears. If I don't laugh, I may start crying."

Entertainment goes on growing in the world, because misery goes on growing. You need more and more new kinds of entertainment. Ordinary movies won't do – they are only for common masses. Those who are rich have special kinds of movies called blue movies. They are very respectable people, honored by the society, but in their homes they are seeing blue movies, which are nothing but sexual orgies. They are created only for the rich who can have a small theater in their own house, a private theater, where they can invite their friends. But that too makes me feel that they *are* in a more tense and anguished state than the ordinary common masses.

The common masses may be poor, they may not have enough food, they may not have enough clothes, they may not have good houses; they may even be sleeping on the streets, they may be beggars...but for centuries it has been known that beggars sleep better than emperors, although the emperor has the best facilities for sleep.

But facilities don't help sleep. The emperor's mind is so worried, so tense – so many problems which seem to be insoluble. And he has to face them the next morning. He has to find some way out of the jungle in which he is lost. The beggar has no problem; at the most he has to beg. That he has been doing – he has become an expert.

One day, a man was passing over a bridge and he saw a blind man. He was in a good mood – he had just got an increase in his pay scale – so he gave one rupee to the blind man. The blind man looked at the rupee, turned it upside down and said, "This is not authentic." The man could not believe it. He said, "You are blind!"

The blind man said, "To tell you the truth, my friend is blind, but today he has gone to see a movie, so I am just tending his shop. As far as I am concerned, I am deaf. In the beginning I also used to be blind, but people were cheating: they would give false coins, and I could not object because of my blindness. I knew that they were cheating, so I changed my profession; I became deaf. But this place is very profitable, and my friend asked me, 'Just for three hours I am going to a matinee show. You just look after my place so somebody else does not occupy it.'"

The beggars don't have many worries. Even if they want to change their profession, it is very easy. And you don't know one thing, that you may be a possession of a certain beggar. That I came to know because I was continuously traveling, and on the station there used to be a old beggar. It had become a routine that whenever I came I would give him one rupee, and whenever I left I would give him one rupee – and I was continually coming and going.

But one day I saw a young man standing in place of the old man. I said, "What happened to the old man?"

He said, "I got married to his daughter."

I said, "That's okay, but where is the old man?"

He said, "He has given his profession as a dowry to me. Now you belong to me."

I said, "Belong?"

He said, "Yes, because all the beggars in the city have their territory. People don't know to whom they belong but we have divided our customers. You just give me one rupee. Don't waste my time unnecessarily, because there are other customers coming. My father-in-law has given me the whole list of those who are his permanent customers and how much they give, and he told me, 'Don't settle for less.'"

I said, "This is a revelation. I will give you more than I used to give to your father-in- law, because you have made me aware of one thing which nobody knows – that people are the property of some beggar – customers. And beggars are giving you in dowries to somebody else; they are not even being asked."

It is the simplest profession. But life is not so simple. You need entertainment because your life is too complex. Once you start becoming simple, peaceful, once you start enjoying yourself, you will not need any entertainment.

Anand Ashubodha, you have not even known for a single moment the watcher, although you have many times thought in your sleep, in your dream that you are a watcher.

Dreams are very protective of sleep. Throughout the whole past of humanity it has been thought that dreams are a disturbance of sleep. But the latest findings of psychology are totally different: dreams are not disturbances of sleep, dreams are protective of sleep; they avoid disturbances.

For example, in the night it is cold and you are feeling like going to the bathroom. Now, getting up in the cold night and going to the bathroom, your sleep will be disturbed. The dream is a protection. The dream will give you the idea that you have got out of the bed, you have gone into the bathroom, you have done whatsoever you wanted to do, you are back and fast asleep. And you have not moved a single inch. The dream protected your sleep from being broken.

In eight hours, if you are sleeping eight hours, for six hours you are dreaming; only for two hours are you sleeping without dreams. And those two hours everybody has to find because they are not fixed: somebody may have them between four and six, somebody may have them between three and five; it differs with each individual.

The person who has them between one o'clock and three o'clock can wake up at three o'clock without any trouble, and he will not feel sleepy in the day; he will not miss anything because he had got up so early. But if the person whose two hours of sleep without dream are between four and six gets up at five, his whole day will be spoiled. That one hour of deep rest will be missed the whole day. He will find himself upset, irritated about small things, becoming angry, tense, feeling to go to bed early; and he will not know actually what is the cause.

People have been asking me, "What is the time in your ashram when everybody has to get up?" I say, "You are talking nonsense, because everybody cannot get up at the same time. Everybody has to get up at the time which gives him a peaceful day, a joyous feeling, a well being."

In Vinoba's ashram in Wardha, Vinoba used to

wake up at three o'clock – perhaps it was suitable for him. He used to go to sleep at nine o'clock. In old age, six hours are enough, and perhaps those two hours were covered. But because he was getting up at three o'clock, he had made the rule that in the ashram, everybody had to get up at three o'clock. And you could see that everybody, the whole day, was feeling sleepy. People's faces were looking dry, dull; they were somehow carrying themselves, waiting for the night to come.

And just as there is a certain time to get up, exactly the same is true about going to bed. And it differs from individual to individual. No general policy or principle, or a discipline is psychologically and scientifically right. Everybody has to find out...and it is not a difficult job. Just try a few different times going to sleep, a few different times waking up, and you will find the right time to wake up and the right time to go to sleep. And that will transform your twenty-four hours.

You are not to follow any scripture – because the man who wrote the scripture may have been right about himself, but he cannot be right about the *whole* universe, for all the coming generations. But this kind of stupidity continues. Somebody may be finding it right to get up at seven; there is no harm, he is not doing any violence to anybody. In fact, if he wakes up early, he may do some violence, some harm, because he will be irritated, he will be always ready to fight. His nerves are not relaxed. The old idea of a discipline for everybody is absolutely out of date. At least my people have to find their own discipline, and they have to remember not to impose it on anybody else.

And that conception, that dreams are disturbances, has been found absolutely wrong. Your dreams are immensely protective. You just watch your dreams, remember them in the morning, and you will be surprised how intelligently your unconscious mind creates a situation and protects your sleep.

Actually that's what is happening, Ashubodha, to you, because you are continuously interested in being a watcher. So the dreams say, "Okay, we will supply it – you can be a watcher." But it is a dream, and you are part of the dream. You are not standing out of the dream, you are playing the role of the watcher in the dream. Don't be deceived by it, because if the watcher is there, the dream cannot be there. So this can be used as a criterion: Either the dream can exist or the watcher can exist.

Mr. and Mrs. Goldberg went on a skiing holiday to Switzerland. On the first day Goldberg told his wife he was going off skiing all day in the high mountains. "Don't worry Becky, I will be back by five or six at the latest."

She waited nervously all day, and when he did not return by seven, she begged for a search party to be sent out. Eventually a Red Cross rescue team, a full complement of guides, Saint Bernard dogs, and army mountaineers set off. They climbed to the high slopes, calling as they went, "Mr. Goldberg, Mr. Goldberg! It is the Red Cross, where are you?"

No reply. Up they went to the high valleys, "Mr. Goldberg, it is the Red Cross!" No answer still. Eventually, almost at the glacier, they called out once more, "Mr. Goldberg, it is the Red Cross!"

And the faint answer came back, "I have given already!"

Beloved Bhagwan,

I took sannyas ten years ago
and felt at home for the first time in my life.
Since then, silence, peace and clarity are growing.
Yet I feel that I am moving more towards death than
towards life and love. My girlfriend tells me I am cold
and know nothing about love. She may be right.
Am I keeping my heart closed? Is my meditation an escape
and a protection from involving myself completely in life?

Deva Sudheer, I do not agree with your analysis. You say, "I took sannyas ten years ago and felt at home for the first time in my life." That is right. "Since then, silence, peace and clarity are growing." That too is right. "Yet I feel that I am moving more towards death than towards life and love." That is not right and that is not your idea. That is your girlfriend's idea.

Because you are becoming silent, peaceful, and a clarity is growing in you and you are feeling for the first time at home in life, it will change immensely all your relationships – particularly the relationship with your girlfriend. You cannot be the same old person who used to be passionately, hotly in pursuit of the woman. You have become cooler, and the person who will note it first will be the woman you are with. She will not think that it is coolness, she will think it is coldness.

You, yourself are saying, "My girlfriend tells me I am cold and know nothing about love. She may be right." She is not right, because you are not cold, you are just cool. And it is not true that you don't know love. But people are accustomed to a hot love, and in their mind there are only two possibilities – either you are hot about them, or you are cold.

The golden mean does not exist for people.

A man of meditation never becomes cold and never remains hot either: he becomes cool, calm and quiet. His love takes a totally new dimension, which will appear to ordinary people as indifference. To those who understand, his love becomes less noisy, less stupid, less retarded, less biological, but starts having a flavor of spirituality, which needs an understanding; otherwise the other person, your partner, is bound to think you have become cold. And coldness is a sign of death, not of life.

You are saying, "Am I keeping my heart closed?" No, your heart is *as* open as it has never been before. But your girlfriend is not growing with you in your meditations. She is no longer a fellow traveller; she has been left behind, and a distance has grown.

You have to help her. But on the contrary, she is trying to pull you back. And it seems she is powerful, because she has convinced you that you are growing and moving towards death and towards coldness, and not towards life and love. And you say, "She may be right."

This is a dangerous idea if you carry it in your mind; then rather than helping her, she will destroy you. Now it is an urgent duty for you to share your meditation, your silence, your clarity, your coolness with your girlfriend. I know it is a difficult job. Particularly if the man goes ahead and the woman is left behind, it is more difficult. She will create tantrums, she will throw things, she will have pillow fights, she will disturb your meditations. She can do anything, because you are slipping out of her hands, out of her possession.

And it is not only about small people, even a man like Socrates…his wife poured boiling water, which she was preparing for tea, over his head and burnt half of his face for his whole life. He was teaching his students – and you will see what I mean by coolness: he wiped the water and continued with what he was teaching.

The students were shocked; they could not believe it. At least the woman could have waited if she wanted to fight with her husband; she had every right, but not before the students who have come from faraway places to seek the wisdom of Socrates. But they were more impressed by the way Socrates responded to the incident, as if nothing had happened.

He simply wiped his face, and started where he had been stopped by his wife – this is coolness, this is calmness – this is suchness. And when a student asked, "We cannot understand, and we have forgotten all that we had come to ask you. Now this question has become more important to us: Your wife has misbehaved, and you have not even taken note of it."

Socrates said, "Whatever she is capable of she has done, and whatever I am capable of I am doing. Our capacities are different – this is nobody's fault." He is not angry about his wife; on the contrary he is very compassionate. He said, "Any woman would have done the same, because I am continually concerned with my students, with philosophers coming from faraway places to visit me, and I am discussing things in which she is not interested at all. Sometimes the whole day passes and I don't have any time for her. She is a poor woman, and she is behaving just as any unconscious human being is supposed to behave."

But if it happens otherwise – my experience is of both the types – if the woman progresses in meditation, in silence, in blissfulness, she manages to pull her husband closer to her state. Husbands are very obedient people.

It rarely happens that the couple grow together; then it has a beauty of its own, no conflict. I would like couples to grow together, hand in hand, dancing the same dance, singing the same song, so as they grow, their understanding about each other also grows and nobody creates trouble. Otherwise, whoever is left behind feels offended.

Your wife, Sudheer, or your girlfriend, is suffering from a natural phenomenon. She has been left behind. You have not cared to keep her hand in your hand; you have grown alone. Now, don't be convinced by her ideas.

You, yourself say, "I feel for the first time that I have arrived home." You feel your serenity, your silence, your clarity, and still you are convinced by your wife that you are moving towards death, and that you are not moving towards love and life because you are becoming cold. Now it is your responsibility.

Love knows responsibility.

Share whatever you have gained in these ten years. Help her to grow; otherwise, she will poison your own mind and destroy your growth. Your heart is not closed; neither is your meditation an escape and a protection from involving yourself completely in life.

Your meditation is a preparation for a higher

life, for a deeper life, for a more divine life. But you will have to be more loving and more compassionate towards your girlfriend, and don't be, in any way, pulled back by her.

A man walks into a department store and goes up to the good-looking woman behind the counter. "Excuse me," he says, "do you keep stationery?" She blushes and says, "Well, as long as I can, but then I go absolutely crazy."

Now the word *stationery*, one would have never thought would be understood in this way. But words are words; how you interpret them, what meaning you give them, becomes their meaning.

Your girlfriend must be troubling you. And I am not condemning her, I am simply saying that it is your fault. If you wanted to remain in a relationship, then you should not go too far away. The distance will destroy your relationship.

Meditate together, and help her to come closer to you. And don't be taken by her attitudes, don't allow her to poison your mind. That's what you are doing, you are accepting her ideas.

It is not yet understood by humanity that women are in many ways stronger than men. Just the other day, Neelam was showing me a woman's picture. I could not believe my eyes. She was preparing for a national competition in Japan, and now that kind of competition is becoming popular all over the world.

The competition is to show that a woman can also be muscular. This has been up to now the monopoly of men. And men have been convincing women all through history, "That is our superiority, our strength: we are muscular; you are weak, fragile, you need protection." Seeing that woman, I could not believe that she was a woman. She was looking like a great wrestler, with such good muscles.

And these competitions are proving it, that to be muscular is not men's monopoly. They have just convinced women that they cannot have muscles; otherwise, there is no reason. They can do the same gymnastics, the same exercises, and they can have a muscular body – although a muscular body in a woman is not beautiful, it looks ugly.

But in every way, the woman is stronger than man. This has to be understood. She lives longer – five years more than man. All over the world, her average life is five years more. And when children are born, a hundred girls are born to every one hundred and fifteen boys, because fifteen boys are going to pop off before the time of marriage comes. At that time there will be a hundred girls and a hundred boys. Girls don't pop off.
They have more resistance against diseases than man has.

Now it all depends what we mean by power. Women fall sick less, men fall sick more. Women remain younger longer than men. Women go mad less than men. One would expect that things should be otherwise – because women behave so crazily they should go mad more. But because they are throwing out their madness every day, in installments, they don't gather it enough. And because man goes on controlling himself, he accumulates his madness, and then one day it is too much and he has a nervous breakdown.

Less women commit suicide than men; although women say almost every day that they are going to commit suicide. They even make attempts – but very safe ones. A few pills, sleeping pills they will take, knowing perfectly well that that is not going to kill them. It is enough to harass the husband and make him condemned by all the neighbors, and the doctor, and the whole crowd: "You should behave, and you should treat her in a more gentlemanly way. This is not right."

But women don't commit suicide. They talk about it, they manage the drama also, but their number of suicides is half the number of men's. Man does not play the drama; he feels that that kind of drama is womanish...it is not good to take sleeping pills and make yourself look stupid in the morning.

And it is strange – if the man takes the pills, then nobody is going to tell the wife, "You should behave better." Still the man will be told, "How stupid you are, is this the way to behave with a poor woman and children?"

If a man is developing spiritually, it is for his own sake that his girlfriend – or wife, or whatsoever is her name – should not be left behind. Otherwise she will go on pulling your leg. She is not worried about your spirituality. In the first place, she does not believe that you are spiritual. Just sitting with closed eyes, she knows you are simply avoiding her. It is not meditation, it is escape.

No woman has any good ideas about her husband or boyfriend. She knows that this stupid guy..."Who does he think he is befooling, that he has become serene, silent, cool, attained clarity?" No woman with whom you are sexually related is going to believe that you have any intelligence. She goes on worshiping people who have renounced the world, who have renounced the woman particularly. That man may have no other qualities, may be just a complete idiot, but the women will go and touch his feet – here is a great saint. So remember that your fellow traveler is not to be left behind.

When Hymie comes back from visiting the doctor, he looks terrible. Hymie tells his wife that the doctor had said that he was going to die before the night was out. She hugs him, and they cry a little, and Becky suggests they go to bed early to make love one more time.

They make love until Becky falls asleep, but Hymie is frightened to sleep because it is his last night on earth. He lies there in the dark while Becky snores.

Hymie whispers in his wife's ear, "Becky, please, just one more time for old times' sake." But Becky keeps snoring.

Hymie looks at his watch, leans over to his wife and shakes her hard, "Please Becky, just one more time for old times' sake!"

Becky simply looks at him and says, "Hymie, how can you be so selfish? It is alright for you, but I have to get up in the morning."

Okay, Vimal?

Yes, Bhagwan.

Session 18

The River Needs No Guide

That "me" is the block.
In suchness there is no "me,"
only a pure isness – no "I," no "thou."
And when there is no searching, no longing,
the ego cannot exist even for a split second.

March 6, 1987
Morning

Beloved Bhagwan,

In discourse I followed past words,
disregarding feelings, into air and the pattern of my being.
Is it really this simple?
Now moving into mysterious depths, no universal visions –
just me, here amongst the birds, the trees, the people
in all its suchness.
No searching, no longing, just living me...
I know this to be true, but I also need Your answer.
In this context, then what is enlightenment?

Dhyan Sarvam, the question that you have asked is not a question, but an expression of what you are feeling. What you are feeling is, "no universal visions – just me, here amongst the birds, the trees, the people – in all its suchness. No searching, no longing, just living me...I know this to be true, but I also need Your answer." Then your knowing is not complete. Your knowing has hidden behind it a doubt; otherwise there is no need of any answer. If you know, then what is the need of my answer?

But I can understand your problem – on the one hand you know the beauty of this moment, the blissfulness of here-now, and yet there is a suspicion underground raising the question, "Is it really true? Is it all? Or is there something more?" And this doubt is arising because of a simple thing. If you had looked at your question a little more deeply, you would have found, "No universal visions – just me." This "me" is the source of your doubt. If you had said, "No universal visions, no me, here amongst the birds, the trees, the people – in all its suchness. No searching, no longing, just living me...." That "me" is the block.

In suchness there is no "me," only a pure *isness* – no "I," no "thou." And when there is no searching, no longing, the ego cannot exist even for a split second. The searching, the longing, the desiring – these are the very heartbeats of the ego.

You say, "I know this to be true." You do not know, your mind is deceiving you, because you are still there – in knowing *you* cannot be. Knowing drowns the "I" and then there is a certainty, "This is true." But wherever you find the "I" lingering in some way, beware of it. Its deception is going too far.

You are asking, "In this context, what is

enlightenment?" In this context there is no enlightenment. But if the "I" and the "me" have also dissolved in the suchness of things, in the *isness* of existence, then this would have been the enlightenment. Just a little more awareness...you are very close to it. But don't take it for granted that you have arrived. The old mind tries to the very end; when you are entering the boundaries of enlightenment, then too, it goes on trying with all its power to hold you back.

The experience is beautiful, but your ego is making it not reach to its ultimate climax. You drop the "me," you drop the "I," and there will be no need to answer; there will be no need for recognition – you will know. But *you* will not be there, only the knowing will be there, that, "This is it."

Everybody has to remember about the old mind. It is such a long habit; for many, many lives you have remained attached to it. So it is not surprising that when you are departing from it, it clings to you – perhaps just the last hug, but the hug can go on being prolonged.

I have heard.... An old Jew is run over in front of a church. A priest runs out and whispers in his ear, "Do you believe in the Father, the Son, and the Holy Ghost?" The Jew opens his eyes and says, "I am dying and he is asking me riddles!"

Although he is dying he has a Jewish conditioning and the priest is asking from the background of a Christian mind.

You were very close. You just missed by inches, not even miles. When you again feel this – and you will feel this.... It is a great achievement to feel the pure space of no searching, no longing, no universal visions, to feel only the birds singing in the trees, the people all around. But *you* are missing; you are no more there. Just gather courage not to be, and this very experience becomes enlightenment.

Enlightenment is not something superhuman, it is your basic right. But your ego goes on postponing it, goes on bringing itself between you and your enlightenment. And in such subtle ways that unless you are very alert, you are going to be deceived. When you felt no searching, no longing, you could have felt just life, just living. Why just "living me"? Why confine living to a small prison of "me"?

Feel the heartbeat of the whole universe and let your own separation be dissolved into it. Then you would have said, "The knowing has happened; this is it and there is no other enlightenment." The absence of the ego and the presence of universal consciousness is what enlightenment means.

Beloved Bhagwan,

I am a student from Japan.
"Where there is a will, there is a way."
Please tell me about it, Bhagwan.

Yasuhiro Janiguchi, the proverb, "Where there is a will, there is a way" exists in almost every language, in every civilization. But nobody has looked into the psychology of it. The will creates its own way, because the will takes you away from yourself. If you ask me, I would rather like to change this proverb to, "No will, no way, and you are at home." Why go unnecessarily traveling around the world? – because no way leads anywhere, no will leads anywhere except into frustration, misery, failure, even if you succeed.

There is another proverb which says, "Nothing succeeds like success." But my own experience is, "Nothing fails like success." But we are such hypocrites, pretenders. When you succeed you know you have not gained anything; on the contrary, this stupid idea of success has taken away all your life, and all its songs, and all its poetry, and all its dances. You sacrifice yourself before the false goddess of success, and now what have you got?

But it needs courage to declare to the world, "You think I have succeeded? That is an outward interpretation of my state. My inner experience is, 'Nothing fails like success.'" But all of our societies have been teaching you to succeed, to have a strong willpower, because, "Wherever there is will, there is a way." You will find the way, but those ways lead nowhere; they are dead-end streets. And meanwhile, your life is slipping from your hands.

But willpower has been supported by thousands of thinkers and philosophers without ever going into the inner reality of it. To will means you are not satisfied with yourself. It means you are not fulfilled, something more is needed, that you are not at ease. You have to go somewhere, you have to become someone. The very existence of will is against your being – it degrades your being into becoming. Then there is search and then there is longing, and naturally you will find a way, just to go away from yourself.

But this is not the right thing to do – this is suicidal; you are committing suicide. The farther you go on that way of the will, the more you will find yourself lost. This has happened to almost the whole of humanity – they have forgotten who they are. They have gone so far away from themselves that they have forgotten their home.

Drop the will, and immediately that way disappears like a dream. It has no reality of its own. The will gives its power to the way, it creates the way.

So the proverb is right, but those who follow it are wrong. One need not have any will, and one need not have any way. Then sit inside your home and play a bamboo flute. There is no need to go anywhere because you are already there, where you would really like to be.

Beloved Bhagwan,

Tears gently falling in rivers down my face...
just so tired of trying, struggling, fighting to be
what I think I should be in order to get what I think I need.
Beloved, even with You I tried so hard.
In this giving up...the gap, the beauty, the unknown...
fears meet trust.
Bhagwan, could it be that this river is flowing
towards life, towards You, towards the ocean?
Thank You, my Master.

Do you see? "Tears gently falling in rivers down my face... just so tired of trying, struggling, fighting to be what I think I should be in order to get what I think I need. Beloved, even with You I tried so hard." This is the way of the will. It simply goes on destroying you.

In the old days there used to be a proverb, "All roads lead to Rome." But in fact, all roads lead to death. And perhaps Rome is the graveyard of the whole world.

Just the other day I heard that one of the archbishops is hiding in the Vatican, because the Vatican is an independent country – just eight square miles – and the Italian police are after him because he has been deceiving the Vatican and the Italian government. He is the treasurer of the pope, and the pope is protecting him. The Italian police cannot enter into the Vatican.

These are your religious leaders! That man has stolen millions of dollars – and he is an archbishop, and a treasurer to the pope! If the pope had any guts, he would have handed him over to the police. But he is hiding him in the Vatican, because the police cannot enter there.

You are feeling tired, full of tears. You have been struggling hard to be what you think you should be in order to get what you think you need. These are the ways of the will: you have to become this, you have to become that, you have to get this, you have to get that. But you are fortunate, greatly blessed that you became tired and you gave up trying; you gave up the will to succeed; you dropped the hardship you were imposing upon yourself.

"In this giving up...the gap," – no will, no way, no you, just the gap. And, "the beauty, the unknown... fears meet trust. Bhagwan, could it be that this river is flowing towards life, towards you, towards the ocean?" Deva Leena, there is no question, because every river is moving towards the ocean. It is only the man who gets frozen, and then the flow stops.... If you melt in trust, the river starts flowing again. And it has never been the case that any river has forgotten the path and has not reached the ocean.

But remember the gap. And remember Chuang Tzu's statement, "Easy is right and right is easy." And when you forget both, what is right and what is easy, you have arrived at the ocean.

The ocean is not far away, Leena. But your ego

is a frozen block – it needs melting. Love melts it, fear makes it more frozen, trust melts it. All that the people who are trying to find themselves have to do, is remain melted and allow the river to move on its own. You should not be the guide; the river needs no guide. Its very nature is to reach to the ocean. It is not an effort, it is its intrinsic quality.

After making the flight information, the Israeli pilot on the El Al jet forgot to turn the intercom off, and his next words were heard throughout the cabin, "I will have a cup of coffee and then I will screw that gorgeous new stewardess, Lee."

Lee was down at the end of the passenger cabin and ran forward to tell the pilot to turn the intercom off. Halfway down, an old man tripped her up.

"Can't you wait, Lee? Let him have his coffee first!"

Leena, be at ease, have your coffee. And there is no need to run towards the ocean. Just slowly enjoy the trees, and the birds, and the people, having a trust in your heart that every river has always reached the ocean. And you cannot be the exception; existence does not allow any exceptions. You will also reach the ocean.

Beloved Bhagwan,

Thank You for throwing most of my questions in Your garbage bin.
At first it hurts the ego, but not really that much.
You are showing me how my questions are unnecessary.
Either I'm trying to be smart, trying to write an unusual question,
or trying to be funny, hoping to make everybody laugh.
But I realize I'm always trying to prove something, which is nonsense.
My beloved Master, it occurred to me that maybe You want me to stop
asking questions and simply shut up.
Has the time really come?
Sometimes I have wondered if that time had not come already a long time ago.

Chidananda, it is true, I have been throwing your questions away because they were not authentic; they were not coming from your necessity of inner growth. And you have received the answer. Unless I had thrown them, you would not have understood what you recognize in this question. Although you have not yet understood the whole point, a glimpse has happened.

You say, "Thank You for throwing most of my questions in Your garbage bin. At first it hurts the ego, but not really that much." That means you will be still asking those questions. And the fear is that you may become slowly, slowly immune, because it hurts only just a little. By and by it will not hurt at all.

You say, "You are showing me how my

questions are unnecessary. Either I'm trying to be smart, trying to write an unusual question, or trying to be funny, hoping to make everybody laugh. But I realize I am always trying to prove something, which is nonsense." Just remember what you are writing in this, because man's memory is very superficial. Tomorrow you may forget again and fall into your old habits.

You don't know that almost one hundred questions come every day, and I have to throw away almost ninety-five. Not that I don't have time – if I feel that they are sincere and you need it urgently, I will find the time – but they are so obviously unnecessary. But throwing them away was also my answer to you.

George Bernard Shaw used to reply only once a month to his letters. For one month he would go on piling up all those letters – and he was receiving thousands of letters from all over the world.

His friends were worried, "What kind of method have you found? You go on piling up the letters; you don't even read them." He said, "I have decided, on every first day of the month, I read them. Most of them already have answers. The few that still remain relevant, I answer – and they are very few."

Not answering a question is also an answer. And it is good that some insight happened to you, Chidananda. Now remain aware of it, because I have unnecessarily to read your questions. I may not answer, but I cannot be so uncompassionate as George Bernard Shaw.

You say, "It occurred to me that maybe you want me to stop asking questions and simply shut up." No, I want you to ask authentic questions. I want you to ask something that is going to help you in your growth. You are forgetting yourself completely in your questions. They are meant for others – they should be funny, they should make people laugh. How are you going to be helped by this?

I don't want you to shut up. The time has not come for it yet. And when the time comes, I will not need to tell you to shut up. You suddenly will find there are no questions to be asked; you have received the answer; you have found the answer.

But the mind is so cunning, Chidananda, that you are saying, "Has the time really come? Sometimes I have wondered if that time had not come already a long time ago."

You have not even begun the journey. You are concerned with unessential things. The time has certainly come for you to be sincere and authentic and ask those questions which will expose your wounds and heal them.

A KGB agent sees a Jew reading a Hebrew grammar book on a bench in Moscow's Gorky Park. "Hey, Jew," he shouts, "Why are you reading that? You know we will never let you go to Israel."

"Well," said the Jew, "I am reading it in case they speak Hebrew in heaven."

"And what if you go to hell?," said the KGB man. "Oh," sighed the Jew, "I should be okay. I already speak Russian."

You need not worry, Chidananda, that people should laugh. When I feel it necessary, I find a way for them to laugh. These laughters are not meaningless. I don't want to make your head too burdened with heavy, serious, existential problems, so I go on telling jokes here and there. A good laughter clears the clouds, and then you are ready again to hear something serious.

One thing you can do, Chidananda – and I have been using your jokes – if you cannot find any authentic question, you can go on writing your jokes. Anybody who feels like writing something and does not have any question to ask, he can write a joke. Because from where am I going to find the jokes?

Beloved Bhagwan,

In my mind there is a very subtle conditioning,
and that is: giving and receiving always have to be balanced.
You say that action and reward are two sides of the same coin, but still sometimes
I feel that to receive so much from You is not right. Thank You!

Deva Sukhkanda, are you a Jew? Or perhaps you may have been a Jew in some of your past lives? From where did you get this conditioning?

You are saying, "In my mind there is a very subtle conditioning, and that is: giving and receiving always have to be balanced. You say that action and reward are two sides of the same coin, but still sometimes I feel that to receive so much from you is not right." But you don't know that I am receiving more from you than you are receiving from me.

You *are* my life, otherwise I have no reason at all to exist another day. You are my dreams, You are my hope. It is through you I go on believing that perhaps humanity can be saved.

What you are receiving is very small. What I am receiving from you is my very life, my very heartbeats, my breathing – because the day I feel that it is a hopeless task, I will simply cover myself in my blanket and disappear.

It is your joy, your laughter, your silence, your effort to be aware that goes on giving me hope.

In the whole world nobody is concerned about the calamity humanity is going to face. I can see it approaching every day closer and closer. And I want you to be ready to fight against it, to revolt against all those forces which are rotten, old, ugly, animalistic – but they *are* in power. And such destructive power...then these poor birds will not be able to sing anymore, these trees will not be able to have a sunbath every morning, a dance in the wind, in the rain. They are not concerned that the moon will still go on rising but there will be no poet to sing about it. There will be sunrises and sunsets, but no painter to paint it.

This is the only planet where we are absolutely certain that life has come to the highest peak. Scientists guess that at least fifty thousand other planets also must have life of some kind – but that is guesswork, and you cannot depend on it. This is the only reality that we know and that we are certain about.

So you need not be worried. In fact I should be worried that I am taking too much and giving too little. But my problem is that I cannot worry, and your problem is that you cannot stop worrying; you will find something or other to worry about.

Goldberg meets Ginsberg at the station. "Tell me, Ginsberg, we meet here every day and often at the synagogue and the golf club, and you never ask me, 'How is business?'"

"Okay," replies Ginsberg, "tell me Goldberg, how is business?"

"Ah," replied Goldberg, "don't ask."

Okay, Vimal?

Yes, Bhagwan.

Session 19

Awareness
Will Not Go To War

*Nation itself is an immoral idea,
because it divides humanity –
and war is certainly immoral.
You may find good names, good words –
sometimes it is religion,
sometimes it is political ideology,
sometimes it is Christianity,
sometimes it is communism – good ideas,
but the reality is turning human beings into butchers.*

March 6, 1987
Evening

Beloved Bhagwan,

Please talk about morality.

Shantam Divyama, the question about morality is immensely significant, because morality is not that which has been told to you for centuries. All the religions have exploited the idea of morality. They have been teaching in different ways, but the basic foundation is the same: unless you become moral, ethical, you cannot become religious.

By morality they mean that you have to be truthful, you have to be honest, you have to be charitable, you have to be compassionate, you have to be nonviolent. In one word, all these great values have first to be present in you, only then you can move towards being religious.

This whole concept is upside down. According to me, unless you are religious you cannot be moral. Religion comes first, morality is only a by-product. If you make the by-product into the goal of human character, you will create such a troubled, miserable humanity – and for such a good cause. You are bringing the cart before the bullocks – neither the bullocks can move, nor the cart can move; both are stuck.

How can a man be truthful if he does not know what truth is? How can a man be honest if he does not know even who he is? How can a man be compassionate if he does not know the source of love within himself? From where will he get the compassion? All that he can do in the name of morality is to become a hypocrite, a pretender. And there is nothing more ugly than to be a hypocrite. He can pretend, he can try hard, but everything will remain superficial and skin-deep. Just scratch him a little bit, and you will find all the animal instincts fully alive, ready to take revenge whenever they can get the opportunity.

Putting morality before religion is one of the greatest crimes that religions have committed against humanity.

The very idea brings a repressed human being. And a repressed human being is sick, psychologically split, constantly in a fight with himself, trying to do things which he does not want to do.

Morality should be very relaxed and easy – just like your shadow; you don't have to drag it with you, it simply comes on its own. But this has not happened; what has happened is a psychologically sick humanity. Everybody is tense, because whatever you are doing there is a conflict about whether it is right or wrong. Your nature goes in one direction, your conditioning goes just in the opposite direction, and a house divided cannot stand for long. So everybody is somehow pulling himself together; otherwise the danger is always there, just by your side, of having a nervous breakdown.

I do not teach morality at all. Morality should come on its own accord. I teach you directly the experience of your own being. As you become more and more silent, serene, calm and quiet, as you start understanding you own consciousness, as your inner being becomes more and more centered, your actions will reflect morality. It will not be something that you decide to do, it will be something as natural as roses on a rose bush. It is not that the rose bush is doing great austerities, and fasting, and praying to God, and disciplining itself according to the ten commandments; the rose bush is doing nothing. The rose bush has just to be healthy, nourished, and the flowers will come in their own time, with great beauty, effortlessly.

A morality that comes with effort is immoral. A morality that comes without effort is the only morality there is.

That's why I don't talk about morality at all, because it is morality that has created so many problems for humanity – about everything. They have given you ready-made ideas about what is right, what is wrong. In life, ready-made ideas don't work, because life goes on changing, just like a river – taking new turns, moving into new territories...from the mountains to the valleys, from the valleys to the plains, from the plains to the ocean.

Heraclitus is right when he says, "You cannot step in the same river twice," because it is always flowing. The second time you step in, it is different water. I agree with Heraclitus so much that I say unto you, you cannot step in the same river even once – because when your feet are touching its surface, the water underneath is flowing; as your feet are going deeper, the water on the surface is flowing; and by the time you have touched the bottom, so much water has gone...it is not the same water, that your step can not be said to be entering into the same river.

Life is just like the river – a flux. And you are all carrying fixed dogmas. You always find yourself unfit, because if you follow your dogmas, you have to go against life; if you follow life, you have to go against your dogmas.

Hence my whole effort is to make your morality spontaneous. You should be conscious and alert, and respond to every situation with absolute consciousness. Then whatever you do is right. It is not a question of actions being right or wrong, it is a question of consciousness – whether you are doing it consciously or unconsciously like a robot.

My whole philosophy is based on growing your consciousness higher, deeper, to the point when there is no unconsciousness inside you; you have become a pillar of light. In this light, in this clarity, to do anything wrong becomes impossible. It is not that you have to avoid doing it; even if you want to do it, you cannot. And in this consciousness, whatsoever you do becomes a blessing.

Your action out of consciousness is moral, out of unconsciousness is immoral...it may be the same action.

I am reminded of an old story: A king was getting old, and he told his only son, who was going to succeed him, "Before I die you have to learn the art of morality, because a king has to be a model for everyone else in the kingdom; nothing should go wrong in your actions. So I am sending you today to my old master. I am old, he is even older than me, so don't waste time. Learn everything intensely, totally, without wasting a single moment."

The prince went to the master and he was surprised – surprised by the fact that the master was a master of archery: "And what has archery to do with morality? Has my father gone senile?" But he had come to the mountains, so he thought, "It is better to see the old man at least once."

He went in. The old man was immensely beautiful and graceful, surrounded by an aura of silence and peace. He had been thinking he was going to meet a warrior, an archer, but here was a sage. He was getting even more puzzled. He asked the old man, "Are you the master archer?" He said, "You are right."

The prince said, "I have been sent by my father, the king, who is your disciple, to learn morality from you. I cannot see any connection at all between morality and archery." The old man laughed and he said, "Soon you will see."

The prince said, "I am in a hurry. My father is old, and before he dies I want to fulfill his desire." The master said, "Then get lost, because these things cannot be learned in a hurry. Patience, infinite patience is the very foundation of learning any art, whether it is archery or it is morality."

Looking at the old man's eyes the prince remained, and he said, "When are my lessons going to start?" The old man said, "Just now they have started. Patience is your first lesson. And about the second lesson I should make you aware. The second lesson is that you will be cleaning the floors, cleaning in the garden, collecting the old leaves, throwing them out. Be very careful, because I may hit you with a wooden sword at any moment. Although it is wooden, it hits really hard. It has given many people fractures."

The prince said, "But I have come here to learn morality, not to get fractures!" The old man said, "That will come in its own time, this is only the beginning." Puzzled, confused...but he knew his father, that if he went back empty-handed the old man would be really enraged. He had to learn. On both sides two mad, old people.... "And this man is trying to teach me morality by hitting me! But let us see what happens."

And the master started hitting him. He would be washing the floor, and suddenly a hit would come. He would be cleaning the path in the garden, and suddenly a hit would come. But he became surprised, within a week, that a certain intuition was arising in him. Even before the old man had approached him, he would jump out of his way. Whatever he was doing, some part of his consciousness was continuously alert to the old man, where he was. And the old man used to walk so silently that it was almost impossible to remain conscious. But he started being conscious, because getting so many hits, his whole body was hurting.

It continued for one month. But in one month he became so capable that the old man was no longer able to hit him. The old man said, "You are really the son of your father. He was also very keen, intense, and total in learning; it won't take much time. Your first lesson is finished today, because for twenty-four hours I have been trying to hit you, but you have been found always alert, and saved yourself.

"From tomorrow morning you will have to be more alert, because the wooden sword will be replaced by a real sword. The wooden sword at the most could have given you a fracture, but the real sword may even cut off your head. So more awareness will be needed."

But this one month had been of such great learning...he was never aware that inside him there was so much possibility of intuitive awareness. He was trained, well-trained intellectually, but he had no idea of any intuitiveness. And he was not afraid even of the real sword, because he said, "It is the same. If you cannot hit me with the wooden sword, you cannot hit me with the real sword either. It makes no difference to me."

For one month the old man was trying in every possible way to hit him with the real sword, and naturally the prince became more and more alert – had to become, there was no other alternative. And one complete month passed, and the old man could not even touch him. He was very happy, and he said, "I am immensely satisfied. Now the third lesson. Up to now I was hitting you only while you were awake. From this evening, remember that in the night when you are asleep I may hit you at any time. Again it will start with the wooden sword."

The prince became a little worried – awake it was one thing, but when you are asleep? But these two months had given him tremendous respect, trust in the old man and his art, and also a confidence about his own intuition. And he thought, "If he says it, then perhaps intuition never sleeps."

And that proved to be the truth. The body sleeps, the mind sleeps, but the intuition is always awake; its very nature is awareness, but we never look at it. He had to look, he had to remain alert, even asleep.

The old man started hitting him, and a few times he got really bad hits. But he was grateful, not angry, because after each hit he was becoming more and more alert, even in sleep – just like a small flame, something remained alive in him, alert and watchful. And just in one month he was again able to protect himself even in his sleep. As the old man would come close, very silently, making no noise, no footstep sounds, the young man would jump up out of his bed. He may have been fast asleep, but something remained awake.

And in the next lesson the real sword appeared in his sleep. The next morning the old man said, "Now the last lesson – I will be hitting you with a real sword. And you know my sword, just a single hit and you are finished. You have to gather all your consciousness." The young man was a little worried, a little afraid, because the game was becoming more and more dangerous.

In the early morning sun the old man was reading a book, sitting under a tree in the rising sun, and the young man was gathering the old leaves from the garden. Suddenly a thought came to him, "This old man has been hitting me for months; it will be a great idea...I should try to hit him and see whether he is alert or not."

And he was just twenty or twenty-five feet away, when he was just thinking this in his mind – he had not done anything yet – and the old man said, "Boy, I am very old, and your teaching is not finished yet. Don't have such ideas." The prince could not believe it. He came and touched his feet, and said, "Forgive me, but I had not done anything, I was only thinking... just an idea."

The old man said, "When you become fully

alert even the sound of your thoughts is heard. It is the question of awareness. You don't have to do anything, you just think and I will know. And soon you will become capable of the same – just a little more patience."

And soon the day came when he started suddenly becoming aware that the old man was thinking of hitting him...for no reason. The old man was sitting reading his book, but the idea came so clearly that he went to the master, and said, "So you are going to hit me again? Just a few seconds before I heard the idea." The master said, "You are right, I was just thinking to finish the page and come. Now there is no need for you to be here. I know your father is old and is waiting for you."

But the young man said, "What happened about morality?" The old man said, "Forget all about it. A man who is so alert can only be moral. He cannot harm anybody, he cannot steal, he cannot be unkind, cruel; he will be naturally loving and compassionate. You forget all about morality!"

This awareness is what I call religiousness. The prince went back. The father was waiting and waiting, and he said, "Have you learned the whole art of archery?" The young man said, "You sent me to learn the art of morality. From where have you got the idea of archery?" The king said, "I sent you to learn morality, archery was only a device."

There are many devices, many ways and methods of meditation to create awareness, to wake up your sleeping intuition. And once it is awake, then there is no need to tell you what is good, what is moral, what is bad, what is immoral; your awareness will be decisive on its own. And it will be spontaneous, fresh and young, and always to the point, because all principles become dead. And if you try to fit your life according to principles, you also become dead.

That's what has happened to Christians, to Hindus, to Mohammedans, to Jainas, to all the people around the world – they are living according to dead principles. And those dead principles don't fit with the reality – they cannot fit. Only a spontaneous consciousness.... The difference is something like this: you have a photograph of yourself of the last year, or maybe of your childhood, and if you don't know that it is your picture of your childhood, you may not even recognize it – because you have changed so much. That picture is dead, it is not growing; you are growing.

Morality is like photographs. Religion is like a mirror. If a child is facing it, it reflects the child; if an old man is facing it, it reflects the old man. It is always spontaneous, in the moment, responding to reality. A conscious human being is just like a mirror – he reflects reality and responds accordingly. His *response* is moral.

So I am changing the whole emphasis from action to awareness.

And if more and more people can become aware, the world will be a totally different place. A man of awareness will not go to war. Although religious scriptures say that to sacrifice yourself for your nation, for your religion is virtuous, a man of consciousness cannot follow that dead idea. To him, the nation itself is an immoral idea, because it divides humanity – and war is certainly immoral. You may find good names, good words – sometimes it is religion, sometimes it is political ideology, sometimes it is Christianity, sometimes it is communism – good ideas, but the reality is turning human beings into butchers.

You are killing people whom you have never even met. And you know perfectly well that just as you have left a wife behind, crying, who will be waiting for you, just as you have left your old mother and father back at home, hoping that their son comes back alive, just as you have left small children... the man you are killing has also a wife, has also children, has also an old father and mother. And he has done no harm to you; neither have you done any harm to him.

If the world becomes a little more conscious, soldiers will throw away their arms and hug each other, sit down together under a tree and gossip. The politicians cannot force all the armies to kill, to murder. Neither can the popes, the religious leaders convince anybody that, "For God's sake you have to kill." Strange...because God has created everybody. Whomsoever you are killing, you are killing God's creation. If it is true that God created the world, then there should be no war – it is one family; there should be no nations.

These are immoral things: the nations, the religions, anything that discriminates against people and creates conflict.

A man of awareness will not be greedy, because he will be able to see that his greed will create poverty; and the people who will be starving and dying through poverty are his brothers and sisters. It does not matter whether they live in Ethiopia or in India; it does not matter whether their skin is white or black.

Authentic morality is a by-product of consciousness. And the art of consciousness is religion. There is no Hindu religion, there is no Christian religion, there is no Mohammedan religion; there is only one religion, and that is the religion of consciousness – becoming so aware, so enlightened and awakened, that you have eyes to see clearly and can respond according to that clarity.

A man of consciousness cannot be deceived by words. Mohammedans say that if you die in a religious war...how can there be a religious war? War is basically irreligious. But Christians, Mohammedans, and all other religions say that if you die in a religious war, your reward will be great in the otherworld. For this immoral act of killing people, you will be rewarded. Beautiful words "religious war", cover it up.

A man of awareness sees deeply and penetratingly through your words. Neither your God can deceive him, nor your holy books can deceive him, nor your nations, nor your politicians. He lives according to his consciousness. He has an individuality, a very crystal clear individuality – a pure mirror, unclouded by anything, with no dust covering it.

But for thousands of years just mere words, and sometimes such stupid, trivial causes, have been killing people. Christianity in the middle ages burnt thousands of women. They created a fiction – the fiction of the devil. There is no devil. There is no God! But people have lived in unconsciousness, and whatsoever the leaders, the so-called saints, go on saying, people have been told to believe: if you don't believe you will suffer in hell; if you believe you will be rewarded.

People's intelligence has been destroyed. They have been kept retarded. Otherwise it would be impossible to burn thousands of living women for a strange reason – that these women are having sexual intercourse with the devil. Now nobody is having sexual intercourse with the devil. Only in the middle ages, suddenly, the devil became so much interested in women, and that too, only in Europe...!

A special court was created by the pope, so that if anybody suspects any woman, that she is having some friendship with the devil, you have just to report to the court and the woman will be immediately imprisoned, tortured. And the torture was so intense. They had invented special methods of torture.

Just five, six years ago, something went wrong with my back. There were so many body –

workers in the commune, and they all tried, but nobody succeeded in fixing it. Finally the best expert in the world from London was called, and he suggested a machine called traction. The machine was brought, and I was put on the machine. And while they were fixing their belts, I remembered that I have read that this traction machine was created in the middle ages by the Christian priests, to torture women. It pulls your legs to one side and your hands to another side. Naturally it pulls your backbone – so if the backbone has slipped somewhere it comes into line.

It was just an accidental invention. One old woman they were torturing had been suffering for twenty years from a bad back, and after their traction, she could not believe it when she stood up – her pain was gone. That's how the traction machine was transferred from the church to the hospital. It is really torturous, and if you are using it just to torture, then you can go on pulling....

Sometimes even hands were broken, legs were taken out. The torture was so much that the women thought it was better to confess, because while they went on saying, "I have nothing to do with the devil, I don't know the devil," the torture continued. It would stop only when they confessed that they were having sexual intercourse with the devil.

Thousands of women confessed that they had been having sexual intercourse with the devil. And once they had confessed before the court, then there was no problem. The punishment was to burn the woman alive at the crossroads in the middle of the city.

Nobody ever bothered about whether there was any devil. It was just a word – nobody had seen the devil. If you had tortured these women to make a confession that they are having intercourse with God, they would have confessed that too! There is a limit to what one can tolerate in suffering.

Just mere words...but why have people enjoyed killing, suffering, torturing? – because they themselves are unhappy...so unhappy, so miserable. They cannot see anybody else being blissful, being joyous. They want everybody else to suffer more than they are suffering.

Morality has been a very good device to torture people: you don't have to torture them, they torture themselves – even to make love to your own wife is a sin. They don't say it about somebody else's wife, *sex* is sin; and anything connected with sex becomes sin. Now, sex is something natural – there is no way to avoid it. So you are putting man into a dilemma: fixing in his mind that sex is immoral, and giving him a nature which is sexual and sensuous.

It has been discovered that millions of men around the world suffer from migraine after making love. And I was reading a report of a Christian scientist – because he is Christian, his mind is conditioned. He is trying to find all kinds of causes why men suffer from migraines.

He has been working on the project for one year continually. Just now he has produced his report, giving many, many causes – physiological, chemical – and the reality is so simple, there is no need of any investigation. The reality is that you have divided men's mind into two parts. One part says, "What you are doing is wrong. Don't do it"; the other part says, "It is impossible to resist the temptation. I'm going to do it." These two parts start struggling, conflicting.

Migraine is nothing but a conflict, a deep conflict, in your mind. No aboriginal suffers from migraine after making love. Catholics suffer more than anybody else, because their conditioning is so deep that it creates a split in their mind. What they have been saying for centuries is without any base, without any evidence, but they go on repeating it. And once...even if a lie is repeated too often, it starts looking as if it is true.

One should be very much aware about words.

A man goes into a bar and begins to tell a Polish joke. The man sitting next to him, a big, hulking, powerhouse of a man, turns and says menacingly, "I'm Polish. Now you just wait a minute till I get my sons."

He then calls out, "Ivan, come out here; and bring your brother." Two men, bigger than the first, appear from the back room. "Joseph," the man calls out, "You and your cousin come in here," Two more men, the biggest of all, come in through the back door. All five men crowd around the man with the joke.

"Now," says the first Polish man, "Do you want to finish that joke?"

"No," says the man.

"No? And why not?" says the Polish man, opening and closing his fist, "Are you scared?"

"No," says the man, "I just don't feel like having to explain it to five men."

People are very clever with words. They can hide any kind of reality. He is afraid – those five men can kill him – but he finds a beautiful excuse: "I don't want to bother myself, explaining to five people the meaning of the joke"

All the religions have been playing with words, and have not allowed man to be intelligent enough to see through the words. They have created a jungle of words and theologies and dogmas and creeds and cults. And poor man is simply carrying the whole load of it in the name of morality.

I want to tell you, *never bother about morality*. The only concern for a sincere seeker is awareness, more consciousness. And your consciousness will take care of all your acts. Without any effort, your acts will become moral – just like flowers without any act, without any effort they will blossom around you.

Morality is nothing but a conscious man's lifestyle.

Beloved Bhagwan

What is it, that when I sit in Your presence
tears start to run from my eyes?
They are not tears of sadness or happiness.
They come from an unknown space in my being, and they leave me
open and vulnerable, as if I have just been born.
And I find myself looking at the world with new and fresh eyes.
Beloved Bhagwan, would You please say something about tears.

Prem Madhu, tears are one of the most mysterious phenomena in our life. Most people of are aware only of one dimension – that of pain, suffering, misery, sadness. Few people are aware of a second dimension too: that when you are too happy, too blissful, tears come to your eyes. So tears are not confined to sadness and misery; they can be of joy, they can be of blissfulness.

You are talking of a third dimension which is very rare. Very few people have ever come to know the third dimension.

You are saying, "What is it, that when I sit in your presence tears start to run from my eyes? They are not tears of sadness or happiness. They come from an unknown space in my being, and they leave me open and vulnerable, as if I have just been born. And I find myself looking at the world with new and fresh eyes."

This third dimension is of innocence. You feel so innocent, so overflowingly innocent and fresh that tears come to your eyes, out of gratitude. One thing is common – whether pain, or happiness, or innocence – one thing is common, that is overflowingness. Sadness, when it is too much and you cannot contain it, comes out through the tears. Happiness, when it is too much and you cannot contain it, overflows through the tears.

Your experience is very rare, because very few people feel so full of innocence that tears just of pure gratitude, just the feeling of so much grace towards the whole existence...you don't have anything else to give; you pour out your heart in your tears.

It is something tremendously great that is happening to you. Never make any effort to stop it. The society teaches everybody that tears are signs of weakness – so women can be allowed, but men should not cry and weep. Even small boys are told, "Don't be girlish!" Girls are allowed to cry – they are weaker; they cannot contain with as much power as men can contain. And slowly, slowly it has become a part of our heritage, that if you see a man crying he feels embarrassed. Even you feel embarrassed: "A man, and full of tears? You should be strong enough to control them." This is something absolutely absurd.

Tears should never be controlled, because they are always cleansing you. Even if they are of sadness, they will take away your sadness; they will leave you more calm and more quiet. They are always of great help. If they are tears of joy, then the dimension changes. In sadness they will take away your sadness, in happiness they will increase it. They are just like flowers.

And the third dimension of innocence, which you are feeling, is the highest of all. It will cleanse your heart, it will cleanse your mind, it will make you feel fresh, new. That's what you are feeling – as if you are newly born. The same old trees and the same old people start looking so fresh. The green of the trees becomes greener, and the rosiness of the roses becomes rosier, and the beauty of the human face takes on something of the divine. The same eyes of poeple start becoming windows to their soul.

It is a great experience, unique and very rare. Prem Madhu, allow it, help it, enjoy it. Dance when the tears come, sing songs, play on your guitar. You have to rejoice in these tears, because they are opening a new door into your life: the door of pure innocence. The only people who have known anything of godliness in existence are those who have attained to this innocense of the eyes.

The beauty, the truth, the good, they are not far away, just your eyes are so covered with dust that you cannot see. They are all around you; they are everywhere, only you have to clean your eyes. And you cannot do that except when this third dimension of tears happens to you. It happens to all those who enter deep into meditation.

It is happening to you just in my presence. Perhaps my presence is becoming a deep meditation in you, a deep silence, a great love, a tremendous trust. Rejoice in it and be grateful.

Just don't be bothered by the word *tears*, because it has a connotation of sadness, misery, anguish, anxiety – because most people are aware only of one dimension.

A Jew is having a drink at the bar of a hotel, when an oriental gentleman accidentally knocks over his drink. "You dammed Japanese," yells the Jew, "first you gave us Pearl Harbour, now this!"

"Hold on a minute, I am not Japanese, I am Chinese," says the man" Chinese, Japanese, so what's in a name?" Replies the Jew.

"And you Jews," replies the Chinese, "you can talk. You sank the Titanic!" "We sank what?" asked the astonished Jew. "The Titanic was sunk by an iceberg."

"Iceberg, Goldberg! So what is in a name?"

But there is much in a name – its associations. The moment you say tears, suddenly the idea arises of sadness. My people have to change that association absolutely.

Let tears mean always blissfulness.

And if possible, let tears mean innocence, overflowing gratitude to all that existence has done and given to you.

We cannot give anything back. At least tears of gratitude will be a good prayer. Prayers consisting of words are useless; prayers consisting of tears are meaningful.

Beloved Bhagwan,

I am afraid of being nobody. Would you please comment?

Shunyam Anurakt, everybody is afraid of being nobody. Only very rare and extraordinary people are not afraid of being nobody. A Gautam Buddha is needed to be a nobody. A Nobody is not an ordinary phenomenon; it is one of the greatest experiences in life – that you are and still you are not, that you are just pure existence with no name, with no address, with no boundaries...neither a sinner nor a saint, neither inferior nor superior, just a silence.

People are afraid because their whole personality will be gone; their name, their fame, their respectability, all will be gone; hence the fear. But death is going to take them away from you anyway. Those who are wise allow these things to drop by themselves. Then nothing is left for death to take away. Then all fear disappears, because death cannot come to you; you don't have anything for death.

Death cannot kill a nobody.

Once you feel your nobodiness you have become immortal. The experience of nobodiness is exactly the meaning of nirvana, of nothingness, of absolute undisturbed silence, with no ego, with no personality, with no hypocrisy – just this silence...and these insects singing in the night.

You are here in a way, and still you are not.

You are here because of the old association with the body. But look within, and you are not. And this insight, where there is pure silence and pure isiness, is your reality which death cannot destroy. This is your eternity, this is your immortality.

Shunyam Anurakt, enjoy as much as you can moments of nobodiness. And it is such a simple, uncomplicated experience – because you *are* nobody; you have just to sink within yourself a little deeper. Your personality is only on the surface. Inside is only a vast sky – infinite.

Once you taste it without fear, you would love to go back again and again into the experience. Whenever you will have time, you would like to dive deep into your nobodiness.

When you are nobody you are a Gautam Buddha. When you are nobody you are the whole existence.

There is nothing to fear. There is nothing to lose. And if you think anything is lost – your name, your respectability, your fame – they are worthless. They are playthings for children, not for mature people.

It is time for you to be mature, it is time for you to be ripe, time for you, just to be.

Two drunks are walking down the streets of London with nothing to do, as all the pubs have closed long ago. They come by a street light and both stop to stare at it. After a few moments, one of them mumbles, "Is not the moon beautiful tonight?" The other one turns to him in surprise, and says, "The moon? That is the sun you are looking at."

They argue for a while, and just as they have decided to get an opinion, another drunk come stumbling around the corner. One of the first drunks asks him, "Excuse me, is that the sun or the moon?" The drunk shrugs his shoulders, and says, "Sorry, I don't know. I don't live around here."

All your name, and all your fame, and all your degrees and qualifications, and your richness, and your respectability and prestige, are nothing but different kinds of alcoholic beverages.

Only one who is nobody is not drunk. Only one who is nobody is fully awake, fully alert. And in his alertness he gains the whole world; in his nobodiness the whole universe can disappear. It is so vast.

Your somebodiness is so small. The more you are somebody, the more small you are. The more you are nobody, the bigger....Be absolutely nobody, and you are one with the existence itself.

Okay Vimal?

Yes Bhagwan.

Session 20

Each Human Being Is A Longing Of Existence

*Life does not owe anything to you.
You owe everything to life.
This is a great misunderstanding
which should be dropped.*

March 7, 1987
Morning

Beloved Bhagwan,

The more I am here with You,
the more I am confused, excited and amazed that You exist.
I have been a sannyasin for seven years
and realize now that I took You for granted.
Beloved Bhagwan, how is it possible
that it took me seven years to start slowly, slowly seeing You?

Anando Visarjano, seven years or seventy years, it makes no difference. Whenever you realize, from that very point your authentic life begins. Before that you were asleep.

And always remember, every individual has his own pace. A few run fast, a few go slowly – in fact going slowly has its own quality. The slower you go, the more established you become, the more centered you become. The person who goes very fast never comes to such crystallization as the person who goes slowly.

You are saying, "The more I am here with you, the more I am confused, excited and amazed that you exist. I have been a sannyasin for seven years and realize now that I took you for granted. Beloved Bhagwan, how is it possible that it took me seven years to start slowly, slowly seeing you?"

Seven years is not a long time as far as seeing clearly without any prejudice, without any conditioning, is concerned. It is a small period in the long journey of thousands of lives behind you. You may have come across many living masters in your past lives and you did not realize.

It has to be remembered that thousands of people came to Gautam Buddha, but only a few remained with him. The others could not see that a great phenomenon was present just before their eyes. They remained concerned with their own minds, with their own chattering thoughts – and there is so much rubbish in the mind that covers your eyes.

Seven years are not long. You should not feel confused; you should feel rejoiced. Now begins your real sannyas. Seven years before you had taken sannyas perhaps just out of curiosity. There was no trust, no love, but only a curiosity to know what it is all about. Now you are feeling my presence, now your heartbeats are in harmony with my heartbeats. This is the beginning of a new and a real sannyas.

It is certainly amazing that out of millions of people who are all capable of becoming self-realized, it happens rarely, to very few people. It is as if you are sowing seeds, thousands of seeds, and only one seed becomes a sprout, comes to foliage, brings flowers and fragrance.

What happened to the thousands of other seeds? They never gathered courage to disappear in the soil. They remained protective of themselves. The protection became their death. The one who dared to die in the earth began a new life, started rising upwards against gravitation, started transforming the earth into green foliage, into the beautiful colors of the flowers, into great fragrance.

But the first step was the most difficult – to drop your defenses. A seed is a defense measure. Inside is the potential, and the seed is defending it. It is good, as long as it has not found the right soil. That's why I continuously emphasize the fact that as the context changes, what was good becomes bad, what was bad becomes good.

A seed needs total protection, because it is carrying a womb, a child within itself. But only to the point when it comes to meet with the soil. Then it has to drop the protection. Now the protection should not become its imprisonment. It was good up to now, but now it is evil. At the moment it drops its defenses, the earth takes it into its own heart and pours all its juices into it. And a miracle starts happening – the seed is gone, but the potential of the seed starts becoming a reality.

I call it a great miracle, because it has to grow against gravitation. And if the tree grows one hundred or one hundred and fifty feet high.... The scientists in the beginning were very much puzzled, that it has no pumping system for the juices to reach one hundred and fifty feet high. But slowly they discovered that the tree has its own mechanism, a very subtle mechanism, by which it becomes capable of going against gravitation.

The tree consists of millions of layers, and the strategy the trees have used for millions of years is very simple, non-mechanical, more natural. When the uppermost layer becomes dry, the layer just beneath it gives its juice to it. Now that it has given its juice to the upper layer, it becomes dry, so the layer beneath it gives its juice to it. And this way, from the roots to the flowers, a continuous flow of juices, water goes on rising against the tremendous force of gravitation.

And when the tree comes to its maturity, it is again amazing, that in the small seed so much was hidden – all these branches, all these leaves, all the flowers, all the fruits. The small seed was carrying them in a miniature form – so small that they are not available even to scientific instruments. If you cut the seed, you will find nothingness there. But that nothingness is fullness, you just have to give it the right soil, the right water, the right help to be itself. Because it is happening all around you, you don't feel amazed. You feel amazed when it happens to one man amongst millions, and every man has the same potential.

Every man has a birthright to become a Gautam Buddha. But people go on sleeping. A seed is fast asleep; the tree has awakened. And the awakening brings all the fruits and all the flowers. Remember not to remain asleep. Wake up!

You are not what you appear to be. You are much more, immensely much more. You have to be provoked, challenged, to find that "much more" within you. But because the whole crowd goes on living sleepily, you also go on imitating them.

There are societies in South Africa which are cannibal. Living in thick forest, the child is born amongst the cannibals, and from the very beginning he starts eating human flesh – because everybody else is doing it; this is the right thing to do. He never becomes aware that to eat human flesh is so ugly that even animals feel ashamed of it. No animal eats the flesh of its own species; no lion will eat another lion, no bird will eat another bird of its own species.

Man seems to be perverted in many ways.

One cannibal tribe, just in the beginning of this century, had three thousand members. Now there are only three hundred left. Because nobody passed through that forest, afraid that they may be caught, they started eating their own people, their own mothers, their own fathers, their own children. From three thousand to three hundred...now three hundred...now three hundred will not take much time to disappear.

I have heard that one Christian missionary was very adamant to go to the tribe and teach them the right way of living, and preach to them that cannibalism is the ugliest thing you can do. As he reached there he was welcomed, because the cannibals had been waiting for somebody to come for many days. And this missionary was so fat that the whole tribe started dancing. The missionary thought, "These people seem to be very good people, very nice."They gave him a good welcome, garlanded him with flowers, took him on their shoulders, and went inside the jungle where there was a big pot of boiling water.

Seeing the big pot and the boiling water, the missionary thought, "Perhaps these poor people don't have bathrooms and they have prepared hot water – it is very cold here – just for me to take a bath." But instead of giving him a bath, they threw him in the pot. He could not believe it. Still he was thinking that they were giving him a bath. Just standing in the pot, as it was getting hotter and hotter, he asked them, "Have you ever tasted something of Christianity?"

They said, "Not up to now, but soon, as you become a soup, we will have our first taste of Christianity." Even small children were dancing and enjoying – what a great foodstuff they have found.

In different societies people are imitating the crowd; but on the whole, the whole world is asleep, because everybody else around them is asleep. Hence it seems amazing, when you come across a Gautam Buddha, or a Mahakashyap, or a Bodhidharma, or a Chuang Tzu.

The amazing part is how they avoided the gravitation of the society, how they made it possible for themselves to get out of the grip of the crowd. But even if one man can get out of the crowd, he shows you the path. He indicates to you that you are also capable – just a little courage, just a little intelligence....

Solly has been tossing and turning all night long, unable to sleep. "Solly, what is the matter?" asked Becky. "It is that five hundred dollars I owe Benny. I have to repay him tomorrow, and I have not got it." Becky opens the window wide, and yells at the house opposite, "Benny, Benny, you know that five hundred dollars Solly owes you? He is due to pay you back tomorrow, right? Well, he has not got it." She shuts the window and says, "Now, let him do the worrying. You go to sleep."

Somebody has to wake you up...not to send you to sleep. The whole society is geared for sleep, because the people who are asleep are not rebellious, are not disobedient, are not against any stupid superstitions that the society thinks are great truths.

What does it matter to a man who is asleep,

what is truth and what is untruth? He moves like a drunk in his life.

This mystery school is just to wake you up, not to send you to sleep. I don't give you any doctrine, any belief system, any scripture; I simply give you only one thing: a hard shaking, so that the dormant, the asleep potential starts becoming aware of its own reality.

The master cannot give you anything except a kind of seduction. He can seduce you that wakefulness is beautiful, that wakefulness is blissful, that wakefulness is the ultimate ecstasy.

Forget about those seven years; they don't count. Start counting your life from today.

This recognition of my presence will soon become a realization of your own presence.

Beloved Bhagwan,

In his book *The Fourth Way,* Ouspensky says,
"In the work, the first condition is understanding
what one wants to gain and how much one is prepared
to pay for it, because one has to pay for everything."
In the marketplace we accept that nothing is free;
yet as far as the non-material things are concerned,
like love, happiness, meditativeness,
we tend to think this law does not apply.
We seem to take them for granted, as if they are our due –
things that life owes us, because we have been good enough
to grace existence with our presence.
Would You please comment?

Maneesha, Ouspensky is right. In the work, the first condition is understanding what one wants to gain and how much one is prepared to pay for it because one has to pay for everything.

I can understand your doubt about Ouspensky's statement. You say, "In the marketplace we accept that nothing is free; yet as far as non-material things are concerned, like love, happiness, meditativeness, we tend to think this law does not apply." This law still applies, but in a more subtle way, in a more invisible way.

For example, you cannot get love if you are not ready to give up your ego – that is the payment. You cannot be happy unless you drop things that are preventing your happiness from arising. You cannot be meditative unless you disperse all your thoughts. Nothing is free; one has to pay for everything, material or immaterial.

Of course, in the marketplace you have to pay for commodities in a material way. You can see that you are paying something for getting it. But in a non-material world, also you are paying something for getting something; but because it is non-material, you need a deeper insight to see this.

Meditation is not free. That does not mean that you have to pay the way you pay to Maharishi Mahesh Yogi two hundred and fifty dollars – but you have to pay by dropping your thoughts, by dropping your emotions, by dropping your moods. Only then you can be silent, still.

You have to pay with your mind, only then you can get meditation. You cannot keep both, the mind and meditation together; either you are in the mind or you are in meditation. And there is always a subtle balance.

Ouspensky is right, that one has to be clearly aware of what he wants and how much he is ready to pay. His statement is very significant, because if God is free, everybody would like to have it. What is the harm? You don't have to pay for it; if meditation was free, I don't think anybody would like not to have it. But it is more arduous than paying for something with money. You have to pay with mind, you have to drop your ego, you have to drop your unconsciousness – because these things are inner and not visible to the eyes; hence your question has arisen.

You are also saying, "We seem to take them for granted, as if they are our due." They are our due, but you cannot take them for granted; you will have to prepare yourself to receive them. And that very preparation is the payment. You are also saying, "Things that life owes us...." Life does not owe anything to you. *You* owe everything to life.

This is a great misunderstanding which should be dropped: "things that life owes to us, because we have been good enough to grace existence with our presence." The reality is just the opposite. Existence has been generous enough even to accept you, even to make a place for you. It is very rare that existence feels your grace, because you don't have grace. Yes, when a man becomes awakened, existence starts owing something to him.

There are beautiful stories...not historical of course, because the East has never been interested in history. History consists of trivial facts. The East has paid its attention not to facts, but to the essential values. Those essential values can be expressed only in parables. For example, it is said that when Mahakashyap became enlightened, flowers showered on him like rain. This is not a fact – this cannot be a historical fact – but it is not untrue. It is absolutely true. It is something greater than facts; it is a truth.

When a man becomes enlightened, the whole existence feels that it owes something to this man. He has graced the whole existence. His blissfulness has spread all over the existence; his finding the truth, his finding the ultimate reach of consciousness is a joy to the whole reality. It is a poetic way to express this – that when he became enlightened, suddenly he was puzzled – what is happening? Thousands of flowers raining over him... flowers not of this world, flowers of the unknown that he had never seen, and the fragrance of which he is not at all acquainted with. He is drowned in that fragrance and in those flowers.

You would not have seen them if you were present while Mahakashyap became enlightened. It was seen by Mahakashyap himself. It would have been possible for you to also see, if you were in the same space, in the same consciousness, in the same enlightenment. Then you would have seen the flowers, then you would have felt the fragrance.

But ordinarily, Maneesha, you are neither good enough nor do you have any grace. On the contrary, existence is so compassionate to you that even though you are not good enough, it continues to support you, to keep you alive in the hope that some day you may be good enough. Although you don't have the grace right now, existence goes on dreaming and hoping that the potential of grace that is in you, one day.... Somewhere, some place, your grace will start overflowing your being.

Existence has not to be thankful to you; you have to be thankful to existence – thankful that, "I do not deserve even to be alive, I do not deserve even to be born," but existence gives you out of its abundance, life and all the potentials that can make you blissful, ecstatic, knowing, experiencing the truth.

Existence is almost like a gardener who goes on sowing seeds with the hope that one day the spring will come and there will be flowers. It is not necessary, it is not inevitable – still existence trusts its own dreams, its own longings.

Each human being is a longing of existence. You should be grateful to existence. And you should remember that to have love you will have to drop many things – you will have to drop jealousy, you will have to drop possessiveness, you will have to drop the desire to dominate.

To have meditativeness you will have to drop your whole mind, your whole thinking process. To be blissful you will have to drop your old habits of being miserable. They are very deeply ingrained in you, because you have been miserable for so long that you have started taking the misery for granted – that this is how life is.

You will have to change your whole attitude and approach. And this is what Ouspensky is saying: you have to pay for everything; nothing can be taken for granted, and nothing can be taken without paying the right amount to have it.

Mr. Smith and his wife were on their first cruise. Mrs. Smith wanted to go to bed early every night, but Mr. Smith wanted to join in the fun and games – but he did not want to upset his wife. After three days, he tells his wife that he is going to a discussion group while she sleeps. She thinks for a moment and then agrees.

In the discussion, everybody drew a piece of paper from a hat and had to speak for five minutes on the subject written on the paper. Mr. Smith's paper said: Sex. He speaks about sex and makes everyone laugh at his jokes.

When he returned to his wife later that evening, she asked what the discussion was about. He said, "Sailing." She grunted and went back to sleep. The next morning a large-breasted young woman stopped Mrs. Smith and said, "Your husband was very funny last night. I did not realize he was so experienced." Mrs. Smith was annoyed, "Experienced?" she said, "he has only done it three times – three times in all the years we have been married. The first time he complained because his hat flew off and he lost it. The second time he got all his clothes soaked, and the third time he fell in and nearly drowned!"

Maneesha, it is just a misunderstanding. Ouspensky is a disciple of George Gurdjieff and he speaks a different language than I speak. He approaches the same truth, but the concepts and the philosophy and the direction is totally different from mine. So I cannot say that he will agree with what I am saying about his statement. But whether he agrees or not, one thing is certain, that I am making his statement more significant than he himself would have been able to make it.

In Gurdjieff's groups you will be surprised, it was really paying for everything in a very materialistic way. Gurdjieff himself has written one book, *All And Everything*. It is a one thousand page book and absolutely unreadable. And he himself gives the recognition to the fact that it is unreadable. Only one hundred pages are cut and open; nine hundred pages are still joined and uncut!

The book begins with a statement. The statement is, "you read first one hundred pages – it is the introduction. If you feel you can manage to understand what is being said, you can open the other pages. If you feel it is beyond you, you can return the book and take your money back."

And how much money was he charging for that book in those days? One thousand dollars – because Gurdjieff and Ouspensky both believed that unless a person pays for something, he is not going to be deeply involved in it. When a person pays one thousand dollars, he has to read the book. And because there were nine hundred uncut pages, even people who could not understand the introduction were curious about what was inside the book; and they had already paid one thousand dollars, so it was better to cut it and see.

But the book goes on becoming more and more difficult – difficult in the sense that Gurdjieff used to make words of his own. So first you cannot find their meaning in any dictionary. Those words have never existed in any language. He would mix three languages and make one word. And his words are so long that sometimes the whole sentence is one word. You cannot even pronounce it. His paragraphs are so long that one paragraph may take the whole page. By the time you come to the end of the paragraph, you have forgotten with what it had begun. Sometimes even lines run into whole pages.

Gurdjieff had his own ways. And when he says you have to pay for everything, he means it in a very materialistic way.

One countess was introduced to Gurdjieff by another of his rich followers, and the same evening Gurdjieff sent a message to the countess, "You give all your ornaments, diamonds, and money and everything, so that from tomorrow your teaching can start." She was worried, "What kind of teaching is this? Even if there is some fee I can pay, but all my diamonds and all my ornaments?" She was very rich, and she had very valuable stones.

She asked her friend, "What to do? What kind of man is this Gurdjieff? He wants everything, and then only tomorrow morning will the teaching begin." The other woman laughed; she said, "Don't be worried. He also asked me for all. I gave all my ornaments, all my money, everything that I possessed, and next day, when the teaching started, the first thing he did was he returned all the money, the whole bag. So you need not be worried."

So the countess collected all her diamonds and ornaments and money in a bag, and sent them to Gurdjieff. The next morning she was waiting, that before the teaching starts...but the bag never came back. She was very much puzzled – he has taken everything, she is now a pauper. She asked her friend, "You were saying that he returned yours."

She said, "That is absolutely true. You can see, all my things are with me. I am also amazed about what has happened. Perhaps he forgot or something, that's why he has not returned them." Those things were never returned, and when the woman asked, "I had given them because of my friend's assurance that they will be returned tomorrow morning, but three days have passed. The teaching has started, but I cannot concentrate on the teaching; my whole mind is thinking about my money and my diamonds and my ornaments, because that was all that I had."

Gurdjieff said, "The first woman's things were returned because she offered them with love and trust. Yours will not be returned because you offered them with the idea that they will be returned – and first you made sure of it by asking your friend. You have not given out of trust and love. This is your first teaching, that if you are going to be with me, you will have to trust. And nothing is free."

So perhaps Ouspensky will not agree with my interpretation. But I am absolutely certain that my interpretation is far more spiritual, far more poetic, far more mystical, far more Eastern. And I don't care whether Ouspensky agrees with me or not.

I am not here to teach you the philosophy of Ouspensky or Gurdjieff; my path is totally different. Their path never crosses my path. Still, I love those people, because they created a tremendous desire for a spiritual search in the West.

Many of you might not have come here if Gurdjieff and Ouspensky had not existed. You may not have heard their names, but they created the climate for spiritual search, and I have tremendous respect for them both.

But I do not agree with them as far as the path is concerned.

I have my own understanding, how you have to become awakened, enlightened.

Beloved Bhagwan,

Each day, each word, each gesture penetrates unknown layers...
unimagined flowers opening, unexplained music dancing.
And with each, a deeper longing for something missing,
like a target that cries for the arrow
that has just fallen short.
Beloved Master, am I dwelling too much on what's missing?

Deva Abhiyana, you are dwelling too much on what is missing. And your focus should be on what is growing. Attention is nourishment; if you give attention to what is missing, you will find that more and more things are missing. And that will create a misery in you, a pain.

If you focus your attention on what is happening to you, what is growing within you, it will grow faster. And perhaps with its growth, what is missing will not be missing anymore.

You say, "Each day, each word, each gesture penetrates unknown layers...unimagined flowers opening, unexplained music dancing. And with each, a deeper longing for something missing."

It is natural that as you start on the path, as new experiences start showering on you, a desire for more arises simultaneously – because this is what we have been accustomed to for centuries in the ordinary world... our mind is always asking for more.

In India, we have an ancient parable: A king had a very beautiful man, very happy and joyous. His only work was to give the king a good massage early in the morning, and he used to get one gold coin every day. That was his whole work, and then the whole day he was free. He used to live just in front of the palace; and he was a lover of playing on his flute.

Having nothing else to do, and one gold coin was too much, he was living the richest and the most comfortable and luxurious life. And one gold coin was absolutely certain every day, so he never saved anything. The king was always puzzled, "This poor man looks so joyous, even when he is playing on his flute. You can feel his joy and his blissfulness. And here am I, a king of a great country, continuously worried, problems upon problems, cannot sleep in the night, and when he comes in the morning to give me a massage I feel jealous of him. He is in a far better condition than I am; and I am the king, and that poor fellow gets only one gold coin."

He asked his prime minister, "What is the mystery? I have such a big kingdom, such a great treasure, and the treasure goes on becoming bigger and bigger. But I don't feel any happiness; I have not smiled for years – I don't even remember when I have smiled. What is the mystery, that this poor guy goes on playing on his flute in the daytime, in the full moon night.... He is so healthy, with no worry in the world, and he has nothing because whatever he gets in the morning he finishes by the evening."

The prime minister said, "Just give me a little time, and I will solve the mystery." And that morning, when the man came to give a massage to the king he was looking sad. This was the first time his face had lost the joyous aura. And every day he was becoming more and more miserable.

The king called his prime minister and asked, "What is the matter? What have you done? Now I don't hear the flute. Perhaps he does not feel like playing on the flute and he has become a miserable person, just like me."

The prime minister said, "Nothing, just a simple thing. I threw in his house a bag containing ninety-nine gold coins." The king said, "I don't understand, what can your bag do? He should be more happy, that he has got ninety-nine gold coins."

The prime minister said, "You don't understand a simple psychological fact. The next day he was sad, because he thought, 'Ninety-nine coins...if I can save one coin, I will have one hundred coins.' So that day he did not eat anything. He said, 'There is no harm in fasting one day just to save one coin; don't waste it.' And since then the desire for more – one hundred and one, one hundred and two, one hundred and three.... Now he is eating less, not living the way he used to live. Saving has become his problem. And he is hoping that soon he will have two hundred."

The king said, "But this is not...you will kill the poor man!" The prime minister said, "You had asked, what is the mystery? The mystery is, the mind goes on asking for more and more and more – the more you get, the more it goes on asking for. And there is no end to it."

Your accumulation becomes great, but your desire for more also becomes great; this is the habit of your mind. When you enter into the spiritual world, you go on keeping the old habit for more and more, unconsciously.

You are saying, "Each day, each word, each gesture penetrates unknown layers...unimagined flowers opening, unexplained music dancing. And with each, a deeper longing for something missing."

Nothing is missing. But if you become concerned about the missing, all that you are experiencing will be destroyed. You have to drop the old habit...just a little intelligence. Enjoy that which you are getting. Pour all the nourishment into that which you are getting, so it becomes stronger, with more flowers, with more beauty.

And don't be bothered about the missing. Those missing flowers will grow on the same tree. But if you think only of the flowers that are missing and forget the tree, and forget to give nourishment to it, those flowers will never be attained; on the contrary, you may miss even the tree, the tree may die. But mind is a strange thing. It is always concerned about that which you have not got. That which you have got you don't rejoice in, and you are miserable for that which you have not got.

A sannyasin has to shift his whole focus. It is a simple matter of understanding. Deva Abhiyana, don't behave stupidly. You are growing in the right direction, but if your mind becomes worried about something more which is missing, you will go astray. And not much intelligence is needed.

But we are all living with a very small fraction of our intelligence. We don't use our whole intelligence; otherwise, everybody will have such grace and such beauty and such joy and such love – so much of it that he cannot contain it within himself; he will have to share it.

Two Polish men are driving along and they have to stop at a shopping mall. So they find a parking space, get out of the car, slam the doors and the driver says, "Oh, shit, I just locked the keys in the car." "What we are going to do now?" says the other man. "I don't know," replies the driver, "I guess we will have to break the windshield and get them out."

"No," says his friend, "you can't break the windshield. Maybe you can find a coat hanger and open the door that way." "That is too difficult," says the driver. "Well," says his friend, "you had better think of something fast, because it is starting to rain and the top is down."

But this is the standard of the whole humanity. Nobody seems to be using intelligence at all. You are not supposed to use it; you are supposed always to rely on the advice of your bosses, of your father, of your mother, of your teacher. Slowly, slowly you forget that you also have intelligence.

Always asking for advice is a disease.

First try your own intelligence; give it a chance to become sharp. And about your problem, it is very simple. I can understand your longing for more and more. It will be coming, you need not worry about it, but right now relish, rejoice, dance, with all that is happening to you.

Your rejoicing will create more space, more capacity for many more things to happen. And anyway, you had better think of something fast, because it is starting to rain and the top is down.

Okay, Vimal?

Yes, Bhagwan.

Session 21

What Am I Doing Here?

*People always feel good walking on the superhighway
where the whole crowd of millions of people are walking.
They may be going nowhere,
but just because so many people are going,
you feel a certain confidence
that so many people cannot be wrong.
But my whole teaching is
that unless you start moving alone,
dropping the crowd....*

March 7, 1987
Evening

Beloved Bhagwan,

Why is it so difficult for me to take sannyas?
Ever since I saw You in an interview on TV one year ago,
I've never been so nervous before in my whole life.
Sometimes I wish I'd never heard of You, and, on the other hand, I'm happy
that there is someone like You to show me the way.
But to take sannyas...I feel such an egoist – jealous, lazy –
that maybe I shall never be a good sannyasin.
Can You please give me a hint to find a way out of this dilemma?

Rita, sannyas is always difficult. But only the first step, because it is a transformation from one style of life to a totally different style of life. Mind always finds it difficult to adjust to new ways of life. The old way you seem to be well-acquainted with; you can walk on it with closed eyes, almost asleep, like a robot. But the new way will need alertness, awareness; the new way will need learning life from scratch.

Sannyas is simply an initiation into new spaces within you, a change from the head to the heart, from logic to love, from your ordinary conditioning, to an unconditioned mind, to a freedom which you are not even aware that you are capable of.

Sannyas is something like a bird which has remained in a cage – the cage is golden, very artistic, very valuable, but to the bird it is nothing other than an imprisonment. But the bird has lived long in the cage, although it is taking away its freedom, its whole sky, its flights across the sun, its joy; it has almost destroyed the bird's capacity to be on the wing. Perhaps the bird has already forgotten that it has wings. But the cage has security, safety from the unknown. The bird need not to be worried for the coming days – it need not worry about its food.

Even if you open the door of the cage, the bird will hesitate to get out of it. So much is involved – the security, the safety. And who knows about this vast sky, and where he will land? And he has forgotten completely that he has wings. You know something only if you use it. If a bird has never used its wings, how can it remember them?

The English word *sin* is very beautiful. Christians have destroyed its beauty, they have made it ugly; otherwise its original root means "forgetfulness." There is only one sin, and that is forgetfulness.

The doors are open, the sky is inviting, the other birds are flying, it is only a question of a little courage. That's why I say that only the first step is difficult. If the bird can gather courage and take a jump into the air, the wings that he has no awareness of suddenly open.

He's on the wing.

The whole sky is his.

Now the faraway stars can be his pilgrimage. Sannyas is initiation into freedom, making you aware about your wings, making you also aware that the whole sky, with all its stars is yours. You need not worry about security and safety; existence is taking care of so many birds, so many trees, so many stars – it can take care of you too.

Sannyas is trust in existence. And the moment you trust, there is no fear, there is no worry, and there is no difficulty. Life becomes the most enjoyable, relaxed phenomenon.

You are asking, Rita, "Why is it so difficult for me to take sannyas?" My suggestion is that you cannot deliberately take sannyas; it is something like love that happens, it is something like sleep that comes. You cannot make any effort for the sleep to come, nor can you make any effort for love to happen – these are not part of the world of doings. Your first difficulty is that you are thinking of taking sannyas. Drop that idea, and sannyas will take you. Suddenly you will realize, "My God, I am a sannyasin."

It simply comes – and it comes so silently, so gracefully. But the idea of taking sannyas is basically wrong; hence it becomes difficult. Even if you take it, it will be false, it won't be the true sannyas; you will be simply dreaming that you have taken sannyas. The authentic sannyas simply comes one moment and possesses you – it springs up from your very heart, and there is no way to avoid it. It is your very heartbeat.

So the first thing you have to drop is the idea of taking. Just be here, enjoy for a few days. Just watch other birds opening their wings in the sky. Participate in their songs, in their dances, without bothering about sannyas. And if you start feeling that it is already happening, in a moment when you are lost in singing and dancing, when you are not there...it occupies your innermost being.

It is not something that you have to do, it is something that simply grows in you. It is not a commodity that you have to purchase, it is a quality, a grace, a search which starts growing inside you – just like a seed disappears into the soil and in its place a plant starts growing. That plant was asleep in the seed; now it has awakened.

Sannyas is asleep in you, just asleep. So dance madly, sing madly, meditate, enjoy all these people, this crazy communion, and the moment will come on its own. When you are ripe you will find that there is nothing more easy than sannyas.

You are saying, "Ever since I saw you in an interview on TV one year ago, I've never been so nervous before in my whole life." It is a good sign. I touched your heart. Your nervousness, that you have never felt before, is simply an indication that something new has started happening in you. You don't know what it is, you don't know where it is going to lead you; hence the nervousness.

People always feel good walking on the superhighway where the whole crowd of millions of people are walking. They may be going nowhere, but just because so many people are going, you feel a certain confidence that so many people cannot be wrong. But my whole teaching is that unless you start moving alone, dropping the crowd...because the crowd has never reached anywhere, and one has never heard of a crowd becoming enlightened. A crowd always remains a crowd – blind, deaf, without direction. It just goes on because it always finds somebody ahead of it is continuing on.

One scientist was trying to experiment in South Africa on a very rare species of insect which always follows the leader; they always move in a long line. If you pull one out of the line it becomes nervous, it starts feeling that it has lost its moorings, its roots. Put back in the line it is perfectly at ease. Somebody is ahead, somebody is behind, they must be going somewhere, and so many cannot be wrong.

The scientist tried one experiment and captured almost a dozen insects of that species. He put them onto a big plate, a round plate, and they started moving round, and round, and round. Somebody was always ahead, somebody was always behind, and out of their conditioning of centuries, unless the leader stops.... And there was no leader because it was a circle. They are very obedient people – unless the leader stops, nobody is going to stop. They went on and on for sixty hours, until they all fell dead.

Where is the crowd going?...but it is cozy to be part of it. People are very nervous in being alone, and sannyas is the art of being aloneness. Unless you learn to be alone, you will never be an individual in your own right; and unless you learn to be alone you will never be able to enter within yourself, because the crowd cannot go there. Even your most intimate friend, your lover, your beloved, cannot go with you inside you; there you have to go alone. That path is absolutely private. That is your privilege, nobody can interfere there, and that is where your source of life is. You can call it life, you can call it God, you can call it truth – names don't matter.

You became nervous – it is a good sign. From that very moment I have been haunting you, and unless sannyas happens I am going to haunt you your whole life. You can go anywhere, you can escape to the moon, but it won't help.

You say, "Sometimes I wish I'd never heard of you." Nobody desires disasters, but they happen. And it has happened already; now there is no point in crying for the spilled milk. "And, on the other hand, I'm happy that there is someone like you to show me the way." You will remain in a dilemma: half of you is already ready to take the jump, and the other half is clinging to your past.

One thing has to be remembered, that the past is no more, and clinging to the past is clinging to the dead. It is very dangerous, because it hampers and hinders your life, in the present and for the future. One should always go on freeing himself of the dead past. That is one of the fundamentals of sannyas, to go on renewing yourself every moment, to die to the past and be born anew. That which is gone is gone – don't even look back. Looking back is not a good sign.

Small children never look back, they always look ahead. They don't have anything in the past to look back on – there is no past, they have only the future. Old men never look at the future, because in the future there is only death, and they want to avoid it, they don't want to talk about it. They always look back. They decorate their memories; they make them look very beautiful. All that they have is a collection of memories, and they go on improving on those memories, but when they were actually living them, they had not enjoyed them. But now the future is darkness; one needs some consolation. They can find consolation only in the past.

A person who lives in the present – neither bothering about the past, nor bothering about the future – is fresh, young; he is neither a child nor an old man. And one can remain young to the very last breath. The body may be old, but the consciousness remains fresh, just like a fresh breeze, cool, fragrant, in the early morning sun.

The whole problem is that we are caught up with our past. It is holding us back, it does not allow us to go against it. And if you don't go against it, your whole life will be simply boredom, because you will be repeating and repeating the same past, the same routine.

The most important philosophical school of our age is existentialism, and they have brought a few new problems for the philosophers to think about. One of their problems is boredom. If you look into an existentialist treatise you will be surprised: God is not talked about at all; there is nobody concerned about the soul, about heaven and hell, and angels and the devil. The things that they are talking about are boredom, anguish, meaninglessness, society – strange subjects, but in fact far more significant than God, the devil, heaven and hell, because they were all fictions, and these are realities.

A man who lives according to the past remains in the grip of the past. He is bound to feel boredom, meaninglessness, and a kind of anguish, "What am I doing here? Why am I continuing to live? What is there in tomorrow? – another repetition of today? And what was in today was a repetition of yesterday." So what is the point? Why go dragging yourself from the cradle to the grave, in the same routine?

It is perfectly good for buffaloes and donkeys because they don't think, they don't have the memory of the past, they don't have any idea of the future. So they are doing the same thing every day – the buffaloes go on chewing the same grass their whole life; they don't change even the grass – but they are not bored, because for boredom a certain consciousness is needed. This consciousness is aware that you have done it before, you are doing it again, and you will be doing it tomorrow also – because you don't move from the past, you don't let it die, you keep it alive.

This is the dilemma that everybody faces in life, and the only solution is to let the past die. There is a beautiful story in the life of Jesus. He comes to a lake; it is early morning, the sun has yet not risen, and one fisherman is just going to throw his net into the lake to catch fish. Jesus puts his hand on his shoulder and says, "How long are you going to do this thing, every day – morning, afternoon, evening – just catching fish? Do you think this is all life is meant for?"

The fisherman had never thought about it – a simple, poor fellow. He said, "I have never thought about it, but because you have raised the question, I can see the point, that life must be something more."

Jesus said, "If you come with me I will teach you how to catch men, rather than catching fish."

The man looked into Jesus' eyes...such depth, such sincerity, so much love that you cannot doubt this man, such a great silence surrounding him that you cannot say no to this man. The fisherman threw his net into the water and followed Jesus.

As they were getting out of the town a man came running and told the fisherman, "Where are you going with this stranger? Your father who was ill for many days has died. Come home!"

The fisherman asked Jesus, "Just give me three days so that I can do the last rituals which a son is expected to do when his father dies."

And this is the statement that I want you to remember: Jesus said to that fisherman, "Let the dead bury their dead, you come with me." What does he mean, "Let the dead bury their dead, you come with me.... The whole city is full of dead people; they will manage to dispose of your dead father. You are not an absolute necessity to them. You just come with me." People like Jesus have such a certain authority in their very presence –

the fisherman followed him.

Every moment something is becoming dead. Don't be antique collectors; that which is dead, leave it. You go with the life, you flow with life, with your totality and intensity, and you will never face any dilemma, any problem.

Sannyas is such a simple happening, but it is a simple happening only to the intelligent, not to the retarded. It is not for idiots...at least, I have never seen any idiot even thinking about sannyas. The idiots belong to the world of the buffaloes. They are perfectly at ease, although their life has no meaning, no flowers, no fragrance. No song ever arises in their heart; they don't ever feel like dancing to abandon. Their life is very lukewarm. It never gets to such an intensity where one becomes almost a flame – a torch burning from both ends simultaneously. And only these few people have known the truth of life and the beauty of life and the ecstasy of life.

You are saying, "But to take sannyas...I feel such an egoist – jealous, lazy – that maybe I shall never be a good sannyasin."

Who told you that you have to be a good sannyasin? Here are only sannyasins; nobody is good, nobody is bad. We don't believe in those categories. Have you ever seen a deer which is beautiful or a deer which is ugly? Those categories don't exist – all deer are simply so alive.... Here nobody takes note whether you are a good sannyasin or a bad sannyasin. You can be a good Christian or a bad Christian, a good Hindu or a bad Hindu. But sannyas is not a religion; it is a search.

What do you mean when you say, "I cannot be a good sannyasin?" To be a sannyasin is to be *good*! It is its intrinsic quality. A person who is so courageous to take the jump and come out of the old bondage into the open sky...this love for freedom and this risk for freedom is what goodness is.

And as far as laziness is concerned, sannyas is exactly the art of how to be spiritually lazy. I call myself the lazy man's guide to enlightenment – because I teach nothing but sitting silently, doing nothing, and the spring comes and the grass grows by itself. You don't have to pull the grass, it grows by itself; you have just to wait.

Laziness is not a bad quality. I have always been condemned by my elders, by my teachers, by my professors, by my colleagues, friends, "You are good for nothing." And I said, "That's actually how I want to be: good for nothing" – because in this world you cannot find a lazy man becoming Adolf Hitler or Ronald Reagan or Alexander the Great or Nadir Shah or Tamerlane or Genghis Khan. The world has suffered from active people, not from lazy people!

If two dozen people in the world would have been lazy, just two dozen more – people like Joseph Stalin and Benito Mussolini and Adolf Hitler...just two dozen people in the world, and the world would have been a paradise, because there would have been no wars. Lazy people cannot fight.

I am reminded of a small story. In India there is one state, Rajasthan, which is the most ancient place of warriors; it has created great warriors. In a small village there was a great warrior, and in India, to have your mustache pointing upwards is thought to be the sign of a great warrior. He was such an arrogant and stubborn fellow that he had told everybody in the town, "You can have your mustache, but they should be always pointing downwards. If I see anybody having his mustache pointing upwards, I will kill him!"

And he had killed at least two, three people. Then the whole village became afraid, "This is a strange man; we cannot even keep our mustaches upwards." But what to do? The man was dangerous and he was powerful.

And then came a new stranger to live in the village. He was a very lazy man. People told him, "You are a stranger, you don't know the law of this town. The great warrior...if he sees you, your head will be chopped off. You have to put your mustache downwards."

He said, "I am so lazy that I will prefer it if he chops off my head. But I am not going to make that much effort, because it will take hours...for my whole life my mustache has been trained to remain upwards; to change its direction is not easy. If he chops off my head, that finishes all my anxieties and problems." People said, "Are you mad or something?"

As he was sitting outside his house, the warrior came and he said, "It seems you are a stranger in this town."

He said, "That's right."

The warrior said, "Stranger or no stranger, pull down your mustache!"

The lazy man said, "That is not possible. But if you are going to have a fight with me, then I will suggest one thing – because one never knows, I may be dead, you may be dead...because it is not going to be just that you chop off my head; I also have my sword, although I have never used it. But if that moment has come I will give it a try. There is no harm; anyway I am going to die.

"Before we enter into a fight to kill each other, my suggestion is that I should go inside my house and kill my wife and my children, because more or less I will be killed, and after me my children will be orphans, my wife will be a widow, and who will take care of them? And I suggest the same thing to you: that you go home, kill your wife, kill your children, so if you are killed there is no problem; there will be nobody left behind you in misery and pain."

The warrior said, "The idea is right." He went back and immediately cut off the heads of his wife and his six children and came back. Just on the way he met the man. He was coming without the sword and he had put his mustache downward. The warrior said, "What happened?"

He said, "I thought, I am a lazy man, it is more simple to put the mustache down than to kill the wife and the children. And I have never killed anybody. So I changed my mind." The warrior said, "You idiot! You changed your mind. And I have finished my family!"

He said, "That is not my responsibility. Just, I had to choose between two things, whichever was simpler. I thought, putting the mustache down is simpler."

Basically I am a lazy man. Lazy people have not done any harm in the world. It is the too active, the hyperactive, who have driven the whole world into misery, madness, slavery. So as far as laziness is concerned, it is very supportive to meditation because meditation needs a very quiet, calm, silent mind. A lazy man is so lazy that he cannot even be bothered to think. Thinking is also part of the active mind.

So, you don't be worried about your being a good sannyasin, because to be a sannyasin is to be good. You don't worry about being lazy – that is a great quality that has to be developed, and you already have it!

As far as your ego is concerned and your jealousy is concerned, my whole work here is to help you become so loving that the energy that becomes jealousy is transformed into love. And you know perfectly well that jealousy always follows your love. You are not jealous without love. A man who does not love is not jealous.

Jealousy is almost like a shadow of love. If we can grow our love, it takes over the whole energy of jealousy and transforms it into love. It is an alchemical change. And I can say it with guarantee, because it has happened in me, it has happened in my thousands of sannyasins who have forgotten what jealousy is. Their love is so much.

And as your silence, your peacefulness, your relaxedness, your love, deepen, your ego disappears. Ego is a false entity. One need not be worried about ego. Meditation is the medicine to kill the ego. So I accept all kinds of people: egoist, jealous, angry, violent, depressed, because I have seen that a simple meditation transforms all these baser metals into gold. This is the alchemy of sannyas.

So that should not be your worry. Once you are a sannyasin, that has to be my worry – your jealousy, your ego. I have to take care that they don't leave you too quickly, because then one starts feeling a gap. One starts feeling that something is missing. So my whole concern is that before you start missing your ego, I should provide at least a little glimpse to you of your real individuality, your self. Then you won't miss the ego. I have to provide you with a few new flowers in your loving energy, so that you won't miss your jealousy.

And these things are not alone – there are many, many things. Ego is surrounded with depression, with anxiety, with anguish, with all kinds of sick ideas. My problem is that your sick ideas should not disappear suddenly; otherwise you will start feeling yourself empty. They have been there for so long, and you have been feeling so full.

Before they disappear I have to give you new experiences, which are not difficult, which are lying dormant in you. Just a little push and your heart becomes so full of songs that, who cares about jealousy?

Your own life becomes so graceful that you forget all about somebody else being more beautiful, somebody else being more intelligent. All your competitiveness, all your jealousies simply disappear; otherwise, you go on accumulating more and more problems, and when death comes you are nothing but a huge collection of problems. You don't have anything to feel grateful for towards existence. You are angry because this existence has given you only problems and nothing else – and they go on growing.

It all depends on you, whether you want to grow roses or you want to let any weeds grow in your being. Ordinarily, people never bother: weeds go on growing, and they go on suffering.

A lady is sitting on the bus with her baby, when a drunk staggers over in front of the woman, looks down and says, "Lady, that is the ugliest baby I have ever seen!"

The woman starts crying and everyone on the bus kicks the drunk off. They are making such a big fuss that the bus driver pulls over and stops. He goes to the back of the bus and asks, "What is the matter?" The woman is inconsolable and can't even talk. She just keeps crying.

"Look, I don't know what he said to you", says the driver, "but to help calm you down I am going to go get you a cup of tea."

He gets off the bus, goes into a nearby hotel and comes back with the tea. "Calm down", says the driver. "Everything is okay now. See? I brought you this cup of tea and I also brought you a banana for your pet monkey!"

Things go on growing. Whatever you have is not going to remain the same, because everything in life is always growing. If you have thorns, then thorns will be growing; and if you have roses, then roses will be growing.

Sannyas is only the opening of a new door, dropping the past and starting your life from ABC. If your past life had jealousy, egoism and other problems, you can start a new life with roses. It is absolutely in your hands. You *are* what you have made yourself, and you *will be* what you are going to make yourself.

Beloved Bhagwan,

I am a very new sannyasin.
I came here to experience You and Your love
and the atmosphere around You. Something is confusing me.
It is the fact that I feel my love to You
and Your presence in my heart much more when I am doing meditation
than when I am sitting with You in discourse.
How is this possible?

Gyandip, it is not a very complex question. When you are sitting silently in meditation your mind relaxes, there are less thoughts, and your heart starts feeling more love. The mind with less thoughts, the heart with more love, and you will feel my presence very easily, because then your own being is very close to the loving heart.

We may be different as minds, we are less different as hearts, and we are one as beings. So what is happening inside you is that you are feeling your own being more intensely, more clearly, more transparently. The same happens here, to people who have been sitting with me for years. Their very sitting with me is a meditation. You are a new sannyasin. When you are sitting with me you are not absorbing my presence, you are more interested in what I am saying, not in what I am.

And it is natural. Because you are new, you want to be acquainted with my philosophy, so your mind starts working. You are more thoughts and in the head, and less love and less in the heart and farther away from your own being. The distance from your own being is the same as the distance from me.

Slowly, slowly you will become aware that what I am saying is not so important, but what I am is more important. You have not just to listen to my thoughts, you have to drink me, you have to absorb me. It takes a little time for every new sannyasin, because you have come here, first, because you were convinced of my thoughts, and you are enchanted with new thoughts, new arguments, new ways of thinking.

As you will become more and more acquainted with me, you will be surprised that I am not a philosopher and I am not a theologian. And what I am saying is only a device, so that you can sit with me silently. I do the talking, your mind remains silent and your heart starts coming closer to me. Slowly, slowly there happens a synchronicity between your heart and my heart.

Beyond that is the meeting of the being. Then

thoughts don't matter at all. Then what matters is simply the light that I am hiding in my being, the juice that I am spreading all around. Once you become aware of it, my presence becomes a nourishment, a food. Then the whole situation will change. Your meditation will be deepened as it is now, but you will miss me. You will miss me more in your meditation than at any other time, because you will find the temple in the meditation but the temple will be empty.

It will take a little time more, when slowly, slowly your temple itself becomes full of godliness. Then you don't need me. Then you have become me, or I have become you, or perhaps I and you, both have disappeared into one entity.

So don't be confused – what is happening is natural; it happens to every new sannyasin, and particularly to male sannyasins. To female sannyasins it is just the opposite: when they are here in my presence they feel me more; sitting in meditation they remember me, but they don't feel me. And remembering is one thing, and feeling is another. Remembering is of the mind and feeling is of the heart. Remembering brings a sadness and feeling brings joy. But that's how men and women are different. Their energies function in a different way.

But nothing is wrong with you. Everything is going right. Just a little time is needed, a little patience, a little more waiting.

A Jew comes home – it is midnight – and finds out that his wife has been unfaithful. He tells a friend that he's going to kill her. "Don't do that", says the friend. "If you kill her you will go to jail and be hanged. It is better you should screw her to death."

So the Jew makes love to his wife day and night for a year. His friend comes round to visit him and is shocked to find him a haggard and shaking old man, but his wife looks wonderful, shining with health.

"How is it you are so ill and she is so well?" asked the friend.

"Sh, don't say anything, she does not know she is dying."

Just a confusion. You cannot kill a woman by making love, you will kill yourself. The energies are so different. By making love man loses energy and the woman gains energy; she is the receiver. So the more you love, the more you are bringing your death closer. The woman will become more and more healthy.

It is unfortunate that no great psychologist has yet bothered to go into deep research about the energies of men and women and their differences. They don't have the same energy. It is not only that their bodies are different; their energy bodies are also different, their functioning is also different. When a woman comes here, her contact with me is through the heart; when a man comes here, his contact with me is through the head.

And the contact with the head is not very reliable. It will take a longer time because a small doubt and the whole edifice can fall down. But the woman has no question of any doubt. Love knows no doubt. As time passes it becomes more and more deep, to the point where it becomes trust. Trust is the highest development of love.

For men the journey is long, because he has to begin with doubt and reach to trust. The woman begins with love; her journey is short – short and not with many possibilities of going back. There are not many pitfalls on the path. Beginning with doubt and moving towards trust is just moving towards the opposite of doubt. Trust is diametrically opposite to doubt. Love is not opposite to trust, love is the beginning of trust.

So the path for the woman is simpler, cleaner,

shorter. It is because man has repressed women for centuries that you don't have so many mystical women, so many enlightened women. But one thing perhaps you have never thought about: every great master has been betrayed by his male disciples, but he has never been betrayed by his female disciples. You cannot find a Judas in women.

Gautam Buddha was betrayed by Devadatta and Devadatta tried to kill Gautam Buddha many times – many attempts were made on his life – but you will not find a single woman parallel to Devadatta or Judas. Jesus was also surrounded by women, but they simply served.

I remember a small incident: Jesus is staying in the house of one of his female disciples, Mary. There were two sisters, Mary and Martha. Martha was preparing food and other arrangements, and Mary was washing the feet of Jesus with very precious oils from Egypt. Judas was very angry, and he said to Jesus, "You should stop Mary, because she is wasting such precious oils. This much money can be used for the poor people."

Before Jesus could say anything, Mary said one thing that I have never forgotten. Mary said, "The poor will always be here, but Jesus will not always be here. Please don't say such a thing. I can serve the poor, they will always be here. And you can serve the poor, there is no lack of poverty, but where will you find Jesus again?"

The woman has a different outlook. Judas is perfectly socialistic, mathematical, and logically right. Mary is not logically right, neither is she a socialist, but she knows how to love, she knows the art of devotion.

Gyandip, you are a man; you have come here with your mind. It will take me a little time to chop it off...just a little waiting, a little patience. I have to move your mind energy towards your heart, and then things start becoming better. Then you have moved from the desert to the garden and then everything starts becoming better.

Okay Vimal?

Yes Bhagwan.

Session 22

Don't Be Worried – The Worst Will Also Happen

*One never knows when the right time comes.
And by the right time I mean the vulnerability, the openness,
when you are ready to receive, when you are not afraid,
when you drop all your defenses.*

March 8, 1987
Morning

Beloved Bhagwan,

Since You first spoke about
subjective and objective art, the artist and the mystic,
a deep reflection has been triggered in me.
I'm confused concerning meditation and doing.
I have always felt my art to be my meditation,
but is it still not a doing?
I notice the difference when sitting in vipassana.
Must art and sculpture even, fade away into non-doing?
Can creativity on the material plane be truly meditative?
Will my art remain solely subjective
until the ego agrees to commit suicide?

Deva Darpana, the distinction between the subjective and the objective art is basically based on meditation. Anything that comes out of the mind will remain subjective art, and anything that comes out of no-mind, out of silence, out of meditation, will be objective art.

This definition is simple and will destroy your confusion. Whether you are creating something – you may be a sculptor, you may be a carpenter, you may be a painter, a poet, a singer, a musician – all that has to be remembered is that it is coming out of a silence within you, that it has a spontaneity. It is not prearranged, preprogrammed, pre-thought. As you are creating something you go on being surprised yourself – you have left yourself in the hands of existence.

Now your hands are not your own hands. They are simply following what the existence longs for. You are not to interfere, you have just to be a watcher – a watcher of your own creative activity. From the doer you have to shift to being just a watcher.

The ancient *Upanishads* are one of the best expressions of objective art – tremendously meaningful statements, immensely beautiful poetry, yet we don't know the name of the poet, the name of the mystic. They have not mentioned their names for the simple reason that they are not the doers; they are just instrumental in the hands of existence.

Mind is a doer, so when you are doing something according to your mind, it will be subjective art – subjective in the sense that you are pouring your own thoughts onto the canvas in colors, singing your own thoughts on the flute, but it cannot be sacred. Your mind is so full of trivia, your mind is concerned with absolutely nonessential things. It is a mess.

Just sit silently in a corner one day. Close the door – lock it so that you can be confident that nobody is going to see what you are doing – and then go on writing whatsoever arises in your mind. Don't edit it; don't try to make it better. Don't even complete the sentences – if they remain incomplete and another sentence intrudes, leave it as it is. It has to be photographic. Just a small ten minute exercise – and then read what you have written. And you will be surprised: are these your words? Is this your mind? This seems to be the mind of a madman!

But twenty-four hours, day in and day out, those thoughts go on rushing in your mind. When anything is created out of this madness which you call mind, it is going to reflect it. That's why even a great painter, a genius like Picasso, has never attained to what I am calling objective art. All his paintings are subjective.

And if you watch his paintings, sitting silently, looking at them, the paintings will create not silence in you, not beauty in you, not grace in you, not a feeling of the divine in you, but you will start feeling a little crazy. Those paintings *are* crazy. They have come out of a mad mind. It does not matter that the mad mind was a genius.

On the other hand, if you sit silently on a full moon night near the Taj Mahal and watch it, you will be surprised how your mind becomes calm and quiet. The Taj Mahal has a totally different effect, because it was created by Sufi mystics. It is an example of objective art.

The subjective art is a kind of vomiting. You are filled with so much rubbish; you want to get rid of it, and the only way to get rid of it is to throw it on the canvas, on the musical instruments. Objective art is coming out of a silence so deep... it is almost an expression, to convey to you that this silence is possible in everybody.

Objective art has a message.

Subjective art has a madness.

You need not be worried. You are asking, "Since you first spoke about subjective and objective art, the artist and the mystic, a deep reflection has been triggered in me. I am confused concerning meditation and doing." There is no need to be confused. If doing comes out of your mind, full of thoughts, then it is subjective. If your doing pours out of silence, blissfulness, serenity, ecstasy, then the same doing has a different flavor, a different significance; it becomes objective.

You must have heard about the haikus of the Zen masters of Japan. They are examples of objective art. One of the famous haikus of Basho...and Basho is a genius, but he is not writing through the mind. Whatever he is writing is growing within him in his silence like a flower, and he gives it as a gift to the world.

Listen deeply to this haiku. You have to visualize it; then only will you be able to feel its freshness, its beauty, and its penetration into your own being. Just visualize:

An ancient pond.
A frog jumps in.
This sound.

Just these three lines...not even lines.

An ancient pond.
A frog jumps in.

Naturally, he creates a certain sound.

This sound.

If you visualize it, you will find yourself sitting by the side of an ancient pond...a frog jumps in. You will hear the sound of the frog jumping in, and after the sound, an immense silence. That silence is the message. Basho is trying to give you the message which he has lived, felt, and he feels a responsibility that it should reach to anybody who is in search of it.

In comparison to Basho, Picasso is not

concerned with you. He is burdened in his head and he wants to unburden it. And when you look at Picasso's paintings you will feel a certain burden, a tension arising in you. If you keep Picasso's paintings in your bedroom you will have nightmares. Each of his paintings is a nightmare. He has relieved himself of his nightmare, given it to the painting. The distinction is very significant.

Before you do anything, let your doing come out of your silence. Before you sing, let your song come out of your silence. Before you paint you should meditate. Unless you come to the point where you feel you are no more, and now existence can use you as its instrument....

You say, "I have always felt my art to be my meditation." Just a little change – let your meditation be your art. You have always felt your art to be meditation. Art has the priority, and you are calling it meditation because you get absorbed in it, involved in it, and you forget yourself.

Just a little change – let your meditation be the art. First cleanse yourself; let fresh breezes pass through you, let new flowers of silence blossom in you. Then you know the spring has come, and now you are in the hands of the unknown. Just leave your hands in the unknown, allow them to move not according to your wishes, but according to something bigger than you, something vaster than you. You will be surprised that they move, and you will be surprised that that movement is not coming from you – it is coming from the beyond.

Darpana, just a little change – let your meditation be your art...but meditation has the priority; art is only a by-product. Meditation cannot be a by-product of anything.

You are asking, "I have always felt my art to be my meditation, but is it still not a doing?"

It is. If art has the priority then it is a doing. If meditation has the priority then it is a non-doing. Just a small change makes such a tremendous change – so mysterious, so beautiful, so delicious. You have given yourself into the hands of eternity. It is a deep offering.

This is the only prayer I know of. All your other prayers are just rubbish coming from the mind.

"I notice the difference when sitting in vipassana." It it good that you have noticed the difference, that meditation is a totally different thing. "Must art and sculpure even, fade away into non-doing?" They don't fade away, they simply go through a transformation. They start having a sacredness about them; something of the divine enters in them.

"Can creativity on the material plane be truly meditative?" The question of material plane or immaterial plane does not matter. What matters is that whatever you do should be born out of meditation. It can be material – a painting is going to be material, a statue is going to be material.

If it is coming from deep meditation it will have that radiation for centuries. And anybody who knows how to sit silently a little bit and just to watch it, will receive your message. The gap of centuries will disappear – he will start feeling the same meditation in which the sculpture or the painting was created.

"Will my art remain solely subjective until the ego agrees to commit suicide?"

The ego never agrees to commit suicide.

The ego *is* suicide.

Because of ego you have forgotten your authentic being. Don't be concerned with the ego, be concerned with searching for your authentic being. The moment you find your real being, the ego will disappear. There is no question of suicide, because the ego is not a reality; it is only an absence of your being. Because you have not entered into your being, the shadow of the being has been misunderstood as the being itself.

So don't be worried about suicide, and don't be worried about what will happen to your ego. I can understand that every artist, every creative person has a very strong ego. Painters, poets, singers, dancers, actors – all have very strong egos. But they are unaware that their egos are not allowing their genius its total actualization. They are not friends; they are your enemies. And because you are identified with them you will never look for the real one.

To be identified with anything false is very dangerous, because then the search for the real stops. The false has to be dropped. The false has to be understood at least as false, so that a process of search is triggered in you for the real. The real belongs to existence. You have come with it at your birth.

Ego is your nurture, not your nature. Ego has been produced by your family, by your friends, by your education, by your talents. It is just a false creation, and if you become identified – as almost everyone is identified with it – this is the greatest barrier. Disidentification with the ego will immediately give you a new insight to enter into your own being – that which is a gift of nature. Finding it, who cares about old junk? – your ego, your thoughts, your personality; you have found the real diamonds.

And because vipassana has given you a sense of what meditation is, don't miss this opportunity. Use that sensitivity to go even deeper. At the deepest you can go, something of immense beauty and grace will be created by your hands, but not by you.

As far as the suicide is concerned, I will take care of it – you just…. I have seen so many suicides. My whole business is to help people to commit suicide, because unless you commit suicide as an ego, you will never find your soul.

A doctor calls his patient to give him the results of his test. "I have some bad news and some worse news," says the doctor. "The bad news is that you only have twenty-four hours to live." "Oh no," says the patient. "What could possibly be worse than that?"

The doctor answers, "I have been trying to reach you since yesterday."

Don't be worried. The worst will also happen. Perhaps it has started happening, because even a small experience of the real, just a small candle in the dark night is enough to dispel all darkness.

Beloved Bhagwan,

Being here with You
I feel so fresh and light like a newborn child.
All the German heaviness is gone.
Sitting in front of You I feel totally drunk.
No more thoughts and worries about the future and the past.
Never before was being with You so strong and fulfilling.
But the other night, when You were talking about aloneness,
a shadow came over me – the fear to be without You,
the fear of getting stuck again in all my old worries.
This shadow falls on me again and again.
Beloved Bhagwan, can You lighten this up so that I can understand?

Dhyan Kavish, whatever you are feeling in this moment, trust that the next moment is going to be born out of it. If it is beautiful, the next moment is going to be more beautiful. If it is nourishing, the next moment is going to be more nourishing. I have been watching you, I have been seeing in your eyes that the German is dead. You need not worry about it.

You have become a pure human being. German or Indian or Chinese or Japanese, all this is nonsense. The simple reality is that you are a human being with no adjective attached to you. I know the German glue is a little stronger, but I have been destroying so many Germans that you can call me almost an expert in killing Germans! Even the parliament of Germany is afraid.

I have not applied for any visa to enter Germany – I don't have to. Whoever wants to die comes here. This way it is easier; otherwise how am I going to find out who from all over Germany is ready to die, disappear, become a nobody? The chosen ones travel themselves.

But the German parliament must have been afraid. Their problem is that any German who comes to me never returns. And naturally, the parliament is worried – what is happening? Their young people, men and women, educated people, suddenly disappear. And even if they come back they are no longer German; they have dropped all that idiocy.

Kavish, you are sayng, "Being here with you I feel so fresh and light like a newborn child." This freshness, this lightness, this feeling of being newborn will remain with you. It is not going to disappear; it has come forever. These are qualities that once you become aware of them, you cannot lose them. They have always been within you, just you never looked at them. They are not coming from outside; they are growing within you.

"All the German heaviness is gone." That's great! "Sitting in front of you I feel totally drunk." Inform the German parliament!

"No more thoughts and worries about the future and the past. Never before was being with you so strong and fulfilling." One never knows when the right time comes. And by the right time I mean the vulnerability, the openness, when you are ready to receive, when you are not afraid, when you drop all your defenses.

"But the other night when you were talking about aloneness, a shadow came over me – the fear to be without you." Don't be worried about it. If you are open, alive, fresh, I am within you. You may be alone, but if you close your eyes you will find me there, more real than you can see with your eyes open, more real than you can see me now. There is no question of any anxiety.

"...the fear of getting stuck again in all my old worries." Once you have experienced something of the beyond, you cannot fall back. Nature has a certain law: you can go only forward, not backward. Nature has not put any reverse gear in your consciousness.

When Ford made his first car he forgot to put in a reverse gear; so it was a very troublesome job. Even if you had passed your house by ten feet, you had to go round for miles to come back again and stop exactly before your house. People said, "This takes more time; walking seems to be easier – at least you can go back." And then he added the reverse gear.

God has also forgotten to put in a reverse gear. You cannot go back; you cannot go back in time, in consciousness. If you are young you cannot become a child, if you are old you cannot become young. God thought He had completed the creation. And after six days He could not be found. So perhaps He does not know that man is living without a reverse gear. Perhaps He Himself does not have the reverse gear, so He cannot come back! He must be going on and on, trying to find out, "Where is my creation?"

In this vast emptiness, to find this small earth is very difficult. The earth is really very small. Our sun is thousands of times bigger than this earth, and our sun in comparison to the stars is a very mediocre sun. Those stars are thousands of times bigger. Our earth is just a small place. If you have missed it, there is not much possibility to find it again.

Kavish, I am certain you will remain fresh, light, innocent like a small child, whether you are here or in Germany.

"This shadow falls on me again and again." Don't be worried about shadows. That is just the old German which is trying again to catch hold of you. But I have not seen any sannyasin again being caught by the German ghost. That shadow is a ghost, a German ghost!

You just enjoy your innocence, your lightness, and don't take any note of these worries. They happen to everybody in the beginning. Just old companions...they don't know that you are changed, and they go on knocking on your doors. They don't know that you are no longer interested in them, that you are not going to be a host to them. But slowly, slowly they will understand.

Right now you enjoy, dance and sing as madly as possible. Seeing you dance and sing madly, all those German shadows will go back to Germany to find some member of the parliament, to tell them, "You were right to decide that this man is dangerous and should not be allowed on German land."

The German parliament is so afraid – I have never thought that Adolf Hitler has left such weaklings. They have decided that my jet airplane cannot even land at any German airport just for refueling. They must be really afraid!

And just two days ago I received a letter from a sannyasin who had written to the German parliament saying, "Now it is almost one year since you passed an order that Bhagwan cannot enter in the country. And he had not even asked you; there was no need to pass an order. You could have denied him a visa any moment. Now it is time that you should withdraw your order – it looks stupid."

But the committee that receives any appeals against the parliament has stated, "The order should remain....the man is dangerous; he corrupts the minds of people."

But the German parliament cannot prevent me from corrupting the minds of the people. They don't know the exact word: I *destroy* the minds of people, so that they become simply heart – because all that is beautiful happens in the heart and all that is eternal happens in your being. Mind is just a wastepaper basket. Anything of no use you go on throwing in the mind. It has a tremendous capacity to collect...a great computer.

Kavish, you enjoy, laugh, and laugh totally. And that laughter will help you. Whenever in Germany you feel something of the German disease is entering in you, just dance and laugh and the disease will escape from you.

Germany has forgotten laughter; it has forgotten rejoicing, it has become so hard. Just for your laugh:

A man and a married woman are making love when her husband comes home unexpectedly. The poor man has no choice – the husband can come in any moment – so, naked as he is, he jumps out of the bedroom window. Outside it is cold and raining, and a group of joggers are running by. Having nothing better to do, he joins in.

After a while a man running next to him asks, "Hey, do you always run naked?" "Yes," says the man as he keeps jogging along. "And do you always wear a condom when you run?" asked the other man.

"No," he answers, "only when it is raining."

Beloved Bhagwan,

A therapist once told me
that we can get stuck in our feelings just as much as in the mind
and that feelings too have to be dropped or gone beyond.
I often wonder about this,
as my feelings are usually my guide in life
and also, I feel things very intensely.
Would you please comment?

Anand Trinda, it is a significant question you have asked: "A therapist once told me that we can get stuck in our feelings just as much as in the mind and that feelings too have to be dropped or gone beyond. I often wonder about this as my feelings are usually my guide in life and I feel things very intensely."

There are three centers from which all your actions come: the head, the heart, and the being. The head is the most superficial. It has to think about things – even if you fall in love the head thinks about it, am I really in love? And if it decides that yes, it seems you are in love, the head is going to propose to the woman, "I think I am in love with you."

But thinking is base. Man functions from the head. It has its utilities – it has created all the sciences, and all the technologies, and all the nuclear bombs; and perhaps is bringing a global suicide soon.

The woman functions from the heart. She cannot say, "I think I love you." It has never been heard in the whole history of humanity. She simply says, "I love you." Thinking plays no part. The heart is enough unto itself; it does not need any help from the head.

If one has to choose between the head and the heart, one should choose the heart, because all the beautiful values of life belong to the heart. The head is a good mechanic, technician, but you cannot live your life joyously just by being a mechanic, a technician, a scientist. The head has no qualities, capacities for joy, for blissfulness, for silence, for innocence, for beauty, for love, for all that makes the life rich – it is the heart.

But the therapist who told you was not wrong. You can get stuck in your heart, in your feelings too, just as people get stuck in their thoughts. But perhaps the therapist was himself not aware that there is a deeper center than heart, and that is the being – which has all the qualities of the heart and still more qualities, more riches, more treasures: blissfulness, silence, serenity, centeredness, rootedness, sensitivity, awareness...a certain insight into the godliness of existence.

First drop from your head to your heart. But don't stop there; it is only an overnight stay, a *caravanserai*. You can have a little rest there, but it is not the goal. Drop from the heart into the being.

And this is the secret of meditation, that wherever you are – in the head, in the heart – it doesn't matter, meditation brings you from the head, from the heart, to the being. Meditation is the way to your own center of existence, where there is no question of getting stuck. You are it. Who is going to get stuck in what? There are not two things, only you – you and your absolute glory.

But Trinda, you are a woman, and naturally afraid that your feelings are your guide in life, and you feel things very intensely. But it is easier to reach to the being from the heart than from the head. You will not lose guidance; in fact you will not need it at all. You will be so full of light, so full of clarity....

Guidance is needed by the blind. You will have new eyes to see – to see even that which is not visible to your ordinary eyes. And you will be able to feel new experiences which are not available even to the heart.

So there is nothing to be worried about. Your worry is simply that of a woman, a natural concern that feelings are your guide and you feel intensely; if you drop them then who will guide you? Then how will you feel things intensely? You don't know there is still a deeper center in you where guidance is not needed at all, where you *are* the guide, and where intensity becomes total, one hundred percent. And not only about those things that you have felt in the heart, but about universal experiences of enlightenment, of awakening, of divineness. You will not be a loser; you need not worry at all.

But a woman, after all, is a woman.

I have heard, a group of Jewish women decided to improve their intellectual level. No more talk of mates or children or sons-in-law, but only politics and social questions: Poland, El Salvador, Afghanistan, the bomb. Then one said,

"And what about Red China?"

"I love it, I love it!" said Sarah, "Especially on a nice white tablecloth!"

They were trying to be very intellectual about great problems of the world, but when the words "red china" came, immediately the woman asserted – forget all about intellectuality! To a woman, red china means not the Red China that is a problem, but Sarah said, "I love it, I love it! Especially on a nice white tablecloth!"

A man was reading in the newspaper that amongst every five people in the world, one is Chinese. The wife said, "Then we have to be very alert now. We already have four children, and I don't want any Chinese to be born to me."

The woman has her own way of feeling and thinking and looking at things. You became worried, how can you drop your feelings? You need not drop them; you simply learn the art of meditation and they will drop by themselves, just like dry leaves are dropping from the trees. When the wind blows strong...just yesterday I was sitting and the wind was blowing strong, and the dry leaves were showering like rain.

When meditation deepens in you, your thoughts, your feelings, all start disappearing. Meditation makes you a silent pool without any ripples – so silent that it looks like a mirror; you can see your face. And it takes nothing from your intelligence or from your feelings; it only makes everything more authentic, more real, more total, more pure. Intelligence reaches to its highest peak, just as love reaches to its highest peak.

To know your being and to be centered in your being you have found the meaning of life, you have found the purpose for which you have come here on this planet. The intention of existence is revealed to you.

Socrates has said, "Know thyself." In those two words are contained all the scriptures of the world.

Okay Vimal?

Yes, Bhagwan

Session 23

It Is A Carbon Copy

*A bird on the wing looks so beautiful,
so representative of freedom.
The whole sky belongs to it...no limits, no boundaries.
You can catch the bird; you can keep it in a cage.
It is the same bird in a way,
but it is not the same bird because,
where is its sky?
Where is its freedom?
Where is its joyful dance in the air?
All that was alive in it is gone.*

March 8, 1987
Evening

Beloved Bhagwan,

Would you talk some more
on the art of how to be fully alive?

Prem Rudra, the art of living fully, totally, and intensely is not something arduous or difficult, but it has been made almost impossible. It is so simple and so obvious that there is no need to learn it.

One is born with an intuitive feeling, intrinsic in life itself. The trees know it, the birds know it, the animals know it. Only man is unfortunate. Man is the highest peak of life, and he wants to know the art of living. There has been a continual conditioning against life. That is the basic cause why the art is needed.

All the religions of the world which have dominated humanity for centuries are anti-life. Their very fundamental is that this life is a punishment. According to Christianity, you are born in sin because Adam and Eve disobeyed God. One cannot believe how long you can stretch fictions. Even if Adam and Eve disobeyed God, I don't see any relationship with you or with me. And secondly, disobedience is not necessarily a sin. Sometimes it may be the most virtuous thing to do.

But all cultures, all societies, want obedience. That is another name of slavery, spiritual imprisonment. What wrong had Adam and Eve done because they had eaten the fruit of knowledge? Is wisdom a sin? Is ignorance a virtue? And God had forbidden them to eat from two trees; one was of wisdom and the other was of eternal life. Who is committing the sin, Adam and Eve, or God? Neither is wisdom wrong, nor is the longing for eternal life wrong; they are absolutely natural. The prohibition is wrong, and their disobedience is absolutely right. They were the first revolutionaries of the world, the first human beings with some dignity.

It is because of their disobedience that all

civilization, science, art, everything else has become possible. If they had not disobeyed, we would have been still naked in the Garden of Eden chewing grass – even chewing gum would not have been possible.

It is not only Christianity; other religions find other reasons to condemn life. Hinduism, Jainism, Buddhism all say you are suffering, you are miserable, and you cannot get out of it because it is a punishment for your evil acts of the past life. Now, what has been done in the past life cannot be undone; you have to suffer it. This misery, this suffering, this anguish has been created by yourself, and all that you can do is patiently suffer so that in the future life you are rewarded. A strange argument!

If you do something wrong in this life, you should be punished in this life. In fact, cause and effect are always together. You just put your hand into fire – do you think you will be burnt in your coming life? You will be burnt here-now. Every act either has its own reward or has its own punishment. This distance of lives is a cunning idea to make you accept life at the minimum, and all these religions teach you to renounce life. The people who renounce life become saints; they are worshiped. The people who live fully, totally – nobody worships them; nobody even appreciates them. They are, on the contrary, condemned.

Our whole upbringing is such that it goes against pleasure, against joy, against the sense of humor, against rejoicing in small things of life – singing a song or dancing or playing your flute. Nobody is going to call you a saint because you play the flute so beautifully – except me.

I will call you a saint if you dance so totally that you disappear in the dance and only the dancing remains; the dancer is completely merged, melted and has become dance. If you play the flute so totally that you completely forget yourself, only the song remains, and you are not the singer but only a listener, then the flute is on the lips of God.

If you love, it is condemned.

It has been told by all the religions that love is animalistic. Although I have been watching animals, I have never seen any love in any species of animals. Love is absolutely human. Animals may indulge in sex, but have you watched animals while they are indulging in sex? You will not see any joy. You will find them absolutely British. Such hangdogs, as if they are going through a misery. And in fact they *are* going through a misery. It is a biological necessity, and they feel it – that they are being forced to do something by some unknown force in which they are not interested.

That's why, except man, no animal makes love all the year round. Only when their mating season comes, when biology compels them: "Now you have to do it..."under enforcement, as if somebody is standing with a gun and ordering you, "Make love!" Just watch the animals, their eyes – they are not feeling any joy.

Talking about love as animalistic is such nonsense. Animals don't know what love is. Even millions of human beings don't know what love is. Love needs, as a base, a certain centering, a certain grounding in your own being, because unless you are centered in your being you will not know all the treasures that you are carrying within yourself. Love is only one of those treasures. There are even greater things – there is truth, there is ecstasy, and there is the experience of the divine. Unless one is deep in meditation he cannot love, and he cannot live.

You are asking me, Rudra, about the art of being fully alive. Start with meditation so that you can know the source of your life, and you can be at the source of your life...and it is an amazing experience. Suddenly you become aware that you have so much, such an abundance that if you want, you can love the whole world. You can fill the whole world with your love.

In your small body there is the seed that can create millions of flowers, that contains all the fragrance possible.

The art of life begins with meditation. And by meditation I mean silence of the mind, silence of the heart, reaching to the very center of your being and finding the treasure that is your reality. Once you have known it, you can radiate love, you can radiate life, you can radiate creativity. Your words will become poetic, your gestures will have grace; even your silence will have a song to it. Even if you are sitting unmoving, you will be in a dance. Each breath coming in, going out, will be a joy, each heartbeat so precious because it is the heartbeat of the universe itself – you are part of it.

To know yourself as part of existence...and you will start living fully, without any fear of religions and the priests and all the anti-life teachings which want you to be, rather than rejoicing, *renouncing* life, escaping from life. Once you are free of your conditionings – and meditation is almost like fire which burns all the rubbish that the past has given you as heritage – you are born anew. And you will not need any art to learn. It will arise spontaneously within your being.

Right now there are so many hindrances, so many barriers. You have been poisoned for so long, and you have been taught so many wrong things, that it has become almost a dragging. Rather than being a dance, life has become a dragging from the cradle to the grave. People go on living because, what else to do? They don't commit suicide because if life is so miserable, how can they hope death is going to be better?

So rather than focusing on the art of living, focus on where your life arises, in the very roots from where it gets its juice. Go deep within yourself searching for the roots of your life, and suddenly you will come across what mystics have called enlightenment, awakening, or the experience of the divine. After that experience you are a totally different person.

Then each act will have your totality behind it. Then you will not be schizophrenic. Then you will not hold anything back.

If you are dancing, then you are dance. If you are singing, then you are song. If you are loving, then you are love. If you are listening, then you are just ears and everything else has disappeared. Then each moment becomes so full, and this fullness goes on expanding.

Otherwise, people are somehow making themselves satisfied with the minimum, consoling themselves with "Blessed are the poor. Blessed are the meek." Nobody needs to be poor and nobody needs to be meek.

Life gives you so much that you are capable of being an emperor. To be an emperor you don't need an empire; to be an emperor is just an authentic and total way of life. Otherwise your emperors are also beggars. They are not living, they are in the same boat in which you are; inside they are as hollow as you are. You are asking for more, they are asking for more.

I am reminded of an ancient Sufi story: A great emperor had gone for a walk in his garden early in the morning, and suddenly he found himself encountered by a beggar who was waiting in the garden, knowing that every day before sunrise he comes. Otherwise who is going to give an appointment with the emperor to a beggar? And he always comes alone, so there is no problem. The emperor said, "What do you want?"

The beggar said, "This is my begging bowl and I want it to be filled. And this is my condition: if you cannot fill it...and I am not asking with what – gold, silver, diamonds, or stones or mud – I am not saying anything about with what. My condition is that it should be filled completely. If you accept my condition, then only, try; otherwise I can go."

It was a great challenge to the emperor. He said, "What do you think? – I cannot fill your begging bowl?" He immediately called his prime minister and told him, "Fill his begging bowl with the most precious diamonds."

The beggar said, "Once again I say to you, beggar to beggar, that there is still time, I can go." The emperor said, "What do you mean by, 'beggar to beggar'?"

He said, "You will understand it a little later on. Just let your prime minister come."

And he came with a bucket full of diamonds and poured all the diamonds in the small begging bowl. The emperor and the prime minister both could not believe...as the diamonds fell in the begging bowl, they disappeared. The begging bowl remained empty – as empty as it was before. But the emperor was a man of great pride. He said, "Even if my whole treasury has to be poured, this beggar has to be defeated. I have defeated emperors; I cannot allow this beggar to defeat me. And he has already called me 'beggar to beggar.'"

As the sun was rising, the rumor went around the capital that the emperor was in great difficulty. His treasure was being swallowed by the begging bowl. Crowds gathered; nobody could believe it. But the emperor was stubborn. Diamonds and rubies and emeralds and sapphires disappeared, then gold, then silver. By the evening the emperor said, "You were right. Now I am as much a beggar as you are." The beggar said, "That's why I was saying, 'You will understand.'"

The emperor said, "You have deceived me. This is not a begging bowl and you are not a beggar. You seem to be a magician!"

The beggar said, "No, I am not a magician, I am simply a beggar. But this begging bowl is really magical. And I will tell you the secret, beggar to beggar.

"I found this – just come close and have a look. This is the skull of a man. I have polished it, made it clean. I found it in the cemetery. I am so poor that I cannot buy a begging bowl from the market, so I said, 'This is perfectly good.' I washed it, cleaned it, polished it, but because it is the skull of a man, it is never satisfied, it is always asking for more. There is not much mystery in it. Your skull is doing the same. Everybody's head is doing the same, 'More!'"

In asking for more you go on missing that which you have.

A meditator neither bothers about the past that is gone, nor bothers about the future that has not come yet. He is focused in the present, and whatever he has, he enjoys it to its full. He squeezes the juice of the present moment to its maximum. Naturally, his life is not the life of a beggar. He is never asking for more, although he is living at the maximum with totality and intensity. Otherwise, you have to be satisfied. That's what your religions teach you – to be satisfied with little.

Satisfaction and contentment have been raised to great values. They are simply opium to the people so that you can at least tolerate the suffering that surrounds you and the misery in which you are drowning continuously.

A man is playing golf, and he hits his ball into the woods. He goes to retrieve it and comes upon a witch stirring a large cauldron of brew. "What is in there?" he asks.

"This is a magic brew," the witch cackles. "If you drink this, you will play the best golf in the world. Nobody will be able to beat you."

"Give it to me," says the man. "I want to drink it!"

"Wait a minute!" she warns. "You will also have the worst sex life in the world."

The man pauses to consider and then says, "Okay give me the brew." The man drinks it down, goes back to his friends, wins the game and becomes the champion of the club. He goes on to play tournaments and becomes the best golfer in the country.

A year later he is playing at the same course and he decides to go to see if the witch is still there. He goes into the woods and finds her in the same place. He asks her, "Do you remember me?"

"Ah, yes, I remember you," she says, "tell me something, how is your golf game?"

"You were absolutely right," he says. "I win all the time. I am the best golfer in the country!"

She cackles and then says, "So how has your sex life been?"

"Not bad," he replies.

"Not bad?" she says, surprised. "Tell me, how many times did you have sex in the last year?"

"Three...maybe four," says the man.

"Three...four?" says the witch. "And you call that 'not bad'?"

"Well, no," he says, "not for a Catholic priest with a very small congregation."

So one thing, Rudra, don't be a Catholic priest! If you want to live life fully, don't be part of any organized religion and don't be dominated by the dead. Live according to your own light. Find your own light within and live according to it without any fear. It is *our* existence, we are part of it, and whatever existence wants us to be, it has given us potentially. Use it! Actualize it! Never hold back, and never be miserly in living, in loving, in sharing, in singing, in dancing, in anything that you are doing or not doing.

If you are sitting silently, then be totally silent.

If somebody wants to learn the art of living, he will have to forget all religious scriptures, all doctrines which teach nothing but anti-life attitudes, which are in the service of death, not in the service of life.

I want my people, the first people in the world, to have a life-affirmative religiousness.

Beloved Bhagwan,

It is strange...the closer I come to You,
the more ordinary it feels.
It is a calmness and a coolness and a nothingness,
and yet out of this space I find myself dancing,
clapping, laughing, and rejoicing with You.
But it feels so different- -as though something has gone,
but I can't remember what.
And if I look for words to describe this new feeling,
I can only say, "love." But I say it uncertainly, insecurely.
Oh, Beloved Bhagwan, what is going on?

Sarovara, the observation that you have made is right and shows immense clarity. You are saying, "It is strange." It appears strange only in the beginning. The more you become acquainted with it, the more the strangeness will be gone.

You say, "The closer I come to you, the more ordinary it feels." It *is* ordinary. Do you think the stars are not ordinary? Do you think the moon is not ordinary? Do you think the roses in the garden are not ordinary? Do you think these beautiful trees are not ordinary? This whole existence is ordinary! Even to say that it is ordinary shows a desire that it should have been extraordinary.

But if everything were extraordinary, it would look very ordinary. And that is the situation. Everything is very extraordinary...but everything. Extraordinariness is the ordinary quality of existence. It is nothing special, it is simply the way things are.

So the closer you come, the more understanding you will become. Your imagination will start dispersing, and you will know the extraordinary ordinariness of everything that surrounds you.

You say, "It is a calmness and a coolness and a nothingness, and yet out of this space...." You are already feeling that this ordinariness is not what you have always thought to be the meaning of the word *ordinary*, because out of this ordinariness is coming calmness, coolness, nothingness. How can this ordinariness be ordinary?

"I find myself dancing, clapping, laughing and rejoicing with you. But it feels so different- -as though something has gone, but I can't remember what."

Something has really gone, and it always goes in such a way that you become aware only when it is gone. And then, too, you don't know what it is that has gone. It is your ego. And because the ego is so non-substantial, when it goes it makes no sound; you don't hear its footsteps going away. It is just like your shadow: you are standing in the sun and there is a shadow; you move under the shadow of a tree and your own shadow disappears. But there is no noise, no footsteps of your shadow going away. To which direction has it gone? But something has disappeared, and that is making it different.

Your dancing, your singing, your clapping, your laughing, your rejoicing...it feels so different for the simple reason that it is happening spontaneously; it is not your doing. In these beautiful moments of dancing and singing and clapping, it is not that you are doing them, they are happening. You are just a witness, at the most. The doer, the ego, is absent; hence, the difference.

And your observation is correct, "...as though something has gone, but I can't remember what. And if I look for words to describe this new feeling, I can only say 'love.'" People think hate is against love. That is not right, because hate can be transformed into love. It is the other side of the same coin. The real enemy of love is the ego, and because the ego has disappeared, although you are not certain what has disappeared, you are feeling a new arrival, a new guest within you which you can only describe as love.

"But I say it uncertainly, insecurely." Love is such a great phenomenon. You cannot say it with certainty; it is not mathematics. And you cannot say it with security. It is so vast and so fragile. How can you be secure about it? A moment before, it was not there, and who knows what is going to happen a moment afterwards? Suddenly it has descended upon you. You are in its possession, but security is not possible and neither is certainty. And if you want to make it certain and secure, you will kill it.

A bird on the wing looks so beautiful, so representative of freedom. The whole sky belongs to it...no limits, no boundaries. You can catch the bird; you can keep it in a cage. It is the same bird in a way, but it is not the same bird because, where is its sky? Where is its freedom? Where is its joyful dance in the air? All that was alive in it is gone. It is only a faraway echo of the real bird that you had seen in the sky. It resembles it, it is a carbon copy, but it is not the original.

When love comes to you – and it comes only when the ego is absent – when love comes to you, you cannot be certain about it and you cannot be secure about it. You can only be grateful. You can only be amazed – amazed at the generous existence, because you don't deserve it, and it has suddenly poured over you so many flowers. You never earned it. You cannot demand tomorrow, "Again you have to shower those flowers." That's why there is no certainty, no security.

Your observation is very clear, and I am happy; everybody's observation has to be so clear. You are simply in a state of awe. You are asking, "Oh, Bhagwan, what is going on?"

It is better not to be rational about it, not to intellectualize it, not to label it. "What is going on?" I can say only that whatever is going on is tremendously beautiful. Allow it – no need to have any explanation. Experience it – no need to understand it, to explain it. Be totally possessed by it, and this total possession by love will bring a new birth to you, a new life, and a new world all around.

You are passing through the most beautiful space every meditator has to pass through. Unafraid, go dancingly into the unknown without ever being concerned where it is going to land you. If love is the guide, then you need not be worried; if the ego is the guide, then you have to be really concerned and worried. Love can take you only to the ocean. The ego always tries to go upwards, up-current, against the current.

Love goes with the current.

Love is a relaxation, a rest, the peace that passeth understanding.

Don't start looking for that which is missing – it was not anything valuable, it was not your friend. That which you have lost, that something that you feel has gone, was your enemy. Say goodbye to it, and allow this new state to become more and more deep. There are depths beyond depths. There is no end to growth; there is no end to the mysteries of existence. Doors after doors go on opening. This is the infinity of the miracle of the universe. You should not be bothered about rationalizing your experiences, just drink them, and dance and sing and rejoice. And thank existence that it has been your fortune.

A Sicilian woman is standing in a crowded bus, having been shopping in the market. Suddenly she realizes that her purse has been stolen and she begins to cry. The bus stops and the conductor asks her, "What is wrong?"

The woman explains that in all the confusion and crush of people, her purse has been stolen. The conductor, trying to console her, asks, "But where did you keep your purse?"

The Sicilian woman blushes and touching her lower belly says, "Here, in my underpants."

The man looks at her, amazed, and says, "And you did not realize that someone was touching you there?"

The woman replies indignantly, "Of course I did. But I thought he had good intentions!"

So wherever you were hiding your ego, it is gone. Even if it comes with good intentions, don't let it come back in. And take care, because it will not leave you so easily. It is not that somebody has stolen it, it is just that in your totality, you dropped it. It must be looking for you, so be careful! It happens again and again: one loses the ego and the next day again it is back – and with good intentions! But you simply keep your doors closed, good intentions or no intentions.

Just tell the ego, "I am finished with you." Or give it as a present to some friend, because there are a few people who will really enjoy having two egos! One is not enough for them.

Beloved Bhagwan,

Is there a possibility that the disciple's love for the master
will not be the last barrier
if love and awareness can grow together?

Prem Shunyo, the possibility is there, but it is one of the most difficult things in existence, to let love and awareness grow together. People find it difficult even to grow one. So ordinarily, people either choose the path of love or the path of awareness.

But the possibility cannot be denied, because there is no intrinsic antagonism between awareness and love. In fact, my effort here is exactly for what Shunyo is asking. I want you to grow in your love *and* in your awareness together – to be a Zorba and to be a Buddha, together. Zorba is love; Buddha is awareness. It is easier to grow one, but is far more juicy to grow both together. And if both together can be grown, then the master will not be the last barrier, because in love and awareness you will become one with the master.

On the path of awareness the master is a barrier. That's why Buddha said, "If you meet me on the path, cut my head immediately." That is the answer on the path of awareness, because in Buddha's teaching there is no place for love.

There have been schools of love like the Sufis. A Sufi will not agree with this. He will say, "If the master meets you on the way, become one with him." But if you are understanding my approach...it is a little bit complex, because I am trying that your love and your awareness both go hand in hand.

The reason for my insistence that both should grow together is that the people who have grown in love have not reached to the ultimate peaks of consciousness. They have enjoyed existence tremendously, but they have not become like Everest, pillars of awareness. Love makes them more drunk, less aware. And the people who have followed only awareness have become desert-like, dry. Nothing grows, not even grass. There is no oasis on their path, only the desert, which goes on becoming drier and drier; but they have reached to the highest peak of awareness.

The effort to create a synthesis between love and awareness is my contribution to the world, because I would like you to be as aware as Gautam Buddha, but not so dry.

I would also like you to be like Meera – so juicy that even today her songs are unparalleled. She is like a garden in the spring. And I don't see that there is any contradiction. Why have people chosen only one? They have chosen one because it is simpler to manage one. To manage both is a little difficult, but it is worth it. If you can grow roses on top of Everest, you have fulfilled my dream of being a new kind of sannyasin, a new seeker of truth. And love and awareness together means you don't have to renounce life.

Love will prevent you from renouncing life, and awareness will help you to *be* in the world and yet not be of the world. As I see them, they can be complementary and we can create Zorba the Buddha – whose feet are on the ground and whose head is touching the stars. When you can have both, why unnecessarily be poor and have one? I want you to be the richest sannyasins the world has ever known.

The world has known both kinds of people – the lovers and the meditators – but the world has never tried both together. This synthesis will bring a new kind of man. For this kind of searcher, the master is not a barrier at all.

Okay, Vimal?

Yes, Bhagwan.

Session 24

No Heaven, No Hell, No Doubt

*Love takes up your whole energy – nothing is left
for anything else. It is total and intense;
that's why, except for love, everything disappears.
It is a very simple phenomenon in a way,
just you have to understand that love has a magnetic force
which neither doubt nor shame nor fear
nor self-condemnation have.*

March 9, 1987
Morning

Beloved Bhagwan,

One night in darshan I suddenly saw You sitting there
as not only one person. It was more like one part of You
was speaking to us, and another part was doing something
with the whole atmosphere and energy around us and inside of us.
Beloved Bhagwan, how many are You really?

Deva Karunesh, I am as many as you are; my heart is beating in you. Without you I don't have any purpose to be here. Just a thin thread of love is keeping me amongst you. It all depends on you – as you grow more, I am more.

I am reminded of Ramakrishna...he was a strange mystic. It was difficult for the Indian-conditioned mind to accept him. Many came, but very few remained with him. After he died, then millions followed him. The problem that was preventing people was so trivial, but for the conditioned mind, even something trivial becomes immensely important if it goes against its conditioning. And Ramakrishna was an absolutely free individual.

One queen had made a beautiful temple in Dakshineshwar, near Calcutta. But the queen belonged to the sudras, by caste the lowest – they are untouchables. So no brahmin was ready to become a priest in her temple – as if the God in the temple had also become a sudra, an untouchable.

The queen, Rani Rasmani, was very cautious about it. She never entered the temple; she always stood outside the door and from there she gave her gratitude and thanks to God. But the brahmins were all absolutely against becoming a priest in a sudra temple. The temple had also become sudra. But Ramakrishna, when he heard about it, accepted the post. He was a high-caste brahmin, and all of the brahmins condemned him, boycotted him. But he laughed. He said, "Whoever makes the temple cannot change the quality of God." Against his whole society, he accepted the post.

And his worship was also strange. He was a strange man...very colorful. Sometimes he will worship the whole day, from morning till evening. People were amazed... sometimes he will worship the whole day from morning till evening, and sometimes he will not worship at all – he will not even open the doors of the temple, he will keep them locked.

It was reported, and Rasmani could not believe it. She asked Ramakrishna, "What kind of worship is this?" He said, "I am not a man of rituals; I trust in love. When God behaves well with me I worship the whole day, and when He is adamant, stubborn, then I boycott Him completely – I don't even give Him food. Just within two, three days, He comes to his senses." Rasmani must have been a woman of great understanding. She could see the innocence of Ramakrishna, that he was not a priest in the ordinary sense.

Then it was reported that first, before offering food to God, he tasted it and then he offered it. "This is sacrilegious, this is too much," people said. Again he was called, "What are you doing? Don't you know that you should not taste the food first. First God has to take it, it has to be offered to Him; then you can distribute it, and you can take it."

He said, "You can accept my resignation, but I cannot do anything against my heart. My mother used to taste food first, and then she would give it to me. If it was really delicious she would give it; if it was not that good she would prepare it again. I cannot be cruel with God. I love Him. How can I offer Him something which I have not tasted?"

Rasmani understood this too. She was not only wise, she was also a woman. But the third thing was very difficult for people, and that was: Ramakrishna would be giving a discourse, and in the middle of the discourse – talking about God, talking about the ultimate, talking about prayer – he would suddenly stop and he would say, "Excuse me, I will be coming back." And he would go to the kitchen to enquire of his wife Sagar, "What are you preparing today? Make something really good."

This was too much. Even Sagar objected, saying, "This cannot be supported in any way – talking about God, and suddenly in the middle you remember about food, what will people think? – what kind of man is he?"

His closest circle of disciples believed that he had arrived, but even they were suspicious. Everything was okay, but this continuous disruption in the discourse, going to his wife to enquire...and the kitchen was not far away, so everybody was hearing what he was enquiring about. Back again, he would start talking about God. They said, "This you should stop. It discredits you." He would simply laugh, and would not answer.

One day his wife said, "Unless you answer this question, I am not going to prepare food today at all; we will all fast." He said, "If you insist, I can tell you. The day I am not interested in food, the day you feel that I am not interested in food, remember, only three days are left for my life. This is the last thread, very thin and fragile, that I am holding." Even if he was resting, lying down on the bed, as his wife entered with the food, he would jump – just like a small child – and just look at the plate: "What have you made?"

The wife said, "You should behave like a grown-up, you are not a child!" He said, "Who is going to see here? Don't be worried, just tell me what you have prepared. You make such delicious things that most of the time I am meditating on them. But remember, the day I show no interest only three days are left."

And it happened one day that he was resting, looking at the door; the wife entered, and he turned to the other side. Usually he would have jumped, but he did just the opposite. The plate fell down from the wife's hands. "Only three days?" And that very day it was discovered that he had cancer of the throat.

For the coming three days he was not able to eat or to drink. One of his closest disciples asked him, "You are so close to the sources of life, you can just ask, 'Remove this cancer.' If you are not eating, not drinking, none of your disciples are drinking or eating. How can we?" When they all insisted, he said, "Okay, I will try. The problem is, when I close my eyes I forget, because thoughts disappear, and I forget what I was supposed to ask. But I will do my best."

It was the third day, the day he died. He closed his eyes and his face became radiant. He smiled although the pain was immense and he opened his eyes and said to his disciples, "I asked, but the answer that I received was, 'Now, Ramakrishna, you should eat from every mouth that loves you, you should drink with every mouth that is connected with you. Why are you insisting on having only one body? All these bodies of your lovers are your bodies.' So if you want some nourishment to reach me, drop your fasting."

Sadly, the disciples ate that evening, but that was the last.... Ramakrishna came out of his room and enjoyed seeing his disciples eating. But he said, "Why are you sad? You know me, I love food. If you are eating on my behalf, just behave like me."

He made them laugh and rejoice in a situation when they were full of tears – because it was the third day and by the evening Ramakrishna was gone, he was dead. Just before dying, he told Sagar and his disciples, "I am only leaving the body, nobody should say that Ramakrishna has died. I will be here, and you have to remember to behave in this room as you behave in front of me – with the same love, with the same respect, with the same gratitude, with the same joy."

He said to his wife, "You need not be a widow, because I am not dying; I am only moving from body into bodilessness. Now it will be easier for me to be in all of you, wherever you are."

Karunesh, your hands are my hands, and your eyes are my eyes, and *only* if this happens, you rise from discipleship to the status of a devotee. So your feeling is perfectly correct. I am talking to you just to keep you engaged so that I can work in other ways on you, on your heart.

It is spiritual surgery. Unless you are silent, quiet, calm, just absorbed in listening to me, I cannot do the subtle work. My speaking is nothing but anesthesia.

Saint Peter was on vacation from guarding the pearly gates, so Jesus was his stand-in. An old man arrived, tired and downhearted. "Cheer up, old man, you have reached heaven," Jesus said. "Why are you so sad?"

"Well," replied the old man, "I am just a poor carpenter; but once I had a very special son who had a miraculous birth and became world-renowned. He left me many years ago and I have been searching for him ever since."
"Father!" exclaimed Jesus, hugging him.
"Pinocchio!" said the old man.

Beloved Bhagwan,

Doubt, shame, fear, self-condemnation –
all disappear in the mystery of Your love.
Would You care to comment?

Love is the greatest alchemy there is, the most profound science of transformation. If you love, your whole energy is gathered, becomes one-pointed. Doubt needs energy, shame needs energy, fear needs energy, self-condemnation...they all need energy.

If you do not love, then all these things can go on living in you; you are nursing them. As the great miracle of love happens, all the energies rush towards love, just as all the rivers rush towards the ocean. Doubt remains empty, and without energy it is dead. It was your energy that was keeping it alive.

Shame and fear and self-condemnation, they all need energy from you, your support. On the surface you think you want to get rid of them, but deep down you are supporting them; otherwise, they cannot exist. They are parasites.

Love takes up your whole energy – nothing is left for anything else. It is total and intense; that's why, except for love, everything disappears. It is a very simple phenomenon in a way, just you have to understand that love has a magnetic force which neither doubt nor shame nor fear nor self-condemnation have.

Love is your very being, and all these things have come from the outside. Doubts have been created by people who are giving you beliefs. If you don't have any belief, you don't have any doubt. Have you ever thought about it?

In a small school a teacher is telling the small boys and girls what qualifications are needed to enter into the kingdom of God. She explained in every possible way so that they could understand, that unless you drop sin you cannot enter into the kingdom of God. And afterwards she asked, "Now can you tell me, what is needed to enter into the kingdom of God?"

One small boy raised his hand. It was rare, because he never used to take the initiative to answer; this was the first time. The teacher was very happy; she said, "Yes, what is needed to enter into the kingdom of God?" The boy said, "First you have to commit sin." The teacher said, "You have to commit sin? For a whole hour I have been trying to teach you that you have to drop sin, and you are saying that you have to commit sin."

The boy said, "But unless I commit sin, how can I drop it? And without dropping sin, nobody enters the kingdom of paradise. So the first thing is, commit sin; then drop it and enter into the kingdom of God."

Doubt arises because you have been forced to believe. If you are not given any belief system, you will not have any doubt. For example, a Christian, a Mohammedan, a Hindu – all have doubts about God, because they have been conditioned that God exists. But they have no evidence, no proof, no argument, no eye-witness, and they themselves don't feel anything about God. The belief is creating a doubt in them. But there are religions like Buddhism, Taoism,

Jainism, where God is not a belief; it is not part of their religions.

I have never come across a Jaina or a Buddhist who doubts the existence of God. How can you doubt if you don't believe? It looks strange, but it is not. Belief is an effort to repress your doubt. So underneath every belief there is doubt. But if there is no belief system, there is no place for doubt to exist.

In countries like the Soviet Union or China, where there is no heaven, no hell, nobody doubts. One of my friends was visiting the Soviet Union, and just out of curiosity – he was a professor in the University of Varanasi – he asked a little boy, the son of his host, while walking in the garden, "What is your idea about God, about heaven, about hell?"

The boy laughed. He said, "In the past, when people were ignorant, they used to believe in such things; now nobody even bothers about them. They are part of a dead history." The boy is not doubting. He is absolutely clear.

Beliefs create doubt. You are trained from the very beginning to feel ashamed of this, ashamed of that; you are never accepted in your simple naturalness. That's why shame exists, and with it the fear that you may do something wrong, you may go astray, you may miss the train – although there is no train and the question of missing it does not arise.

In India, all the trains run so late, and for twenty years I was continually traveling all over the country. I was surprised that one day in Allahabad the train came exactly at the right time. It was almost a wonder. I went to the driver to thank him: "This is something of a great feat," but he looked very ashamed.

I said, "What is the matter? You have done a great job, bringing the train, exactly to the second, at the right time on the platform. In twenty years this is the first time that I have seen a train coming to the platform at the right time."

He said, "Don't make me more ashamed."

I said, "You are a strange person. I have come to show my gratitude to you."

He said, "Don't show your gratitude, because this is yesterday's train; I am twenty-four hours late. So just go away, don't make me feel so ashamed."

I said, "I was not trying to make you ashamed; I had not even imagined that it is yesterday's train. But anyway I have got in it at the right time, who cares which day's train it is!"

All the religions live on fear; they make every child fearful. And the fear becomes the psychological atmosphere of your being. So you are never total in doing anything, you are always hesitating – whether it is right: what you are doing, is it going to lead you towards reward or towards punishment; are you coming closer to God or going farther away? Each step is full of fear. And because of this, religions have been able to exploit you.

A man who has no fear cannot be exploited. He lives his life according to his own light. He has a lifestyle which is his, not borrowed, not given by somebody else. Nobody has ever accepted you as you are. And because everybody wanted you to be somebody else other than who you are, slowly, slowly you have also become self-condemnatory: I am always a failure; my arrow always falls short, it never reaches the target.

There is an ancient story of a great king who was also a great archer. And he used to think that there was no parallel to him. As he was traveling in his golden throne, on a golden chariot – he was going to a meeting with another emperor – he passed through a village, and he was immensely surprised. For the first time he felt, "Perhaps there is a greater archer than me in this small village, and I have never heard about him" – because on every tree, on the fences, there were arrows exactly at the center of a circle.

It seems the man had never missed the center of the circle. He enquired from the people...he stopped the chariot and he asked, "Who is this archer?" and they started laughing. He said, "Why are you laughing? I love archery and I want to reward this man, because I used to think I am the greatest archer – once in a while I miss – but here I have seen that on every tree there are arrows exactly at the center of a painted circle."

They said, "We are laughing because you don't know; this archer is the idiot of this town." He said, "Idiot? It does not matter, but he is a great archer, you bring him."

They said, "You don't understand. First he shoots the arrow and then he goes and makes the circle around the arrow – this is not archery. But he is always happy, and anybody who passes through this village almost always enquires about that idiot; nobody enquires about anybody else. His archery is all over the town; the whole day, that is his business. There is no target, wherever the arrow hits, he will go there and make an exact circle around it, so it is always in the center.

"So you go, and don't be bothered about him, he is just an idiot and nothing else. We have been telling him, if you want to be an archer then learn archery. He said, 'What is the point? The archer can hit in the middle of the circle – it does not matter whether the circle is made before or after – but my arrow is always in the middle.'"

This society is utterly condemnatory. Whoever you are it is not acceptable, something better.... Slowly, slowly you become infected with the disease of self-condemnation.

But love is a miracle. If it happens, and you are totally involved in it, then it takes all the energy from fear, from self-condemnation, from doubt, from sadness, from misery, from anxiety. And once the energy is taken away, all those concepts are only corpses; they lose their grip on you.

Hence I say to you: Love is the golden key to transformation. But it should not be a superficial, ordinary love. It should not be so small that doubt can also exist by the side, self-condemnation can also exist, misery can also exist, hate can also exist, because your love needs only very small energy. It has to be life-absorbing. The moment your love is almost your very life, it becomes prayer.

To me there is no other prayer than love possessing you so totally that nothing else can remain inside you; love needs all the space and you have to throw all junk out of your being. A great love is the only prayer, the only true prayer. And Jesus is right when he says, "God is love." Just a little improvement is needed, because for two thousand years the statement has remained the same. Statements don't grow with the evolution of consciousness, we have to change them, give them higher dimensions.

Jesus says, "God is love." I would like to say to you, "Love is God." On the surface you will not see much difference, but there is a great difference. "God is love" implies that he can be many other things, love is not his totality – he can be just, he can be all-powerful, he can be all-seeing, he can be present everywhere; love does not exhaust his whole being, love is only one of the attributes of God. But if you change it into "Love *is* God", then God becomes an attribute of love.

And love has no other attributes. Love is the only experience on the earth which is not of the earth, which is not of this world, the only experience which can give you a taste of the beyond.

God cannot be proved because it is an attribute of love. But love can be proved. Love cannot only be proved, it can be lived. And as you live love you will know, something divine has entered into you. You are no longer just an ordinary human being. Something in you, in your consciousness, has gone beyond humanity. And that beyond-ness, the taste of that beyond-ness, is the only argument and the only evidence of something which people have called God.

I myself like to use the word *godliness* because the word God looks dull and dead – frozen, as if there is no possibility of any growth in God; he has come to the full stop. But godliness is a quality, a riverlike flow. It can become more and more and more; it need not be limited.

God is limited, godliness is infinite. And because godliness is a quality, you need not worship it; you have to develop it. You don't have to make statues of godliness – you cannot. And you cannot reach godliness directly, because it is an attribute of love. All these are the implications. You can forget all about God and the churches and the organized religions.

There is no one who has dared to deny that love does not exist. There is almost half of the population of the world which denies the existence of God; but there has been nobody, not a single person, who denies the existence of love. Because love is a potential in your heart, you can grow it. And when it comes to its blossoming, when the spring comes and the fragrance comes to the flowers, you will know what godliness is. It follows love just like a shadow.

You have been told to do strange things: "Love God!" – and God is only a quality of love. I cannot say such a stupid thing, "Love God." I can only say to you, "Love, and you will find God. Love, and God will find you. Love, and as your love will mature, it will turn into something superhuman, into something divine."

It is not a question of belief; you cannot believe in God. And there is no need to believe in love because you can experience love. In the temple of love, the very silence of the temple, the very spaciousness of the temple, is godliness.

But all the religions have been, in a very strange way, giving distorting ideas to humanity. Otherwise, religion can be so simple – just like music or poetry or singing or dancing. The priority should be of love. And you can forget all about God, it will happen on its own accord if you manage to be full, to be abundantly full of love. Otherwise, you can go on believing. Just the other day I came across a small joke: What are the three reasons that prove that Christ was a Jew? Firstly, he was thirty-three years old and still lived with his mother; secondly he believed his mother to be a virgin; and thirdly, his mother believed her son to be a god.

Let Jewish mamas believe their sons to be gods, but just by anybody's belief or your own belief, God cannot be discovered. I want you to deeply understand it, that God is not a person but only a presence. When love is abundant, overflowing, a presence surrounds you. You cannot catch hold of it, but you can feel it.

The presence transforms you from the world of human beings into the world of eternity, immortality, from all kinds of lies that religions have been preaching to you, to the naked truth of existence.

Okay, Vimal?

Yes, Bhagwan.

Session 25

The Same Vicious Circle

*Knowing the being, is bringing a light
into the darkness of your inner world;
and unless you are enlightened inside,
all the light outside is of no use.
Within you, there is just darkness,
abysmal darkness, unconsciousness,
and all your actions are going to arise
out of that darkness, out of that blindness.*

March 9, 1987
Evening

Beloved Bhagwan,

You always talk against the mind –
that we should drop it, tell it to shut up,
that it is not needed in the search for truth.
You seem to regret that none of your sannyasins
is a Nobel prize winner and You give us
unfertilized eggs to nourish our brains.
Hence I almost feel guilty when I make an attempt
to become informed about one thing or another,
though it seems almost impossible
to survive in the marketplace totally ignorant.
What is the mind for?
Is it really totally mischievous?

Prem Mandira, mind is one of the most significant thing in life, but only as a servant, not as a master. The moment the mind becomes your master, then the problems arise; then it displaces your heart, displaces your being, takes over the whole posession of you. Then rather than following *your* orders, it starts ordering you.

I am not saying to destroy the mind. It is the most evolved phenomenon in existence. I am saying beware that the servant does not become the master. Remember your being comes first, your heart comes second, your mind comes third – that is the balanced personality of an authentic human being.

Mind is logic...immensely useful, and in the marketplace you cannot exist without the mind. And I have never said that you should not use your mind in the marketplace – you should use it.

But *you* should use it, you should not be used by it. And the difference is great....

It is mind which has given you all technology, all science, but because the mind has given so much, it has claimed to be the master of your being. That's where the mischief begins; it has completely closed the doors of your heart.

Heart is not useful, it has no purpose to fulfill. It is just like a roseflower. The mind can give you bread, but the mind cannot give you joy. It cannot make you rejoice in life. It is very serious, it cannot even tolerate laughter. And a life without laughter has fallen below human standards. It has become subhuman because it is only man, in the whole existence, who is capable of laughing.

Laughter indicates consciousness and its highest growth. Animals cannot laugh, trees cannot laugh, and the people who remain encaged in the mind – the saints, the scientists, the so-called great leaders – they cannot laugh either. They are all too serious, and seriousness is a disease. It is the cancer of your soul; it is destructive.

And because we are in the hands of the mind, all its creativity has gone in the service of destruction; people are dying from starvation, and the mind is trying to pile up more nuclear weapons. People are hungry, and the mind is trying to reach to the moon.

Mind is absolutely without any compassion. For compassion, for love, for joy, for laughter...a heart, freed from the imprisonment of mind, is needed.

Heart has a higher value. It is not of any use in the marketplace, because the marketplace is not your temple; the marketplace is not your life's meaning. The marketplace is the lowest of all the activities of human beings.

Jesus is right when he says, "Man cannot live by bread alone." But mind can only provide bread. You can survive, but survival is not life. Life needs something more – a dance, a song, a joy.

Hence I want you to put everything in its right place: the heart should be listened to first if there is any kind of conflict between mind and heart. In any conflict between love and logic, then logic cannot be decisive, love has to be decisive. Logic cannot give you any juice – it is dry. It is good for calculations; it is good for mathematics and good for scientific technology. But it is not good for human relationships, not good for the growth of your inner potential.

Above your heart is your being. Just as mind is logic and the heart is love, being is meditation. Being is to know yourself. And by knowing yourself, to know the very meaning of existence.

Knowing the being, is bringing a light into the darkness of your inner world; and unless you are enlightened inside, all the light outside is of no use. Within you, there is just darkness, abysmal darkness, unconsciousness, and all your actions are going to arise out of that darkness, out of that blindness.

So when I say anything against mind, don't misunderstand me. I am not against mind, and I don't want you to destroy it.

I want you to become an orchestra. The same musical instruments can create a hell of a noise if you don't know how to create a symphony, how to create a synthesis, how to put things in their right place.

Being should be your ultimate...there is nothing beyond it – it is part of God within you. It will give you that which neither mind can give, nor the heart can give: It will give you silence. It will give you peace. It will give you serenity. It will give you blissfulness, and finally, a sense of being immortal. Knowing being, death becomes a fiction and life takes wings into eternity. A man who is unaware of his own being cannot be said to be really alive. He may be a useful mechanism, a robot....

Through meditation, search your being, your *isness*, your existence. Through love, through your heart, share your blissfulness – that's what love is all about: Sharing your blissfulness, sharing your joy, sharing your dance, sharing your ecstasy.

Mind has its own function in the marketplace, but when you come home, your mind should not continue chattering. Just as you take off your business coat, your hat, your shoes, you should say to the mind, "Now be quiet, this is not your world." This is not being against the mind. In fact, this is giving rest to the mind.

In the home, with your wife, with your husband, with your children, with your parents, with your friends, there is no need for the mind.

The need is for an overflowing heart. Unless there is love overflowing in a house, it never becomes a home; it remains a house. And if in the home you can find a few moments for meditation, for experiencing your own being, it raises the home to the highest peak of being a temple.

The same house...for the mind is only a house; for the heart it becomes a home; for the being it becomes a temple. The house remains the same; you go through the changes – your vision changes, your dimension changes, your way of understanding and looking at things changes. And a house that is not all three, is incomplete, is poor.

A man that is not all three, in deep harmony – the mind serving the heart, the heart serving the being, and the being belonging to the intelligence spread all over existence.... People have called it God; I love to call it godliness. There is nothing above it.

I will read your question, Mandira. Do you remember the meaning of your name that I have given to you: Prem Mandira, "Love Temple". In your question there are many misunderstandings.

You are saying, "Bhagwan, you always talk against the mind." I have to talk against the mind, because of you, because you are clinging so much to the mind. You drop clinging and I will never even mention the word.

I am tired of talking against it. It has not done any harm to me, it is not my enemy; it has served me perfectly. It is because of you that I have to go on and on, until one day you decide, "Let us try to put the mind aside." And you say to it, "Shut up for the moment." Unless you all get out of the cage of the mind, I will have to talk against it; although I am not against it.

"You are saying that we should drop it, tell it to shut up." I say drop it if you want to meditate. And the moment you are going to the marketplace, pick it up. Who is preventing you? Is there a need that you should continually cling to it for twenty-four hours? – because tomorrow you are going to the marketplace, so in the night you also have to keep it with you, under your blanket? Are you afraid that it will escape?

I say drop it because I want you to feel that you are the master. If you want to drop it you can drop it, and if you want to pick it up, you can pick it up. It is just a mechanism.

"You are saying that it is not needed in the search for truth." It is not needed. As far as the search for truth is concerned, it is not needed. On the contrary, it is a hindrance.

And truth is not available in the marketplace; it is not something you can purchase, not something that you can steal, not something that you can borrow – it is something within you. But it is beyond the reach of the mind. The reach of the mind is only to outside things. As far as your inner world is concerned, mind is absolutely impotent. It is not its fault; it is not made for that purpose.

As far as truth is concerned, you need a state of no-mind – I mean no thought, not even a ripple in your consciousness, no disturbance – just absolute silence.

One discovers one's truth only in silence, in aloneness. Even your mind will not be a witness to it.

And Mandira, you are absolutely wrong in saying, "You seem to regret that none of your sannyasins is a Nobel prize winner." Where you got the idea from, I don't know.

I have certainly said that the vegetarians have not been able to get a single Nobel prize. And the reason is that intelligence needs certain chemicals, certain proteins, which are not available in their vegetarian food. But I am not regretting it, I am simply stating a fact.

A Nobel prize does not necessarily prove that somebody has achieved the highest consciousness. J. Krishnamurti did not receive it; Raman Maharishi did not receive it. Meher Baba did not get it. And these were people who reached to the highest peak; they belong to the same category as Gautam Buddha.

Even if Gautam Buddha was alive, he would not receive the Nobel prize because the Nobel prize is a political game. It is not decided by the height of your intelligence; you need some political reasons. Even politicians like Kissinger have received the Nobel prize, yet Krishnamurti's name was never even mentioned.

One of my sannyasins works on the Nobel prize committee. He is a member who chooses who is going to be the Nobel prize winner for certain subjects; he is the expert for economics on the committee. And because he is my sannyasin, he just mentioned my name to the president of the Nobel prize committee, and wanted to introduce my books to the members.

The president said, "This should be the first and the last time that I hear this name! And if you want to keep your post, you should never mention this man's name again. He is dangerous."

He informed me, saying, "I was shocked. They were not even ready to read books. They were not even ready to consider...."

"It is not a question of giving, I was not insisting," he said, "that my master should be given the Nobel prize. Seeing that the committee is giving the Nobel prize to politicians, to people who do not deserve it, I simply mentioned your name. And I was threatened that, I would be thrown out of the committee and would lose a good job. They said if I went on working silently, perhaps I might get the Nobel prize for being a great econonomist, but I was never to mention the name of my master."

I don't have any political support. On the contrary, I have all the political antagonism from all over the world. Every politician, and it does not matter to what country he belongs, is going to oppose me.

Just today I was seeing a press cutting about an address of Rajiv Gandhi, the prime minister of India, saying that there should be an open discussion all over the country about one very significant subject. The subject suggested by him is: "Religion should not interfere with politics."

I said, "This is perfectly good, but if it is an open discussion, then the other side should also be allowed: 'Politics should not interfere with religion,' and there should be an absolute freedom of expression."

They have created laws so there are a few things you cannot even say. The moment you say them, you will be thrown into jail without any trial. Then how you can conceive of an open discussion? And do you think politics is a higher value than religion? The higher *should* not interfere with the higher; the higher should interfere with the lower.

I am ready for an open discussion with Rajiv Gandhi anywhere; it would be perfectly good in his parliament. What does he know about religion? And what does he know about politics? And just giving an address saying that all over the country there should be an open discusssion – how is it going to happen? Who is going to arrange it? Let it begin from the parliament – I am ready. If Rajiv Gandhi has guts, then I am in favor – religion *should* interfere with politics! And by religion, I don't mean Hinduism or Buddhism or Christianity; by religion I mean religious values – truth, sincerity, honesty, compassion.

If these values cannot interfere with the politicians, then politics will go from bad to worse – it is already in the gutters. If anybody can pull it out of the gutters and give it a good shower, it cannot be anything other than religious values.

I stand for religiousness. I don't belong to any organized religion, and I will not say that organized religion should interfere with politics because organized religion *itself* is politics.

Religiousness is always individual. And whenever there is a religious person, he should be heard by all the politicians because although they may have been able to get votes from the ignorant masses, that does not make them wise.

Even if the whole world votes for you, you cannot become a Gautam Buddha; getting votes does not transform your consciousness. A Gautam Buddha should be heard....

When I was seeing the address of Rajiv Gandhi, I remembered a story about Gautam Buddha. Buddha was entering into the Kingdom of Vaishali and the prime minister told the king, "It will be absolutely appropriate that you should receive Gautam Buddha when he enters the boundaries of our empire."

The king was a young man, arrogant.... He said, "What do you mean? He is just a beggar and I am an emperor? If he wants to see me, he can make an appointment. But why I should go to receive him...who is he?"

The prime minister was very old. He had been the prime minister for the king's father. The father had died and he had brought up the child and crowned him as a king.

Listening to his arrogant and egoistic attitude he said, "Now you are mature enough and you can make decisions on your own. Please retire me, accept my resignation; I cannot work under you anymore. I have fulfilled my duty to your father. I had promised that until you become king I would not leave my post. That promise is fulfilled."

But the king became worried because the prime minister was really a very wise man, and to find a substitute would not be easy – and he has loved him almost like a father. So he said, "Just because I am not going to receive that beggar...."

The prime minister said, "Don't insult me any more." He said, "I am not insulting you."

The prime minister said, "You are insulting me, my age, and you are insulting the whole Eastern concept of what is higher and what is lower. The man you are calling a beggar was once a prince of a many-times-bigger empire than you are the king of. He was also going to be the king. He was the only son of his father and he renounced the empire; he is no ordinary beggar. He is far higher than you.

"If you want me to remain as prime minister to you, you will have to come with me to receive Gautam Buddha. Not only that, remember when I touch his feet, you will have to touch his feet too. Because it is not a question of how rich you are. It is a question of how conscious you are. And this man happens only once in thousands of years, this Everest-like consciousness. You are the beggar.

"What have you got? Death will take it away. What he has is beyond the reach of death. Now his empire is not of this world, but of eternity; he will be the king forever. You are king only for a day, or today. Don't be lost in this momentary, phenomenal, illusory greatness. Your greatness is made of the same stuff as dreams are made of. Come with me."

When I saw the address of Rajiv Gandhi, I remembered the story of Gautam Buddha, and the king of Vaishali.

I do not regret that none of my sannyasins is a politician. I am immensely happy that my sannyasins are not politicians. And the Nobel prize has not been given, at least up to now, even to a single meditator. Meditation does not come into their consideration.

A novelist can get a Nobel prize. A film director can get a Nobel prize. A scientist can get a Nobel prize. A politician can get a Nobel prize. But there is no category in the Nobel prize for a man like Jesus, or Gautam Buddha, or Zarathustra, or Lao Tzu.

And even if these people are given Nobel prizes, they will laugh. To them your Nobel prizes are just like toys; they are good for children to play with. In what way can they enhance Gautam Buddha?

This is how people go on hearing things which are not sane...I have never regretted....

And you are saying, "I feel almost guilty when I make an attempt to become informed about one thing or another...." You are misunderstanding me completely. Who has told you, "Don't become informed"? I have been telling you that by informing yourself you cannot attain to self-realization. But if you want to be an electrician, I will not suggest: Meditate, and you will become an electrician; meditate, and you will become a mechanic in a factory – you will need information.

There is no need to feel guilty. This is how your mind goes on making distortions, interpretations, and you go on carrying in your mind things which I have never said.

You are saying, "...it seems almost impossible to survive in the marketplace totally ignorant." But who has said to you that in the marketplace, be totally ignorant? Be as knowledgeable as possible. In the marketplace innocence is not needed, neither is silence needed, nor is self-realization needed. The more you are knowledgeable, the more you will be successful.

I have been talking, not about the marketplace, I have been talking about the realization of who you are. This is *not* possible through gathering information; this is *not* possible through becoming knowledgeable – this is possible only if you become innocent.

And remember, innocence is not ignorance. There is a very fine demarcation, but the difference is immense. Ignorance means absence of knowledge, and innocence means presence of silence, presence of clarity. Ignorance is a negative thing. Innocence is a positive phenomenon. They don't mean the same thing.

You can be innocent as far as your inner growth is concerned, and you can be knowledgeable as far as your outside world is concerned. They are two different things; they don't clash with each other.

I have heard...two cowboys come upon an Indian lying on his stomach with his ear to the ground. One of the cowboys stops and says to the other, "You see that Indian?" "Yah," says the other cowboy.

"Look," says the first one, "he is listening to the ground. He can hear things for miles in any direction."

Just then the Indian looks up, "Covered wagon," he says, "about two miles away. Has two horses – one brown, one white – a man, a woman, a child, and household effects in the wagon."

"Incredible!" says the cowboy to his friend. "This Indian knows how far away they are, how many horses, what color they are, who is in the wagon, and what is in the wagon. Amazing!" The Indian looks up and says, "Ran over me about a half hour ago."

Prem Mandira, when you are listening to me, be alert that your mind does not start interpreting it. Just listen exactly to what I am saying; otherwise you can go on listening to me for years and still remain in the same vicious circle, moving round and round but going nowhere.

I really mean business. I want you to be the

new man. The whole of humanity needs the new man; it is not only your need. It used to be the need of the individual in the past, but now we have come to a point where the new man is needed for the survival of the whole of humanity, for the survival of life itself on the earth.

Beloved Bhagwan,

Your thinking frequently reminds me of Nietzsche's realism;
yet he didn't believe that man was intrinsically good or bad.
Would You please comment.

Mathilda Argyll, Friedrich Nietzsche is a great thinker. I am not. When he says that man was intrinsically, neither good nor bad, he is right. Man is born a tabula rasa, just a clean sheet of paper, nothing written on it. But he brings seeds, and if he is allowed freedom and support, he will become a unique individual.

Nobody can predict what is going to be his destiny, but one thing is certain: if he is not interfered within his growth, whatever he becomes, he will be immensely contented. He may become a musician, just a bamboo flute player, but he will have a richness in his being which even the richest people cannot have, a fulfillment. His seed has not been destroyed. He has come to become his own self, not somebody else's carbon copy.

He may not be a lotus flower; he may be just a marigold, or even a grass flower without any name, anonymous, a nobody, but still he will dance in the rain, and in the wind, and in the sun, with the same joy as any roseflower.

But this has been one of the most difficult problems: people grab every child as he is born and start making something out of him. Nobody cares to allow his nature to have its own say, to sing its own song. With all good intentions, the parents, the priests, the teachers, the whole society is trying to make somebody according to their own conceptions.

And this is the sole cause of humanity's misery, because nobody is what he would have been if left in freedom – supported, accepted, nourished. But everybody has been distorted. And the problem becomes more complex because the people who are distorting children are distorting them for their own good.

Every child comes with tremendous energy and potential, but the whole of society around the child starts moulding him, giving him ideals: you have to be a Jesus Christ or a Gautam Buddha; you are not acceptable as you are; if you want respectability, honor, respect, recognition, then you have to become somebody according to the ideas of the society in which you are born. So everybody is led astray, away from his nature, away from his being, and the farther away he goes from his being, the more miserable he will become.

I have heard about a great surgeon who was retiring at the late age of 75. It was not customary to keep somebody in service for that long, but that surgeon was a master surgeon. In the whole country there was nobody who even came close to him. Even at the age of 75, he was the best surgeon. So rather than getting retired at the age of 60 he was persuaded to continue.

At 75 he said, "Enough is enough. Now, I want to rest and relax. I'm utterly tired."

The day he was leaving his service, his friends gave him a farewell party, and they were all drinking and dancing and rejoicing. But he was standing in a corner, sad and miserable. One of his friends reached to him and asked, "What is the matter? We have come here to give you a joyous festive farewell, and you are standing here in the corner as if somebody has died. Why you are looking so miserable?"

He said, "You have touched my wound. I have been carrying that wound for almost 60 years. I never wanted to be a surgeon. My father was a doctor, my mother was a doctor, and they both forced me to be a surgeon. I wanted to be a musician. And they both hammered me,'Are you mad? If you become a musician, at the most you will be a street singer. But if you listen to us, we will send you to the best educational institutions, to the best medical college, to the best surgical institute. We will make you one of the great surgeons. You will leave a name behind you in the history.'

"I was helpless, as every child is. They forced me; I became a surgeon. And they were right, I became world famous. But I have never felt any joy. I have been working like a robot. Perhaps that is the reason why I am such a good surgeon, because I have lost my human heart. My heart is almost dead. If I had become a musician, perhaps nobody would have ever heard my name, but what does that matter. I would have felt fulfilled, satisfied. I would have been my own self."

This has happened to almost everybody. Only once in a while, by accident a child escapes, survives, protects his own destiny and does not allow anybody to drag him into other directions.

Nietzsche is right, but he provides no cure. His diagnosis is right because he is only a thinker, a great thinker. And I have always loved him for his insights. But this is the poverty of the West.

It is not only the question of Friedrich Nietzsche; none of the philosophers in the West are meditators. They are only thinkers. By thinking, they come to certain conclusions. By logic, by argument, they try to find something closest to truth, but it is never the truth.

You cannot think about truth; either you know it or you don't know it. How can you think about love? Either you love and know, or you don't love and you don't know. There is no third alternative.

Nietzsche lived just in thoughts. Otherwise he had the potential of being a Gautam Buddha for the West. He had the capacity, the caliber, but the West has missed the very dimension of meditation. Their philosophers have remained only thinkers.

The East has not produced great philosophers like Frederich Nietzsche – there is no parallel in the East. The East has never bothered about polishing, sharpening, thinking, knowing that by thinking you cannot arrive at your being, to your truth, to your godliness, to self-realization.

Nietzsche lived a miserable life, full of worry, anxiety, anguish, angst. This is strange. Such a great thinker, but his life is nothing but anguish. Gautam Buddha may not have been such a great thinker. He was not, but his life was so calm, so quiet, so peaceful.

And the strangest phenomenon is that the Western philosopher has been thinking, "What is truth?" and has never been able to find it. And the Eastern mystic, non-philosopher, has never been thinking about truth. He has been on the contrary, dissolving thoughts, getting out of the mind, finding a space in himself where no thought has ever entered. And in that space he has encountered God Himself. The Western philosopher creates great edifices of thought, but his whole life is so poor.

Nietzsche went mad...you cannot conceive of Gautam Buddha going mad. Not a single mystic in the whole ten thousand years of history in the East has ever gone mad. The deeper they have entered into themselves, the more sane they have become. But the Western thinker almost always, if he's really a great thinker, ends up either being mad or committing suicide.

The old proverb is, "A tree is known by its fruit." A philosopher or a mystic is also known by his fruit. What is his ultimate flowering, madness or enlightenment? suicide or self-realization?

Mathilda, you are saying, "Bhagwan, your thinking frequently reminds me of Nietzsche's realism...." There is some similiarity, but there is also a great difference. Nietzsche's realism is only a conclusion of logic. My realism is an experience of silence. His realism is based on arguments. My realism is based on my experience. His realism leads him towards madness. My realism has led me beyond mind into a state of no-mind, into utter sanity, from where you cannot fall back.

A medical student is taking a test, and one of the questions is, "Name the three best advantages of mother's milk." The student immediately writes, "1. It has all the healthful nutrients needed to sustain a baby. 2. It is inside the mother's body, and therefore protected from germs and infections." But the student can't think of the third answer. He tries hard, and finally he writes, "It comes in such nice containers."

What else to do? He did his best, thinking about the third best quality.

Thinking has always been leading people, societies, cultures, into very ridiculous conclusions. Thinking has not proved a blessing to humanity, while meditation has proved a tremendous ecstasy, and the ultimate experience of deathlessness. I am all for meditation.

Nietzsche was very much against Jesus and against Gautam Buddha too. Although he had no idea, at least about Gautam Buddha, his antagonism was based on Gautam Buddha's support of feminine qualities – compassion, love, silence, non-violence, kindness, grace.

Nietzche was absolutely in favor of the qualities of a warrior. The warrior cannot be compassionate, cannot be kind, cannot be graceful; he has to be inhuman, cruel. And it is not a coincidence that out of Friedrich Nietzsche's realism Adolf Hitler got the idea of his Nazi philosophy. You cannot distort Gautam Buddha's words into a Nazi philosophy – that is impossible. However hard you try, you cannot derive from his philosophy a second world war.

Nietzsche cannot be absolutely forgiven. Adolf Hitler was not a great thinker – he was almost retarded – and he chose parts of Nietzsche and distorted them. But still some responsibility of Frederick Nietzsche *is* there, and the reason is that he himself did not live a life of peace, joy and love. He was very frustrated, utterly against existence, not grateful at all to existence, but irritated – why have I been given life?

I can understand, he was a troubled man, but nobody else is responsible for it. He never tried to find a simple fact: " What is the secret of the peaceful life of Lao Tzu, Chuang Tzu, Mahavira, Bodhidharma, Tilopa? All these Eastern mystics who have lived so joyously and so dancingly, what is their secret?

Western philosophers have remained almost blind; even today the same is the case. It will be a great day in the history of man when Western philosophy starts to enter into the mysteries of the Eastern achievement. Perhaps that will be the beginning of East and West meeting.

The East is outwardly poor, but inwardly has a richness. The West is outwardly rich, but inwardly is very poor. Both can meet, and in their meeting the whole of humanity can be rich – outwardly, inwardly. And when you can be rich so totally, why be rich only halfheartedly? Yet the other half remains poor.

If one has to choose – if there is no other way, and these are the only alternatives – then I will say the East has chosen well. It is better to be outwardly poor, and inwardly rich, but I don't think that is the only possibility.

My approach is to create a third alternative, where East and West can meet and merge. And I don't see any difficulty at all.

Okay, Vimal?

Yes, Bhagwan.

Session 26

Live Fearlessly, Die Fearlessly

*If you live fearlessly,
you will die fearlessly.
And the man who has no fear
has no God, has no hell, has no heaven,
because he knows one thing: wherever he is,
he will be able to live as beautifully,
as artistically, as aesthetically as possible.*

March 10, 1987
Morning

Beloved Bhagwan,

I feel so imprisoned by the fear of being intimate
and totally losing control with a man.
This outrageous woman is locked up inside.
When she comes out once in a while, men usually freak out,
so she goes back into hibernation,
plays safe, and is totally frustrated.
Could You please talk about this fear of intimacy?

Shantam Lani, mankind, especially womankind, suffers from many sicknesses. Up to now all the so-called civilizations and cultures have been psychologically sick. They have never dared even to recognize their sickness; and the first step of treatment is to recognize that you are sick. The relationship between man and woman has been especially unnatural.

A few facts have to be remembered. Firstly, man has the capacity for only one orgasm; woman has the capacity for multiple orgasms. This has created a tremendous problem. There would not have been any problem if marriage and monogamy had not been imposed on them; it seems it was not the intention of nature. The man becomes afraid of the woman for the simple reason that if he triggers one orgasm in her, then she is ready for at least half a dozen more orgasms – and he is incapable of satisfying her.

The way that man has found is: don't give the woman even one orgasm. Even take away from her the conception that she can have an orgasm.

Secondly, man's sex is local, genital. The same is not the case with woman. Her sexuality, her sensuality is spread all over her body. It takes a longer time for her to warm up, and before she even gets warmed up, the man is finished. He turns his back towards her and starts snoring. For thousands of years, millions of women around the world have lived and died without knowing the greatest natural gift – of orgasmic joy. It was a protection for man's ego. The woman needs a long foreplay so that her whole body starts tingling with sensuality, but then there is the danger – what to do with her capacity for multiple orgasm?

Looked at scientifically, either sex should not

be taken so seriously and friends should be invited to give the woman her whole range of orgasms, or some scientific vibrator should be used. But with both there are problems. If you use scientific vibrators, they can give as many orgasms as the woman is capable of; but once a woman has known...then the man's organ looks so poor that she may choose a scientific instrument, a vibrator, rather than a boyfriend. If you allow a few friends to join you, then it becomes a social scandal – that you are indulging in orgies.

So the simplest way man has found is that the woman should not even move while he is making love to her; she should remain almost like a corpse. And man's ejaculation is quick – two minutes, three minutes at the most; by that time the woman is not at all aware of what she has missed. As far as biological reproduction is concerned, orgasm is not a necessity. But as far as spiritual growth is concerned, orgasm is a necessity.

According to me, it is the orgasmic experience of bliss that has given humanity in the early days the idea of meditation, of looking for something better, more intense, more vital. Orgasm is nature's indication that you contain within yourself a tremendous amount of blissfulness. It simply gives you a taste of it – then you can go on the search.

The orgasmic state, even the recognition of it, is a very recent thing. Just in this century, psychologists became aware of what problems women are facing. Through psychoanalysis and other psychological schools the conclusion was the same, that she is being prevented from spiritual growth; she remains just a domestic servant.

As far as reproducing children is concerned, man's ejaculation is enough – so biology has no problem; but psychology has. Women are more irritable, nagging, bitchy, and the reason is that they have been deprived of something that is their birthright; and they don't even know what it is. Only in Western societies has the younger generation become aware of the orgasm. And it is not coincidental that the younger generation has gone into the search for truth, for ecstasy – because orgasm is momentary, but it gives you a glimpse of the beyond.

Two things happen in orgasm: one is, mind stops the constant yakkety yak – it becomes for a moment no-mind; and second, time stops. That single moment of orgasmic joy is so immense and so fulfilling that it is equal to eternity.

In the very early days man became aware that these are the two things which give you the greatest pleasure possible, as far as nature is concerned. And it was a simple and logical conclusion that if you can stop your chattering mind and become so silent that everything stops – time included – then you are free from sexuality. You need not depend on the other person, man or woman; you are capable of attaining this state of meditation alone. And orgasm cannot be more than momentary, but meditation can be spread over the whole twenty-four hours.

A man like Gautam Buddha is living every moment of his life in orgasmic joy – it has nothing to do with sex.

I have been asked again and again why very few women became enlightened. Amongst other reasons, the most important reason is: they never had any taste of orgasm. The window to the vast sky never opened. They lived, they produced children, and they died. They were used by biology and man, just like factories, producing children.

In the East, even now, it is very difficult to find a woman who knows what orgasm is. I have asked very intelligent, educated, cultured women – they don't have any idea of it. In fact, in the Eastern languages there is no word which can be used as a translation for "orgasm." It was not needed; it was simply never touched.

And man has taught woman that it is only prostitutes who enjoy sex. They moan and they groan and they scream, and they go almost crazy; to be a respectable lady you should not do such things. So the woman remains tense, and feels humiliated deep down – that she has been used. And many women have reported to me that after making love, when their husband goes on snoring, they have wept.

A woman is almost like a musical instrument; her whole body has immense sensitivity, and that sensitivity should be aroused. So there is a need for foreplay. And after making love, the man should not go to sleep; that is ugly, uncivilized, uncultured. A woman who has given you such joy needs some afterplay too – just out of gratitude.

Your question, Lani, is very important – and is going to become more and more important in the future. This problem has to be solved; but marriage is a barrier, religion is a barrier, your rotten old ideas are barriers. They are preventing half of humanity from being joyous, and their whole energy – that should have blossomed in flowers of joy – turns sour, poisonous, in nagging, in being bitchy. Otherwise all this nagging and this bitchiness would disappear.

Men and women should not be in a contract, like marriage. They should be in love – but they should retain their freedom. They don't owe anything to each other.

And life should be more mobile. A woman coming into contact with many friends, a man coming into contact with many women, should be simply the rule. But it is possible only if sex is taken as playfulness, as fun. It is not sin, it is fun. And since the introduction of the pill, now there is no fear about having children.

The pill, in my opinion, is the greatest revolution that has happened in history. All its implications have not yet been made available to man. In the past it was difficult, because making love meant more and more children. That was destroying the woman, she was always pregnant; and to remain pregnant and give birth to twelve or twenty children is a torturous experience. Women were used like cattle.

But the future can be totally different – and the difference will come not from man. Just as Marx said about the proletariat, "Proletariat of the world unite, you have nothing to lose..." and everything to gain.... He had seen society divided into two classes, the rich and the poor.

I see society divided into two classes, man and woman.

Man has remained the master for centuries, and woman the slave. She has been auctioned, she has been sold, she has been burnt alive. Everything inhuman that can be done has been done to women – and they constitute half of humanity.

The whole future can be a totally different phenomenon. All the women of the world just need to fight for a separate voting system, so that a woman will vote only for a woman, and a man should vote only for a man. Then in every parliament there will be half women and half men.

And men are divided into small parties. Women have to be aware not to create divisions, but to agree on fundamentals – because it is a question of thousands of years of slavery: you cannot afford parties. There should be only one international party of women, and they could take over all the governments of the world.

That seems to be the only way to change the

status of women: to allow science full freedom to transform the relationship between man and woman and to drop the idea of marriage, which is absolutely ugly because it is simply a kind of private ownership. Human beings cannot be owned, they are not property. And love should be just a joyful play. And if you want children, then children should belong to the society, so the woman is not labeled as mother, as wife, or as prostitute. These labels should be removed.

Lani, you are asking, "I feel so imprisoned by the fear of being intimate and totally losing control." Every woman is afraid, because if she loses control with a man, the man freaks out. He cannot handle it; his sexuality is very small. Because he is a donor, he loses energy while making love. The woman does not lose energy while making love – on the contrary, she feels nourished.

Now these are facts which have to be taken into account. Man has for centuries forced the woman to control herself and has kept her at a distance, never allowing her to be too intimate. All his talk about love is bullshit.

"This outrageous woman is locked up inside. When she comes out once in a while, men usually freak out, so she goes back into hibernation, plays safe, and is totally frustrated." This is not, Lani, only your story; it is the story of all women. They are all living in deep frustration.

Finding no way out, knowing nothing about what has been taken away from them, they have only one opening: they will be found in churches, in temples, in synagogues, praying to God. But that God is also a male chauvinist.

In the Christian trinity there is no place for a woman. All are men: the father, the son, the holy ghost. It is a gay men's club.

I am reminded that when God first created the world he created man and woman from the mud, and then breathed life into them. He created them equal. But looking at the world, you can understand – whoever has created it is a little stupid. He created man and woman, and made a small bed for them to sleep in. The bed was so small that only one person could sleep on it. They were equal, but the woman insisted: she would be on the bed – he should sleep on the floor. And the problem was the same with the man – he was not willing to sleep on the floor. You will be surprised to know that the first night in existence was the beginning of pillow fights.

They had to go to God. And the solution was very simple – just make a king-size bed; any carpenter could have done it. But God is a man, and is as prejudiced as any other man: he demolished the woman, destroyed her. And then he created Eve, but now woman was no longer equal to man – she was created from one of Adam's ribs; so she was just to serve man, to take care of man, to be used by man.

Christians don't tell you the whole story. They start their story from Adam and Eve – but Eve is already reduced to a state of slavery. And since that day woman has lived in slavery in thousands of ways. Financially she has not been allowed to be independent. Educationally she has not been allowed to be equal to man – because then she could be financially independent. Religiously she has not been allowed even to read the scriptures or listen to somebody else reading the scriptures.

Woman's wings have been cut in many ways.

And the greatest harm that has been done to her is marriage, because neither man nor woman is monogamous; psychologically they are polygamous. So their whole psychology has been forced against its own nature. And because woman was dependent on man she had to suffer all kinds of insults – because man was the master, he was the owner, he had all the money.

To satisfy his polygamous nature, man created prostitutes. Prostitutes are a by-product of marriage.

And this ugly institution of prostitution will not disappear from the world unless marriage disappears. It is its shadow – because man does not want to be tied to a monogamous relationship, and he has the freedom of movement, he has the money, he has the education, he has all the power. He invented prostitutes; and to destroy a woman by making her a prostitute is the ugliest murder you can do.

The strange fact is, all religions are against prostitution – and they are the cause of it. They are all for marriage, and they cannot see a simple fact – that prostitution came into existence with marriage.

Now the women's liberation movement is trying to imitate all the stupidities that men have done to women. In London, in New York, in San Francisco, you can find male prostitutes. That is a new phenomenon. This is not a revolutionary step, this is a reactionary step.

Lani, the problem is that unless you lose control while making love, you will not have an orgasmic experience. So at least my people should be more understanding, that the woman will moan and groan and scream. It is because her whole body is involved – total involvement.

You need not be afraid of that. It is tremendously healing: she will not be bitchy towards you, and she will not nag you, because all the energy that becomes bitchiness has been transformed into an immense joy. And don't be afraid about the neighbors – it is their problem if they are worried about your groaning and moaning, it is not your problem. You are not preventing them....

Make your love a really festive affair, don't make it a hit and run affair. Dance, sing, play music – and don't let sex be cerebral. Cerebral sex is not authentic; sex should be spontaneous.

Create the situation. Your bedroom should be a place as holy as a temple. In your bedroom don't do anything else; sing and dance and play, and if love happens on its own, as a spontaneous thing, you will be immensely surprised that biology has given you a glimpse of meditation.

And don't be worried about the woman who is going crazy. She *has* to go crazy – her whole body is in a totally different space. She cannot remain in control; if she controls it she will remain like a corpse.

Millions of people are making love to corpses.

I have heard a story about Cleopatra, the most beautiful woman. When she died, according to the old Egyptian rituals her body was not buried for three days. She was raped in those three days – a dead body. When I first came to know about it, I was surprised – what kind of man would have raped her? But then I felt, perhaps it is not so strange a fact. All men have reduced women to corpses, at least while they are making love.

The most ancient treatise on love and sex is Vatsyayana's *Kamasutras*, aphorisms about sex. It describes eighty-four postures for making love. And when the Christian missionaries came to the East, they were surprised to realize that they knew only one posture: man on top – because then man has more mobility, and the woman is lying like a corpse underneath him.

Vatsyayana's suggestion is very accurate, that the woman should be on top. The man on top is very uncultured; the woman is more fragile. But why men have chosen to be on the top is so that they can keep the woman under control. Crushed under the beast, beauty is bound to be under control. The woman is not even to open her eyes, because that is like a prostitute. She has to behave like a lady. This posture, man on top, is known in the East as the missionary posture.

A great revolution is ahead in the relationship between man and woman. There are institutes evolving around the world, in the advanced countries, where they teach you how to love. It is unfortunate that even animals know how to love, and man has to be taught. And in their teaching, the basic thing is foreplay and afterplay. Then love becomes such a sacred experience.

Lani, you should drop the fear of being intimate and totally losing control with a man. Let the idiot be afraid; if he wants to be afraid, that is his business. You should be authentic and true to yourself. You are lying to yourself, you are deceiving yourself, you are destroying yourself.

What is the harm if the man freaks out and runs out of the room naked? Close the door! Let the whole neighborhood know that this man is mad. But you need not control your possibility of having an orgasmic experience. The orgasmic experience is the experience of merging and melting, egolessness, mindlessness, timelessness.

This may trigger your search for finding a way that, without any man, without any partner, you can drop the mind, you can drop time, and you can enter into orgasmic joy on your own. I call this authentic meditation.

So you have to stop going into hibernation, stop playing safe, and all your frustration will disappear. Why should you be worried about the man? Let him ask the question, "What am I supposed to do? Lani goes crazy, jumps on top of me, starts scratching my face...!" But here in my place, among my people, you cannot make much fuss about it. You have to accept it as a natural phenomenon. Otherwise simply meditate – who is telling you to make love to a woman?

Women have not discovered meditation. Perhaps it was these freak-outs who discovered meditation to avoid the woman and all the problems...and just sit silently, doing nothing – and the spring comes, and the grass grows by itself. You can do that.

I have heard...a fat American walking down the street saw a sign: "Amazing Slimming Treatment! Twenty-four-hour cure – one thousand dollars; Six-hour cure – five thousand dollars."

Curious, he went inside and asked the receptionist about the twenty-four-hour cure. He was shown inside a large room, and there stood a beautiful naked girl with a sign around her neck, "You catch me, you make love to me; but first you have to catch me."

That was the process of slimming! He was very impressed, and thought, "If this is the one-thousand-dollar cure, the five-thousand-dollar one must be five times as good." So he immediately signed up for the five-thousand-dollar, six-hour cure.

He was undressed and taken into another large room, and the door was locked behind him. Alone in the room with him was an enormous gorilla, with a sign around his neck saying, "I catch you, I make love to you."

Don't be worried, enjoy the whole game – be playful about it. If one man freaks out, there are millions of men.

One day, Lani, you will find some mad guy who does not freak out. And anyway, freaking out and running all around the bed will give him a slimming treatment – and without paying a single dollar!

Beloved Bhagwan,

You look into my eyes, and I disappear into Yours.
I experience a communication happening beyond words,
beyond this world. I am so in love with You,
all other things have lost my interest.
I have heard so many times
that all good things must come to an end.
Please, Bhagwan, tell me again that this is not going to end.

Prem Devika, the proverb, "All good things must come to an end," must have been invented by unenlightened people. In the ordinary, unconscious life, it is true. But the really good things, which can happen to you only in immense consciousness, never end. This proverb belongs to the crowd.

But if you ask the awakened ones, they will say that good things only begin, they never end. There is a statement of Gautam Buddha to the same effect. He says, "Bad things don't have any beginning, but they have an end. Good things have a beginning, but they don't have an end." Now that is coming from a very conscious man.

You are saying, "You look into my eyes, and I disappear into yours. I experience a communication happening beyond words, beyond this world. I am so in love with you, all other things have lost my interest."

Hence the fear has arisen in you; the proverb arises out of that fear: "I have heard so many times that all good things must come to an end" – it is not necessary; it depends on your consciousness. Just a very small part of your being is conscious – one tenth of the whole; that's why good things are very momentary. As your consciousness grows deeper, the experiences of the good, of beauty, of joy, of ecstasy, start becoming longer.

When you are fully aware, then the ecstasy remains with you twenty-four hours a day, awake or asleep.

So don't be worried about it. Just make an effort to be more alert, to be more aware; and whatever is happening to you will become more intense, will become juicier, will become your permanent quality – a part of your very being.

But it always happens; whenever something good happens to you a fear is lurking by the side, that perhaps soon it will end. And because of this lurking fear, you cannot even enjoy it while it is there; the fear destroys the moment. Don't be bothered about proverbs created by the ignorant masses. They are expressing their own experience – in their lives it is very rare that anything good happens. And it remains for such a short time that later on, looking retrospectively, they cannot convince themselves whether it has happened or they have dreamt about it. Was it a reality or only imagination?

And the whole of humanity is living in fear – fear about everything: you cannot live fully, because there is death.

My logic is totally different: because there is death, live as totally as possible. Because you cannot be certain about tomorrow, you have got only this moment, you cannot afford to postpone living – because there may not be any more time left.

One of the disciples of Confucius asked him, "Master, can you tell me something about death, and what happens afterwards?"

Confucius said to him, "Do you want to die? Are you preparing for death?"

The man said, "No, I am not preparing for death, I am very much afraid of death. I want to be certain that there is nothing to be afraid of."

Confucius said, "Don't be stupid. While you are alive, be alive! And be totally alive, and enjoy life in all its dimensions; and when you are dead, be totally dead. And if you want to think about death, in your grave you will have enough time; lying down, go on thinking about death. But don't waste your life thinking about death."

But man has been made so afraid – about his actions, about his living, about his respectability – that there is no time left for living. Fear takes all the time.

Rain is pouring over Warsaw. Mr. Cohen and Mr. Goldberg are rushing back home, wrapped up in their dark, orthodox Jewish coats. But the rain is getting too strong, and they look around for shelter. The only place available is a butcher's shop. They look at each other, look at the dark, black clouds, and walk into the shop. Everybody stares and they are totally embarrassed. Mr. Cohen tries to break the ice, and asks casually, "Hmm, how much is it for a kilo of pork?"

Right at that moment, an incredible thunder clap echoes in the air. Mr. Cohen rushes out, looks at the sky and says, "I was just asking for the price."

Even God is nothing but your fear. It is not your love, it is your fear.

Have you ever watched? Whenever you are in misery, anguish, suffering, you remember God. Whenever you are joyous, happy, with a feeling of well-being, you never bother about God.

God is a creation of man's fear.

If a man is fearless, he does not have any conception of God. Gautam Buddha has no conception of God. Mahavira has no conception of God. Lao Tzu has no conception of God. Where has God disappeared? As their fear disappeared, the projection of their fear, God, also disappeared.

One of the fundamentals of sannyas is: Go on dropping your fear, don't waste time. Enjoy life so totally that there is no space left for fear. And I give you the guarantee that even when death comes, you will not be afraid; your whole life-long training in fearlessness will not allow you to be afraid of death. On the contrary, you will feel excited because you are moving into an unknown space.

An exploration – that's how Socrates took his death. He was condemned to death by poison by the court of Athens. Exactly as the sun was setting, his disciples gathered around him. They were crying, and Socrates told them, "I have always been teaching you to enjoy every moment. I am not crying, and I am dying; you are alive, and you are crying – this is very strange. I am feeling very excited, after a long time, because life I have lived, I am well acquainted with it – but death is a new experience, so new that it is a challenge for me to explore it."

The man who was preparing the poison outside the room had killed many people in the past by preparing this poison. He was the expert. But he was delaying the preparation of the poison because, listening to Socrates in the court, he had fallen in love with the man.

The court had no argument against him; they were all pygmies, and he was a genius. And finally, seeing that by arguing with this man you cannot win, they decided that it was taking too long, it was better to take a vote.

This was a cunning strategy. And a vote was taken to decide whether Socrates should be sentenced to death or not. They had not proved any crime. He had argued so well, and destroyed all the slurs on his character – they had not been able to prove a single crime. They resorted to a different device: to vote.

And fifty-one percent of the people voted that Socrates should be killed – just fifty-one percent. Forty-nine percent of the people were voting for his life – even the man who was to prepare the poison had voted for his life. But it was his job.... He was delaying, the sun had set....

And Socrates was asking again and again, "What happened? At sunset the poison was to be given to me. It is getting late." He went out of the room, and asked the man, "Why are you delaying?"

He said, "You are a strange fellow! I have fallen in love with you – and now you are making it even more difficult for me. People enjoy if some delay happens, at least that much more they have been able to live. Why are you in so much of a hurry to die?"

Socrates said, "Life I have lived. And I have lived so totally, I have squeezed all the juice out of it. Now there is no more to explore. Death opens a new door, a new mystery. Don't delay, I am feeling so excited. I am feeling young again."

If you live fearlessly, you will die fearlessly. And the man who has no fear has no God, has no hell, has no heaven, because he knows one thing: wherever he is, he will be able to live as beautifully, as artistically, as aesthetically as possible.

Okay, Vimal?

Yes, Bhagwan.

Session 27

This I Call The "Razor's Edge"

Going without any fear, risking everything.
There is every possibility
that you will be one of those very few fortunate ones
who attain to the ultimate truth.

March 10, 1987
Evening

Beloved Bhagwan,

What is the false in me?

Atmo Khirad, everything is false in you. The false and the true cannot have a mixed existence. There is no compromise possible; either you are true or you are false.

Your whole personality is false because it has been given to you; it is not a growth. It is like plastic flowers – you have put them on a rose bush. They are not part of the bush and they don't get any nourishment from the bush, although they can deceive people.

One thing is strange, that the false is more permanent than the real. The real is almost like a river, a continuous change. Springs come and go, nothing remains the same. But the false, plastic flower is permanent; whether spring comes or goes does not matter to it. It is not alive, it is dead. Because of this strangeness humanity has depended more on the false, because the false is more reliable – tomorrow also it will be the same.

The real is unpredictable.

One thing can be certainly said about it, that tomorrow it will not be the same. It *must* have changed, because everything living goes on changing.

You are asking me, "What is the false in me?" Your question implies that there is something real too. As far as you are concerned, everything is false; and when the false disappears, you will also disappear. The real has no ego, no feeling of I-ness. The real is pure is-ness. It is there, in its all-glory, in its all-golden glamour, in its all-eternal beauty. But it is so vast that you cannot say, "It is me." It is God, it is the existence, it is reality itself.

You are the symbol of the false. Just look at your personality – it has all come out of nurture, training, discipline, education.

You have not been allowed to be natural for

the simple reason that nature cannot be relied upon. There is no guarantee about nature, there is no security, no safety. Hence every society before the child even comes to know who he is, starts forcing a false mask over his original face, giving him a name, giving him qualities.... And the child is so helpless and so dependent on you that it is almost impossible for the child to rebel. He simply becomes imitation; he starts learning whatever you want him to learn.

You give him a false name, you give him a false identity, you give him a false pride. You teach him to be obedient; you teach him to be good, whatever is your definition of good; you teach him to be religious, whatever religion you belong to – you make him a Christian, a Hindu, a Mohammedan. And the poor child goes on being covered by layers of falsities.

Have you ever thought if your being a Christian or a Jew or a Hindu is your choice? Has it been your discovery? Have you ever looked at why you are a Christian? Just because of the accident that you were born to two persons who were Christians. They were also accidentally Christians, just as you are. One accident goes on giving birth to another accident. Neither was Christianity their discovery, nor is Christianity your discovery. And a religion that has not been discovered by you, how can it be real? How can it become a song in your heart? How can it transform you?

That's why the whole world is religious, but still there is no religiousness anywhere. Somebody is Mohammedan, somebody is Jaina, somebody is Buddhist – except my people, who are searching for who they are. And the miracle is, when you search you never find that you are a Christian or a Hindu or a Mohammedan.

If you search, you find that you are part of God. You are divine – and who bothers about being Christian or Hindu or Mohammedan? You have reached to the very source of religiousness. You will not belong to any organized religion. And then whatever religiousness you have found will be authentic, true. It will show in your actions, it will show in your eyes, it will show in your relationships, in your responses to situations.

You will not go to a church or a temple or a mosque or a synagogue, because you have found the real temple of God within yourself. So whenever you want to go to the temple, you will close your eyes and be silent. In that silence you will start falling deeper and deeper...finally to your very center. And *your* center is also the center of the whole universe. Only on the periphery we are different; at the center all differences are lost, just a blissfulness remains.

Atmo Khirad, remember this as something very basic, that you cannot be something of the false *and* something of the true. Just as in this Chuang Tzu Auditorium, if there is light it is not possible that half of the auditorium will remain dark and half will become full of light – either the whole will remain in darkness, or the whole will become full of light. There is no co-existence between light and darkness, and there is no co-existence between reality and the false.

An Irishman was condemned to receive forty lashes, but the more they whipped him, the more he laughed. "Why are you laughing?" they asked him. "You don't understand," he told them, helpless with laughter, "you are whipping the wrong man."

You are also living the wrong man. Even when you are in love, which is your most precious moment, there are four persons, not two. The real two are hiding, and the false two are making love. And the false two are absolutely incapable of love – how can love arise out of falseness? Hence love gives you so much hope and frustrates you almost a thousand times more. But the problem is so deep that you never become aware of why you go on condemning the other person. You go on changing lovers, but with each lover the same thing is going to happen.

Even a man like Jean-Paul Sartre lives in the same fallacy; he calls the other the hell. The other is not hell, but there is some meaning when he calls the other the hell. You never come in contact with the *real* other; you always come in contact with the false other. The false has a quality of giving you great promises, but it never delivers any goods.

There is an ancient parable in India: A man was a great devotee, but as devotees are, his devotion was not a gratitude but a greed. He was asking God, "Give me something so that I can perform miracles. Just one small thing I am asking. For years I have been praying, and there is no response." And finally it happened. God must have become bored and tired, because every morning, every evening, the same prayer: "Give me some power of miracles."

So he gave him a small seashell and told him, "This is no ordinary seashell, it is magical. If you ask for something, that thing will immediately be presented to you." He tried and it worked. He asked for something and immediately the thing appeared. He created a big palace, gathered all kinds of luxuries, and became the richest man of his land. But one day he got into great trouble.

A sage was passing through the city. He was very famous, very much respected, and naturally, the richest man invited him to stay in his guest house. And in the night he saw that great sage sitting outside the guest house on the lawn, with a similar kind of seashell but of double the size. And he was asking the seashell, "Give me one hundred rupees," and the seashell would say, "I will give you two hundred."

The rich man thought, "This is.... I was thinking that I have got the most miraculous thing in the world, but this man has got something which even answers and asks, 'Are you ready to receive two hundred?'" He thought, "It will be good... he is a sage, perhaps he may be willing to exchange."

He went to him with his shell, and he said, "You are a sage; I am a worldly man. I also have got this miraculous seashell, but it only gives what I ask. Your seashell...I have never even dreamt. But you are a sage, you can do well with my shell and you can give me your shell."

The sage said, "There is no problem, you can have it." The man rushed into his palace. He had a small hiding place where he used to ask the seashell for things. With the new seashell he entered there, locked the door from inside, and asked the seashell, "Give me one crore rupees." And the seashell said, "No, I will give you two crore." He said, "That's very good. Give me two crore."

The seashell said, "No, I will give you four crore." The man said, "Okay, give me four crore."

The seashell said, "Now I have changed my mind, I will give you eight crore." This went on – nothing was given, just it was doubled. He became afraid; he said, "What is the matter? Whatever I say, you simply double it." The seashell said, "That is my quality, I don't give anything."

He rushed out to get his old shell back, but by that time the saint had disappeared. He was so miserable, but the seashell said to him, "Why are you so miserable? I am ready to do whatever you say, just say it."

He tried it again, but again the same thing: "I want a great palace to be made." The shell said, "No, I will make two palaces." The tired man said,

"Okay, make two." But the seashell laughed and he said, "No, not less than four."

It is just like your false personality: it goes on promising but it never delivers anything. And the people you are with, they are in the same track. They also go on promising – because the false is very articulate in promising, but absolutely incapable of giving anything. Between two real persons there is no need of any promise. The real persons are overflowing with joy, overflowing with blissfulness. Before you ask, you receive; before you knock, the doors are opened; before you seek, you have already found it.

That is the quality of the real. The search here in this mystery school is how to get rid of the false, which is not yours, and to find out that which you have brought with yourself from the womb of existence itself. Your mother's womb was only representative of the existential womb.

The discovery of oneself in its total reality is so ecstatic and so eternal that you cannot conceive there can be more blissfulness, more benediction. The desire for more disappears, because you cannot even conceive that more is possible. The false goes on asking for more.

Neither it gives anything, nor does it receive anything; it is a beggar. The real is an emperor.

So remember, all that you are right now is just a thick layer of falseness around you. In your thoughts you are false, in your feelings you are false, in your actions you are false. And you are not responsible for it; you have been prepared, disciplined with great skill, education. Almost one third of the life of a man is wasted in making him false. But you can drop it in a second, in a split second – just a sheer understanding: "This is borrowed, others have given it to me. It is not my own intrinsic nature."

Drop it! There will be a little fear, because with it your safety, your security, your respectability will also disappear. But something greater will come: your authenticity, which is such a tremendous fulfillment that only in that fulfillment does one come to know the tremendous meaning and significance of life.

So just watch. Whatever you find is borrowed, drop it. The moment you become empty of everything that was borrowed you will become the light of the world, a light unto yourself and to others.

Beloved Bhagwan,

You are so much in me, it's just more and more amazing.
You are the most surprising friend I ever dreamt of having.
I find myself talking to You inside, sharing.
Sometimes I have the urge to ask so many essential things,
just like an ongoing intimate affair.
I feel You in every corner of my being, in the here and now,
in all moments, and yet it's very subtle; who are You, who am I?
Do You hear me, or am I just getting off the wall?

Kavisho, I hear you, and you are not just getting off the wall. It is not your imagination; you are mature enough, centered enough. To imagine, to dream...you may have done it in the past, but not now. Whatever you are describing in your question is absolutely true. Only one problem is there which I cannot answer.

You are asking, "Who are you, who am I?" I don't know. Neither has anyone ever known; and this unknowability is the beauty of our being. You are saying, "You are so much in me, it is just more and more amazing. You are the most surprising friend I ever dreamt of having. I find myself talking to you inside, sharing. Sometimes I have the urge to ask so many essential things, just like an ongoing, intimate affair. I feel you in every corner of my being, in the here and now, in all moments, and yet it is very subtle."

This is only the beginning, Kavisho. Soon your questions will disappear, my answers will disappear. The dialogue will remain, but it will be not in words, but in silence. Soon you are going to have a much more surprising experience. The friend that you have found will disappear, and at the same moment you will disappear too, and there will be just a nothingness – not empty, not negative, but overflowing with joy.

You have taken the first step towards reality, now never look backwards. And however dangerous it seems...because as questions and answers and me and you start disappearing, you will find yourself entering into a more and more unknown space.

This I call the "razor's edge." Those who are courageous – and as I feel you, you have every potential to be courageous – enter into the unknown; but the unknown is not the end. Very soon the unknown starts taking you into the unknowable, and that is the exact space of mysticism. In that unknowable you will know who you are and who I am.

But there are no words to express it. One simply has a good laugh, because this unknowable has been always within you, your most intimate inner reality, and you have been searching for it all over the world in many, many lives.

It is strange that the guest was in your home – to be more exact, the host was the guest – and you were searching. And every search was going to be a failure, was bound to be a failure, was destined to bring frustration. The moment you find that the host is the guest, that, "I am that which I have been searching for," all that remains is just to have a good belly laugh.

In Japan, a great mystic, Hotei, is called the laughing Buddha. He is one of the most loved mystics in Japan, and he never uttered a single word. As he became enlightened, he started laughing, and whenever somebody would ask, Why are you laughing? he would laugh more. And he would move from village to village, laughing.

A crowd will gather and he will laugh. And slowly – his laughter was very infectious – somebody in the crowd will start laughing, then somebody else, and then the whole crowd is laughing – laughing because.... Why are they laughing? Everybody knows, "It is ridiculous; this man is strange, but why are we laughing?"

But everybody was laughing; and everybody was a little worried, "What will people think? There is no reason to laugh." But people would wait for Hotei, because they had never laughed in their whole life with such totality, with such intensity that after the laughter they found their every sense had become more clear. Their eyes could see better, their whole being had become light, as if a great burden had disappeared.

People would ask Hotei, "Come back again," and he would move, laughing, to another village. His whole life, for near about forty-five years after his enlightenment, he did only one thing and that was laughing. That was his message, his gospel, his scripture.

And it is to be noted that in Japan, nobody has been remembered with such respect as Hotei. You will find in every house, statues of Hotei. And he had done nothing except laugh; but the laughter was coming from such depth that it stayed with anyone who heard it and triggered his being, created a synchronicity.

Hotei is unique. In the whole world there is no other human being who has made so many people laugh – for no reason at all. And yet, everybody was nourished by the laughter, and everybody was cleansed by the laughter, felt a well-being that he had never felt. Something from the unknowable depth started ringing bells in peoples' hearts.

Kavisho, if you can go without looking back at all, passing through the unknown into the unknowable, where everything will be lost – questions, answers, me and you – all that remains is pure existence, infinite and eternal. And I am saying it because it is possible. You have come a long way with me.

Thousands of people have come with me, and somebody drops out after a mile, somebody drops out after the second mile; I don't complain about them, I just feel sorry for them. They were not courageous enough. There came a point where they stopped.

But you have been like many of my sannyasins – going without any fear, risking everything. There is every possibility that you will be one of those very few fortunate ones who attain to the ultimate truth.

Before you come to the laughter of Hotei, start laughing more and more deeply, more and more madly. This joke is just for you, Kavisho:

A young couple have been trying for ages to have a baby, but with no success. Finally they decided to go to the doctor with the problem. After a detailed interview he suggests that maybe they should not make love every day, to avoid love becoming a routine. They should make love only spontaneously. Not as if they have to do it, but only when they are possessed by it.

"You have to find the right, spontaneous moment," the doctor says, "when you feel the moment is right, do it."

A few months later, sure enough, the woman

is back and the doctor confirms her pregnancy. "May I enquire if my advice was of any help?" "Oh, doc," she says, "it was terrific. We were having a romantic candlelight dinner with French wine and soft music, and suddenly our hands met. We were looking deep into each others eyes and we both knew, 'this is it!' We simply threw off the tablecloth and made love right on the table."

"Amazing," says the doctor. "Yes, it was great," she says, "the only sad thing about it is, that we can never go to that restaurant again."

Beloved Bhagwan,

What is the difference between "easy" and "lazy"

Satyam Svarup, the difference between easy and lazy is the difference between the positive and the negative. Easiness is a positive feeling; it is not empty. You are overflowing with energy, but you are simply enjoying the energy with ease. The very flow of energy is becoming an inner dance. In this very sense, Chuang Tzu says, "easy is right and right is easy."

Out of this easiness everything is possible, because it is not lack of energy, it is a fullness of energy, without tensions. It is energy relaxed. And the more relaxed it is, the more fresh, the more young, the more potential to be creative.

Laziness is negative; it is just feeling drained, having no energy, a kind of emptiness – no longing to do anything, no desire to create anything. One is simply tired, exhausted, spent.

The distinction is very subtle. One can be confused. When Chuang Tzu says, "Easy is right," you can think that perhaps laziness is right. Easiness is just the opposite of laziness – diametrically opposite. Easiness has a grace and an overflowing aura of energy. Laziness makes you almost appear like a corpse.

One ancient parable in India is: Two lazy persons are lying down underneath a tree; it is the season for mangoes to become ripe and a mango falls just by the side of one lazy man. A few minutes pass and nobody moves. Finally the man on whose side the mango is lying, says to his friend, "This is a great friendship. You know the mango has fallen just by my side, and you are so utterly lazy that you cannot even put the mango in my mouth – great friendship!"

And the other lazy man says, "Yes, it is a great friendship. Just a few minutes before, why had you closed your eyes – remember? A dog was pissing in my ear, and you could not even stop the dog or shoo the dog away, and you are talking about great friendship."

These are utterly spent people – as if much of their soul has left the body. Just somehow they are breathing, with great difficulty. They are breathing only because nobody else can breathe on their behalf. If it was possible that somebody else could breathe on their behalf, they would have stopped breathing.

Easiness means disappearance of tensions, anxieties, disappearance of all kinds of perversions, of all that is unnatural, and just becoming a natural human being – so relaxed that no energy is being unnecessarily wasted, not even thoughts are destroying your energy...utterly silent.

A Gautam Buddha is easy. Only in meditation will you find one day the exact meaning of easiness – not in any dictionary. When you feel so full like an ocean, everything is possible if you want, but there is no desire; the ocean is silent, resting. And just the feel of resting energy is so blissful, so peaceful, that if you come close to a man who is easy, you will start feeling yourself, a certain relaxedness.

Satyam Svarup, avoid laziness and create yourself a pool of energy without any ripples, and the small statement of Chuang Tzu, "Easy is right" will be understood in its essential meaning. Anything that is not easy and creates tensions in you, anxiety and anguish, is not right – don't do it. Follow the easy way to the point that you forget that it is easy. It becomes so natural to you that there is no need to remember that it is easy, or to remember that it is right. This is the state of enlightenment.

Easy flows the river of consciousness towards the ocean.

Dirty Ernie is sitting in the back of his first grade class, a can of beer in one hand and a cigarette in the other. The teacher says, "Okay class, today we are going to play a game. I am going to say a few words about something and you try to tell me what I am thinking about, okay? Here we go: The first thing is a fruit; it is round and it is red."

Little Billy raises his hand and the teacher calls on him; little Billy stands up and says, "An apple." The teacher says, "No, it is a tomato, but I am glad to see you are thinking. Now the next one is yellow and it is a fruit."

Bobby raises his hand, and after the teacher calls on him, he stands and says, "It is a grapefruit." The teacher says, "No, it is a lemon; but I am glad to see you are thinking. Okay, the next question is round and it is a green vegetable."

Little Mary stands up and says, "It is a lettuce." "No," says the teacher, "It is a pea. But I am glad to see you are thinking." then she says, "Okay, that's enough for today." Just then, Ernie raises his hand and says, "Hey teach, mind if I ask you one?" "No," she replies, "go right ahead."

"Okay," says Ernie, "I got something in my pocket. It is long, and it is hard, and it has got a pink tip." "Ernie," shouts the teacher, "that is disgusting." "It is a pencil," says Ernie, "but I am glad to see that you are thinking."

Satyam Svarup, just go on thinking and you will find the difference between laziness and easiness.

Okay, Vimal?

Yes, Bhagwan.

Session 28

Truth:
The Greatest Surgery

*These are the people: Socrates, Mansoor and Jesus,
who have raised the human consciousness
by sacrificing themselves.
They knew perfectly well
that to say the truth was inviting death,
but death does not matter to the man of truth.
He knows there is no death –
the body dies, but your consciousness remains always.*

March 11, 1987
Morning

Beloved Bhagwan,

I am feeling closer and closer to You as my lover and my friend.
My trust in You is helping me to sink deeper and deeper into myself.
Fear is there for the unknown,
and when I relax into it I fall one more step into myself,
and after that, I feel as if something is dying.
Beloved master, am I on the right path?
Could You please say something?

Deva Nirupo, the moment you come closer to me, you are coming closer to yourself, because I am not here as a person. Coming closer to me is coming closer to your future.

People are afraid about the unknown, always, because the known seems so well acquainted that you can remain unconscious with the known; there is no need of any alertness.

The unknown requires you to be more conscious, more alert. And the fear is coming from your false ego, because the more conscious you become, the less is the possibility for the ego to exist. That's why you are feeling that something is dying in you.

This happens only to the fortunate ones, because anything that can die in you, is not you. Your life source is eternal and knows no death. You can take it as a criterion, that whatever is dying, deserves dying. It was false and you were unnecessarily identified with it. With its death you will realize your reality and that reality never dies – it is always there.

Your question is, "I am feeling closer and closer to you as my lover and my friend." You will have to come a little closer, so that even the friend and the lover disappear. These are distant relationships, however intimate, but there is a distance: you are you, I am I. And friendship can be broken and the love can disappear, so don't get stuck rejoicing in the feeling of love and friendship. You have to come a little closer.

The exact closeness is only *one*, when neither you exist nor I exist. As far as I am concerned, I do not exist at all – it is only your imagination. My ego has died decades ago. But unless your ego dies, you will not be able to see the point that ego can die and not only do you still remain alive, you become more alive.

These are the mysteries of life...when the friend disappears, it is not that the enemy appears. When the friend disappears, then you will find the first taste of true friendliness. When love disappears, you will find that now love is no more a relationship, but your very being.

You *are* love.

So whatever is happening, is on the right path, in the right direction.

"My trust in you is helping me to sink deeper and deeper into myself." A little deeper, and the trust in me will become trust in yourself; and only that can be relied upon. Trust in me is going to disappear just as friendship and love. It is certainly deeper than friendship and love, but not the deepest. At the deepest point when your trust disappears, you will suddenly find a trust in yourself – and my work is not to make you a slave, but to make you a totally free individual.

"Fear is there for the unknown, and when I relax into it I fall more into myself." The fear is two-sided. It is of the unknown, in which you are moving, step by step, and it is also of the known, that is leaving you. All that you had known about yourself will be gone, and all that will come, you have never even dreamt about it! But that is your essential self.

That's why you are feeling "...and after that, I feel as if something is dying." Don't hold onto it. That which is dying, help it to die – the quicker, the better. And when something dies, don't carry the corpse with you, because your attachment has been with it for so long, that even though it is dead, you would not like to depart from it. But unless you depart from it, the barrier will not be broken between you and your reality. It is a thin barrier, but very strong.

So rejoice that something is dying, and remember that you are not to collect corpses.

Many things will die; don't be a collector of antiques. You have a much more beautiful future, much more fresh, much more eternal....

And not for even a single moment be worried whether you are on the right path or not. What is happening can happen only if you are on the right path; these are indications, evidences. Just be intelligent: let the dead be dead. Don't look backwards, go ahead.

You are alive, otherwise, who would take note that something is dying? Don't freak out when something starts dying, because that will be going backwards.

Three Irishmen were caught up in the French Revolution and were sentenced to be guillotined. As the first man waited for the blade to fall, it stuck, and he was released according to the old custom. The same thing happened to the second man, and he too was released.

As the third man looked up, waiting for the blade to fall, he shouted, "Hold on! I think I can see what is making it stick."

Don't be an Irishman. Be a little more intelligent. And intelligence always brings with it awareness, clarity. You can see yourself that the dead which is dead, was something false – that you have been taught to be false. Now that you are moving towards the real, the unreal has to fade away.

The unreal cannot encounter the real; the real is the death of the unreal. And there is much more which you will have to see dying – but remember you have never died before. Death is the greatest lie in existence; it is the most fictitious thing.

The real life always continues in different forms and ultimately, when you realize it, it moves into the formless. It becomes universal and that is the most blessed and the most ecstatic moment: you have found the very meaning of life.

Beloved Bhagwan,

I was blind. You gave me light for which I am extremely grateful.
Until now, I did not ask a single question,
but now I cannot hold back.
Bhagwan, it seems that some men of truth,
after contemplating the consequences of telling the truth,
came to observe, "Say the truth, but say the pleasant truth.
Don't say the truth that is unpleasant."
Bhagwan, please say something about it.

Satyadharma, it is a very significant question. There have been men who have been trying not to tell the unpleasant truth and only tell the pleasant truth, but these men do not know what truth is. Once a man knows truth, then he is not concerned about consequences. The concern for consequences is only for the coward, and cowards have never been known to know the truth.

It has to be remembered that truth is almost always going to be unpleasant, for the simple reason that the whole of humanity is living in many lies. The truth itself is not unpleasant, but because people's lies are exposed, it feels to them as unpleasant. And if you try to make the truth pleasant, you will have to make it a lie. Only a lie can be a pleasant thing for the masses because it fits with their conditionings.

My own experience is just the opposite: The man who has experienced truth will say it in its absolute sharpness, so that he can cut through your layers of lies.

All surgery is unpleasant. And truth is the greatest surgery in existence.

I am reminded of a story about Gautam Buddha. One day early in the morning, a man came. He was an atheist; his belief was that there is no God. Now, atheism is one of the lies. You have not explored the outer space, neither have you explored the inner space, and still you have come to the conclusion that there is no God. You have never meditated, you have never given a chance to yourself to feel the divineness of existence – still you go on carrying your belief that there is no God.

The man asked Gautam Buddha, "What is your opinion? Is there a God or not?" Buddha looked at the man. There was a moment of silence and he said, "There is nothing except God."

His intimate disciple Ananda was with him. He could not believe it because Buddha never taught about God, and suddenly, to a stranger, he says, "There is nothing but God."

And in the same day in the afternoon, another man came who was a theist. He believed there is a God; a God who created the world. Now this too is a lie because even if God created the world there cannot be an eye witness. If you accept that there was an eyewitness, that means the world was already there.

And if the God created the world, the world does not show the qualities that God would have given to humanity: constant violence, constant war, jealousy, anger, ego, depression, anguish.

Unless God created these things in you, they cannot be in you. Looking into man it is possible to believe that the devil created man, but not God. And moreover, what was God doing before he created the universe, for eternity? And what was the sudden motive to create the existence?

According to Christians, He created the existence only four thousand and four years before Jesus Christ; so six thousand years are nothing compared to eternity. What was he doing all this time? And why suddenly the motivation to create it? Has the motivation come from somewhere else? That will mean that existence was there before God created it. Otherwise, the motivation....

And finally, if existence needs to be created by God then the question is very relevant. Who created God Himself? And if you can accept the idea that God does not need any creator, then why unnecessarily bring in a useless hypothesis – then existence, can remain without any creator. Anyway, God has to remain without any creator. With existence, we are acquainted – it is there, all around. God is only in the beliefs of people.

And the man wanted to know Gautam Buddha's opinion...and Gautam Buddha said, "God? There is no God anywhere. Existence is self-sufficient; it does not need any creator. Existence itself is creativity."

Now Ananda was getting more puzzled. But it was the routine...Buddha had told him, "Whatever questions arise in your mind, when I am going to sleep and all the visitors have gone, then you can ask. Don't disturb my conversation with the visitors."

And in the evening a third man came. He was neither a theist nor an atheist; he was just an innocent seeker. He said to Buddha, "I don't know whether God exists or not. But there is a great urge in me to seek the truth. Can you be of any help?"

Rather than answering him, Buddha closed his eyes. There was utter silence...and Ananda was surprised. Seeing Buddha closing his eyes and sitting in silence, that man also closed his eyes and sat in silence. Almost an hour must have passed. Then the man opened his eyes, touched Gautam Buddha's feet and said, "Your answer is so precious that I will keep it in my heart forever."

Now it was too much, and as the man left, Ananda was furious. He said to Gautam Buddha, "What is going on? In one day you have contradicted yourself again and again and again. First you say there is only God and nothing else, and then you say there is no God – it is an absolutely useless hypothesis. And to this third man you don't say anything. And that great fellow receives the answer and I was present, but I have not received any answer! He touched your feet in deep gratitude, with tears of joy in his eyes, and he has gone so fulfilled..."

Gautam Buddha said to Ananda, "First, those were not your questions, neither were the answers given to you. You are unnecessarily poking your nose into other people's affairs."

Ananda said, "That I understand, but I am a human being. Although they were not my questions I have heard them; although the answers were not given to me I have heard them. And inside me there is so much trouble – what is the reality? And why should Gautam Buddha go on giving contradictory statements to different people?"

The answer that Buddha gave to Ananda is very important. He said, "The first man has been living in a lie, that there is no God; I had to shatter his lie. Without searching, it is much too egoistic to say that there is no God. And he has not done anything to discover the reality. He had come to me just so that I can support his lie and he can tell people, 'not only do I say that there is no God, even Gautam Buddha has supported me.'

"And the same was the case with the second man – he was also living a lie. He knows nothing about God. He has simply acquired the belief from the atmosphere, from the society, that God exists and God created the world. I had to destroy his lie.

"The third man was very innocent. He had no lie. He had no belief, this way or that. That's why I could not answer him through words. I became silent. And he was an authentic seeker. Seeing me closing my eyes, and sitting in silence, he understood this was the answer. He closed his eyes, sat with me for one hour, and in that silence he understood...felt, not a belief, but something real within himself. Although I had not given him the answer, he has received it."

The man of truth cannot make it pleasant, because the only way to make it pleasant is to make it a lie. Lies are very pleasant; you never deny them. Somebody says, "I love you, you are the most beautiful person I have come across." You accept it, you never even enquire, "Have you ever met all the people of the world? Otherwise your statement is not true."

Say to the ugliest woman, "You are a beauty and I have fallen in love with you," and she will believe you because it is such a pleasure that at least somebody believes you beautiful. She will never doubt the fact, she will never question it. It is so pleasant that any doubt, any question cannot disturb it.

Truth is going to be a very shattering experience; otherwise the people who crucified Jesus were not mad. He was not making his truth pleasant. He was saying it in its utter nudity, in its utter purity, as it is.

And truth can be said only as it is; you cannot edit it, you cannot add something to it, you cannot delete something from it, you cannot distort it. So the people who have been telling pleasant truths are really cowards. They don't know anything about truth. All that they know are your lies, and they support your lies and it is very consoling.

It is a contract: They will support your lies and make you feel good and consoled, and you will give them great respect, as if they are sages, saints, men of wisdom – it is a mutual agreement. And the more respect you give them, the sweeter they will make their lies. And the sweeter the lies are, the more respect you will give to them.

You will not crucify such a person. You may give him a Nobel prize, your universities will honor him with "D.Litt.'s", he will be universally respected. But the man of truth is destined to be crucified. Even if you don't crucify him, the whole world is going to condemn him because he is disturbing your sleep, he is disturbing your lies which were very consoling. And the way of truth that he is telling you about is a great search; you are not ready for it, you don't have time for it.

And why waste your time? Jesus Christ has found...you can believe. Krishna has found...you can believe. Buddha has found – now what is the need for you to discover it again? You can simply believe.

This is the difference between the objective sciences and subjective religiousness. For example, Edison discovered electricity. Now it is not needed that when you electrify your house, you have to discover electricity again. Neither does the electrician who comes to put electricity in your house have any first-hand experience – there is no need. Once it is discovered, it becomes the common property of everybody. This is true about objective reality, but this is not true about subjective reality.

Truth is a subjective experience. Buddha experienced in his own innermost being, and unless you go to the same space within yourself you will not find it. And to go to your own innermost center, you will have to leave all your borrowed beliefs, which hurts, because they were so consoling. Without any effort, beliefs are available in the marketplace.

Satyadharma, you say, "It seems that some men of truth..." – they were not men of truth – "after contemplating the consequences of telling the truth..." No man of truth ever contemplates the consequences. Only cowards think about the consequences... Whether to say it or not to say it, whether to say it in this way or that way so that you can retain your respectability, so that you will not be poisoned like Socrates, or killed like Mansoor, or crucified like Jesus.

These people that you think are men of truth are men of untruth. They are contemplating the consequences so that they can exploit you and gain respectability and nourishment for their egos.

You are saying, "They came to observe,' Say the truth, but say the pleasant truth.'" Do you think there are two kinds of truth, pleasant and unpleasant? Truth is simply truth; two plus two are four. How can you make it pleasant or unpleasant? It is simply there without any fear of consequences.

And truth is such a big experience, the biggest experience, that in that very experience, you will be drowned. Who will remain out of it to contemplate? You will become the truth. And whatever you say, and whatever you do, and whatever is your way of life, is going to disturb millions of people around the world, because it will be just the very opposite of what they have been believing.

Truth makes you absolutely alone, outside the crowd, and the crowd takes revenge.

When Jesus was crucified, Judea, the country where he was born, was under the Roman Empire. A Roman governor, Pontius Pilate, could not see why Jesus should be crucified. But all the rabbis and the highest priest of the Jewish temple were insistent, unanimous, that he should be crucified.

Pontius Pilate could not see any reason – he has not committed any crime, he has not harmed anybody. There is no valid reason to murder this innocent young man, and he is only thirty-three. All that he does...he has certain teachings and those who want to listen to him – and they are not many – it is their freedom to listen to him.

But the problem was that Pontius Pilate was Roman and Jesus was a Jew. Whatever Jesus was saying was going against the Jewish lies. It was not at all concerned with Roman paganism, so it was not hurting Pontius Pilate. So for his consolation, he made a last attempt to save Jesus.

It was the convention that every year when the Jews have their holidays, they were allowed to ask for one man who was going to be crucified, and he would be given freedom – he would not be crucified.

So this was his last hope. Three persons were going to be crucified and Pilate was hoping that they would ask for Jesus because the other two were murderers, rapists – they had done all kinds of crimes. But the whole crowd of rabbis and Jews shouted for a murderer who had committed seven murders to be released. Not a single voice was heard shouting that Jesus should be released.

But the psychology is very simple to understand. Jesus was saying truths which were going against the Jewish tradition. For example, in the old testament, which is a Jewish book, God is made to say, "I am not a nice man. I am very jealous. That I never forgive, and those who go against me will have to suffer. I am not your uncle."

And Jesus said, "But I say unto you that God is love." Now Jews cannot tolerate this; he is turning the whole philosophy upside down. God Himself is saying that He cannot forgive, and Jesus says, "Don't be worried, He is pure love. You will be forgiven."

It was not against the Roman conceptions, Roman beliefs. Truth is simply truth, neither pleasant nor unpleasant. If you silently listen to it, without prejudice, you will not feel that it is pleasant or unpleasant. But your mind is full of prejudices, and if it goes against your prejudices, then it becomes unpleasant. If it supports your prejudices, it becomes pleasant.

Satyadharma, no man of truth ever contemplates the consequences. And it is good; otherwise this world would have been even poorer in spirit, more ugly in its behavior than it is now.

These are the people: Socrates, Mansoor and Jesus, who have raised the human consciousness by sacrificing themselves. They knew perfectly well that to say the truth was inviting death, but death does not matter to the man of truth. He knows there is no death – the body dies, but your consciousness remains always.

So drop this whole idea because this is simply cunningness, not the way of truth.

A new officer arrives in the French foreign legion in the Sahara, and he quickly tries to adapt to the ways of life there. One day he was very puzzled to see all the men rushing off, out of the camp, and he asked, "What is going on?" A soldier explained,"Well, you see, all this time here in the desert, and no women ever come here, so when the camels come, we...ah...take the opportunity."

" Ah yes, I see," says the new officer. "But then tell me, why such a rush?"

"Oh," the man answers, "of course, nobody wants to get stuck with an ugly one."

What you are saying is absolutely ugly. Truth has to be pure, uncontaminated, unpolluted, without any fear of any consequences – only then can it help humanity. Perhaps it may be dangerous for the man who utters it, but it is worth it. To be sacrificed for truth is one of the great blessings, one of the greatest ecstasies.

Socrates was offered three alternatives by the judges because they felt the man was innocent, but the crowd was shouting that he should be killed. Athens in those days was a city-state, and it was a direct democracy. So every citizen – slaves were not counted as human beings, so leave out the slaves, and half of Athens was full of slaves – but the citizens had the right to vote directly on any point. It was not like our democracies where you choose a representative for five years. They had no representatives, they represented themselves directly.

So the whole of Athens was shouting, "Socrates has to be killed because he is destroying our morality, he is destroying our religion, he is corrupting the mind of our youth and we cannot tolerate it anymore."

The chief justice knew that it was impossible to save Socrates, and that the man was absolutely innocent. His only crime was that he said the truth as it is.

So he offered three alternatives to Socrates. He said, "You can leave Athens – it is only a city-state and you can live just outside the city boundary. Those who want to be your disciples can come there and Athens will not have any power to kill you."

Socrates said, "That will be very cowardly. My inner truth will never forgive me. I have to face the consequence, but I am facing it because of truth, and it is a joy."

The chief justice said, "Then you can do one thing. You can go on living in Athens, but stop teaching your truth. If you promise that you will not teach the truth, then there is no need for me to kill an innocent man."

Socrates said, "This is not acceptable. For what should I be living if I cannot teach the truth? Then death is better, far better."

Unwillingly, in spite of himself, the chief justice had to give him the death sentence, death by poison.

Do you think Socrates was not intelligent? Alternatives were offered: he could have moved out of Athens – but truth knows no compromise. He could have stopped teaching, he was already very old. But when you are pregnant with truth, you cannot stop teaching. You have to say it to those who are blind, who are deaf, and who are living in all kinds of lies.

He preferred to die. He said to the chief justice, "Remember, I am choosing death in favor of truth. And because of this death, whatever I have been teaching will remain for centuries. Even the names of your judges, and you, will be forgotten. Nobody will know this crowd who is shouting to kill me, but my death will make it a guarantee that even after my death, my words will go on improving human consciousness."

But the people who are living in lies will always say the same thing, "Morality is in danger, religion is in danger, culture is in danger. Particularly, the minds of the youth are being corrupted."

These are the charges against me too – exactly the same, worded almost the same. And I was amazed that after twenty-five centuries, I was deported from Greece for the same reasons for which Socrates was poisoned. They could not kill me because I was just a tourist. I was not a citizen. I had not committed any crime there, and I had not even moved out of the house where I was living.

But the archbishop of the Orthodox Christian church of Greece, which is the oldest church in the world, threatened the government, and he threatened the owner of my house, my host, saying," If he is not moved immediately out of Athens, I am going to dynamite the house and kill him and the twenty-five people who are staying with him."

I could not believe that in twenty-five centuries nothing has changed – he listed the same crimes. He was giving telegrams to the president, to the prime minister, saying, "This man's presence is going to destroy our tradition, our religion, our culture. And this man is corrupting the minds of our youth." And I had been there only for fifteen days, just on a tourist visa for four weeks. Two weeks had passed and they had no reason to deport me.

But the old mind is still there. When I was arrested and brought to Athens from the small island where I was staying, the chief of the police was there with forty police officers to welcome me. I said, "In the middle of the night, there is no need for forty police officers with loaded guns. I am not a violent man, I don't have even a pistol, and I am under arrest. Why have you gathered this crowd?"

My people in Athens – Amrito, who had invited me to Greece, was there – they were trying hard, that at least for the night, I should be allowed to stay in a hotel. But they were not willing, even for six hours, to let me stay in a hotel. I had to leave immediately.

I used to think that England is a far more developed country... so I told my pilot – my jet plane was there – "It is better you leave Greece and we can rest at the London airport".

But I was amazed that human stupidity is the same all over the world. The London port authorities would not allow me even to stay in the first class lounge at the airport for just six hours. The officer showed me the file saying that the parliament had decided that I cannot do anything there. They were afraid, that from Greece I might come to England, and their fear had proved right.

But I said, "I am not going into England. This is an international airport and from the lounge there is no way to enter England." And the same charges were made: corrupting the youth, destroying the morality, the religion, the culture. I asked the officer, "You just think, how can I do this while I am asleep at the airport, just in six hours?" A culture that has been there for twenty-five centuries, a religion that has been there for twenty-five centuries, a morality that has been taught to every generation for twenty-five centuries – if it can be destroyed by a man within six hours sleeping at the airport, it is not worth much; it should be destroyed.

But I said, "My pilot cannot fly because he has run his whole time; now it will be illegal. You are forcing my pilot to go against the international flight laws."

He said, "I am in a dilemma." And he was continually going in the room and phoning the home minister, the prime minister asking, "What to do now?" And finally they decided that I could stay, but only in the jail for six hours, and in the morning I have to leave immediately.

I had a certain respect for England, it is an educated country with great universities like Oxford and Cambridge. But it seems man remains idiotic. No Oxford, no Cambridge can make any difference.

Truth has to be said.

Just the other day I received a letter from the German parliament. One year before they had passed an order that I cannot enter into Germany for the same reasons. Not only that, my airplane cannot land on any German airport for refueling. One sannyasin has appealed to the parliament appeals committee, saying," Now one year has passed, and this ugly order should be cancelled."

That's why I have received a letter again. A copy of the letter has been given to the sannyasin saying that this order cannot be cancelled because this man is dangerous. They don't mention what danger – just the same old crimes they had imposed on Socrates.

Almost twenty-one countries have decided that I cannot enter in their countries. And these are the most developed countries of the world.

Satyadharma, your name means "truth is religion." And there is no other value higher than truth. Life can be sacrificed for it – but on no account is any compromise possible.

Okay, Vimal?

Yes, Bhagwan.

Session 29

The Answer Is You

*Silence will bring you great gifts.
And the most precious and the first gift is intelligence.
A clarity of vision, a deep understanding of yourself,
and almost all the problems start disappearing –
not that you get answers for your questions,
but just that the questions disappear.
You don't find the answer because you are the answer.*

March 11, 1987
Evening

Beloved Bhagwan,

Waivering between bold action and paralyzing doubt, silent acceptance and useless sabotage, I struggle...waiting. Please comment on silence and death.

Anand Nirvana, it seems you are not clear about what you want to ask. The question seems to be out of confusion. You are saying, "Waivering between bold action and paralyzing doubt, silent acceptance and useless sabotage, I struggle...waiting. Please comment on silence and death." The first thing you have to remember is, no bold action is expected of you here at least. We are not preparing warriors, we are preparing peaceful, loving human beings – not violent, not destructive, not murderers. The question of bold action does not arise.

You have created the problem yourself. First, you think that a bold action is needed, which is a pure fiction of your own. I have been telling you to relax, I have been telling you to be easy, to be natural, to be spontaneous. There is no question of any bold action. In fact, there is no question of any action at all.

My whole teaching is how to be effortless. Even when you are doing something, you should not be the doer. Even when there is action, it should be almost non-action. It should come as a spontaneous flowering, not out of willpower.

But these are the diseases given to every human being by the whole past. Willpower has been taught to everybody as a great value. Every child is told to have willpower. And willpower is something against your spontaneity – then you cannot be at ease, restful. Do you think flowers have to do much to blossom? Are trees taking bold action to grow? There is no action at all.

Lao Tzu used to say, "Look at the trees, look at the rivers, look at the stars, and you will understand 'actionless action.'"

Certainly the river is flowing towards the ocean but you cannot call it action because there is no will forcing it to go towards the ocean. It is very easy-going – no hurry, no haste, not even the longing that it should reach, no competition with other rivers that perhaps they may reach ahead of it. It is simply going, singing and dancing its dance through the mountains, through the valleys, through the plains, not worried whether it reaches to the goal or not. Every moment is so beautiful and precious that, who cares about the tomorrow?

Willpower has been used to create a false personality in you. Willpower is another beautiful name for the ugly entity called ego.

One of the great psychologists of this century, Alfred Adler, based his whole psychological analysis on this simple fact – that all man's problems arise out of will to power. He wants to become somebody, somebody special, somebody higher than others, somebody holier than others. It does not matter whether he is in the marketplace or in the monastery; the struggle is to be on the top.

The more you fight and the more you succeed, the farther away you are from your own being, because you become more and more tense, more and more worried. Your life becomes a constant agony – the fear of failure. Even if you have succeeded, the fear that somebody may throw you away from your position.... Just now ask Ronald Reagan about the tremendous anguish he must be in. A man who lives to achieve something can never be peaceful.

So on the one hand you have created this fiction of bold action. Perhaps you think meditation needs a bold action? or sannyas means a bold action? It needs only relaxation. It needs dropping the very achieving mind, forgetting that there is any future, allowing this moment to be enough unto itself, rejoicing it, and the next moment will take care of itself.

If you can rejoice in this moment, you will be able to rejoice more in the coming moment because you will become more and more expert in rejoicing, in dancing, in singing. And you will become more and more confident about yourself – that you need not be somebody else. Whoever you are, you are capable of enjoying the ultimate ecstasy without being rich, without being in power, without being world famous, without being a celebrity.

You can be just a nobody and yet all the treasures of existence can be yours – because they are not outside you. You are unaware of your own inner richness.

There is no need of any bold action. And with that need disappearing, the paralyzing doubt will disappear. They are two sides of the same coin. First you create the idea that you have to take a bold action and then the fear comes of whether you are capable of taking such a bold action: do you have enough energy and guts? Then a paralyzing doubt arises and you are in a fix. Drop both together, because they are not separate and they are not separable.

You have heard beautiful words but you don't understand their meaning. You say, "...silent acceptance and useless sabotage..." If there is silent acceptance, how can there be useless sabotage? And if the useless sabotage is there, then what do you mean by "silent acceptance"? And apparently, absolutely unrelated, suddenly you ask, "Please comment on silence and death."

From "bold action" to "paralyzing doubt," from "silent acceptance" to "useless sabotage" – and suddenly the question arises about silence and death!

You must be very much split in your mind, schizophrenic. But this is not only your disease, so don't feel bad about it. It is the disease of almost all human beings, more or less...just you are courageous enough to expose the disease.

The others are not so courageous – they keep it down, repressed within themselves. They don't tell anybody; they repress it so deeply that even they themselves become unaware that it exists.

But because you have asked, I would like to say a few things to you. Silence knows no death, it is only the mind that is not silent which falls into the fallacy of death. Have you ever died in your life? You have always seen somebody else dying, but you have never seen yourself dying – although you have died many times, in many lives. But because you don't have a silent mind, each time when death came to you, you became so disturbed that you fell into a coma. You died in unconsciousness; that's why you don't remember your past lives.

If you had died in silence, peace, consciously, you would have been amazed to know that it is only the body that is dying, but not you, not the witness. You would have witnessed your own death. Just as others are witnessing from the outside, you would have witnessed it from the inside.

If a man dies consciously, then he is also born consciously, because death is one side and birth is another side. Death is the beginning of a new life. Within seconds, you will be entering a new womb. And if you die peacefully, without any disturbance, you will enter a new womb with the same silence, with the same awareness. The nine months in the mother's womb will not be of unawareness. And the birth out of the mother's womb will be in full silence and joy, because now you know that neither death matters nor birth; you belong to eternity.

Birth and death are small episodes. But silence has not to be just a word, it has to become your experience, and it will give you a tremendous intelligence.

Right now, all your intelligence is being destroyed by your conflicts, struggles, indecisiveness – bold actions and a feeling of paralysis. You want to accept whatever is happening and yet, deep down, you don't want it, you want to change it; hence, the sabotage.

You are a battlefield. You are not one but a crowd, and not only a crowd, but a crowd which is fighting and you don't know who you are.

Silence will bring you great gifts. And the most precious and the first gift is intelligence. A clarity of vision, a deep understanding of yourself, and almost all the problems start disappearing – not that you get answers for your questions, but just that the questions disappear. You don't find the answer because *you are* the answer.

Just be silent, and all questions disappear. Millions are the questions but there is only one answer, and that is you, in your crystal clear, silent awareness.

But man has been behaving so stupidly. He somehow manages outside to look intelligent, but if you look inside in him....

If the God who created the world was a little more intelligent, he would have made a small window in every head so that others can look at what is going on inside. It would have been really a great entertainment. And you would not be able to hide anything.

I have heard.... Two police officers are having coffee and chatting about their new recruits.

"You won't believe how dumb my new constable is," says one. "Oh, I bet mine is worse than yours" says the other.

So the first officer calls his constable. He comes in and salutes, "Yes, sir!" "Here is a dollar, go and buy me a Rolls Royce." "Yes, sir!" says the constable and he goes out.

"That's nothing," says the other officer and calls his constable. "Go immediately to my house and see if I am there."

"Yes, sir!" says the constable and he goes out.

The two recruits meet in the corridor and one says, "Boy, you won't believe how dumb my officer is. He gave me a dollar to buy him a Rolls Royce. Doesn't he know it is Sunday and the shops will be closed?"

"That's nothing," says the other. "My officer told me to go to his house and see if he is there. Can't he just make a phone call himself?"

Beloved Bhagwan,

I was drawn to Your commune at Rajneeshpuram like to a magnet
about three years ago, not understanding why I was there,
just knowing somewhere inside of my being
that there was no other place on this planet
to experience life in its totality.
I had never read any of Your books, nor any other books
on the search for truth, awareness, or raising consciousness.
I wonder how I keep coming to Your well
when I don't even feel thirsty,
or at least I don't experience this thirst.

Shantam Lani, life is a mystery, and it is not always possible to find explanations for what is happening to you and why it is happening. In the first place, why are you in the world? There is no answer to it. Why does love arise in you, suddenly, without even giving you an advance notice? There is no rational answer for it. Why does the roseflower look beautiful to you? You cannot explain it.

You are saying, "I was drawn to your commune like to a magnet about three years ago, not understanding why I was there." Nobody understands it. You think all these people understand why they are here? Do you think I know why I am here? At the most this much can be said: I am here because of you, and you are here because of me. But that does not explain anything. "...just knowing somewhere inside of my being that there was no other place on this planet to experience life in its totality." That is more than is needed, to be pulled, magnetically.

Everybody is longing in his heart to live life totally, but society does not allow you, the culture prevents you, religion controls you, the family cuts your wings. All around you there are people whose vested interest is that you should not live totally. It is surprising: why are they so interested that people do not live totally? Because their whole exploitation of humanity depends on it.

A man who lives totally will not drink alcohol, or take any other kind of drug. Naturally, the people who are earning millions of dollars out of alcohol and drugs cannot allow you to live totally. To live totally is so joyous that you don't want to destroy your joy by drinking alcohol. Alcohol is needed by miserable people, by people who are troubled, by people who want somehow to forget their problems, their anxieties - -at least for a few hours. The alcohol is not going to change anything – but even a rest for a few hours seems to be an absolute necessity for millions of people.

If a man lives totally, his every moment is such a fulfillment that you will not see queues before movie halls – who wants to see somebody else making love? When you yourself can make love, why should you go to the movie house? When your own life is such a mystery and such a tremendous challenge to discover, who is going to be interested in third-class film stories?

The man who lives totally becomes unambitious. Because he is so happy right now, he cannot conceive that there is the possibility of more. The ordinary madness of man's mind – of desiring for more and more – is because you are not living totally. There is always a gap, something is missing, you know things could have been better. Out of this partial living, all ambitions arise, and then the whole game of the society goes on: people want to become rich, people want to become famous, people want to become politicians, people want to become presidents and prime ministers.

Up to now humanity has depended on not allowing man to live totally, creating all kinds of barriers, because the total man will destroy so many vested interests in the world. The total man is the most dangerous man to the vested interests. You cannot enslave a man who is enjoying his life in its fullness, in its wholeness. You cannot force him to go into the army to kill people and to be killed. Your whole structure of society will collapse.

With the total man coming in, there will be a different structure of society: unambitious but immensely joyful – without great men. Perhaps you have never thought about it: great men can exist only because millions of people are not great; otherwise, who is going to remember Gautam Buddha? If there were millions of Gautam Buddhas, millions of Mahaviras, millions of Jesus Christs, who would bother about these people?

These few people have become great because millions are not allowed to live totally. Who will go to the churches if people are not miserable...to the temples, to the synagogues, to the mosques? Who is going to be there? Who is going to bother about God, and heaven and hell? A man who is living each moment with such intensity that life itself has become a paradise, that life itself has become divine, need not be a worshiper of dead statues, dead scriptures, rotten ideologies, stupid superstitions.

The total man is the greatest risk to your existing establishment in the world.

And you can see, Lani, why I am being condemned by the whole world. It is not without reason. If they crucify me, I will not be able to say to God, "Forgive these people because they know not what they are doing." In the first place, there is no God to whom I can say anything; in the second place, I cannot say they are doing something not knowing what it is. I can only say, they are doing exactly what they want to do and they are doing it *knowingly*. Their whole lifestyle is in danger.

Their lifestyle may not be giving them joy, blissfulness, but it is their lifestyle. Even their misery is *their* misery. These miserable creatures are in such a vast majority, and they cannot tolerate people who have nothing and yet are so happy and so contented, so tremendously joyous that their hearts are full of songs, and they are ready to burst into dancing any moment.

The United States attorney, addressing a news conference, said, "Our priority was to destroy Bhagwan's commune." One wonders why a great nation with so much power should be worried about a small commune of five thousand people, living absolutely aloof from America, in a desert. The nearest American town was twenty miles away.

Why were they so worried? Why, in every Christian church, were they condemning me? For the simple reason that those five thousand people were living life without any inhibitions. They were living really in total freedom; they had dropped all barriers. They were working perhaps the hardest in the whole world – twelve hours a day, sometimes fourteen hours a day – and still they had the energy at night to dance for hours, to sing for hours; and they had the energy in the morning to wake up early and meditate for hours.

This was creating a very dangerous situation. If these people who have nothing are living so joyously, then why are all the Christians of America and all the Jews of America, who have everything, miserable?

We were even celebrating death – they were not even able to celebrate life. Whenever some sannyasin died, it was an opportunity to rejoice and give him a good farewell, dancing and singing. He is going on an eternal journey and perhaps we shall never meet again; this is not the moment to mourn, to be miserable, to cry and weep.

This became the problem for America. That's why it became a priority for them to destroy the commune – and they did everything illegal and criminal and unconstitutional. But these five thousand people were helpless. They had never thought that being joyful could be a danger to their lives, that in a miserable world you should behave just as others are behaving. When everybody is crying and weeping you should not laugh; otherwise, those crying and weeping people will kill you.

Lani, you were pulled towards the commune because you had not read any books and you were not burdened with borrowed knowledge. You were not in search of truth; otherwise, naturally, you would have looked into scriptures, gone to the rabbis, to the bishops, to the learned. Because you were not interested in searching for the truth, and you were not reading my books, or anybody else's books, you had an innocent mind...unburdened.

That was the quality that made you feel a pull towards the commune. And when you were in the commune, you could see that life can be lived in a totally different way, in a more intelligent way, that man has been simply wasting a great opportunity: an opportunity in which he can discover himself, can discover new spaces of being, new flowers of blessings, new love – a love which does not become a bondage but a love that makes you more free than you ever were before, a love that gives you freedom.

And for the first time you must have become aware that five thousand people of all races, of all religions, from almost every country, of all colors can live just like a huge family. Just to see five thousand people eating in one kitchen – and at festival times there were twenty thousand sannyasins eating together – and nobody was worried about who is a Christian, who is a Jew, who is a Mohammedan. Nobody even asked, "What is your religion?"

Everybody understood that our religion is to live totally, fully, and allow everybody else to live according to his own way, according to his likings and dislikings – not to interfere in any way in anybody's life, and not to allow anybody to interfere in your life. Five thousand individuals...yet living as if they are one organic unity.

I was just talking to Niren – that's why I was late coming to you. He was my attorney, fighting for me in America; and he had tears in his eyes as he said, "Bhagwan, I could not do more to save the commune."

And as I said, "Now that Ronald Reagan and his gang of criminals are going down the drain, try to get the commune back again," he became so happy. He said, "I will go and will start working on it immediately."

Lani, you are saying, "I wonder how I keep coming to your well, when I don't even feel thirsty." You don't feel thirsty because you go on coming to the well! Just try for a few days *not* coming, and you will feel thirsty.

An Irishman and a Scotsman were taking an intelligence test. "What bird does not build its own nest?" asked the examiner. "The canary," said the Scot. "He lives in a cage."

"The cuckoo," said the Irishman.

"Very good," said the examiner to the Irishman. "How did you know?" "Everybody knows the cuckoo lives in a clock," said the Irishman.

Lani, you are neither Irish, nor Scottish. You are an intelligent woman, and only intelligent people can be attracted to my well. The unintelligent person is so burdened with the past that he cannot move an inch. Coming to my well is a long journey for him; he is so blind with prejudice that even if you present him truth on a plate he will not accept it.

You can see it here – how many Indians are here? I was telling Niren that coming back to India was not a happy choice for me, because the country is not even contemporary. It is thousands of years out-of-date and the gap is so big that it is very difficult to create a rapport with the Indian mind... It was out of compulsion that I had to come back to India. The world has progressed much, and the Indian mind has not even heard the names of Sigmund Freud or Assagioli, or Alfred Adler; and moreover, they are so afraid of what their society will say if they come to me.

It happened almost every day in America that people who live in Poona would phone from some city in America, saying, "I have come from Poona, and I want to see Bhagwan." And I told my secretary to ask them, "Bhagwan was in Poona for seven years – how many times did you see him?"

They had not come even once. And I am back again, and they have not phoned here to come. And this was not only people from Poona – people coming to America from other cities in India would phone, "I want to come because I come from India and you should not refuse me; I have come from so far away." But they don't phone here. There it was simple for them, because their society, their community, their religious group, their political party...nobody would know that they had gone to see me.

It is not only ordinary people who are so afraid. Even a courageous woman like Indira Gandhi wanted to see me, wanted to come to the ashram, and at least six times the date was fixed and just one day beforehand, it would be canceled: "Some urgent work has come."

Finally her secretary came and told me, "There is no urgent work. The problem is that her political advisers prevent her. They say, 'Going to Bhagwan can affect your political position; so it is better not to go to him, because the old traditional Indian mind is so much against him that if you go to see him, you may lose votes.'" Even the prime minister of the country is afraid to come and see me – she wants to, but her own vested interests prevent her.

Many industrialists who often go to America were continually phoning... "We want to come and see the commune and meet Bhagwan." But what happens to these people? They live in Bombay; I was in Bombay for two months and none of them turned up. I am here – it is just a fifteen minute flight. Such a cowardly mind. Privately they all say that whatever I am doing will be beneficial to the country and to humanity.

Just the other day, Zarin was saying to me that she has been meeting people from the highest society in Poona: "In private they appreciate you, but in public they are against you." Now to live in such an atmosphere, where everybody has a double face...in public, he will condemn me, and in private he is an admirer. In public, he is more concerned with his respectability, less concerned with sincerity.

I have been around the whole world, but perhaps India is more hypocritical than any other country. If people don't like you, they say they don't like you. If they don't agree with you, they don't agree with you. But this is a strange thing: privately they admire and publicly they are against you.

Lani, it is because of your intelligence and your innocence that you have been coming to this well. You have almost become part of me. Wherever you are, you will feel me and my presence with you. And whether you are thirsty or not.... There are thirsts of which your conscious mind knows nothing, they are so deep in your unconscious, but when you come to the well, you will find a great contentment. You may not be aware of the thirst, but you will be aware that something has been quenched in you.

Beloved Bhagwan,

Before coming to India I was Your disciple "in spite of myself."
But since coming here I have fallen so in love with You
that I feel You as my beloved master and not just Bhagwan.
There are times when I feel awed or privileged
or in blissful, painful communion.
But there are also moments when life
seems so utterly futile and hopeless, and I feel such despair
that even one more footstep seems like too much.
Beloved Master, can you provide some insight?

Anand Mayoori, the observation that you have made in your question is relevant to many people. You say, "I was your disciple in spite of myself." The very phenomenon of discipleship is so ego-shattering that anybody who decides to be a disciple has to decide in spite of himself, because his ego gives tremendous resistance.

To be a disciple means putting your ego aside. To be a disciple means to be humble, to be open, to be vulnerable, to be receptive, to be trusting. And ego cannot do these things. These things will kill the ego immediately; hence, the ego goes on giving rationalizations why you should not be the disciple.

But there is a basic and essential need in every human being of finding the meaning of life, the significance of being here in existence.

You may be aware or not, but there is a deep longing to know, "Who am I?" And it is possible only through disciplehood. The word *disciple* is very significant. It comes from the same root as discipline. Its original meaning is learning.

We come into the world absolutely ignorant, and there are two ways one can choose: either one can start becoming knowledgeable, accumulating borrowed knowledge and covering one's ignorance.... As the layer of knowledge becomes thicker and people start thinking of you as learned, as a scholar, as a wise man or a wise woman, you will forget that you are still ignorant. And it is so sweet to forget that you are ignorant; it is so consoling. When so many people are confirming that you are wise, they cannot be wrong – you convince yourself that you are no longer ignorant.

I have been always telling a small story: One journalist died and reached to the gate of heaven. It very rarely happens – being a journalist and reaching heaven is almost unheard of; journalists go directly to hell. But by some bureaucratic mistake, this fellow reached to the gate of heaven and knocked.

The doorkeeper looked through the window and was very much puzzled because he was not expecting anybody. That day nobody was going to come to heaven. He said, "What do you want?"

The journalist said, "There is no question of wanting. Open the door." Journalists are generally very pushy. And he said, "I must introduce myself, that I am a great journalist. And you should be happy."

But the doorkeeper said, "If you are a journalist then it is absolutely impossible. You will have to go to the other place. It is not far away, just on the other side of the road." But the journalist said, "Why is it difficult for me?"

The gatekeeper explained to him, "We have a quota – twelve journalists – and that quota has been filled for thousands of years. Since then, neither has any journalist turned up, nor has the question been raised. Even those twelve journalists are absolutely useless. One newspaper has been started, but only one issue was printed, because in heaven, nothing happens – no rape, no murder, no smuggling, no riots. Here people are just old saints, sitting under their trees, chanting their mantras, that's all. All their photographs and all their mantras have been published in the first issue, and since then nothing has happened.

"So even those twelve journalists are sitting without any work. And I say to you, believe me, they are very miserable because there is no work, no story to write. Saints don't have any story – no love affairs, nobody escaping with somebody else's wife... absolutely nothing happens. You will be far happier in the other place, where every moment, so much is happening. All the criminals, all the politicians, all the murderers, all the artists, all the musicians – everybody is there! And they have dozens of newspapers. You just go there."

But a journalist you cannot get rid of so easily. He said, "Just give me twenty-four hours and I promise you, after twenty-four hours, either I will leave or I will convince some other journalist to leave so your quota remains."

Seeing no possibility that this man was

going to leave, he was allowed in, and twenty-four hours were given to him. Immediately he started spreading a rumor that in hell a new paper is going to be started and they need a chief editor, editors, reporters – very good salary, free houses, cars, servants. What you are doing here? It looks like a desert and the saints are so old, so much dust has gathered on them, that one wonders whether they are alive or dead.

He met all the twelve journalists and they were all very much excited about the news. The next day, when twenty-four hours were over, he went to the gate and he asked the gatekeeper, "What is the situation? Has anyone left?" The gatekeeper said, "Anyone? All have left. And now you cannot leave. We have a quota for twelve; at least one should be here."

But the journalist said, "I cannot. If twelve journalists have gone then there must be some truth in the rumor. Those twelve people cannot be just idiots."

The gatekeeper said, "You are strange, you created the rumor!"

He said, "That's true, I created the rumor, but it seems it is a coincidence – my creating the rumor...and there must be something happening; otherwise twelve journalists cannot be convinced so easily. Anyway, I am not supposed to be here. You open the doors; otherwise I will create trouble for you. Why did you allow me in?"

The gatekeeper got afraid and opened the door and he said, "This man is strange. Just out of compassion I opened the door, and the whole quota is gone. And in the future there is no possibility again to fill the quota."

Man is such, that if others believe that you are honest, that you are very kind, that you are very wise, first you may not believe them, but if they go on insisting, soon you will start believing that you must be. Your whole idea about yourself is just the idea others have about you.

So one way is to accumulate knowledge and cover up your ignorance, which is being followed by pundits, rabbis, bishops, *imams*, all kinds of religious leaders. But their ignorance remains repressed deep down.

The other way is not to allow your consciousness to be contaminated by anyone. Keep one thing as a criterion: unless *I* know something, it is not knowledge; unless *I* encounter truth – Jesus may say it is true, Krishna may say it is true, Buddha may say it is true – it does not matter. It may be truth for them but not for me, because truth is an individual experience, just like love.

Millions of people in this world have loved. Do you think their love is in any way helpful to you? You need not love because so many people have loved? Do you think you will know something about love because millions of people have loved? Unless you love, you will not know anything.

This second alternative is the alternative of the disciple. He goes in search of learning on his own.

You say, "Before coming to India I was your disciple 'in spite of myself'. But since coming here I have fallen so in love with you that I feel you as my beloved master and not just Bhagwan. There are times when I feel awed or privileged or in blissful, painful communion. But there are also moments when life seems so utterly futile and hopeless, and I feel such despair that even one more footstep seems like too much."

It is one of the significant things to understand: as you understand light more, simultaneously, by the side, you also start understanding darkness, because they both go together. Darkness is only the absence of light; without light there will be no darkness.

For example, you may have never thought

about the blind people. Do you think blind people live in darkness? They cannot, because even to see darkness eyes are needed. And because they cannot see light, they cannot see darkness. Blind people live in a totally different space, which is neither light nor darkness. They don't have eyes at all; hence they cannot see anything. But once their eyes are cured, they will see light, and they will see beautiful flowers and colors and rainbows and the sun and the moon, but they will also see the dark night.

The same happens on the spiritual path, on the path of discipleship. As you become more and more aware of blissfulness, you also become aware of a despair of which you were never aware before – because the blissfulness cannot remain twenty-four hours a day in the beginning. At the stage of a disciple it comes and goes, so when you are blissful you are immensely happy and joyous, but when it goes you fall into despair.

There is communion with the master, a heart-to-heart meeting which you call "love," but it cannot be for twenty-four hours a day at the stage of the disciple. So it comes like a breeze, and there is coolness and there is fragrance and then it is gone. Then suddenly you feel life is futile, meaningless – of which you were never aware before. To become aware of despair, futility, meaninglessness, you have to be aware of meaning, bliss, love, joy.

But this is only the beginning of the journey. As you go on growing, there are three stages: first, is the stage of the student; second, is the stage of the disciple; third, is the stage of the devotee.

At the stage of devotee your blissfulness becomes just like your breathing, just like your heartbeat. Then there is no despair and then there is no meaninglessness; then you will not feel that even one more footstep seems like too much. No, you will dance madly – so madly that the dancer disappears in the dance, the devotee disappears into the master. Only in this disappearance of your ego is there the ultimate fulfillment that cannot be taken away from you.

One has to be very intelligent and alert not to stop before one has reached to a twenty-four hour continuous, ecstatic state. The journey is not long, only intelligence is needed – that you should not stop in the middle somewhere, because there are beautiful spots, very scenic. One would like to stop there, thinking that one has arrived – what more can there be? But if your state of consciousness goes on wavering, then remember, this is not the place to make your home. You can stay overnight, but in the morning you have to go on.

Just be intelligent, and remember a simple criterion: unless blissfulness becomes my nature, my very being, there is no way for me to stop.

A pretty blonde is driving along in the countryside in her new sports car, when it breaks down. Luckily, she happens to be near a farmhouse. She walks up to the door and knocks. When the farmer answers, she says to him, "It is getting late and my car broke down. Can I stay here for the night and then go for help in the morning?"

"Well," says the farmer. "You can stay here. But I don't want you messing with my sons, Jed and Luke." She looks behind him and sees two strapping young men in their twenties. "Okay," she says.

But after they have all gone to bed, the woman begins to think about the boys in the next room. So she quietly goes into their room and says, "Boys, how would you like me to teach you the ways of the world?" They say, "Huh?"

She says, "The only thing is, I don't want to get pregnant, so you have to wear these condoms." They agree and the three of them go at it all night long.

Forty years later, Jed and Luke are sitting on the front porch. Jed says, "Luke, do you remember that blond woman who came by and showed us the ways of the world?" "Yeah," says Luke, "I remember."

"Well, do you care if she gets pregnant?" "No," says Luke.

"Me neither," says Jed, "let's take these things off!"

Okay, Vimal?

Yes, Bhagwan.

Session 30

A Little More Courage, A Little More Love

If you have found the deathless in you,
all your fears,
forever
will disappear –
and a man without fear
is truly and authentically dignified.
You will be proud
that you have found the right path.

March 12, 1987
Morning

Beloved Bhagwan,

The other night, following the energy between my eyes,
I went into myself, looking for "Who am I?"
At a certain point I found myself immersed in great nothingness.
The sensation was very strong. I couldn't go on;
I felt so afraid of this emptiness that I stopped.
Bhagwan, what is this energy that is felt between the eyes?
Is it the so-called "third eye"?
If this was the right way, why was I so afraid and trembling?

Deva Ramaprem, this is the right way. That's why you became so afraid, because the right way means a certain death, the death of your ego, the death of your personality as you have known it, and the beginning and the birth of your essential self. But the death comes first, hence the fear and trembling. The resurrection comes later.

You have been in a very beautiful space. This is the third eye that in the East has been talked about for at least ten thousand years. It is only symbolic. You have two eyes to see the world of duality – the day and night, the beautiful and the ugly, the true and the false. The whole world consists of dualities. The third eye is a poetic and symbolic expression that your two eyes have become one, that all duality has disappeared.

For the outside world two eyes are needed, for the inside world only a single clear vision – because inside there is no duality, there is only oneness.

Your question is, "The other night, following the energy between my eyes, I went into myself looking for 'Who am I?' At a certain point I found myself immersed in great nothingness." These are the spaces if you go inside. But this nothingness is not negative; just a little more acquaintance with it and you will be surprised: it appeared as nothingness because there was nothing that you have ever known before or even dreamt before. But once you become acquainted with the nothingness you start feeling an immense fulfillment, an overflowing energy. This nothingness is the beginning of fullness and wholeness.

"The sensation," you say, "was very strong. I couldn't go on; I felt so afraid of this emptiness that I stopped." Just be a little more intelligent.

The nothingness was surrounding you, but you were not nothing. You were witnessing it; you were separate from it. The emptiness may be surrounding you, it may be vast and may create trembling in you, but you are not it; otherwise who will become afraid and who will stop going forward? Who will turn back?

Your being is totally separate from the nothingness and emptiness that you have felt. If you had remembered only this much, "I am not it," the fear would have disappeared. Perhaps next time, remember that you cannot be anything that you come across. You cannot come across yourself; you cannot meet yourself. So whatever you come across is separate from you. There is no need to be afraid.

But Ramaprem, it happens to almost everybody. You are alone, surrounded by nothingness, emptiness, and a deep fear arises that perhaps you are coming close to death, because in our minds the association with nothingness and emptiness is with death. But even death is not you. You pass through it; it is a passage. And if you are alert, you can pass through without any fear. On the contrary, you can enjoy the silence, the peace, the immensity, the infinity that is surrounding you. You are almost in an oceanic state of consciousness.

But now you know the door, the third eye. Travel more into it so that you become more and more acquainted, and nothingness, rather than making you afraid, will make you dance, because it is not destructive. It will give you individuality, it will give you freedom, and if you go on and on you will reach to your innermost center, which is life.

Death always happens to the body, but never to you.

And if you have found the deathless in you, all your fears forever will disappear – and a man without fear is truly and authentically dignified. You will be proud that you have found the right path.

Very few people have traveled inwards because of this fear. As they move in, the fear stops them and they turn back into the mundane world where everything is ephemeral, where everything is going to die, where all that you possess is going to be taken away by death.

Death is impotent only against a person who knows himself. But before you can know yourself, you will have to pass through this beautiful space of nothingness, emptiness, aloneness. So rejoice and be grateful that a great experience has happened to you.

A Catholic priest visited a Catholic family. There was a little boy sitting very happily beside his cat, which had just given birth to six kittens.

The priest asked, "Why are you so happy?"

The boy said, "Because all the kittens happen to be good Catholics." Very satisfied, the priest went home.

Two weeks later he visited the family again. As soon as the little boy saw him, he began crying desperately. "What's the matter?" asked the priest. "Why are you so sad?"

The boy replied, sobbing, "The kittens are no longer Catholic."

"How can you say that?" asked the priest.

The little boy replied, "They have all opened their eyes."

The moment your inner eye starts opening, you will not be a Catholic, you will not be a Protestant, you will not be a Hindu, you will not be a Mohammedan, you will not be a Jew – you will be simply yourself; hence, all the organized religions have been avoiding the very subject.

The science of how to enter into yourself has been known for thousands of years, but no religion wants you to enter into yourself. They want you to look upwards at the sky for a fictitious God. If your inner eye remains closed, you are going to remain a Catholic, a Hindu, a Mohammedan, a communist, but once the inner eye opens, you start becoming free of all these fetters and all these imprisonments.

Every person has the potential, but you have been diverted into looking for God outside yourself – and He is sitting inside you. All the priests of the world are against God, because once you know that God is within you, the whole profession of the priesthood is finished. Churches will be empty, mosques will be empty, temples and synagogues will be empty, and the whole politics of numbers and the power that it brings to the priests will be gone.

You are only an individual without any adjective.

The world will be immensely beautiful if there are only individuals, not belonging to any religion or any political ideology, but belonging to their own inner self. That's enough, more than enough. Belonging to life itself is the only true religion, the only truth that has to be discovered. And it is not far away, just a little fear has to be dropped.

And if you go on trying, as you will become acquainted with the beauties of nothingness, the fear is going to disappear automatically. You have accidentally found the right path – now don't lose it. Don't become again a Catholic. Keep the eye open.

Beloved Bhagwan,

A few months ago, I experienced for the first time in my life
that You are not. I saw the perfect mirror.
It appeared to me that even the physical universe is just an idea;
there are no words to describe the nightmare. Only one sentence
rushed through my head: "He kills us! He kills us!"
Your presence in all of my friends is an immense help
to focus my energy into the heart.
Simultaneously I started to go through the fear in my daily life,
but it seems as if there is no end. I'm not sure anymore
whether this is the right way. Would You please comment?

Dhyan Astiko, the way is right, but *you* are not right – you are in utter confusion. And if you are not right, even the right way cannot help. Just look at your question and you will understand what I mean – that you are in utter confusion. "A few months ago I experienced for the first time in my life that you are not." That is perfectly true. "I saw the perfect mirror." I have been repeating to you continually that I am only a mirror. So if a donkey looks into me, he finds a donkey; if a monkey looks into me, he finds a monkey; and if a Yankee looks into me, he finds a Yankee.

People become angry, annoyed, not knowing that they are being annoyed with their own faces. And even those faces are not authentic, they are masks; they are not originals.

I have heard about one ugly woman who used to destroy any mirror anywhere the moment she would see it. And her logic was very clear – "The mirror makes me ugly; otherwise I am perfectly okay."

The people who are annoyed with me are annoyed with a mirror. If they are a little conscious, they will see that they are annoyed with their own life. They were not aware of it; looking into the mirror, they have become aware of it. Rather than changing their life and its style, they try to destroy the mirror; otherwise, there was no need to crucify Jesus. A mirror was crucified, because the man was becoming a nuisance.

I at least remain in one place; it is your responsibility if you come and look into the mirror.

Jesus used to move on his donkey from one place to another place, showing people who were not ready their faces. He irritated all the Jewish rabbis. Rather than listening to him and changing themselves – because he had brought the whole science of transformation with him – they crucified the mirror.

Poisoning Socrates was poisoning the mirror. He had become a problem in Athens. People had become so worried about him...even to say hello to him was dangerous, because that would start a dialogue. And soon he would get you involved in a discussion in which your old prejudices, nonsense, superstitions that you used to think your great treasure, would start dropping away.

He annoyed so many people in Athens that they finally decided that this man had to be finished.

This has happened to many mystics, but such is the mediocrity of humanity that rather than changing themselves, they start destroying the mirror.

I used to know one of my professors, a certain Professor Bhattacharya. He was a Bengali, and very tradition-oriented. He believed in celibacy and all kinds of unscientific, unnatural ideas, but he would never discuss them. I used to harass him. He lived alone, and I would just knock on his door – he had to open the door, and I would immediately enter his house. He would say, "I don't want any discussion."

I said, "You are starting it! I have entered silently and you have started the discussion. Why don't you want the discussion?"

He said, "My God! How to get rid of you?"

I said, "Just close the door; sit on your chair. Now there is no way; you have started it...."

He used to walk the year-round, any season, rain or summer or winter, with an umbrella so close to his head that he could see only two or three feet ahead, just to avoid people.

In the class he used to speak with closed eyes. And he spoke so fast, without even giving anybody any chance to ask a question. He would come, close his eyes, and start speaking. He was so afraid...no question should be raised against his fragile beliefs. But that is the situation of almost all human beings. They may not be carrying umbrellas, but in a subtle and invisible form they are protecting themselves...against the mirrors.

You say, Dhyan Astiko, "It appeared to me that even the physical universe is just an idea." It is perfectly true. That does not mean that there is no physical universe, but the physical universe of your thinking is just an idea. You don't know the reality of the physical universe. You don't know the reality even of your own consciousness.

A man who does not know himself, all his ideas are going to be empty, without content. What do you know about the trees? What do you know about a roseflower? You may say it is beautiful but that is only your idea, you cannot prove it; you cannot produce any evidence. It can simply be refuted.

Albert Einstein's wife was a poet and he was a mathematician – that was a strange couple. On the first night she wanted to show him a few of her poems, but she could not show more than one because the very first poem became a problem. In that poem she had compared the moon with the face of her beloved.

Einstein said, "Wait! I cannot tolerate such idiotic things: moon? and face? – there is no similarity. The moon is a dead planet and so vast that if you put it on somebody's head, that man will be finished. Do you want to kill your beloved?"

Frau Einstein, the wife, had never thought about it, that somebody would bring this argument. And Einstein said, "What is the beauty in it? – just a rotten piece of land where there is no water, no greenery, nothing grows, no life. Is your beloved dead?"

She was an intelligent woman. She never again mentioned any of her poems to him because poems are not mathematics, not physics, not science.

Your idea of the universe is not the universe. When all your ideas disappear and you also become a mirror, then you see the reality of existence reflected in you. But then it is no longer an idea, it is a true reflection.

I said that you are very much confused, because these were beautiful experiences and you are saying, "There are no words to describe the nightmare." I don't see anywhere any nightmare.

Experiencing me, that I am not, is a truth.
Experiencing me as a mirror is a truth.
Experiencing that the universe is only your idea is a truth. How can truth be a nightmare?

This was not a nightmare; you were coming out of nightmares.

"Only one sentence rushed through my head." Naturally, if it was a nightmare to you, you must have become immensely afraid. "Only one sentence rushed through my head, 'He kills us! He kills us!'" That, too, is true.

To be a sannyasin is to commit suicide – suicide of the ego, suicide of the personality – because only after this suicide can you discover your original face. Every master kills you so that he can give you back your reality that you have forgotten.

The ancient *Upanishads* say, "The master is death" – a tremendously significant statement. Those who come to a master should be prepared to die, because only after death is there a possibility of resurrection.

"Your presence in all of my friends is an immense help to focus my energy into the heart." What happened to your nightmare? What happened to the fear – "He kills us! He kills us!" Suddenly you have reached to the heart. Your mind is jumping like a monkey from one tree to another tree without any relevance.

"Simultaneously I started to go through the fear in my daily life..." and you are back again.

The heart does not know fear; it only knows love.

It is the mind that knows fear; it never knows love.

The mind is the center of fear and the heart is the center of love – don't get confused. You need a clarity about your being, about your experiences, about what you say – because if in this question there is so much confusion, there must be a million times more confusion in your head. This is an edited version.

"Simultaneously I started to go through the fear in my daily life, but it seems as if there is no end. I am not sure anymore whether this is the right way." Neither am I.

Looking at your question, even the right way will turn into a wrong way; it all depends on you.

There is a great statement of Jalaluddin Rumi, a Sufi mystic. One of his disciples asked him, "Are we going to paradise?" Jalaluddin laughed and said, "I cannot say that we are going to paradise, but wherever we are going, there will be paradise. It all depends on us – what we make out of our being, out of our creativity, out of our love, out of our consciousness."

He was right: wherever we are going, don't be worried, it will be paradise.

You are asking about the right way; I am worried about *you*.

First put yourself in a right state of being, then whatever path you follow will be right, because the paths are not outside. We are not talking about highways and superhighways.

The path is inwards.

But with a confused mind you cannot move inwards.

It is good that you asked, Dhyan Astiko, that you exposed your mind a little bit. I know millions more confusions must be there. You have presented just a sample, but it is enough indication that you need to meditate more, go through psychotherapies.... Psychotherapies are just to clean the ground, and meditation is to sow the seeds. Then wait patiently. When the spring comes, you will also have flowers in your being. And to have blossomed is right. It shows that you have followed the right way.

It happened at the AIDS prevention clinic...a German walks in and asks the clerk for six condoms. "Six condoms?" says the clerk. "Why six?"

"Ja!" says the German, and begins to count on his fingers: "Monday, Tuesday, Wednesday, Thursday, Friday, Saturday. Sunday I rest!"

Next an Italian walks in and asks the clerk for eight condoms. "Eight condoms? Why eight?"

"Mama mia! It is for-a Monday-a, Tuesday-a, Wednesday-a, Thursday-a, Friday-a, Saturday-a, and twice-a on Sunday!"

Just then an Englishman walks in and politely asks for twelve condoms. "Twelve condoms?" exclaims the clerk, very impressed, "Why twelve?"

"Simple, old chap. January, February, March...."

Dhyan Astiko, laugh a little more and be a little less serious; there is nothing better than laughter to destroy confusion.

Beloved Bhagwan,

This, my first year of sannyas, is the beginning of living,
and each moment is a fresh opportunity
to dive deeper into myself and into You.
You speak of three phases:
the student, the disciple, and the devotee. As disciple,
Your light draws me closer – my inner flame is burning!
And yet, the mind still interprets and interferes.
A true knowing, merging with You as a devotee,
is a distant, undiscovered star.
Beloved Bhagwan, please shed light
on this gap I am experiencing- -
this phenomenon of disciple transforming into devotee.

Nirava Chandira, the question you have asked is based on a wrong assumption. You have accepted, without understanding the meaning, that you are a disciple. You are not yet a disciple, you are only a student – because only for the student does the distance between himself and the state of a devotee seem to be very big, almost unbridgeable.

And what you say in your question gives enough proof that you are at the stage of the student, not the stage of the disciple. I will read the question and make it clear to you. It is always good to know where you are, because then progress becomes very easy. If you imagine to yourself that you are somewhere else, where you are not, no progress is possible.

"This, my first year of sannyas, is the beginning of living, and each moment is a fresh opportunity to dive deeper into myself and into you. You speak of three phases: the student, the disciple, and the devotee. As disciple, your light draws me closer – my inner flame is burning! And yet, the mind still interprets and interferes. A true knowing, merging with you as a devotee, is a distant, undiscovered star."

This recognition that the mind still interprets and interferes shows that disciplehood has not happened. You are still at the stage of the student. These three stages are parallel to three centers in your being.

The student is in the head.
The disciple is in the heart.
And the devotee is in the being.

The student thinks, interprets. The disciple loves, and simply drinks the very presence of the master. The disciple is in tune, his heartbeat is harmonious with the master's heartbeat. There is no question of interpretation or interference. The heart does not work through thoughts. And from the heart, the state of devotee is not very far, but very close. As love deepens and becomes trust, as harmony with the master grows and becomes one organic unity, the devotee is born.

It will be immensely good for you to be clearly aware that you are still in the head. Perhaps your head feels convinced of what I am saying, but there are underlying doubts. To avoid those doubts, your head interprets in such a way that it fits with your own prejudices, your own ideologies.

The student does not get in tune with the master; on the contrary, whatever the master says, the student tries to make it in such a way that it becomes in tune with his old mind. Hence, interpretation and interference are absolutely necessary, but they are indicative that you have not moved from the head. And it is your head that is going continuously into a desire, into a longing to be a devotee.

To be a devotee is not a desire and is not a longing. The disciple is so satisfied, so contented, that the state of devotion happens on its own accord. It is not a desire, not a longing – because every desire and every longing makes things complex and difficult.

The distance between the disciple and the devotee is almost nil. The disciple is the beginning of relaxing with the master, and the devotee is the fulfillment of that relaxation. The disciple is the beginning, the devotee is the end.

Chandira, whatever is happening is not bad. It is good that you are feeling yourself diving deeper and deeper into yourself. But remember that you are still a student and that you have to get rid of your thoughts. For that purpose there are so many meditations – do any meditation that appeals to you, that feels good to you, because I don't want you to torture yourself. Remember Chuang Tzu's statement, "Easy is right."

So find a meditation which is easy for you, comfortable, blissful, and comes without any effort. It is almost a relaxation, a rest.

If the mind stops its madness, its constant chattering, its distortions of everything, you will become a disciple. The bridge between the student and the disciple is meditation, and the bridge between the disciple and the devotee is love. It is only a question of two steps – one step of meditation and one step of love – and you have arrived home.

But drop the idea completely that you are already a disciple, because that will become a tremendous hindrance. Without meditation coming to a fulfillment, love cannot arise. That's why to be a devotee seems to be a faraway star. It is not only far away, it is impossible. One should be very factual and very scientific in judging oneself, where one is.

Don't feel hurt, because even to be a student is a rare thing. In millions of people around the world, to be a student in a mystery school is a rare, very unique opportunity. And you will become a disciple...but keep your focus on moving away from the head towards the heart. Right now the devotee should not be made a goal.

Once your mind is gone and your heart is singing and dancing with joy and love, you will see that the devotee is just one step more. The love has to become crystallized into trust, and the harmoniousness has to come even closer and become oneness.

The master and the devotee are one. The master and the disciple have a little distance. The master and the student are really far away – but everybody has to begin from being a student. That is the right beginning. Don't start thinking of yourself as a disciple. Start from the right beginning as a student; your goal is to be a disciple.

Once you have reached to the point of disciplehood, you cannot ask such a question, saying that the state of devotee looks like a faraway star. It is just within the reach of your hand – a little more courage, a little more love, a little more risk, a readiness to dissolve into the master, who is not.

Dissolving into the master is only a device.

The moment you dissolve into the master, you will be surprised that you have dissolved into existence itself; the master was only a window. Through the master you can enter into the open sky. Then all the stars are yours and the whole existence is yours. You are part of it.

But be intelligent in recognizing where you are. Only the unintelligent cannot grow; the intelligent have no difficulty in growing – and everybody has the intelligence, but is not using it.

A gum-chewing American and a Frenchman are sitting together in a restaurant. The American feels really proud to be an American, so he starts a conversation. He asks the Frenchman, "When you eat bread, do you eat all of it?"

"Of course," says the Frenchman.

"Well," says the American, "We only eat the soft part of it; the rest we collect in containers, take to a factory and put through a mill. What comes out are little breads that we sell in France."

"And what about steaks?" he continues. "Do you eat all parts of them?"

"Yes, we do," answers the Frenchman.

"Oh, we don't!" says the American. "We only eat the meaty part of the steak; the greasy part we collect in containers, take to a factory, put through a mill, and what comes out are little steaks that we sell in France."

Now the Frenchman gets really upset. He asks, "So what do Americans do with their used condoms?"

"Of course we throw them away," says the American.

The Frenchman replies, "Ha! We collect them all in containers, take them to a factory and put them through a mill. What comes out is chewing gum that we sell in America!"

So don't feel bad about being a student; enjoy it. But don't chew American chewing gum. That is the most idiotic act in the whole world. And soon you will grow...just avoid chewing gum. That chewing gum goes into the head and makes all kinds of ideas, interpretations, interferences, ideologies. Just avoid it...and slip back down towards the heart.

The head is good for science, but not for religion. The heart is not good for science, but it is an absolute must for religion, because it is the heart that finally grows into devotion, into merger, into love, into trust, into self-realization, into the experience of the divine.

Okay, Vimal?

Yes, Bhagwan.

WORLDWIDE DISTRIBUTION CENTERS FOR THE WORKS OF BHAGWAN SHREE RAJNEESH

Books by Bhagwan Shree Rajneesh are available in many languages throughout the world. Bhagwan's discourses have been recorded live on audiotape from 1974 onwards and on video from 1985. There are many audio recordings of Rajneesh meditation music and of celebration music played in His presence; and beautiful photographs have been taken of Bhagwan. For further information and catalog, contact the closest distribution center:

EUROPE

West Germany

Rajneesh Verlags GmbH
Venloer Strasse 5-7
D-5000 COLOGNE 1
Tel. 0221/574 07 43

Nationwide book-shop distributor
VVA Vereinigte Verlagsauslieferung,
Gütersloh

Italy

Rajneesh Services Corporation
Via XX Settembre 12
I-28941 ARONA (NO)
Tel. 02/839 21 94 (office Milano)

Netherlands

Stichting Rajneesh Publikaties
  Nederland
Cornelis Troostplein 23
NL-1072 JJ AMSTERDAM
Tel. 020/573 21 30

United Kingdom

Rajneesh Media
Manor Garden Enterprise Center
Manor Garden 10-18
LONDON N7 6GY
Tel. 01/281 4892

ASIA

India

Rajneeshdham
Rajneesh Mandir
17 Koregaon Park
POONA 411001
Tel. 0212/60953/4

Japan

EER Rajneesh Neo-Sannyas Commune
Mimura Building 6-21-34 Kikuna
Kohoku-ku, YOKOHAMA, 222
Tel. 045/434 1981

NORTH AMERICA

United States of America

Chidvilas Foundation
P.O. Box 1510
Boulder, CO 80306
Tel. (303)665-6611

Also available in nationwide
bookstores of Walden Books
and B.Daltons

BOOKS BY BHAGWAN SHREE RAJNEESH

ENGLISH LANGUAGE EDITIONS

RAJNEESH PUBLISHERS

Recent Releases

Beyond Enlightenment
Sermons in Stones
That Art Thou
The Last Testament *(Volume 1)*
 Interviews with the World Press
The Messiah *(Volume 1)*
 Commentaries on Kahlil Gibran's The Prophet
The Messiah *(Volume 2)*
 Commentaries on Kahlil Gibran's The Prophet
The Rajneesh Bible *(Volumes 1-5)*
The Rajneesh Upanishad
The Rebellious Spirit
Zarathustra: A God that can Dance *(Volume 1)*
Zarathustra: The Laughing Prophet *(Volume 2)*

Compilations

A New Vision of Women's Liberation
Bhagwan Shree Rajneesh On Basic Human Rights
Life, Love and Laughter
Priests and Politicians - The Mafia of the Soul
The New Man: The Only Hope for the Future
The Book *An Introduction to the Teachings of Bhagwan Shree Rajneesh*
 Series I   from A - H
 Series II from I - O
 Series III from R - Z

Books on Bhagwan Shree Rajneesh

Bhagwan Shree Rajneesh The Most Dangerous Man Since Jesus Christ *(by Sue Appleton)*
Bhagwan: The Most Godless Yet The Most Godly Man *(by George Meredith)*
Bhagwan: The Buddha For The Future *(by Juliet Forman)*

Biographies

Books I have Loved
Glimpses of a Golden Childhood
Notes of a Madman

Photobiographies

The Sound of Running Water
 - *Bhagwan Shree Rajneesh
 and His work 1974-1978*
This Very Place The Lotus Paradise
 - *Bhagwan Shree Rajneesh
 and His Work 1978-1984*

The Bauls

The Beloved *(Volumes 1&2)*

Buddha

The Book of the Books *(Volumes 1-4)*
 - *the Dhammapada*
The Diamond Sutra - *the Vajrachchedika
 Prajnaparamita Sutra*
The Discipline of Transcendence *(Volumes 1-4)*
 - *the Sutra of 42 Chapters*
The Heart Sutra
 - *the Prajnaparamita Hridayam Sutra*

Buddhist Masters

The Book of Wisdom
 (Volumes 1&2)
 - *Atisha's Seven Points of Mind Training*
The White Lotus
 - *the Sayings of Bodhidharma*

Early Discourses and Writings

A Cup of Tea - *Letters to Disciples*
And Now, and Here *(Volumes 1&2)*
Beware of Socialism
Dimensions Beyond the Known
From Sex to Superconsciousness
I am the Gate
Krishna: The Man and His Philosphy
The Long and the Short and the All
The Perfect Way
In Search of the Miraculous *(Volume 1)*
The Silent Explosion

Hassidism

The Art of Dying
The True Sage

Jesus

Come Follow Me *(Volumes 1-4)*
 - *the Sayings of Jesus*
I Say Unto You *(Volumes 1&2)*
 - *the Sayings Of Jesus*
The Mustard Seed - *the Gospel of Thomas*

Kabir

Ecstasy: The Forgotten Language
The Divine Melody
The Fish in the Sea is Not Thirsty
The Guest
The Path of Love
The Revolution

Meditation

The Orange Book
   - the Meditation Techniques
   - of Bhagwan Shree Rajneesh

Responses to Questions

Be Still and Know
My Way: The Way of the White Clouds
The Goose is Out!
The Wild Geese and the Water
Walk Without Feet, Fly Without Wings and
    Think Without Mind
Zen: Zest, Zip, Zap and Zing

Sufism

Just Like That
Straight to Freedom
Sufis: The People of the Path *(Volumes 1&2)*
The Perfect Master *(Volumes 1&2)*
The Secret
The Wisdom of the Sands *(Volumes 1&2)*

Unio Mystica *(Volumes 1&2)*
   - the Hadiqa of Hakim Sanai
Until You Die

Tantra

Tantra, Spirituality and Sex
   - *Excerpts from The Book of the Secrets*
Tantra: The Supreme Understanding
   - *Tilopa's Song of Mahamudra*
The Book of the Secrets *(Volumes 4&5)*
   - *Vigyana Bhairava Tantra*
The Tantra Vision *(Volumes 1&2)*
   - *the Royal Song of Saraha*

Tao

Tao: The Golden Gate *(Volumes 1&2)*
Tao: The Pathless Path *(Volumes 1&2)*
   - *the Stories of Lieh Tzu*
Tao: The Three Treasures *(Volumes 1-4)*
   - *the Tao Te Ching of Lao Tzu*
The Empty Boat - *the Stories of Chuang Tzu*
The Secret of Secrets *(Volumes 1&2)*
   - *the Secret of the Golden Flower*
When the Shoe Fits
   - *the Stories of Chuang Tzu*

The Upanishads

I Am That - *Isa Upanishad*
Philosophia Ultima - *Mandukya Upanishad*
The Ultimate Alchemy *(Volumes 1&2)*
   - *Atma Pooja Upanishad*
Vedanta: Seven Steps to Samadhi
   - *Akshya Upanishad*

Western Mystics

Guida Spirituale - *the Desiderata*
Philosophia Perennis *(Volumes 1&2)*
    - *the Golden Verses of Pythagoras*
The Hidden Harmony
    the Fragments of Heraclitus
The New Alchemy: To Turn You on
    - *Mabel Collins' Light on the Path*
Theologia Mystica
    - *the Treatise of St. Dionysius*

Yoga

Yoga: The Alpha and the Omega *(Volumes 1-10)*
    - *the Yoga Sutras of Patanjali*
Yoga: The Science of the Soul *(Volumes 1-3)*
    - *Originally titled Yoga: The Alpha and the Omega*

Zen

Ah, This!
Ancient Music in the Pines
And the Flowers Showered
A Sudden Clash of Thunder
Dang Dang Doko Dang
Nirvana: The Last Nightmare
No Water, No Moon
Returning to the Source
Roots and Wings
The First Principle
The Grass Grows By Itself
The Sun Rises in the Evening
Walking in Zen, Sitting in Zen
Zen: The Path of Paradox *(Volumes 1-3)*
Zen: The Special Transmission - *Zen Stories*

Zen Masters

Hsin Hsin Ming: The Book of Nothing
    Discourses on the Faith-Mind of Sosan
Neither This Nor That
    - *The Sutras of Sosan*
Take it Easy *(Volumes 1&2)* - *Poems of Ikkyu*
The Search - *the Ten Bulls of Zen*
This Very Body the Buddha
    - *Hakuin's Song of Meditation*

Darshan Diaries
Talks between
Master and Disciple

Hammer on the Rock
    (December 10, 1975 - January 15, 1976)
Above All Don't Wobble
    (January 16 - February 12, 1976)
Nothing to Lose But Your Head
    (February 13 - March 12, 1976)
Be Realistic: Plan For a Miracle
    (March 13 - April 6, 1976)
Get Out of Your Own Way *(April 7 - May 2, 1976)*
Beloved of My Heart *(May 3 - 28, 1976)*
The Cypress in the Courtyard *(May 29 - June 27, 1976)*
A Rose is a Rose is a Rose *(June 28 - July 27, 1976)*
Dance Your Way to God *(July 28 - August 20, 1976)*
The Passion for the Impossible
    (August 21 - September 18, 1976)
The Great Nothing *(September 19 - October 11, 1976)*
God is Not for Sale *(October 12 - November 7, 1976)*
The Shadow of the Whip
    (November 8 - December 3, 1976)
Blessed are the Ignorant *(December 4 - 31, 1976)*
The Buddha Disease *(January 1977)*
What Is, Is, What Ain't, Ain't *(February 1977)*

The Zero Experience *(March 1977)*
For Madmen Only (Price of Admission: Your Mind) *(April 1977)*
This is It *(May 1977)*
The Further Shore *(June 1977)*
Far Beyond the Stars *(July 1977)*
The No Book (No Buddha, No Teaching, No Discipline) *(August 1977)*
Don't Just Do Something, Sit There *(September 1977)*
Only Losers Can Win in this Game *(October 1977)*
The Open Secret *(November 1977)*
The Open Door *(December 1977)*
The Sun Behind the Sun Behind the Sun *(January 1978)*
Believing the Impossible Before Breakfast *(February 1978)*
Don't Bite My Finger, Look Where I'm Pointing *(March 1978)*
Let Go! *(April 1978)*

The 99 Names of Nothingness *(May 1978)*
The Madman's Guide to Enlightenment *(June 1978)*
Don't Look Before You Leap *(July 1978)*
Hallelujah! *(August 1978)*
God's Got a Thing About You *(September 1978)*
The Tongue-Tip Taste of Tao *(October 1978)*
The Sacred Yes *(November 1978)*
Turn On, Tune In, and Drop the Lot *(December 1978)*
Zorba the Buddha *(January 1979)*
Won't You Join the Dance? *(February 1979)*
You Ain't Seen Nothin' Yet *(March 1979)*
The Shadow of the Bamboo *(April 1979)*
Just Around the Corner *(May 1979)*
Snap Your Fingers, Slap Your Face & Wake Up! *(June 1979)*
The Rainbow Bridge *(July 1979)*
Don't Let Yourself Be Upset by the Sutra, Rather Upset the Sutra Yourself *(August/September 1979)*
The Sound of One Hand Clapping *(March 1981)*

OTHER PUBLISHERS

UNITED KINGDOM

No Water, No Moon *(Sheldon Press)*
Roots and Wings *(Routledge & Kegan Paul)*
Straight to Freedom *(Sheldon Press)*
Tao: The Three Treasures *(Volume 1, Wildwood House)*
The Art of Dying *(Sheldon Press)*
The Book of the Secrets *(Volume 1, Thames & Hudson)*
The Supreme Doctrine *(Routledge & Kegan Paul)*

Books on Bhagwan Shree Rajneesh

The Way of the Heart: the Rajneesh Movement
 by Judith Thompson and Paul Heelas, Department of Religious Studies, University of Lancaster *(Aquarian Press)*

UNITED STATES OF AMERICA

Dimensions Beyond the Known
 (Wisdom Garden Books)
Hammer on the Rock *(Grove Press)*
I Am the Gate *(Harper & Row)*
Journey toward the Heart
 (Original title: Until You Die, Harper & Row)
Meditation: The Art of Ecstasy *(Original title: Dynamics of Meditation, Harper & Row)*
My Way: The Way of the White Clouds *(Grove Press)*
Roots and Wings *(Routledge & Kegan Paul)*
The Book of the Secrets *(Volumes 1-3, Harper & Row)*
The Great Challenge *(Grove Press)*
The Mustard Seed *(Harper & Row)*
The Psychology of the Esoteric *(Harper & Row)*
The Supreme Doctrine *(Routledge & Kegan Paul)*
Words Like Fire *(Original title: Come Follow Me, Volume 1) (Harper & Row)*

Books on Bhagwan Shree Rajneesh

Dying for Enlightenment by Bernard Gunther *(Harper & Row)*
The Awakened One: The Life and Work of Bhagwan Shree Rajneesh by Vasant Joshi *(Harper & Row)*
The Rajneesh Story: The Bhagwan's Garden by Dell Murphy *(Linwood Press, Oregon)*

FOREIGN LANGUAGE EDITIONS

Chinese

I am the Gate (Woolin)

Danish

Bhagwan Shree Rajneesh Om Grundlaeggende Menneskerettigheder (Forlaget Premo)
 Bhagwan Shree Rajneesh On Basic Human Rights
Hu-Meditation Og Kosmik Orgasme (Borgens)
 Hu-Meditation and Cosmic Orgasm
Hemmelighedernes Bog (Borgens)
 The Book of the Secrets (Volume 1)

Dutch

Bhagwan Shree Rajneesh Over de Rechten van de Mens (Stichting Rajneesh Publikaties Nederland)
   Bhagwan Shree Rajneesh On Basic Human Rights
Volg Mij (Ankh-Hermes), *Come Follow Me (Volume 1)*
Gezaaid in Goede Aarde (Ankh-Hermes)
   Come Follow Me (Volume 2)
Drink Mij (Ankh-Hermes), *Come Follow Me (Volume 3)*
Ik Ben de Zee Die Je Zoekt (Ankh-Hermes)
   Come Follow Me (Volume 4)
Ik Ben de Poort (Ankh-Hermes), *I am the Gate*
Heel Eenvoudig (Mirananda), *Just Like That*
Meditatie: De Kunst van Innerlijke Extase (Mirananda)
   Meditation: The Art of Inner Ecstasy
Mijn Weg, De Weg van de Witte Wolk (Arcanum)
   My Way: The Way of the White Clouds
Geen Water, Geen Maan (Mirananda)
   No Water, No Moon (Volumes 1 & 2)
Tantra, Spiritualiteit en Seks (Ankh-Hermes)
   Tantra, Spirituality & Sex
Tantra: Het Allerhoogste Inzicht (Ankh-Hermes)
   Tantra: The Supreme Understanding
Tau (Ankh-Hermes),
   Tao: The Three Treasures (Volume 1)
Het Boek der Geheimen (Mirananda)
   The Book of Secrets (Volumes 1-5)
De Verborgen Harmonie (Mirananda)
   The Hidden Harmony
Het Mosterdzaad (Mirananda)
   The Mustard Seed (Volumes 1 & 2)
De Nieuwe Mens (Volumes 1 & 2) (Zorn/Altamira)
   Excerpts from The Last Testament (Volume 1)
   Dutch edition only
Het Oranje Meditatieboek (Ankh-Hermes)
   The Orange Book
Psychologie en Evolutie (Ankh-Hermes)
   The Psychology of the Esoteric
De Tantra Visie (Arcanum)
   The Tantra Vision (Volumes 1 & 2)
Zoeken naar de Stier (Ankh-Hermes)
   10 Zen Stories
Totdat Je Sterft (Ankh-Hermes)
   Until You Die

French

Je Suis la Porte (EPI), *I am the Gate*
La Meditation Dynamique (Dangles)
   Meditation: The Art of Inner Ecstasy
L'Eveil a la Conscience Cosmique (Dangles)
   The Psychology of the Esoteric
Le Livre des Secrets (Soleil Orange)
   The Book of Secrets (Volume 1)

German

Und vor Allem: Nicht Wackeln (Fachbuchhandlung für Psychologie)
   Above All Don't Wobble
Der Freund (Sannyas Verlag), *A Cup of Tea*
Vorsicht Sozialismus (Rajneesh Verlag)
   Beware of Socialism
Bhagwan Shree Rajneesh: Über die Grundrechte des Menschen (Rajneesh Verlag)
   Bhagwan Shree Rajneesh On Basic Human Rights
Komm und folge mir (Sannyas/Droemer Knaur)
   Come Follow Me (Volume 1)
Jesus aber schwieg (Sannyas)
   Come Follow Me (Volume 2)
Jesus - der Menschensohn (Sannyas)
   Come Follow Me (Volume 3)
Sprung ins Unbekannte (Sannyas)
   Dimensions Beyond the Known

Ekstase: Die vergessenen Sprache (Herzschlag)
    Ecstasy: The Forgotten Language
Vom Sex zum kosmischen Bewußtsein)
    (New Age/Thomas Martin)
    From Sex to Superconsciousness
Goldene Augenblicke:
    Portrait einer Jugend in Indien (Goldmann)
    Glimpses of a Golden Childhood
Sprengt den Fels der Unbewußtheit (Fischer)
    Hammer on the Rock
Ich bin der Weg (Sannyas), *I am the Gate*
Meditation: Die Kunst, zu sich selbst zu finden
    (Heyne), *Meditation: The Art of Inner Ecstasy*
Mein Weg: Der Weg der weissen Wolke (Herzschlag)
    My Way: The Way of the White Clouds
Nirvana: Die letzte Hürde auf dem Weg
    (Rajneesh Verlag/RFE), *Nirvana: The Last Nightmare*
Kein Wasser, Kein Mond (Herzschlag)
    No Water, No Moon
Mit Wurzeln und Flügeln (Edition Lotos)
    Roots and Wings (Volume 1)
Die Schuhe auf dem Kopf (Edition Lotos)
    Roots and Wings (Volume 2)
Spirituelle Entwicklung und Sexualität (Fischer)
    Spiritual Development & Sexuality
Tantra, Spiritualität und Sex (Rajneesh Verlag)
    Tantra, Spirituality & Sex
Tantrische Liebeskunst (Sannyas)
    Tantra, Spirituality & Sex
Tantra: Die höchste Einsicht (Sannyas)
    Tantra: The Supreme Understanding
Das Buch der Geheimnisse (Heyne)
    The Book of the Secrets (Volume 1)
Die Gans ist raus! (Rajneesh Verlag)
    The Goose Is Out!
Rebellion der Seele (Sannyas),
    The Great Challenge
Die verborgene Harmonie (Sannyas)
    The Hidden Harmony

Die verbotene Wahrheit (Rajneesh Verlag/Heyne)
    The Mustard Seed
Das Orangene Buch (Rajneesh Verlag/RFE)
    The Orange Book
Esoterische Psychologie (Sannyas)
    The Psychology of the Esoteric
Auf der Suche (Sambuddha) *The Search*
Das Klatschen der einen Hand (Edition Gyandip)
    The Sound of One Hand Clapping
Tantrische Vision (Heyne)
    The Tantra Vision (Volume 1)
Alchemie der Verwandlung (Edition Lotos)
    The True Sage
Nicht bevor du stirbst (Edition Gyandip),
    Until You Die
Was ist Meditation? (Sannyas)
    Compilation about meditation, German edition only
Yoga: Alpha und Omega (Edition Gyandip)
    Yoga: The Alpha and the Omega (Volume 1)
Der Höhepunkt des Lebens (Rajneesh Verlag)
    Compilation on death, German edition only
Intelligenz des Herzens (Herzschlag)
    Compilation, German edition only
Kunst kommt nicht vom Können (Rajneesh Verlag)
    Compilation about creativity, German edition only
Liebe beginnt nach den Flitterwochen
    (Rajneesh Verlag)
    Compilation about love, German edition only
Sexualität und Aids (Rajneesh Verlag)
    Compilation about Aids, German edition only

Greek

Bhagwan Shree Rajneesh Gia Ta Vasika
Anthropina Dikeomata (Swami Anand Ram)
    Bhagwan Shree Rajneesh on Basic Human Rights
I Krifi Armonia (PIGI/Rassoulis)
    The Hidden Harmony

Hebrew

Tantra: Ha'havana Ha'eelaeet (Massada)
Tantra: The Supreme Understanding

Italian

Bhagwan Shree Rajneesh Parla Sui Diritti Dell'Uomo
 (Rajneesh Services Corporation)
 Bhagwan Shree Rajneesh On Basic Human Rights
Dimensioni Oltre il Conosciuto (Mediterranee)
 Dimensions Beyond the Known
Estasi: Il Linguaggio Dimenticato (Riza Libri)
 Ecstasy: The Forgotten Language
Dal Sesso all'Eros Cosmico (Basaia)
 From Sex to Superconsciousness
Guida Spirituale (Mondadori)
 Guida Spirituale
Io Sono La Soglia (Meditarranee)
 I am the Gate
Meditazione Dinamica: L'Arte dell'Estasi Interiore
 (Mediterranee), *Meditation: The Art of Inner Ecstasy*
La Mia Via: La Via delle Nuvole Bianche
 (Mediterranee), *My Way: The Way of the White
 Clouds*
Nirvana: L'Ultimo Incubo (Basaia)
 Nirvana: The Last Nightmare
Dieci Storie Zen di Bhagwan Shree Rajneesh:
 Ne Acqua, Ne Luna (Mediterranee),
 No Water, No Moon
Philosofia Perennis (ECIG)
 Philosophia Perennis (Volumes 1 & 2)
Semi di Saggezza (Sugarco), *Seeds of Revolution*
Tantra Spiritualita e Sesso
 (Rajneesh Foundation Italy)
 Tantra, Spirituality & Sex
Tantra: La Comprensione Suprema (Bompiani)
 Tantra: The Supreme Understanding
Tao: I Tre Tesori (Re Nudo)
 Tao: The Three Treasures (Volumes 1-3)
Tecniche di Liberazione (La Salamandra)
 Techniques of Liberation
Il Libro dei Segreti (Bompiani)
 The Book of The Secrets (Volume 1)
L'Armonia Nascosta (ECIG)
 The Hidden Harmony (Volumes 1 & 2)
Il Seme della Ribellione
 (Rajneesh Foundation Italy)
 The Mustard Seed (Volume 1)
La Nuova Alchimia (Psiche)
 The New Alchemy To Turn You On (Vol. 1&2)
Il Libro Arancione (Mediterranee)
 The Orange Book
La Rivoluzione Interiore (Mediterranee)
 The Psychology of the Esoteric
La Bibbia di Rajneesh (Bompiani)
 The Rajneesh Bible (Volume 1)
La Ricerca (La Salamandra), *The Search*
La Dottrina Suprema (Rizzoli),
 The Supreme Doctrine
La Visione Tantrica (Riza)
 The Tantra Vision

Japanese

Bhagwan Shree Rajneesh On Basic Human Rights
 (Meisosha Ltd.)
Dance Your Way to God (Rajneesh Publications)
From Sex to Superconsciousness
 (Rajneesh Publications)
Meditation: The Art of Inner Ecstasy (Merkmal)
My Way: The Way of the White Clouds
 (Rajneesh Publications)
Tantra: The Supreme Understanding (Merkmal)
Tao: The Three Treasures (Volumes 1-4), (Merkmal)
The Beloved (Volumes 1 & 2), (Merkmal)

The Diamond Sutra (Meisosha Ltd./LAF Mitsuya)
The Empty Boat (Volumes 1 & 2),
    (Rajneesh Publications)
The Grass Grows by Itself (Fumikura)
The Heart Sutra (Merkmal)
The Mustard Seed (Volumes 1 & 2), (Merkmal)
The Orange Book (Wholistic Therapy Institute)
The Search (Merkmal)
Until You Die (Fumikura)

Korean

Tao: The Pathless Path (Chung Ha)
The Pathless Path (Vol 1&2)
Theory of Happiness (Vol 3&4)
The Art of Dying (Chung Ha)
The Divine Melody (Chung Ha)
The Empty Boat (Chung Ha)
The Grass Grows by Itself (Chung Ha)

Portuguese

Sobre Os Direitos Humanos Basicos (Editora Naim)
    Bhagwan Shree Rajneesh on Basic Human Rights
Palavras De Fogo (Global/Ground)
    Come Follow Me (Volume 1)
Dimensoes Alem do Conhecido (Cultrix)
    Dimensions Beyond the Known
Extase: A Linguagem Esquecida (Global)
    Ecstasy: The Forgotten Language
Do Sexo A Superconsciencia (Cultrix)
    From Sex to Superconsciousness
Eu Sou A Porta (Pensamento), I am the Gate
Meditacao: A Arte Do Extase (Cultrix)
    Meditation: The Art of Inner Ecstasy
Meu Caminho: O Caminho Das Nuvens Brancas
    (Tao Livraria & Editora)
    My Way: The Way of the White Clouds
Nem Agua, Nem Lua (Pensamento)
    No Water, No Moon
Notas De Um Homem Louco (NAIM),
    Notes of a Madman
Raizes E Asas (Cultrix), Roots and Wings
Sufis: O Povo do Caminho (Maha Lakshmi Editora)
    Sufis: The People of the Path
Tantra: Sexo E Espiritualidade (Agora)
    Tantra, Spirituality & Sex
Tantra: A Suprema Compreensao (Cultrix)
    Tantra: The Supreme Understanding
Arte de Morrer (Global), The Art of Dying
O Livro Dos Segredos (Maha Lakshmi Editora)
    The Book of the Secrets (Volumes 1 & 2)
Cipreste No Jardim (Cultrix)
    The Cypress in the Courtyard
A Divina Melodia (Cultrix), The Divine Melody
A Harmonia Oculta (Pensamento),
    The Hidden Harmony
A Semente De Mostarda (Tao Livraria & Editora)
    The Mustard Seed (Volumes 1 & 2)
A Nova Alquimi (Cultrix)
    The New Alchemy To Turn You On
O Livro Orange (Pensamento), The Orange Book
A Psicologia Do Esoterico (Tao Livraria & Editora)
    The Psychology of the Esoteric
Unio Mystica (Maha Lakshmi), Unio Mystica

Russian

Bhagwan Shree Rajneesh On Basic Human Rights
    (Rajneesh Foundation Europe)

Serbo-Croat

Bhagwan Shree Rajneesh (Swami Mahavira)
    (Compilation of various quotations)

Spanish

Sobre Los Derechos Humanos Basicos
  (Futonia, Spain)
  Bhagwan Shree Rajneesh on Basic Human Rigths
Ven, Sigueme (Sagaro, Chile), *Come Follow Me*
  (Volume 1)
Yo Soy La Puerta (Editorial Diana, Mexico)
  I am The Gate
Meditacion: El Arte del Extasis
  (Rosello Impresiones)
  Meditation: The Art of Inner Ecstasy
El Camino de las Nubes Blancas
  (Editorial Cuatro Vientos)
  My Way: The Way of the White Clouds
Solo Un Cielo (Collection Tantra), *Only One Sky*
Introduccion al Mundo del Tantra
  (Rosello Impresiones)
  Tantra: The Supreme Understanding
(Volumes1 & 2)

Tao: Los Tres Tesoros (Editorial Sirio, Spain)
  Tao: The Three Treasures
El Sutra del Corazon (Sarvogeet, Spain)
  The Heart Sutra
El Libro Naranja (Bhagwatam RMC, Puerto Rico)
  The Orange Book
Psicologia de lo Esoterico: La Nueva Evolucion
  del Hombre (Editorial Cuatro Vientos, Chile)
  The Psychology of the Esoteric
El Riesgo Supremo (Editorial Martinez Roca, Spain)
  The Ultimate Risk
Que Es Meditacion? (Koan/Rosello
  Impresiones/Pastanaga), *What Is Meditation?*

Swedish

Den Väldiga Utmaningen (Livskraft)
  The Great Challenge

RAJNEESH MEDITATION CENTERS ASHRAMS AND COMMUNES

There are many Rajneesh Meditation Centers throughout the world which can be contacted for information about the teachings of Bhagwan Shree Rajneesh and which have His books available as well as audio and video tapes of His discourses. Centers exist in practically every country, including some behind the iron curtain.

Argentina

Niketana Rajneesh Meditation Center
Combate de los Pozos 764
RA-1222 Buenos Aires

Australia

Kalika Rajneesh Meditation Center
25 Martin Street
Cairns 4870

Prabhakar Rajneesh Meditation Center
c/o Post Office
Innot Hot Springs
North Queensland 4872

Rajneeshgrad Neo-Sannyas Commune
P.O. Box 1097
160 High Street
Fremantle WA 6160

Belgium

Indu Rajneesh Meditation Center
Coebergerstraat 40
2018 Antwerp

Suryodaya Rajneesh Meditation Center
Rue de Drapieres 12
1050 Bruxelles

Brazil

Abhudaya Rajneesh Meditation Center
Caixa Postal 2651
Porto Alegre 90000
R/S

Amaraloka Rajneesh Meditation Center
Rua Noel Torezin No. 83
Campo Belo
Sao Paulo SP 04615

Anurag Rajneesh Meditation Center
Avenida Recife 4282
Modulo 4, Apto 314 ES
Tancia-Recife 50000

Jwala Rajneesh Meditation Center
Avenida Nico Pecanta 50, Sala 2315
Edificio Rodoefo
De Padi Centro
Rio de Janeiro

Premadhara Rajneesh Meditation Center
Av. Dep. Paulino Rocha 1001,
Apto 402
Sqn. Bloco H, Castelao
Fortaneza-Ceara 60000

Purnam Rajneesh Meditation Center
Caixa Postal 1946
Rio Grande do Sul
Porto Allegre 90000

Sudhakar Rajneesh Meditation Center
Rua Getulio Vargas 80
Jardim Sao Francisco
Cabo Frio
Rio de Janeiro 28900

Canada

Grada Rajneesh Institute
5161 Park Avenue
Montreal

Samaroha Rajneesh Meditation Center
1774 Tolmie Street
Vancouver B.C. V6R 4B8

Colombia

Padma Rajneesh Meditation Center
Apartado Aereo 4128
Medellin

Denmark

Anwar Rajneesh Meditation Center
Thorsgade 74, 4TV
2200 Copenhagen N

Khalaas Rajneesh Meditation Center
Museumsstien 8
9990 Skagen

Pragya Rajneesh Meditation Center
Kiersplads 6 III TV
8000 Aarhus C

Rajneesh Institute for Spiritual Creativity
Bogballevey 3
Tonning
8740 Braeostrup

Sahajo Rajneesh Meditation Center
Sudergade 26 1
3000 Helsinger

Ecuador

Moulik Rajneesh Meditation Center
Eustorgio Salgado 197, piso 3
Miraflores Quito

Finland

Leela Rajneesh Meditation Center
Merimiehenkatu 16B 24
00150 Helsinki 15

France

Rajneesh Meditation Center
60 Ave. Charles de Gaulle
92200 Neuilly

Greece

Darshan Rajneesh Meditation Center
20 Aribou Street
11633 Athens

Mallika Rajneesh Meditation Center
Nikiforou Ouranour 25-A
11499 Athens

Surya Rajneesh Meditation Center
Oia-Santorini

India

Rajneeshdham Neo-Sannyas Commune
17 Koregaon Park
Poona 411001

Rajyoga Rajneesh Meditation Center
C5/44 Safdarjang Development Area
Opposite ITT, Palam Road
New Delhi 110016

Italy

Devamani Rajneesh Meditation Center
Via Basilica 5
10122 Torino

Divyananda Rajneesh Meditation Center
Pensione Tambo
Alpe Motta

Gautama Rajneesh Meditation Center
Via S. Martino 51
Morosolo Casciago
21020 Varese

Miasto Rajneesh Neo-Sannyas Commune
Podere San Giorgio
Cotorniano
53010 Frosini (SI)

Vishad Rajneesh Meditation Center
Castelvecchio di Compito
55062 Lucca

Japan

Eer Rajneesh Neo-Sannyas Commune
Mimura Building 6-21-34
Kikuna
Kohoku-ku
Yokohama 222

Mahamani Rajneesh Meditation Center
105 Country Heights
635 Shimabukuro
Kitanakagusuku-son
Okinawa 901-23

Sitara Rajneesh Meditation Center
498-218, Teine-miyanosawa
Nishi-ku
Sapporo-shi
Hokkaido

Svagat Rajneesh Meditation Center
1-22-46 Nishi-Nakada
Sendai-Shi Miyagi-Pref. 981-11

Kenya

Archana Rajneesh Meditation Center
P.O. Box 82501
Mombasa

Preetam Rajneesh Meditation Center
P.O. Box 10256
Nairobi

Mexico

Madhu Rajneesh Meditation Center
Rancho Cutzi Minzicuri
San Juan de Vina
Tacambaro
Michoacan

Nepal

Asheesh Rajneesh Meditation Center
P.O. Box 278
Pulchowk
Kathmandu

Rajneesh Teerth Neo-Sannyas Commune
Masina Patan, P.O. Box 91
Pokhara

Satmarga Rajneesh Meditation Center
Mahendra Pul
Pokhara

Netherlands

De Stad Rajneesh Mystery School
Cornelis Troostplein 23
1072 JJ Amsterdam

Mudita Rajneesh Meditation Center
Veldhuizenstraat 2
Gein
1072 Amsterdam

Prakash Rajneesh Meditation Center
Dykhuizenweg 70
9903 AE Appingedam

Alok Rajneesh Meditation and Art Center
Stationsweg 73
2515 BJ Den Haag

Wajid Rajneesh Meditation Center
Prins Hendrikplein 1
2518 JA Den Haag

Rajneesh Humaniversity
Dr Wiardi Beckmanlaan 4
1931 BW Egmond aan Zee

De Nieuwe Mens
Enschedesestraat 305
7552 CV Hengelo (O)

Arvind Rajneesh Meditation Center
Hoge Larenseweg 168
1221 AV Hilversum

Amaltas Rajneesh Meditation Center
Staalwijklaan 4
3763 LG Soest

Padam Rajneesh Meditation Center
Koningsoord 10
9984 XH Oudeschip

New Zealand

Rajneesh Meditation Center
P.O. Box 29132
Greenwoods Center
Epsom
Auckland 3

Shunyadeep Rajneesh Meditation Center
42 Park Road
Mirimar
Wellington

Norway

Devananda Rajneesh Meditation Center
Post Box 177
Vinderen
0319 Oslo 3

Peru

Adityo Rajneesh Meditation Center
Paseo de la Republica 4670 Depto E
Miraflores
Lima 18

Portugal

Karam Rajneesh Meditation Center
Rua Conselhevio Fernando de Mello
3360 Penacova (Coimbra)

Spain

Gulaab Rajneesh Information and
Meditation Center
'Es Serralet'
Estellens
07192 Mallorca-Baleares

Kamli Rajneesh Meditation Center
Apartado de Correos 607
Ibiza-Baleares

Krisana Rajneesh Meditation Center
Futonia S.A.
c/ Juan de Urbieta 61
28007 Madrid

Argayall
Valle Gran Rey
La Gomera-Canary Islands

Sweden

Madhur Rajneesh Meditation Center
Foervattarvagen 40
16142 Bromma

Switzerland

Almasta Rajneesh Meditation Center
9 Av. des Arpilleres
1224 Chene-Bougerie - Geneva

Mingus Rajneesh Meditation Center
Asylstrasse 11
8032 Zürich

USA

Nirakar Rajneesh Meditation Center
2646 Orchard Ave.
Los Angeles, CA 90007

Idam Rajneesh Meditation Center
Sw Moksha Prem (MacGregor)
1151 Raymond (23)301
Glendale, CA 91201

Surdham Rajneesh Meditation Center
The Nest, 75-111
Indian Wells, CA 92210

Nanda Rajneesh Meditation Center
447 Aster St.
Laguna Beach, CA 92651

Chandrika Rajneesh Meditation Center
2477 Louis Road
Palo Alto, CA 94306

Viha Rajneesh Meditation Center
252 Richardson Dr.
Mill Valley, CA 94941

Premsindhu Rajneesh Meditation Center
216 Beryl Street
Mill Valley, CA 94941

Gandharva Rajneesh Meditation Center
121 First Ave.
Santa Cruz, CA 95062

Yakaru Rajneesh Meditation Center
P.O. Box 130
Laytonville, CA 95454

Suranga Rajneesh Meditation Center
5852 Dewey Blvd.
Sacramento, CA 95824

Sukhdhama Rajneesh Meditation Center
1546 28th Street No. 412
Boulder, CO 80303
Chidvilas Foundation Inc.
P.O. Box 1510
Boulder, CO 80306

Vibhakara Rajneesh Meditation Center
P.O. Box 5161
Woodland Park, CO 80866

Devadeep Rajneesh Meditation Center
1430 Longfellow St. NW.
Washington, DC 20011

Dharmadeep Rajneesh Meditation Center
2455 6th Avenue N.
St. Petersburg, FL 33713

Rakesh Rajneesh Meditation Center
P.O. Box 1554
Kapas, HI 96746

Mahima Rajneesh Meditation Center
P.O. Box 1863
Makawao, HI 96768

Virat Rajneesh Meditation Center
Top Floor
2316 W Arthur
Chicago, IL 60645

Hridaya Rajneesh Meditation Center
Rt 4, Box 231
Burnsville, NC 28714

Devatara Rajneesh Meditation Center
155 Spencer Ave.
Lynbrook, L.I., NY 11563

Sangit Rajneesh Meditation Center
2920 Healy Ave.
Far Rockaway, NY 11691

Neeraj Rajneesh Meditation Center
2493 McGovern Drive
Schenectady, NY 12309

Shunyam Rajneesh Sannyas Ahsram
P.O.Box 1197
Post Road
New Paltz, NY 12561

Devadeep Rajneesh Meditation Center
Dicob Road, Box 1
Lowville, NY 13367

Tara Rajneesh Meditation Center
2240 S. Patterson Blvd. 4
Dayton, OH 45409

Ansu Rajneesh Meditation Center
19023 SW Eastside Road
Lake Oswego, OR

Bhagwatam Rajneesh Meditation Center
P.O. Box 21297
Rio Piedras, PR 00928

Fulwari Rajneesh Meditation Center
1726 Hillmont Drive
Nashville, TN 37215

Kafi Rajneesh Meditation Center
1781 Spyglass DT247
Austin, TX 78746

Suravi Rajneesh Meditation Center
1215 E. Aloha
Seattle, WA 98102

Sudhakar Rajneesh Meditation Center
902 S. 11th Street
Wausau, WI 54401

West Germany

Dörfchen Rajneesh Institute for Spiritual
Therapy and Meditation
Dahlmannstrasse 9
1000 Berlin 12

Dharmadeep Rajneesh Institute for Meditation
and Spiritual Growth
Karolinenstrasse 7-9
2000 Hamburg 6

Mani Rajneesh Meditation Center
Johannes-Büll Weg 13 II
2000 Hamburg 65

Mukto Rajneesh Meditation Center
Roonstrasse 79
2800 Bremen

Rajneesh-Stadt
Strickhauserstrasse 39
2882 Ovelgönne

Digant Rajneesh Meditation Center
Philippinenhöferweg 75
3500 Kassel

Purnam Rajneesh Neo-Sannyas Commune
Graf-Adolf Strasse 87
4000 Düsseldorf 1

Uta Rajneesh Institut für Spirituelle
Therapie und Meditation
Venloer Strasse 5-7
5000 Köln 1

Pranada Rajneesh Center for Meditation
and Health
Burgberg 3
5378 Blankenheim-Ahr

Prasuna Rajneesh Meditation Center
Oenekinger Weg 60
5880 Lüdenscheid

Kasha Rajneesh Meditation Center
Eiserne Hand 12
6000 Frankfurt/Main

Nityam Rajneesh Meditation Center
Villa Rödelstein
6551 Altenbamberg

Sirat Rajneesh Meditation Center
Hohbuchstrasse 50
7410 Reutlingen

Rajneesh Academy for Harmonious Integration
and Meditation (RAHIM)
Merianstrasse 12
7800 Freiburg

Sampat Rajneesh Meditation Center
Mendelweg 5
7900 Ulm/Lehr

Geha Rajneesh Meditation Center
Winterstetten 44
7970 Leutkirch

Tao Rajneesh Zentrum
Klenzestrasse 41
8000 München 5

Rakesh Rajneesh Meditation Center
Am Hang 1
8063 Oberumbach

Ansumala Rajneesh Meditation Center
Kaps 1
8219 Rimsting

Nishant Rajneesh Meditation Center
c/o Tassy Family
Hör Rain 6 Weichendorf
8608 Memmelsdorf

Premapara Rajneesh Meditation Center
Asternweg 4
8900 Augsburg 1

For further information contact:
Rajneeshdham
17 Koregaon Park
Poona 411 001 (MS)
India